I0670225

MR. OLCOTT'S SKIES

An Old Book and a Youthful Obsession

By
Thomas Watson

DESERT STARS PUBLISHING

Mr. Olcott's Skies: An Old Book and a Youthful Obsession
by Thomas Watson

Copyright ©2012 by Thomas Watson
All rights reserved.

Desert Stars Publications
ISBN: 978-1475138689
ISBN-13: 1475138687

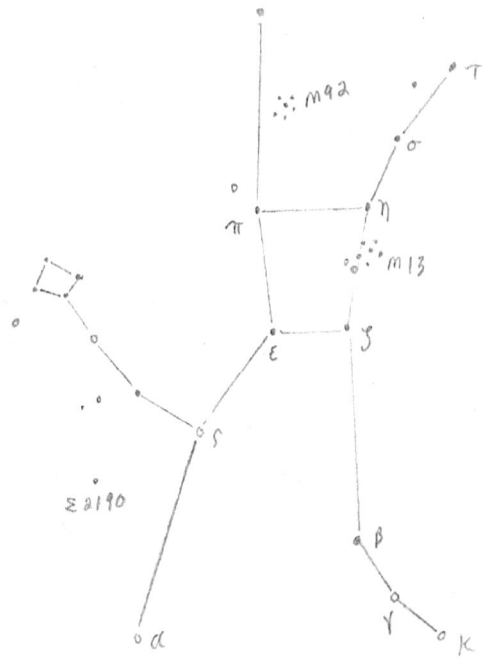

For my wife Linda, who has her own reason to love the Old Scope.

CONTENTS

Special thanks to my wife Linda for proofreading the manuscript and keeping me mindful of hyphenation, and to Erika Gerber-Rix and Stephanie Hansen for their assistance as beta readers.

And many thanks to the members of the Tucson Amateur Astronomy Association and the Cloudy Nights online forum community for their freely offered advice and friendship. I might have gotten this far without you, but it would have taken twice as long, and been half as much fun.

INTRODUCTION

Words are the pigments of the Muses
The writer uses
To paint on the canvas of his pages,
For ages and ages,
Thoughts . . .

- William Tyler Olcott, "The Prism of Thought"

Through the written word it is possible to influence the lives of many people across great spans of time and distance. Written records, especially books in their many forms, provide human ideas and the words that express them with a persistence they would otherwise lack. That persistence allows those words and ideas to reach out to people the writer could never directly address. Writer and reader may never meet, face to face. They may not, and in fact often do not, live in the same episode of history. One result of this persistence is the ability of the written word to influence people long after the writer is dead and gone. This influence has been known to change the course of human history. More often than not, however, it merely shapes the lives of individual men and women.

William Tyler Olcott sought to influence people he would otherwise never meet, by way of the written word. His goal was to share the wonder and beauty of the night sky, as seen through the lenses of eyes and telescopes, and as understood by the science called astronomy. To achieve this end, he wrote books.

Born in 1878 in Connecticut, William Tyler Olcott lived to the age of thirty-two years before the stars took control of his mind and imagination. As the story is told, in 1905 a friend of his wife introduced him to the constellations, an experience that opened a realm of knowledge new to him, and one he found impossible to resist. Within two years of his night sky revelation, he had written the first of the six books he would produce in order to share the adventure of star-gazing with others. *Field Book of the Stars* was published in 1907, and was followed in another two years by *In Starland with a Three Inch Telescope*. All the while, he studied astronomy and made astronomical observations, fueling the obsession that drove his desire to write about the stars.

In 1910 he attended a lecture given by Edward C. Pickering, a professor of astronomy at the Harvard College Observatory. Afterward the two men met, and when Olcott expressed a desire to make observations that might prove useful to science, Pickering explained his need for volunteers to observe and record variable stars. Mr. Olcott did far more than volunteer his time to observe variable stars; with Pickering, he founded the American Association of Variable Star Observers, arguably the longest lasting and most successful pro-am collaboration in the history of astronomy, and possibly in all the history of science. It is therefore no surprise that when amateur astronomers today think of Mr. Olcott's work, they think first of variable stars and the AAVSO.

I became acquainted with the man and his work before I ever heard of the AAVSO, by way of the last astronomy book Mr. Olcott wrote, just seven years before a heart attack would claim his life, far too soon. This last volume, *Field Book of the Skies*, was written in 1929 to be a volume in the Putnam Nature Field Book series, a set of works aimed at folk seeking nontechnical references to various aspects of the natural world. Mr. Olcott's last book survived through four editions, the last being edited by R. Newton and Margaret W. Mayall. Twenty-five years passed between the first and last editions. Sixteen more years would slip away before I came across a copy in my hometown library; there's no telling how long it sat there, or how often – or how little – it was used.

But find it I did, and the power of the written word, bound into a book, to shape at least one aspect of a life was invoked, forty-one years after the words were written . . .

I

BECOMING A STAR-GAZER

"Memory is a complicated thing, a relative to truth, but not its twin." - Barbara Kingsolver.

Astronomy has been a part of my life, in one form or another, for as long as I can remember. Amateur astronomy as a hobby dominated my teenage years, armchair astronomy held and exercised my imagination for a long time afterward, and when I took up visual observing again in my late forties it almost immediately resumed its dominant role among my varied interests. Considering all of this, it's only natural to assume that this fascination is deeply rooted in some childhood experience, a potent event, one of those turning points in a life that shapes all that follows down the course of a lifetime.

Perhaps it was a particular cosmic event, an eclipse or a comet, that filled my imagination with starlight and moonlight. Or maybe an inspirational moment with a parent or a trusted mentor, one that opened my eyes to unsuspected possibilities, and then sent me on a lifelong hunt for wonders in the sky. Surely there is something that looms large in my memory, a life-changing event that sent me on a path lit by the stars and the Moon.

That would indeed make a grand start for this story, but the truth is I *can't* remember exactly how I came to be so interested in astronomy. It seems it was actually a lengthy process, one that unfolded steadily through my childhood. Star-gazing cannot be linked to a single, precise moment of inspiration that shaped this aspect of my life for all the years that followed. The stars and the Moon and the planets have always drawn my mind and imagination up and away from Earthly things. In childhood memories of the books I read, only dinosaurs offered any meaningful competition to outer space for my attention and imagination.

I do, however, have memories of that process as it unfolded through my life, childhood memories of the sky at night. Each added its increment to the mosaic of experience that formed the foundation of the amateur astronomer I am today. Some of these night sky memories are from times when I was very young, so I know my exposure to the celestial sphere, and to astronomy, began at a very early age. My siblings and I were raised by people, my parents and an assortment of well-educated grandparents, aunts, and uncles, who delighted in pointing out marvels of the natural world. They believed that the questions of children regarding that world deserved solid answers, that when a child pointed at a flower or a bird and said, "What's that?" an answer more specific than "flower" or "bird" was called for. They accomplished this in part by learning the answers themselves, where necessary, and by having books for young readers on hand to stoke the curiosity these wonders provoked. My siblings, my cousin, and I were encouraged to look things up for ourselves. The stars at night were just one of many such subjects the adults in my family offered up to us, the one that for some reason sorted out to the top of my list.

I was taught, at a very young age, the location of the North Star. As long as I could see the North Star, they said, I would know how to find all the other directions. Facing that star, west is left, east is right, and south behind you. This knowledge was imparted with such seriousness and gravity that I assumed getting lost was a common event, a clear and present danger for children especially, and that people learned to find the North Star so they could find a way home. For years afterward I was afraid that if I wandered into the woods to the east of the house, I would need to sit and wait for it to get dark before I could find my way out again. When I was a small boy I suffered from an intense fear of the dark. Waiting alone until it was dark in a scary forest so I could figure out which way was north seemed like a really bad plan. It took me a long time to summon the courage to go and explore those woods.

I have an especially vivid memory of a photo of circumpolar star trails, printed in the book *A Primer for Star-Gazers* by Henry M. Neely. (I learned the title long after the fact.) My father used Neely's classic book to learn the names of stars and constellations, so he would be able to point them out and identify them for his children. For some reason that image of stars tracing arcs around Polaris absolutely fascinated me, even though I had no idea at the time what it really meant. (I may have been all of five or six years old at the time.) That picture became so firmly planted in my brain that, many years later, I recognized it when I came across a copy of Neely's book in a used bookstore. Seeing that picture taught me something of the power of memory, as for an instant I was no longer in that bookstore, but in my parents' bedroom, peering at that amazing image in the book, which lay open on the foot of their bed. (And yes, I bought that copy. Of course I did. And if you have a copy of your own, turn to page 13 to see the photo I'm talking about.)

My father was no amateur astronomer, and so was not particularly knowledgeable about star-gazing when he moved his growing family away from Chicago, and out to a small town east of Joliet. Under the darker skies of rural New Lenox, wonders such as the Milky Way and the Big Dipper were easy to see, and the natural curiosity of his children was aroused by such sights. When we asked, "Daddy, what star is that?" he wanted very much to answer, and to answer correctly. He needed to learn a thing or two, beyond knowing how to find the North Star. Neely's book gave him the resource he needed to stay a question or two ahead of us.

The case could be made, I suppose, for Neely's *A Primer for Star-Gazers* being the seed that was planted in my mind, eventually to grow into an inclination toward matters astronomical. I know I found the book at once fascinating and largely incomprehensible. Through it I first became acquainted with the idea that the stars could be used in a sort of connect-the-dots game, one that placed horses, swans, bears, and scorpions in the sky. It was also filled with strange, hourglass-shaped charts that I could not fathom. To whatever degree it influenced me, I can say for certain that *A Primer for Star-Gazers* is the first book I remember holding that dealt with star-gazing. Others followed, and I doubt I'm even close to purchasing the last.

Although he was a man of eclectic interests, the book being in our house did not reflect a growing interest in star-gazing on my father's part. My father had – and still has – rather poor eyesight, and I remember him having trouble seeing anything through telescopes I later owned. With his glasses, however, he could see enough of the night sky to pick out the bright planets and the stars making up the most obvious of the constellations. He could see the Moon, of course, and knew how to find the Pleiades.

As a small boy I endured at least two episodes of truly horrible ear infections. The pain of these infections returns to me in my nightmares even to this day. Little could be done at that time beyond keeping me comfortable with the warmth of a heating pad and child-sized aspirins, while the antibiotics slowly did their thing. The discomfort and fever made for some long, sleepless nights. I was often awake as dawn broke, restless and tired after one of the really bad nights. During one such episode my fidgeting caught my father's attention as he prepared for work. He commuted to Chicago, an insane sixty mile round trip, and so left very early in the morning to make it there on time; depending on the season of the year, it was not uncommon for him to depart before sunrise. On this particular morning he took a moment to try and distract me from the pain I endured. He wrapped me up in a blanket and carried me around for a while in what was probably a vain effort to cheer me up. For some reason he walked outside, into the cool, predawn world, and directed my gaze up and to the east. Over the dark shapes of the woodland between us and the floodplain of Hickory Creek, in a not-quite-dark sky, were a slim crescent Moon and a tiny tangle of white stars. He surely told me we were looking at the Seven Sisters, but I don't remember the exact words he spoke. There's no knowing why he chose to distract me in this way, and he does not recall the event at all, so the question will remain unanswered. I just remember being held up and being told to look at those tiny, bright stars, as if the Sisters and the Moon might together possess some power to restore me. The image of that morning sky, deep blue just above the trees and still dark enough that the Moon and Sisters remained bright and silvery, has never faded from my memory.

Summers in the mid 1960's, in that small town, were as close to paradise as I'm likely to ever experience. The long, slow fade of day into evening, and then night, was a magical time – once my fear of the dark was overcome. Thoughts of that period are lit by stars, and by fireflies which we pursued through the grassy fields around us and caught in bottles for a night's amusement. To this day the stars of summer fill me with feelings of freedom. We were free of school cares and daily chores by the time the brightest of those stars twinkled in the evening sky, and because the days of Illinois summers were so long, we were free to stay out and enjoy them well after dinner. Adults would insist it was too dark to see and play at times when we could see just fine, having been out all the while, steadily adapting to the deepening dusk. To parents in the house, their eyes dazzled by the ball game on TV, it must have seemed we had the eyes of cats, to find our way in that seeming darkness. They would come out wishing for a flashlight, only to find us fielding fly balls or catching lightning bugs with our hands. Before we retired for the night I always looked up and traced out those constellations known to me. We were required to release all fireflies the following morning.

The stars of winter are there in my memory, as well. One winter before my early teens (most likely the mid 1960s), I remember coming home from a particular Christmas Eve celebration at my grandmother's house. The holiday was always a time of joyful madness in our rather large family. Five children, born about a year apart, all filled with the same sort of intense excitement, meant there was no restraining the eagerness for and anticipation of the big holiday party. It was the family gathering of the year, and dwarfed all others – including birthdays – to insignificance. We always came home elated, and at the same time ready for that long winter's nap. Holiday gifts were a delightful mix of things needed and things desired. The adults of the family put a lot of thought into what was given, and were almost always right on target. I was already something of a science geek by then, and as usual came home with several books on the natural sciences. This time, there was something extra special. It was a globe of the Moon, manufactured by Rand McNally. I remember clutching the box containing that fantastic thing as I climbed out of the station wagon, no doubt already thinking of where the globe would look best in the bedroom. The night was as dark and cold as a winter night could be. I breathed in frost, and breathed out steam. My brothers and sister and I played a game as we crossed the yard to the house, each trying to blow steam the furthest. It was perfectly clear, with a sky above like black crystal, bright with stars. It could be seen as a bit ironic that the Moon was not visible, that night. Orion dominated the sky, high in the southeast with its stars twinkling through the bare, dormant twigs of crabapple trees. Lower in the east Sirius gleamed and sparkled, the ultimate Christmas ornament. This was a very special Christmas Eve, for we had thick snow on the ground. It did not always work out to a white Christmas, in north central Illinois. The snow seemed to have a soft and subtle glow, as if the starlight falling upon it was caught and held within. It squeaked and crunched under our rubber boots as we walked through it. As I crossed the yard a flicker of motion, like a ghostly shadow, seemed to move beside me. I paused and looked down, but saw nothing. Only in the corner of my eye, as I walked forward again, could the faint flicker of contrast be detected. It was my shadow, cast by the shining bright stars of winter, invisible if I looked straight at it. On that night before Christmas I had my first experience with averted vision, though at the time the concept was lost on me. It didn't matter. I carried the Moon in my arms.

Growing up in a rural area as I did, I found no shortage of opportunities in which to indulge my curiosity about the natural world. It was a place of open fields and second growth woodland, small streams and creeks, ponds and lakes. The farms and gardens around me were nature of another sort, tamer, but just as fascinating. As I got a bit older, I became freer to wander into those woods to the east, over which the Pleiades sometimes floated, no longer afraid of the dark and not needing a star to guide me out. I became very familiar with the riparian woodland around Hickory Creek, which ran between the woods and the corn fields to the east. Although it was also a playground shared with other kids growing up with me, as often as not I wandered the paths alone, field guides in my back pockets. I was a loner in these pursuits, and did not meet kids my age who shared these interests until late in high school. That was yet to come. Some combination of my innate curiosity, fed by parents and relatives, and the environment in which we lived, turned me into a young naturalist. I collected rocks, pressed leaves, planted seeds in pots, caught insects alive in jars, and learned the names of birds flocking to bird feeders outside my bedroom window. If it had to do with some aspect of the natural world, I was into it. When asked what I thought I would be when I grew up, the answer varied depending on what I was studying at the time, and by turns I was going to be a botanist, a meteorologist, an entomologist, a geologist, and – of course – an astronomer. The last was the answer I gave most often, because no matter what else caught my imagination, sooner or later the sun would set, and – clouds notwithstanding – there would be the Moon and the stars, as always.

Because of this fixation on the natural sciences, holiday and birthday gifts were dominated by books on nature and science, and by "science kits." The books were an eclectic blend of topics, stars and dinosaurs, space exploration and birds' nests, and a gradual accumulation of those little field guides from the

Golden Guides series. (I still have several of these.) The science kits, almost all of them from the Skilcraft line, were prized possessions, and covered a similar range of topics. I remember the one for microscopy and its geology counterpart especially well, each in a metal clamshell case full of wonderful things. Telescopes, of course, figured prominently among these gifts intended to nurture and develop my mind. The first of these were no doubt little better than toys, but I remember them with the same fondness as the science kits. Small and cheap they may have been, but they extended the reach of my vision and were cherished for that – though at the time I doubt I would have put it quite that way. The first of these that I can remember clearly was a spyglass, literally a telescoping tube you pulled out, just as the pirates of old are depicted doing. It was a tiny, brassy thing, and the optics were probably horrible, but I would not have known better. I enjoyed using it. I remember propping it on a car and on the lowest branch of a dwarf apple tree growing in the back yard, seeking to steady it while I studied birds and their nests, clouds, and the Moon. That simple spyglass, in the hands of a small boy, was something like a magic wand.

Other telescopes followed, small refractors mounted on tabletop tripods that frustrated me terribly when I tried to aim them. They fueled the interest, all the same, and left me wanting more. I suppose you could call it a case of ignorance being bliss. I knew nothing of optical quality, and it was a field no one in my family had ever touched upon, so *any* magnified view of the Moon seemed miraculous. I imagine this is how it worked with Galileo and his contemporaries. It was a brand new experience, with nothing against which to judge it, and so they were free to be amazed by what they saw. There was no one available to point out the flaws. And so it was for me as I propped small refractors on tree branches and the roofs of cars. The Moon was my favorite target in the night sky then, and not just because it was so easily found. People were going to fly there, and Moon watching was my way of joining in the fun. I had a map from National Geographic and, later, that globe of the Moon, to guide me. Because of this the Moon was a world to me, with places on it I could name, and not just a bright thing that showed so easily I could look at it through ink-black, frost-rimmed bedroom windows, on winter nights so bitterly cold I was not allowed outside.

Somewhere in the mix came a small *reflector*, the only such telescope I would own for many years, a birthday gift from a well-meaning aunt or uncle. For some reason I can remember that the manufacturer called it 'Satellite Chaser' – it's funny, the things that stick with you. It came on a tall, if wobbly, tripod, and so did not require cars or apple trees to use. Unfortunately all the components (except the mirrors) were made of plastic. Yes, that included the focuser, and you can probably imagine how long *that* lasted. The mount was of the alt-az ilk, and since it too was plastic, it lasted just a bit longer than the focuser. I always salvaged the eyepieces and lenses from old toy telescopes, and had a modest collection of cheap glass that I kept stashed under my socks. I performed numerous 'experiments' with them, mostly involving the focusing of solar radiation. The mirror from that reflector added a unique bit to my collection.

At some point after the gradual demise of the so-called 'Satellite Chaser,' a small refractor was given to me. This telescope also had a 'real' tripod, one originally made for light-weight cameras, but a tall tripod nonetheless. I was once more free of the apple tree. The legs when telescoped out to their full length were locked in place by small, round buttons that clicked into position when the legs were extended. Pushing those buttons back in when it was time to put the tripod away was a real chore. That thing wobbled horribly, but once the Moon was in focus and my hands left the instrument it was steady enough. In terms of optical quality it was likely no better than most of its predecessors (at a guess, I'd say the aperture was no more than 50mm – if that), but it was so much easier to use that I started making serious observations of the Moon with it. I was thirteen years old at the time, a thing I recall because I used that telescope to study the Moon the year Apollo 11 landed. One of the thrills for me that night was the realization that *I knew where they'd landed!* I could easily find it and point to it on the lunar map. The Moon wasn't above the horizon for my boyhood home that incredible night, but as soon afterward as I could, I was out gazing at the Sea of Tranquility in amazement and wonder. My father came out that evening, as I sat perched on an old kitchen stool and peered through the eyepiece.

"Can you see the flag?" he asked with a grin, the first – but not the last – time I ever heard that question.

"No," I said simply, knowing he was pulling my leg. "I just had to come out and look."

He was quiet for a long moment, then nodded and said, "Me, too."

I stepped aside and let him have the eyepiece.

That was also the last telescope I was ever given as a gift. The flimsy, collapsible tripod buckled one evening, shortly after I'd attached the telescope to it. The brassy tubes from which the legs were made were hollow; somehow one had been crimped. It folded completely just as I stepped away to fetch the old kitchen stool. The scope bounced off the front steps before clattering to the short concrete sidewalk outside our front door. The focuser took the brunt of the impact, which jammed components together in a way that ruined it. All I could do was stand there in utter shock and disbelief. I'd had the experience of toy telescopes wearing out in one way or another. It was always a gradual thing, and some of those telescopes had lasted for years. This was more like being struck by lightning. To make matters worse, for some reason the accident was seen as a failing on my part, a result of carelessness and not the failure of a cheap tripod. Of course, I protested my innocence, but to no avail. The message was clear. If I ever wanted another telescope, I would need to earn the money and buy it for myself.

II

THE REFRACTOR

"I have a fine lot of telescopes. I have one with which I can see the Mountains in the Moon."
- Ezra Cornell

Earning the money to buy a new telescope took some time, and almost a full year passed before I was a telescopically enhanced star-gazer again. For the average kid in his early teens, my small home town was not exactly awash with opportunities for employment. Paper routes were few, and spoken for, with a few actually passed down from older to younger siblings. You could mow lawns, shovel snow from driveways, and run errands, but these were somewhat less than lucrative activities. Not being a fan of winter sports, wielding a snow shovel added little to my funds. Fortunately, there were a lot of lawns in my home town, and spring came just in the nick of time. By the end of June, 1970, I had enough for my purposes, using seed money from birthday gifts the previous May, and leaving in my wake a great pile of grass clippings. My goal was the smallest of the refractors that taunted me from the pages of a J.C. Penney's catalog, my family's department store of choice. There were several refractors of varying size and sophistication available through their catalog, but the prices went up dramatically past that 60mm model, and each issue of the catalog that landed in the mail revealed that the price of *all* models had risen yet again. Patience is not generally a teenage virtue, and I was not at all unusual in this regard, but I believe I can be forgiven if my frustration in dealing with a moving target lowered my sights just a bit. In any case, on a day in early July (according to the faded sales receipt that somehow stayed in the box for almost a quarter of a century), in the summer between leaving middle school behind with the grass clippings and heading on to high school, I found myself headed home from a J.C. Penney store in Joliet. My father was in the driver's seat, my mother beside him, while I sat in the back seat with a long, rectangular green and black box beside me. Excitement caused my mouth to runneth over; according to my father I talked *all* the way to the store, and *all* the way back, full of plans and expectations. That telescope may have been the smallest of the lot, but it was larger than any telescope I'd ever owned before, and I had earned it for myself. I did not need adult approval to grasp the importance of this. I don't remember anything being said by either of them that might even remotely have dampened my enthusiasm, but my giddiness must have been amusing!

I was not at all discouraged by the size of the aperture. Larger telescopes were out there; I knew this only too well, having seen them in those catalogs. For my earning power and level of patience, they were out of reach. But this did not change the fact that my new telescope represented a significant improvement over what I'd been using. That refractor was a step up in more ways than one. It was a telescope with two eyepieces and a solid wooden tripod that was actually meant to hold up a telescope. No jury-rigged camera tripod under this baby! And there was a finder scope! I was *really* looking forward to using that finder scope. In other words, I had what looked and felt like a *real* telescope. Possibilities seemed to be, and my excitement certainly was, boundless.

New out of the box, and to the eyes of a 14-year-old boy flush with the power of earning his own cash, the 60mm refractor that turned me from a casual star-gazer into an amateur astronomer was truly a thing of beauty. The thin cardboard box was decorated by a photo of the telescope pointing its dew shield boldly toward the heavens, represented by black and white images of Saturn, the Moon, and the Andromeda galaxy, among other things. I seem to recall that the packaging displayed panels of black and an odd shade of gray-green, close to the shade of green used to paint department store telescopes back then, including – of course – mine. All of the telescope's attributes were printed on the box, in italics, including claims for magnification higher than any experienced amateur astronomer would believe (but what did I know then?) and a list of the included accessories. The packaging all by itself looked absolutely wonderful to my young eyes. The outer cardboard box opened by lifting away the top part, that portion with the illustrations and exaggerations. Resting in the white lower box half was a brown wooden case. A wooden storage case; this was getting serious! After removing the bottom of the cardboard box and freeing the case, I flipped the latches and lifted the lid of the wooden case back on its hinges. The first things I saw inside were the extendable wooden legs of the tripod which, after the skinny sliding tubes of the previous and ill-fated refractor, looked as sturdy and solid as pillars of stone.

Setting those aside and pulling out the top halves of the fitted styrofoam pieces that protected the rest of the contents, the telescope itself was revealed, already attached to its black anodized cast aluminum mount. Nestled beside the telescope tube was a clear, heavy-duty plastic bag that contained various bits and pieces, and the instruction booklet. (Also the obligatory packets of silica desiccant bearing the ominous warning "Do Not Eat.") At this point, parental warnings against getting ahead of myself were issued. So I sat cross-legged on the living room floor and read the instruction booklet cover to cover, and then set out the various parts of the new telescope. When I was sure all was in order, I began that first assembly. This sort of patient approach was not exactly my normal modus operandi, and in past moments of eagerness I'd wrought significant havoc. But not this time, no way! There was something about the look and feel of that refractor that raised it well above the level of a "toy" in my eyes, and it just seemed to deserve a serious treatment as a scientific instrument. Or maybe it was the fact that I'd paid for it myself. So I worked carefully, followed instructions in place of impulses and in the end, even though I was an all-thumbs teenage boy who never developed the fondness for tools so often found in my half of the species, it soon stood before me. Assembled in the living room, to my eyes it stood proudly, as if eager for starlight! Moving it around on the mount reinforced the feeling of solidity, with those stout wooden legs further braced by the black plate of the accessory tray. Every aspect of appearance, material, and construction emphasized that this was something different, related only by a technicality to telescopes past. Everything moved smoothly, everything smelled of new metal, stained wood, and grease. The eyepieces and diagonal were bright and shiny, the Barlow lens was impressively long and black, and the filters – one for the Moon, and one for the sun – had a weighty feel to them, as if they meant business.

I carried the assembled telescope out to the back yard, where I set about getting a feel for the way the telescope moved, how it was aimed, and how it focused. It was a typical summer day with a high blue sky and flocks of fair weather cumulus clouds drifting peacefully overhead. I traced the edges of cloud and studied leaves fluttering atop distant trees. I focused on Francis Road, a mile or more to the north across gently sloping fields of timothy grass, and watched cars pass back and forth through my field of view. Everything was sharp and clear, alive and in living color. I even figured out, using the instruction booklet, how to align the finder scope, which I very carefully did in anticipation of a night's exploration of the heavens.

The fair weather cumulus thickened and darkened, and the phrase "fair weather" could no longer be applied to the day's clouds. There was lightning and thunder and raging wind, and then rain and hail. A typical summer thunderstorm, of a sort I normally found quite exciting. That night it was vexing, to say the least. In the face of my evident disappointment, following a day of eager anticipation, my father merely shrugged and said, "The lawn needs water."

The stormy weather persisted, and put off the moment of first light several days, leaving me in an agony of anticipation. I believe I pretty much memorized the instruction booklet by that point. I also practiced assembling and disassembling the components. Concerns were expressed – facetiously, no doubt – that I might wear something out before I had a chance to use the telescope for its intended purpose. I probably didn't find that very amusing.

First light finally came on a warm, humid summer evening. The Moon set too soon after sunset to be a first light object, but Jupiter was a bright beacon in the twilight, low in the southwest, and I settled on the King of Planets for the big event. I aligned the finder using the knob atop a neighbor's flagpole (apparently just hanging a flag from their porch post didn't make a strong enough statement) and swung the scope down and centered the crosshairs on old Jove. At the eyepiece, the planet was nowhere to be seen. I tried to double-check through the finder scope, but in my haste, managed to bump the telescope proper in the process. Moving more carefully, I re-centered Jupiter in the finder, and went to the eyepiece, but still saw nothing. I nudged the telescope ever so slightly, but Jupiter did not appear. I nudged it the other way, and a small, fuzzy ball of light slid into view. I was using the low-power eyepiece, 20mm focal length with true field of view that was right around a degree and a half, things I would not have known about that night. I did, however, know the magnification was 35x. That much math I could manage. For a moment, I forgot about the finder and just stared at Jupiter. My best effort at focusing left the image blurred and watery, but the concept of seeing conditions *was* something I understood at that point (I'd read every astronomy book I could check out from the middle school and town libraries by then), so I was not surprised, much less disappointed. After all, Jupiter *was* rather low in the sky.

When I looked through the finder with Jupiter centered in the eyepiece, I discovered the bright spark of the planet just off the cross hairs, displaced by roughly the width of the knob atop the neighbor's flagpole. Obviously my technique required refinement.

Jupiter that night was a pale ball of light, set in a sky still touched by the long summer twilight. I could easily see the equatorial bands and the four Galilean satellites, which were surprisingly sharp points of light arrayed around the planet. (I can remember seeing all four, but I'm not clear on how they were distributed. Memory so often paints the past with a broad brush, and at most inconvenient times.) The planet slowly drifted across the field of view; with a gentle touch on the diagonal, I put it back in the center. The previous telescope had resisted adjustment, and then lurched in the direction I wanted it to go, but well past where I *meant* to go. More often than not, this meant relocating even something as bright as the Moon, not an easy thing to do with a setup that had no finder scope. It lacked any sort of mechanism for aiming, aside from sighting up the length of the tube. The new refractor was a completely different sort of beast, and seemed to glide when I moved it. A light touch was all it took, and it went right where I wanted it, no further. I experimented with the silvery metal slow-motion controls, but soon decided I could do a better job just nudging the telescope. And nudge I did, keeping Jupiter in sight as I experimented with eyepieces until the planet was carried by the deepening dark of the summer night down below the tree tops. I remember being alarmed that I might have smudged the eyepiece, only to realize that I was peering through twigs and leaves.

I did not ignore the rest of the kit, that first night out. I switched eyepieces, putting the 6mm in place of the 20mm. At first, it seemed a repeat of the finder dilemma experienced earlier. A careful nudge brought the planet back in view, much larger and *much* fuzzier. Focusing with the higher magnification was a serious hassle. In the first place, I wasn't sure how to tell I'd gotten the image as focused as could be; I didn't know when to quit. I would not have known, that night, that thick air wasn't the only problem, that an optical matter played a role. I did notice immediately that vibrations caused by my touching the focuser were greatly magnified with that eyepiece. So was the speed with which the image flew across the field of view. When I was finally convinced that I'd done as well as I could, I found the image of Jupiter at 117x less than inspiring. I could see the equatorial belts and some of the moons, but the quality of the image was pretty bad.

The Barlow lens, which doubled the magnification possible with each eyepiece, worked well with the 20mm eyepiece, but not at all with its 6mm counterpart. I learned the reason for this before the summer's end. At the time, I recall being puzzled by the result, but not terribly disappointed. I knew I had a lot to learn, and after all, it was only the first night out.

For any non-astronomers who might read this, the numbers in millimeters are the focal lengths of the eyepieces. Divide that number into the focal length of the telescope itself, 700mm in this case, and the number you get is the amount of magnification provided by each eyepiece.

Those first views of Jupiter in the new telescope made the sort of impression that stays in the memory. The memories for the rest of that night are a little less detailed, but I know I didn't just stop when Jupiter passed from view. After I lost Jupiter for the night I more than likely went to various brighter stars, taking in Arcturus and gazing at Vega in all its chromatically aberrant glory. I knew about chromatic aberration – false color some of the books called it – and so was undismayed by its presence. I *do* recall, quite clearly, looking at zeta Ursae Majoris, which I no doubt referred to them simply as Mizar and Alcor. This naked-eye double star has always been a favorite object, ever since I was told it was used as a test of vision in ancient times. It pleased me, for some reason, to think that because I could see both stars so easily, I could have been an archer in the Roman Legion, among other things. This connection with the past tickled something in my imagination. I knew from reading various books, most notably my well-worn copy of *The Sky Observer's Guide* (one of those little nature guides by Golden Press) that there was more to Mizar and Alcor than met the naked eye. On that night of first light with the new refractor I finally saw, with certainty, that the brighter star was itself a double star. Earlier telescopes did not reveal its binary nature. Why this would be so, I can't say. Several of them surely had the resolving power to do so. That night I focused on Mizar and Alcor and spotted the companion of Mizar, tucked up close beside it. The stars, unlike Jupiter, were sharply focused in that 20mm eyepiece. I remember putting dots in a notebook to replicate what I saw, right under the crude sketch of Jupiter and its moons. I've repeated that double star observation many times since that night. I never fail to recall that first time when I do so.

Although I packed up that night puzzled by how a few things worked out, I was nonetheless enormously pleased with the result of all my lawn mowing and birthday frugality. I repacked the new telescope and its assorted gear with great care, polishing away every fingerprint and trace of dew dampness as I did. That some aspects of the kit seemed to have fallen short I wrote off to a lack of experience. After all, I'd never owned a telescope with this level of sophistication. It may sound more than a little ridiculous to put it that way, but remember before you laugh or shake your head where I was before that night, and what it took to move on.

Starting with that night, and then through the years of nights that followed, I learned a great deal about that telescope and, through it, about telescopes in general. As my experience grew, that small telescope revealed wonders sufficient to keep me well motivated. The night sky was open to me at last.

Of course, as time passed I also discovered that some of the first light problems were not due to my lack of experience, but due to imperfections introduced by the accessories that came in that handsome wooden box. The mount and tripod, while orders of magnitude better and more stable than anything I'd used in the past, still produced some shaking when I focused the image. In time, I became adept at turning the focus knobs gently enough to minimize the vibration, and usually had no trouble achieving focus. Somewhat later I discovered that adding weight to the tripod made a significant difference. This was an accidental discovery. One night I placed my small notebook on the accessory tray, since at the time I lacked anything like an observing table. The evening breeze kept flipping and damaging the pages; annoyed, I scrounged up a fist-sized rock and set it on the notebook. The telescope vibrated less, noticeably so. The accessory tray could not manage a heavier weight, so future experiments involved suspending various weighty items from a cord looped around the points of attachment between wooden legs and metal mount. I don't remember how I came by the thing, but in the end I settled on a rather hefty sash weight to do the job. The improved stability made an enormous difference in my ability to focus objects cleanly.

By trial and error – and some of the errors were a sore trial, I must admit – I learned which eyepiece and (more rarely) eyepiece and Barlow combination worked best for specific types of objects. The longer focal length (20mm) eyepiece gave grand views of many double stars, the Moon, and open star clusters. It was my eyepiece of choice for just slowly scanning the sky and taking in the view, which accounted for much of my astronomy time. The 6mm eyepiece worked very well on the Moon. On nights of good seeing it did a pretty good job on Jupiter and Saturn as well. The 2x Barlow, matched with the 20mm eyepiece, was another useful lunar observing tool. Used with the 6mm eyepiece . . . Well, I didn't use that combo much after that first summer. The views provided by that combination were everything the detractors of small telescopes love to hate.

After much fiddling, I did indeed abandon the chrome-plated slow-motion controls. They were awkwardly placed, and using them shook the scope so much that keeping an object in view was a moot point. I did a much better job just nudging the focuser end of the telescope. I was soon very good at aligning the finder scope, especially when I learned the trick of following up a daylight alignment with a bit of fine tuning on a bright star. The finder was, however, very limited in capability, as only the Moon, the naked eye planets, and the brighter stars showed clearly through it. Although it was much better than dead reckoning, most of the time the finder only got me into the ballpark, after which slow and patient sweeping were all I had to work with. The slow part I managed well enough, but patience . . . Well, I was fourteen years old, after all. I got better at it over time, but developing the patience necessary took more time than any other skill acquired for the sake of star-gazing. I learned to both focus the telescope and observe while my targets drifted (or raced!) across the field of view. It was tricky, and sometimes frustrating, but it was what I had to do, so I did it and became pretty good at it. Long before I was ever struck by the ever pernicious 'aperture fever' I yearned for a motor to move the telescope and keep it on target. Somewhere I read of a thing called a clock drive, while missing completely the fact that I would need an altogether different sort of mount in order to use such a device. Lacking any way to satisfy that desire, I learned to put my target object just off the east edge of the field, and observe as that target drifted through the field of view.

The only bits of gear left to discuss are the pair of filters that came with the kit. One was labeled "Moon" and the other "Sun." The lunar filter, a neutral density filter, was my second least used accessory, after the Barlow lens. For a while I used the Moon filter when the Moon was at or near full. I quickly learned that I did not need it early or late in the lunar cycle, or when I used the higher power eyepiece. In fact, at such times it dimmed the Moon too much to be of use. (I did experiment with it on Venus, and was able to see that planet's phases for the first time.)

The solar filter, on the other hand, saw plenty of action. Whether yet another case of ignorance being bliss, or the small aperture limiting the amount of light and heat to reach the filter, I observed and tracked many a sunspot with that thing, without incident. The lurid green cast it lent the sun pleased the slightly weird comic-book-reading, sci-fi B-movie-watching side of me. My notebooks from that time included many sketches of sunspots, umbra and penumbra carefully delineated in each, and just as carefully labeled. This all took place without any damage to either filter or eyesight. When I tell people this they roll their eyes and say I just got lucky. I wonder. I used it regularly for more than six years without mishap. That's rather hard to write off to mere luck. Maybe the modern counterparts that generate so much alarm are simply less robust. To be sure, I wouldn't dream of using a *new* filter of this sort, these days. Everything *else* is made more cheaply on my refractor's descendents. Given the alternatives now available, all of which provide much better views, it would be a completely unnecessary risk.

The feeling of accomplishment that came from having earned the cash and purchased the telescope for myself provided a sense of what is now called empowerment. Boy was I ever empowered! I hauled that telescope out to the back yard on every clear night that summer. I felt I finally had the tools I needed to begin exploring the night sky. I was ready for the voyage to begin.

Well, almost...

III

THE SHORT, FAT BOOK

Learning is not attained by chance, it must be sought for with ardor and attended to with diligence.
- Abigail Adams

I soon learned that I fell short in one important regard; I lacked the charts and references necessary to guide my explorations. My astronomical reference library at that time consisted of a recently acquired but seldom used Whitney's Star Finder, a copy of *Stars* by Zim and Baker, and *The Sky Observer's Guide* by R. Newton Mayall, Margaret Mayall, and Jerome Wyckoff. (The copy of *A Primer for Star-Gazers,* which had helped my parents introduce me to the stars had long since gone back to its owner. I never did learn the identity of my father's stargazer acquaintance.) The closest thing to star charts I owned were the small ones in the back of *The Sky Observer's Guide*, which for the most part depicted only the brighter stars, and very few deep sky objects. Funding remained an issue, but also a moot point. The lawns grew as such things do, and I spent many days bathed in the exhaust of inefficient gas-powered mowers. I could earn the money I needed. Unfortunately, the only bookstore within my reach did not carry such material, and in fact, did not seem to understand what I was talking about when I paid a visit for the purpose. (They did not have much of a newsstand, and did not stock Sky & Telescope, or any other science-related magazine that I can recall.)

So I gave our local small-town library a look. Mind you, I was already thoroughly familiar with their shelves of books on the sciences (as well as science fiction, which the librarian was convinced held an unhealthy attraction for me), and I did not actually expect to find anything there. But I asked what could be *acquired*, having been told that a thing called "interlibrary loan" existed. The librarian just shrugged, not knowing exactly what she would be requesting, and then looked thoughtful and led me back to the reference section. These were all books that could only be used in the library, and not checked out, so I was not all that familiar with what sat on those shelves. I thought it was a collection of old dictionaries. She ran her hand along the book spines, then plucked out a short, fat, hardcover volume with a yellow and black cover.

It was a copy of *Field Book of the Skies* by William T. Olcott, the 1954 updated 4th edition of a far older book from 1929; the editors of the revised edition were the very same Mayalls whose *Sky Observer's Guide* had so far been my primary resource. I took the book and flipped it open, and found to my delight that it was just full of individual constellation charts and lists of things to see, all arranged by season. Each constellation was covered on two levels: things to be seen by naked eye and binoculars, and objects of interest to small telescope owners – people, or so I assumed, like me. There were deep sky objects plotted, but mostly it was a catalog of double stars, with some information on objects in the solar system, and some miscellaneous materials at either end. Of course, at first nothing really registered on me except for those charts.

Field Book of the Skies seemed to be just what I needed, and the discovery pleased me no end. At that point the kindly librarian reminded me that I could only use the book *in the library*. I couldn't take it home with me to study, much less carry it out at night under the stars. I asked politely if an exception could be made, but there was nothing for it. I was more than welcome to sit and read it at the library, perhaps – as she suggested – taking notes as I did so. I was a polite boy to my elders, so although my disappointment was no doubt quite obvious, I did not insist, much less make a scene. But somewhere on the bike ride home, as I considered the possibility that my parents might be able to intervene on my behalf, the idea of taking notes transformed itself into a plausible course of action. At home, taking the germ of an idea and making things up as I went, I sorted through leftover school supplies and came up with pencils, a protractor (the half circle type), a big pink eraser, and a stash of paper, both lined and plain. The plan came together in its final form the moment I saw the package of blank paper. My mother seemed puzzled that I wanted anything to do with school supplies, so close to midsummer, but did not object when I laid claim to these things. I went back to the library that afternoon and set to work reading the book and copying the charts and tables that seemed most useful to me.

The way the book was shaped and bound made simply tracing the charts a problem, and the librarian was quite right when she objected to what she *thought* I meant to do, fearing damage to the binding. But being from early on a lover of books I was not inclined to risk damage to it by pressing it flat and tracing the charts. This is where that protractor came into the plan. I measured the lengths of lines connecting stars in the constellation diagrams, and then measured the angles they made as they connected the star dots. With those two measures, I could duplicate the charts accurately, if slowly, and without placing unnecessary stress on the binding. I knew which constellations were visible at that point in the summer, and started with those, duplicating the charts on the blank paper, and scribbling notes from the text as seemed needful. By summer's end I'd duplicated *all* the star charts, and filled a loose-leaf notebook with material that described what those charts contained. I did everything except, I'm afraid, actually read the entire book.

I must have been in the library on a daily basis, for varying amounts of time, for several weeks. The librarian pretty much left me alone, so I can't remember if she found my diligence admirable, or if she recommended that my parents consider sending me to a shrink. Nothing was said to discourage me, however, and at any rate I was so obsessed with having the material available scope-side as soon as possible, it's most unlikely I could have been derailed. And besides, it was a hot, muggy July and the library was one of the few air-conditioned buildings I knew of in the town. People may have been talking behind my back, but I didn't sweat it. (Actually, such a thing would have upset me a great deal, had I known.)

Needless to say, I came to know certain aspects of William Tyler Olcott's book very well, both through the effort of copying material and then using that material at the eyepiece. That some of what I copied was out of date (this most recent edition being sixteen years old) more than likely never crossed my mind. The only books to which it could be compared in my experience were Golden Press nature guides, which is to say I really lacked any meaningful context in which to make comparisons. Nor was my knowledge of astronomy deep enough that I could see shortfalls in the science contained within the book. It was what it was, and it was the closest thing to what I needed to be found where I lived, and so I took it very much at face value.

What I remember from that time most clearly are the charts and lists of objects, which makes perfect sense, considering what I did to duplicate them. My initial impression that the lists were made up largely of double stars proved correct. There was a good reason for this, but I would not understand that for many years after the fact. I did not question it, and after I tracked down and observed some of those binary stars, and was smitten by their beauty, it did not occur to me to wonder that there were so many in the book. This was, for me, amateur astronomy. To the best of my knowledge – which by the end of that summer came largely from Olcott's book – double stars were what most of amateur astronomy was about. That was fine; I enjoyed finding and observing these double and multiple star systems, so it all made perfect sense.

The scattering of deep sky objects also included in the book were of the brighter variety. Those I was able to locate were generally visible in my 60mm refractor, though more often than not it was necessary to settle for the thrill of discovery, as the views were something less than photographic. Galaxies in a small refractor redefine the idea of a "faint fuzzy." Star clusters, especially open star clusters, were a lot more fun. The emphasis on double stars and bright deep sky stuff made the book very suitable for my situation, and when combined with my already deep fascination with the Moon, I had plenty to do on those muggy summer nights. My interest in visual observing began to develop and grow rapidly at this point, and my frame of reference as an observer was largely shaped by using Olcott's book with my small telescope.

Field Book of the Skies opened another door, as well, for the author included in his book the myths and legends associated with the constellations. This led me to look up books on mythology, and by the time my freshman year began in the fall I'd read Hamilton and Bullfinch – courtesy of that very same library. So quite by accident Olcott's work put me in touch with a different realm of intellectual pursuit altogether, one that in its storytelling power made some of the fiction I was reading back then seem pretty anemic.

I used the material as I copied it, having wisely chosen not to simply begin at the beginning, deciding to copy the summer constellation charts first of all. This meant that the time between realizing I lacked the information I needed to best use the telescope and having that information was very short. One of the first constellations I drew from Olcott's book was Hercules, which I did for an even more specific purpose. There was something in Hercules I was sure the new telescope could show me, but in the brief time since first light I'd had no luck. I hoped the carefully copied chart would make the difference.

I don't remember if the night after making the copy was clear, or if my first use of an Olcott chart came sometime later. Either way, I do remember that experience, as clearly as I recall the adventure of first light. I had that shiny new telescope set up in the back yard, ready and waiting as the long twilight of the Illinois summer slowly faded. Darkness and the stars always seemed overdue on such nights. Beside it stood an old wooden kitchen stool, the origin of which now escapes me, and an old card table around which my grandmother and her "church ladies" had once played bridge. The table was old and battered, recently replaced by something newer, and so had been up for grabs. I grabbed. The card table held various and sundry, including eyepieces, the copied chart, my books, a flashlight, and a small transistor radio. (Remember when those were high tech?)

I know now, years after the fact, that the neighbors looked out at me in the middle of that field and shook their heads, wondering what had gotten into "that Watson boy." Had I been aware of this, it would have left me profoundly self-conscious, and might well have derailed my interest in amateur astronomy. It's just as well I did not know then what I know now. Oblivious to the head-shakers, I watched as the brightest stars pricked the darkening sky. I would note their names and when they managed to attain naked eye visibility and then focus the telescope on them. I no longer recall why I performed this particular exercise, but it was for some reason a source of great interest to me to know and to record which stars appeared first as night came on.

I stood at the north end of our half-acre lot. North of me was a wide field of waist-high timothy grass, east a vacant area of mixed thick grasses and leafy shrubs, beyond which lay woodlands topped by a sky that showed a steadily deepening shade of blue. South was the rest of our recently mowed yard and the house I grew up in, and beyond that more woodland that created my rather high southern horizon. Toward the sunset were the yards of neighbors, sloping down into a hollow that rose again just as gently half a mile away to form the western horizon. The hollow often filled with mist as the night cooled down. The yards were mostly unfenced, and dominated by kitchen gardens. The hazy summer air cooled as the light faded in the west, and was heavy with the scent of damp vegetation. Mosquitoes shared the night with a few late fireflies; I wore foul-smelling DEET – still a novel product at that time – to ward off the blood suckers. The fireflies were a more welcome aspect of the natural world. Night was not yet fully dark when they began to glow, soft slow pulses of greenish light in the grasses and low shrubs, more rapid flashes tracing shallow arcs in the sky.

When there were more stars than fireflies visible I decided to once again seek out the globular star cluster M13 in Hercules. Up to that point I had been completely unsuccessful in doing so. I was puzzled by this, because I could see where in the sky it should be. Although I often found the charts in *The Sky Observer's Guide* a bit confusing, I was reasonably sure I'd picked out the shape in the sky called the Keystone. (The tricks of celestial navigation that I now use without thinking too hard were yet to be learned at that point.) I'd gotten the impression from the books that I should at least be able to *see* M13 with a 60mm refractor and so was determined to find it. On this night, I had an Olcott chart to aid me, and my as yet scarcely used Whitney's Star Finder planisphere.

The Star Finder came to me on my fourteenth birthday, but for some reason I'd made little effort to use it – for reasons I cannot now recall with any certainty. The arrival of the telescope prompted a reassessment of available resources, and so the Star Finder wheel was pulled out and added to the rest of my meager astronomy kit in a sort of 'just because' manner. This prompted a stern lecture from my mother, who felt I'd neglected the gift and should put it to use in order to show proper appreciation.

I repeated my earlier effort to find M13, but failed yet again. The chart from *Field Book of the Skies* appeared to validate my sense for where the cluster should be. Feeling more than a little let down, after all the anticipation that had built while copying that chart, I finally picked up the planisphere. I would mess with the thing a while, and then be able to say in all honesty that I'd used the well-intentioned gift. It didn't take long to figure out how to set the thing to the current date and time; more than likely, I'd done so at least once before by then. Making sense of the tiny renderings of constellations, connected by spidery lines, wasn't easy. I can't help wondering if that might be why I set it aside in the first place? I held a small flashlight, with red tape over the lens, in one hand, and the planisphere in the other. It took an embarrassingly long moment to realize that I needed to spot a constellation I already knew well and hold the planisphere so the two patterns were in agreement. So many things are obvious after the fact. Lyra was right there, riding high in the north-northeast, so I made use of the mythical Lyre for this purpose. As soon as my eye and mind made the necessary connections I tilted my head back and to my delight other constellations fell into place. It finally dawned on me how useful a planisphere could be. My eyes flicked from planisphere to sky and back, matching patterns on the wheel to patterns in the sky – the Northern Crown, Bootes, and a bit west to Hercules.

Except that Hercules was not where I thought I'd found it previously. It seemed too far south. I looked at the sky, looked at the planisphere, and looked more carefully at my chart copied from Olcott's book. I took aim with the telescope one more time. And so it was that, on a night sprinkled with fireflies and with the high whine of mosquitoes in my ears, I discovered that I'd somehow mistaken the head of Draco for the Keystone! The magnitude of my blunder was all too apparent, after the fact, but its impact was blunted when I had my first ever look at a globular star cluster. The accomplishment came that quickly, and that easily, once I knew the *right* place to look. It was little more than a fuzzy gray ball of pale light, but that didn't register as keenly as the fact that I'd been able to find it at all. Here was a sight that was not readily apparent to the naked eye, something far less obvious than a planet or bright star, revealed to me in the eyepiece of my new telescope. I had proven to myself that, with the right information, I could find things in the night sky. I sat there peering at that pale patch of light for a long time, reluctant to put the telescope on anything else, afraid that I might not be able to relocate it again.

On the card table the radio was tuned to a rock-and-roll station in Chicago. They had been playing a canned interview with the musician Donovan, the talk interspersed with tunes by the artist. As chance would have it they were playing "Hurdy Gurdy Man" while I sat there enjoying my breakthrough moment. These memories unfold now, each time I hear that tune. The mellow music rolled into the cool, moist summer air from that little radio, and I kept my eye fixed on the eyepiece. *The Sky Observer's Guide* described the process of using averted vision to see things more clearly, and the cluster did indeed seem to swell slightly in size if I didn't look straight at it. And then, as I watched, a pulsing green glow suddenly filled my field of view. Startled, I looked up from the eyepiece and saw . . . Nothing. No aircraft, no UFOs (oh, how I wished in those days to see one!), no heat lightning. Puzzled, I returned to the eyepiece and had only watched for a moment when the pulse of cold, pale green light was repeated. As quickly as I could I looked up along the length of the telescope. Still nothing. Back to the eyepiece and sure enough, there it was again.

I sat back on the stool, completely baffled. At that moment the firefly wandered up and around the rim of the dew shield and flashed. He had been down inside, on or near the objective lens and out of sight from where I sat.

The summer of the telescope unfolded from that night, until coping with being a high school freshman derailed me for a few weeks. I did my chores, mowed more lawns, read a pile of books, and dabbled in tropical fish for the first time. Every chance I had I loaded my chart-copying supplies, and the notebook that now held the results, into the baskets on the back of my bike, then rode off to the library. I made these trips until all that I wanted from that short, fat book had been duplicated to my satisfaction. And when the nights were clear I set up the refractor and set about finding binary stars and star clusters. I plotted the positions of Jupiter's moons until old Jove was gone for the season. I also acquired the habit then of "working" a constellation. The book was set up to depict the sky one constellation at a time, and that's how the charts were copied – one per sheet of paper. And so I learned the telescopic view of the sky one constellation at a time. That summer passed all too quickly, and other priorities came to compete with the stars for a night's attention. But the pattern had been set, and I did not let any more time pass between observing sessions than I could help. Star-gazing had assumed a new level of importance, and maintained this all through high school, a major commitment for me at the time.

Looking back now, of course, it seems like such a short time, after all.

IV

INCIDENTS OF OBSERVATION

The secret of a good memory is attention, and attention to a subject depends upon our interest in it. We rarely forget that which has made a deep impression on our minds.
- Tryon Edwards

In that relatively short time during my younger visual observing days, I had a number of experiences that remain alive in memory to this day. Each season held its challenges and rewards, and oddities that came along the way – the stuff of memories. Over the course of my high school years, by way of these experiences, I set the foundation for the amateur astronomer I would one day become. Just as I could not have been aware of how short those years would be, I could not have known at the time just how deeply the roots of that foundation would go.

Spring

Of all the seasons, the stars of spring are the ones I remember with the least clarity. My familiarity with constellations such as Leo and Gemini, Corvus and Coma Berenices in those days comes from following those stars down into the west, as the stars of summer rose high behind them. That familiarity did not run deep. Spring was always a messy time in north central Illinois, with weather that was often bad for any outdoor activity, and early in the season mixed rain and snow – sometimes on the same day – in significant quantities. It never seemed to quite dry out or warm up more than necessary to make a fresh batch of mud. It was, if possible, cloudier in the spring than in the winter, more years than not. Winter was actually a better time for observing in many ways. Arctic high pressure systems gave some very clear skies, and if it was not technically drier, the ground was usually frozen solid. After the thaw, but before the mounting sun took the chill out of the air, the yard was a sponge, and I only set up on the gravel driveway, when I set up at all. This seriously limited the view, putting our house and that of a neighbor in my way. The telescope didn't get out much between the last freeze and the first flowers of May.

When it did aim its dew shield into the night, the emphasis was on the Moon. I say this with some confidence because, when I think back on observing the Moon in those days, the image of the Moon riding high in the sky comes to mind. Since I was not much for early rising, except to go fishing, that means I likely did a lot of Moon watching in the Spring – March, April, and May – when the Moon was conveniently high in the sky in the evening, and so at its best in terms of viewing quality. Any evening that weather, chores, and school work permitted, I was out gazing at the Moon, learning the names of craters and watching the play of shadow and light that changed so dramatically from night to night.

It's a bit ironic that my spring telescope memories are dominated by the one aspect of amateur astronomy uninfluenced by *Field Book of the Skies*. Olcott's treatment of the Moon, in addition to being quite dated, offered little of use to a long-time Moon watcher. The lunar maps in the book were inferior to the maps and books I'd acquired during that time of adventure known as Project Apollo. I copied and used nothing from that portion of *Field Book of the Skies* dealing with the Moon, my own small collection being far more detailed.

This particular memory might have been of the first spring after my purchase of the refractor, or any spring thereafter. Sometimes the memory of an incident comes to you without attachment or a strong frame of reference. I was still in Illinois, at any rate, which argues for the event taking place while I was in high school. I was out under a gibbous Moon, not far from full, so bright it cast shadows that left no doubt as to their reality. I would have been taking in the features being revealed by the terminator near the western limb of the Moon. Aristarchus surely caught my eye; the Aristarchus Plateau has always done so.

I was looking at the Moon with low magnification, all the Moon in one eyeful. As I watched, I heard geese high above me in the night, lost to sight in the darkness between the stars. This was not a new thing. Living in that quiet countryside I often heard migrant geese overhead, after dark. They flew over us twice each year, southbound in the autumn and then again headed north with the spring. It was cold and damp, but I shivered from something other than the chill of a foggy night. There's something wild and miraculous in the sound of such calls floating down from the darkness, long distance voyagers heard but not seen. If you hear those calls you feel the thrill, if you have any spirit in you at all.

Usually heard but not seen. Not the case this night. Even as the wild sound of those invisible geese floated down to me from the moonlit sky, I put my eye back to the eyepiece. In that moment, as I gazed at the familiar face of my old friend, something happened that had not happened before. A skein of geese crossed the face of the Moon. They were there and gone in another moment, but the sight of them marked my memory in an instant with photographic clarity. It was the classic pattern for geese in flight, an elongated V with one arm somewhat longer than the other. Each bird was a silhouette against the

Moon, tiny and precise in appearance, the movements of wings quick and determined. I looked up and faced the sky, and heard them honking far above me, fading away to the north. All I could do was stand there looking up, on the ground in a land of farm fields and small houses, as wilderness passed overhead. The Moon seemed farther away, somehow, removed and remote.

There are moments in life that require no thought while you are in them. You scarcely have *time* to think. You simply exist and experience them. And then try to remember.

Summer

As a teenage amateur astronomer, I went out under the night sky any chance I could, but though my intentions were good, this did not mean I was out *every* clear night. Nights with clear skies were limited at the outset by the needs of the average school year. I was a good student, but I was not especially quick at getting things done. I tended to be meticulous with my schoolwork, which made it somewhat time-consuming. It often occurred to me back then that it would be good to be free of school, to be an adult, and have my evenings free to do with as I pleased. The realities of adulthood were some years ahead of me, and only then would I know the truth, that adults are far less free in their use of time than teenagers. (That's the thing about being young and naive. When you're young, you lack the experience you need to recognize naiveté in others, or in yourself.) Friday nights and weekends would, of course, present opportunities (when the weather was clear), but there were other demands on my time. I was not the most socially active boy in my teens, but I did have friends, and we did things together. So on Friday and Saturday nights I was often torn between going out and, well, going out. The stars drew me, but many times their lure simply was not powerful enough, especially if girls were involved.

Come summer, however, and it all changed. Many of my high school friends lived a fair distance away. It was a rural township, and the high school drew students from several small towns. When the school buses stopped running in early May, many of us were cut off from each other. The seasonal segregations faded as we learned to drive, but the much vaunted driver's license, that token of maturity we waved at each other so proudly, was not much help unless a vehicle was available. For most of us, being able to borrow the family car was a different sort of challenge altogether. So some of us said goodbye in May and hello again in September.

This pretty much left me on my own, especially since the friends I had *in* town tended to go on lengthy vacations, visiting family elsewhere for weeks at a time. As spring turned to summer and the world grew warm and hazy, I found myself free to use any clear night that came along to explore the celestial sphere. It was in summer that I was most serious about astronomy, summer when I was *free* to be devoted to it, and so it was the summer sky and its constellations I knew best. I had the nights to myself, and no serious obligations the following morning, and so if I stayed up late, there were no problems. Just a bit of teasing from my parents and siblings when I dragged myself out of bed and stumbled through the morning like a zombie.

Of the summer constellations so designated by Olcott, I was *least* familiar with those fairly low in the south. At 41° N latitude, the Scorpion practically dragged its tail on the horizon, and at times *did* drag its tail through the trees. Libra to the west and Sagittarius to the east, were also only partly accessible. I couldn't see the southern portions of my universe for the trees. Ophiuchus, Serpens, and others "higher" or more properly, farther north, provided easier access, and ended up better studied. Some of my fondest summer star-gazing memories are of splitting double stars in Delphinus, cruising the summer Milky Way with binoculars, and trying to convince myself I'd seen the Ring Nebula in Lyra. Or that what I'd seen – I did indeed spot it – looked like a ring, and not a tiny bubble of smoke.

I tended to stay out fairly late when I observed in the summer. In the middle portion of the season this was actually necessary; twilight lingered far into the night. You didn't get an early start on star-gazing in Illinois, in the summertime. And so on clear nights, at about the time my parents were wrapping up the affairs of the day, I hauled my make-shift and sometimes improvised gear to the far end of the half-acre back yard. There was the old card table, and with it the worn wooden kitchen stool, my radio, notebooks and pens and pencils, and of course, the binder full of star charts hand-copied from *Field Book of the Skies.*

Much of this stuff was kept on a board stretched between two cinder blocks, under the card table, where it was as safe from dew as possible. The sudden onset of clouds could certainly be a problem, one that often shut me down all too soon on what might otherwise have been a productive night. But the onset of dew was a constant problem, even for a high school science geek who knew why dew happened. An understanding of radiative cooling, relative humidity, and dew points gave me a fighting chance, but it was often still a struggle. There were nights when dew dripped from the telescope, when the sodden grass soaked my sneakers and gave me a serious case of cold feet, and when the shield provided by the old card table could not prevent paper from becoming so damp a pen would not write on it. I remember a night when, between the dew and the guttational water oozing from grass blades, a notebook I dropped to the ground came up dripping. The next morning the paper had swelled like a sponge, and I spent several days transcribing the notes and sketches it contained into a more legible form.

It was not unheard of for the cheap plastic flashlights I covered with red tape to succumb to the moisture if dropped. You'd think they fell into a pond, the way they dripped when I retrieved them. The moisture of the grass in the yard leached the stain from the lower four or five inches of the tripod legs, pallor that brought back damp memories when the Old Scope was exhumed and put to use again many years later. Every now and then I would forget to wipe off the old stool I used and, sitting down, would find that I was perched in a shallow bowl of cold water. That was always awkward, especially if I needed to go into the house for some reason, and someone was still awake at that hour.

I was not always alone out there, and was not always glad of the company I kept. Of the creatures of the night I encountered my most unpleasant memories are, of course, of mosquitoes. They may not have been as large as the insects of Alaskan myth and legend, but they were hungry little beasts and they had an advantage in numbers. I was apparently quite tasty. Mosquito repellants were available by then, and I used them liberally. Somehow I managed to do so without damaging any of the lenses of the telescope, but I don't recall if this was caution on my part, or if I just got lucky. I was surely careful, of course, given what that telescope meant to me. I doubt I needed to be told such products were bad for optics to realize I didn't want something that sticky landing on the lenses! The stuff did not last as long as I wanted, and I often resorted to wearing a thin nylon windbreaker, with the wrists held shut by rubber bands. No matter what I did, however, the night was often marred by the high whine of mosquito wings close to my ears.

And then there were those things that go bump in the night. When you are an imaginative boy, such sounds can do more than raise a little gooseflesh. My interest in science, and my love of astronomy, went hand in hand with a love for books, especially those containing escapist adventures on other worlds. This was all in the days before Star Wars, but during the great space race between the United States and the Soviet Union. The science fiction I read was a reflection of those Cold War times, heavy on spaceships blasting things to bits, aliens staging remarkably unsuccessful invasions, and the dangers posed by radioactive mutants. Lots and lots of radioactive mutants. I was also fond of sci-fi B movies of the fifties and sixties that somehow managed to be lurid, even when displayed on a black-and-white television screen. Some of these movies, when I saw them on television (there was no theatre in my home town) were patently absurd, amusing but not taken too seriously. Others, however, while equally implausible, somehow managed to eat into my brain, infecting my own imaginings and (sometimes) intruding on the waking world in those places where imagination leaks through.

One such film (I can't remember the title now) involved invisible creatures powered by nuclear radiation that ambushed people from behind and sucked out their brains. I watched it for the first time late one night while waiting for the skies to clear and grow dark. I can't tell you much about the plot of the film, if there was one, but the gruesomeness of these invisible, unstoppable creatures slurping brains out of the backs of people's skulls certainly gave me the creeps. This most likely explains why I was watching the thing in the first place. These monsters moved by hitching themselves along and sometimes hopping like one-legged rabbits, and the only warning characters in the film received were mysterious slitherings and thumps just as the monsters leaped upon a victim.

The final credits rolled, leaving me with a delightful dread of things imagined but unseen, a feeling as contradictory as it was titillating. I glanced out the door and saw a sky full of stars, and, taking great care not to wake anyone up, I slipped out the back door and into the quiet night. My observing kit, such as it was, occupied a bit of space in the garage, and so I could haul things out onto the already wet grass without disturbing the household. It was cool and moist and very dark, and almost completely silent. There wasn't a breath of wind at all. The grass was wet with dew, of course; I might as well have been wading through a pond. I remember standing there and taking in the sight of the summer Milky Way just clearing the eastern woodlands. I started out by just scanning the richness of the Milky Way, slowly sweeping the telescope from south to north and back. It was so easy to imagine myself flying through space as I did so. And as I slowly panned the telescope across the heavens, fighting off sleep while slipping into a sort of waking dream filled with stars, I heard something rustle the uncut weeds and grasses in the vacant yard next door.

Now, I was a country boy, and knew very well that the woods and fields around me were populated by raccoons, opossums, deer, rabbits, and assorted pet cats. In fact, I assumed it was our house cat Honey, and called softly to her, but no cat appeared. When nothing happened for a time, I went back to the eyepiece.

The grasses just past the edge of our freshly mowed lawn rattled and shook again. Something was obvious pushing through them, and whatever it was, it was coming right at me. Still more curious than alarmed, I walked to the edge of the yard for a look. I had taken out with me the huge flashlight we kept by the back door, and had it in my hand just in case. I was reluctant to turn it on, though, since it lacked the red tape I put on my own flashlights. I knew quite well that, after using the light, I would be blind for several minutes. So I worked by the soft glow of starlight, with young, dark-adapted eyes, and held the flashlight as a last resort. And all I could see was pale grass in the starlight and the dark shadows under trees and shrubs. The yard to the east of us had long since been abandoned, and the house there was falling into decay. The woods to the east were gradually spreading into the grassy space, with hawthorn and oak saplings near the edge of the woods, and mounds of wild raspberries rising from the timothy grass further west. It all looked slightly wild but harmless, and the process of succession unfolding next door as the trees reclaimed this bit of land was a source of endless fascination to a young naturalist. During the day, at least. At night, with my mind on the stars, it usually did not command my attention. Usually.

There was no sign of any sort of animal, and certainly nothing bolted to escape the approaching human. Still reluctant to lose my night vision, I lowered the flashlight, tried to shrug off the prickling of unease that crept over me, and headed back to the telescope. It was as I turned my back on the vacant lot that I heard that thump.

Something hit the ground directly behind me with a soft, muffled thump, landing where I'd been standing a moment before. In a triumph of overactive teenage, hormone-charged imagination over reason and reality (not such a hard thing to do, actually), aided and abetted by lack of sleep and B-movie willies, I knew with absolute certainty that "*something*" was out there with me, and that it wasn't friendly. The realization flashed out of my imagination and shorted out what few critical thinking circuits a teenager may possess. I whirled around, poking the flashlight out in front of me as if it might somehow fend off the threat from behind, flicking it on as if I were firing a phaser, straight out of an episode of Star Trek. And I fired a dud; something was wrong with the thing, and where I expected a shaft of bright white light I saw only a feeble glow that barely illuminated the ground at my feet. All I could see were shadow-filled irregularities of the lawn, and the gray-green shadowy wall of timothy grass beyond. Like the victim of just about every cheap horror movie ever filmed, in which flashlights invariably fade and fail at exactly the wrong moment, I shook the flashlight harshly. The light flickered a bit brighter, and then returned to its feeble glow.

A low, growling groan reached my ears, from something *right in front of me!* I was terrified, absolutely frozen in place, unable to see what made the noise, but acutely aware that there was *something* there. I heard another soft thump and with it came the ghastly sense, some bare hint of motion not quite seen, that something invisible had moved toward me! I wanted to turn and flee, to run and lock myself into one of the cars in the garage. The back door to the house was so near, yet so far; I knew that if I ran that way I would be overtaken before I turned the knob.

Another thump. It was closer!

Desperate, I shook the balky flashlight with all the violence my adrenalin rush could provide. A bright beam of light stabbed out from it and with a hand shaking like a palsy victim, I jabbed the now bright white beam of light out at whatever the intruder was.

A dark, squat, rounded shape in the grass grumbled at me. A pair of eyes gleamed. Then it leaped to the side to escape the light, long hind legs flailing out behind as it did so. And I knew my foe. I stood frozen with fear, terrified of having my brains sucked out of the back of my head by . . .

A bullfrog.

Fall

Autumn shared many of the disadvantages of spring for a teenage amateur astronomer, along with one unique to the season. It started out fine enough, and some of the clearest skies I would see in Illinois were in the first part of autumn. But as the season rolled on and the days became steadily shorter, the weather changed, and so did my mood. As a boy and a teenager I had a tendency to "melancholy humors" as my grandmother once put it. At the time I wrote it off to school being a problem, and high school certainly was a trial for me. Looking back from a more informed perspective, I know now that as the days became shorter I was ever more influenced by the day length, or rather the lack thereof. I endure a condition – one more common than most people realize – called seasonal affective disorder (SAD). No one knew that, then, and thought my emotional ups and downs were simply the hormonal storms of adolescence. And that was there, too, no doubt. It just became stormier in late autumn. I would, among other things, become very short-focused, lacking in motivation, going through expected motions because that provided the path of least resistance. I did school things. I did what I needed to do, and nothing else, except to read science fiction novels. I practiced that form of escapism long before I knew what escapism was.

Before my strange annual depression came on, during the time between summer's end and the bleak end of autumn, I could still take advantage of those fine evenings for observing. I was still charged up by the long days of summer. The catch was the school year being underway, once again limiting me to weekends. My first real after-school job added to the complications. When I could get out with the telescope I explored the Great Square of Pegasus, the double stars and open star clusters of Cassiopeia, and on one memorable night searched for the Andromeda galaxy.

Field Book of the Skies still referred to M 31 as the "Great Nebula" on the chart and in the text devoted to the constellation Andromeda. It was known to be a galaxy well before the year of the last revision, and yet no change was made. No mention is made of M 31 being extra-galactic. Other books in my possession cleared the matter up, though, and from what I read it sounded like the "Great Nebula" was my best chance at seeing a galaxy through a telescope of my own.

Of the objects I viewed with that small telescope, galaxies seemed the most out of reach, a belief that became such a matter of reflex that it took a while to make them a priority when I had a larger telescope. I'd read about the big galaxy in Andromeda, knew a fair amount about this near neighbor, a giant whirl of stars, but aside from photographs in books, had not glimpsed it. Like the Keystone in Hercules, it seems more than a little ridiculous to me now that finding and viewing M 31 presented any sort of challenge. How do you *not* find something bigger (albeit fainter) than the Moon in a dark, rural sky? And yet I needed more than one try.

Looking back on it all, I now have a much better understanding of the cumulative nature of experience. When I first seriously explored the night sky with that 60mm refractor I was filled with a powerful enthusiasm, but had none of the object location skills I now take for granted. I was also on my own. None of my friends shared this passion, nor did my parents or siblings. If there were any other amateur astronomers in my home town, I never met them, so I lacked an experienced mentor. My enthusiasm somehow kept me working at it through times of frustration, allowing me to acquire the experience that in turn would permit me to look back years later and wonder just what took me so long.

Just as I did in confusing portions of Draco and Hercules, I managed once again to confuse myself with patterns in the sky. I convinced myself that beta Andromedae was mu Andromedae, and so dutifully pointed the refractor between the long lines of Andromeda as usually depicted on star charts. I slowly swept back and forth through the area, probably fast enough to fly right past that pale glow, if I *had* crossed it. (The dual concepts of slow and careful have somewhat different meanings for a teenager.) I had enough experience by then that the inevitable frustration did not derail me; I'd been down this road through the stars before. Stepping back for a moment, I looked up at the stars, Whitney's wheel in my hand, trying to make sense of it all. A thought occurred. Somewhere I'd read you could see the

Andromeda "nebula" with binoculars. At some point shortly after acquiring the telescope my grandmother, with whom I shared an interest in bird watching, had given me a pair of 7x35 binoculars. I'd used them already to scan the Milky Way in summer, but had not yet acquired the habit of keeping them with me scope-side. I brought them out and, after my eyes re-adapted to the darkness, scanned where I thought the galaxy should be.

I was still looking in the wrong place, of course, but with the much wider field of view of the binoculars, it was near enough. I found in that dark autumn sky a pale, oblong glow, and knew I had succeeded. I could also, due to the field of view, see mu Andromedae as well and only then realized I'd played connect-the-dots with the wrong stars when I traced out the constellation. I kept my eyes directed toward the galaxy as I lowered the binoculars, to better get a fix on the location for telescopic aiming purposes. And then just stood there, mouth open, looking up into the night.

I could still see the galaxy.

There was a faint but clearly visible smudge up there. Now that I knew where to look, and had an idea of what to expect from its appearance, it was hard to miss. And yet I had done so, many times, missed it all the while, not knowing quite what to look for. Sometimes, with astronomy at least, you can't really *see* until you *know*.

A few moments later I had that hazy gray football in the 20mm eyepiece. I know now that what I saw was merely the core of the galaxy. But it was a galaxy! I found it and I could see it – a galaxy – with my eyes alone! The wonder of such a thing has never faded.

Winter

The stars of the winter sky posed the greatest challenge to me as a young observer. Observing on week nights was a problem, of course, with school in session, but weather was the major difficulty. Stars of winter were alternately hidden by cloudy weather, and then put out of reach by the bitter cold that often moved in behind major storm systems. For my mother, ever the worry-wart, the idea that I might be allowed out on a sub-freezing night, however effectively bundled, was absolutely appalling. Many a clear winter night passed me by simply because mother declared it "Too cold!" I learned early on that it was not a fight I could win. Being trapped in a house each winter with five children prone to every sneeze and sniffle-causing virus known to medical science (actually, I think we bred some new ones), my mother was more than a little paranoid when it came to our health. If she *perceived* a risk it was a *real* risk, end of story. Looking back at it now, it's hard to hold this against her.

I'm not honestly sure whether or not my father always agreed with her, or simply (and perhaps wisely) deferred to her judgment in these matters. As time passed and I became a little older and obviously less fragile than she believed, he did eventually intercede on my behalf. That he did so only *after* my mother went back to work and wasn't always there in the evening when permission was requested, is a tribute to his common sense. I remember no few occasions, after I started high school, on which she drove up to the garage, headlights glaring off the snow, and found me peering up at Orion, Perseus, or blazing Capella. "What do you think you're doing out here?" she demanded the very first time this happened. My defense was that Dad said it was okay for "a while," that conveniently indeterminate unit of time so often used by parents.

To be honest, I was never all that fond of cold weather, or standing in the dark in the snow. There were times when the lure of starlight was too great and I just *had* to be out there. I was not inclined to push it, my motivation being limited by that aversion to cold, the difficulty of using a telescope with heavy gloves on my hands, and the fact that short days pulled the wind out of my sails. I surely did less winter observing than was actually possible. And yet there are, among the sights of the winter night sky, those that I know as well as any from late spring or the summertime. Chief among these, of course, is Orion the Hunter.

My fascination with the Hunter, an attraction that predates meaningful telescopic examination of its vicinity, was most likely due to being able to identify it so readily. The depictions of Orion in Neely's *A Primer For Star-Gazers* caught my imagination and stuck in my memory. The sheer size of the constellation reinforced knowledge of its identity. It looms over you in the winter night sky, and anything that looms makes an impression on small children. So by the time I reached my telescope-wielding teen years, Orion was *the* constellation of Winter. On those clear winter nights when I could get out of the house, Orion received much of my attention. It's a rewarding constellation for a small refractor, containing as it does so many bright double stars, and the Great Nebula of Orion itself.

Of course, the Pleiades and the Bull were also well known to me, as was Canis Major, impossible to ignore with brilliant Sirius flashing low in the south. I can remember standing alone out there, in the frigid winter dark, struggling to focus the refractor with fingers that slowly went numb even with a good pair of gloves to protect them. I split Mintaka, saw three stars of the sigma Orionis system, and tried very hard to make out all the stars in the Trapezium while contemplating the awesome idea that I was staring at a place where stars were born. The sky in which these, and other, wonders were set, especially in mid-winter when domes of dry, transparent arctic air settled over us, would be as black a setting for stars as any I've seen since. The same conditions that made diamonds and jewels of the stars, hard and bright in a transparent black sky, also sent the temperatures plunging. I came in more than once because of ice crystals on the eyepieces, frost on my eyebrows, and with a touch of frost nip in my fingertips causing them to burn and sting when I went back inside.

My mother may have over-estimated the risk I was taking, but she was not entirely wrong. It grew dangerously cold, some nights, but as these were often the best of nights, I would bundle up and take that challenge. Eventually both my parents came to trust my common sense in the matter. Under completely different circumstances, I once endured a touch of actual frostbite, and the pain of it was not something I ever forgot. So I was very careful. I dressed like an arctic explorer and carried the telescope out to an area cleared of snow while wearing snowmobile boots, thick mittens over fingerless gloves, and a wool ski mask that itched something awful. All you would have seen of me was my eyes and mouth, the latter being concealed frequently by steam. I would go out before dark, when the world was marked by long, blue snow shadows and the sunset glowed low in the southwest. The air *smelled* cold, strange as that may sound. If there was any breeze at all it would be a short night; calm nights I lasted longest. The snow squeaked and crunched under those thick-soled, clunky old boots.

Twilight did not last long, that time of year, and darkness settled in quickly. Out at night in the winter, darkness always held a slightly spooky quality for me, no doubt the result of SAD warring with my motivation to do astronomy. It's more than a bit awkward to be enamored of the stars, and to be (in a way) afraid of the dark at the same time.

Toward the end of high school a few of my classmates acquired vehicles of their own, which led to one of the few instances I can recall in which one of them shared the view through the eyepiece. I was not far off the back stoop with only the telescope and the 20mm eyepiece, not doing any serious observing, merely moving the telescope from one old favorite to another. A car came up the drive and stopped, the headlights went out, and one of my friends stalked through the snow over the frozen backyard. He probably made a sarcastic comment about me being out there in the cold and dark, but by then I'd heard them all. There was no ill intent, and so no sting. This incident stands out because for some reason, in addition to the usual harassment, he challenged me to show him something "interesting."

I moved the scope and pointed it at the Great Nebula in Orion, and then set the nebula just off the edge so there would be time to switch observers and still get a good look. My friend peered into the eyepiece. There was some back and forth as we got things focused for his eye, and I demonstrated how to gently nudge the scope to keep the nebula in view. He naturally wanted to know what he was seeing, and so I rattled off everything I could off the top of my head regarding the Great Nebula. It was probably a good deal more than he wanted to know, and I'm sure I got carried away a bit with the part about those four tiny, gleaming stars being new suns, born in that cloud of gas and dust. After a while, he looked up at Orion and nodded. "Far out," he said quietly. And then, as if nothing unusual had taken place, he suggested we drive over to another friend's house and hang out. A little disappointed, though not honestly surprised, by his reaction, I packed up the scope, obtained parental permission for the jaunt, and we went elsewhere to spend the evening.

The following Monday morning, a couple of classes into the day, that same friend and I found ourselves sitting in English class. The emphasis for that semester was on writing creatively, part of the grand effort to prepare us for college. On Monday morning the week's writing assignment theme would be determined by taking an idea from what we experienced over the weekend. To stimulate discussion and ideas, we were encouraged to share the experiences about which we intended to write our essays. My friend was one of those called upon for this one. What had he seen or done over the past two days that stood out, the teacher asked?

He told her he had seen a place where stars were born.

There's a curious thing about these fragments of memory that have survived the decades, somehow following me around along with the old 6omm refractor. They are not always about the stars or the Moon or the planets specifically. For the most part, individual observations are lost in the ever growing depth of time behind me. What I recall instead, and at times vividly, is the experience of being out there, of being alone out in the gentle dark. I know I sought and, sometimes split, double stars. I know I studied the dance of Jupiter's moons and the shadow play of our own Moon. I learned the constellations, all of them I could see above the trees to the south, then over and down to the bare northern horizon, where the glow marking Chicago hugged the distant ground. It never occurred to me I would need to remember any of these things specifically, because I wrote them all down. I took notes and made crude sketches. I duplicated and annotated the charts from *Field Book of the Skies*. The notebooks and folders holding this precious trove piled up over the years following the purchase of the refractor, kept safely on a shelf given over to me for that purpose.

But times and circumstances change, whether you're ready or not, and even the most precious of things can be lost.

V

HIATUS

"They always say time changes things, but you actually have to change them yourself."
- Andy Warhol

I could not have known it at the time, but graduating from high school put me about a year away from dropping the visual observing part of amateur astronomy for many years. I was done with high school in 1974, but utterly at a loss for what was to come next. My fascination with the various sciences did not provide a clear goal or direction, in part because I could not focus entirely on any one branch (not even astronomy), but also – okay, mostly – because I'd developed a powerful math phobia along the way. How this came to be I do not know; it was simply a fact of life, like the color of my hair, and something I was apparently unable to change on my own. The teachers I had back then addressed my situation by putting notes such as "needs to try harder" on report cards, as if I were simply a lazy student. Those notes were the closest thing to mentoring I can remember receiving. Whatever the root causes of the problem, lack of effort on my part wasn't it. At some point I signed up for a basic algebra course, determined to overcome the problem by beating it to death, in a manner of speaking. I passed the class, but just barely. The effort I put into that class, and the disappointing result that came of it all, put me off anything to do with mathematics. Since my reading at that point had already made very plain the profound and powerful role of mathematics in all branches of the sciences, I sought other options.

Like many who drift out of high school without any plans or meaningful guidance, I enrolled in a local community college. School was what I knew, and so I stuck with things familiar, and soon enough found what seemed to be an obvious path to follow. I was, if anything, more in love with words and writing than I was with any particular branch of science. Whatever I did, wherever my interests took me, I wrote about it. My observing notes have always taken the form of essays, and for most of my adolescence I kept a natural history journal, inspired by the writings of Edwin Way Teal. Declaring myself an English major (my goal was journalism, but they lacked such a program) took very little soul-searching. It should come as no surprise that most of the electives I chose were in the sciences: biology, ecology, geology, and (of course) astronomy. I was still an observer at that time, and so the astronomy course was especially meaningful. For the first time in my life I found myself in the company of another person who shared my enthusiasm for star-gazing. He was the instructor of the non-majors Astronomy 101 "Descriptive Astronomy" class I took.

The class was held in a small planetarium, the first and to date still the only experience I've had with such an environment. (I keep meaning to change that.) I found it mesmerizing. I can't claim to remember the exact content of most of the lectures, but I do remember vividly the effect of that fascinating artificial sky. Because of my long hours under the stars, I was right at home, unlike many classmates who found the display either disorienting or – hard to believe from where I sat – boring. No small number of classmates dozed off during lectures that involved displays under the dome, with the largest number zoning out the day he explained coordinate systems on the celestial sphere. The instructor, as mild-mannered a man as you could imagine meeting, took this in stride and with a quiet, knowing smile. He would bring the lights up gradually and raise his voice just a bit to arouse those who had succumbed without startling them. For myself, I was appalled that anyone could fall asleep with such a show going on. But of course, as the instructor himself pointed out one day, I was accustomed to staying awake in the dark, under stars.

This first attempt at a college degree ended unceremoniously after two semesters, when my father found out that his many years of making that insane commute to and from Chicago had come to an end. They were closing down his place of employment. In response to this potentially disastrous turn of events, various members of my family decided this would be a good time to move elsewhere and launch a small business. How exactly my father and my aunt (his partner in the venture) arrived at the conclusion that this was a viable course of action is not something I can explain, as I was not in that loop. I did not initially intend to join in their planned relocation.

Those first two semesters, and the short summer courses I took in 1975, were a turning point for me. First, I found myself with people who knew nothing of me, and taking me at face value, did not treat me as the class science geek and resident misfit. Of course, with such a large and diverse student body, I could not have stood out much from the crowd, not the way I did in my smaller high school population. This allowed me to grow up more in a year, socially and emotionally, than I'd done in the previous four. As soon as I adapted to the varied and sundry stresses of being a college student, I realized I was having the time of my life. At the same time, I discovered that the recent sale of a hobby-related article to a small magazine was not a fluke. I could string words together with enough style and accuracy to put a little money in my pocket. Life was transformed. I felt I was on my way. I wasn't entirely sure where I was headed, but surely it wasn't to Arizona.

So when it was announced that the family was moving west, I quietly set about trying to find a way to cast off and do my own thing in Illinois, without them. I immediately ran into serious trouble. I did not have a car of my own, and the work I could find with my limited skill set at the time was not going to put me in the driver's seat. I had offers of places to stay, some with and some without rent, but in each case I would have been dependent on someone else for transportation – not a workable solution. The inability to render myself in any way self-sufficient in the short time before the family pulled up stakes eventually made it necessary to change my mind, and join the exodus. Once that decision was made, I brought myself up to speed on their plan, and then became rather excited about the possibilities it seemed to hold.

All the same, when the time came to hit the road I did so with a heavy heart. Leaving the place that holds every single memory and experience of your life to that point is not a thing done lightly, even when you are willing to make that move. So at the end of November 1975 I drove with great reluctance away from Illinois, driving one of three vehicles in a caravan barely fit for the open road. The trip was a nightmare that put me off road trips for a very long time, sending us into the teeth of blizzards, and marked by delays due to the weather, car troubles, and flu. I've been back to the old home town just once, since that time.

The end of the journey was Phoenix, Arizona, set in the northern portion of the Sonoran Desert. To say the change in environment was a shock to the system would be a monumental understatement. With very little life experience to guide me, I was quickly lost in that urban environment. The climate was an enormous departure from what I'd known all my life, almost intolerably hot from April to October (and at times, later) and with no real winter to speak of. I did in time become attuned to the subtler seasons of that climate, but that took a while. And it was crowded. It seemed as if more people lived around me in the immediate neighborhood than had lived in my entire home town – unlikely to be literally true, but a good description for how it felt. And yet, few of them seemed to know each other; the concept of 'neighbor' seemed a very different thing in the suburbs.

I found myself intensely focused on the activities surrounding buying and re-establishing a struggling pet shop. The place had the somewhat absurd name of Spawn Shop and emphasized aquaria and exotic fish, which up until then was a modest hobby of mine (nowhere near the prominence of astronomy, or natural history generally). Lacking the resources to enroll immediately in either the local community college or the nearby university, I leaned into that business in an effort to form some sort of foundation for my life in that new place. I also began to write in earnest, and for a time found it provided a healthy supplement for my meager family business income. For a long time I held out the hope that these two sources of revenue would ultimately add up to enough money to put me back on the degree path.

In this jumble of events, astronomy was literally lost in the bright lights of the big city. Part way along the journey from Illinois to Arizona, we stopped for a night in a hotel just outside Las Cruces, NM. That evening, before turning in, I stepped outside for a few minutes. The trip had been a rough one, to that point. I was worn out, mentally and emotionally, from dealing with stressful experiences way outside my frame of reference. Standing in the hotel parking lot, as the very last trace of daylight faded away in the west, I was as tired and depressed as I'd ever been in my life to that point. I looked up and saw the stars, the familiar and unchanging stars, looking just as I had known them a few days before, and for all of my life. They were certainly displaced somewhat to the north, considering my significant change in location, but I don't recall actually noticing this. All that registered was a reassuring sense of familiarity and belonging. However far I might be from the place I had always thought of as home, when the sun went down these old friends would be there. Always. That thought calmed me considerably, and for a little while at least I found my center, enough that the next day, as I passed through Tucson for the first time, I could appreciate and even become intrigued by the sight of the cactus desert.

In truth, when I settled into Phoenix the stars were surely there. But what I could see of them was a source of deep disappointment. Only the brightest, along with the Moon and the planets, could easily be picked out, and right from the start the expected comfortable familiarity of the night was lost to me. The city sky glowed at night, as if giving off a light of its own. What I could see of the celestial sphere was depressingly anemic compared with the dark rural skies I'd left behind.

At first the novelty of my new urban situation, and the effort that went into establishing the family business, blunted the impact of this less-than-positive aspect of city life. I was busier than I'd ever been in my life, and massively distracted. But as each day came to an end and the night grew as dark as it was going to get, there was a sense of disappointment and loss. I indulged in Moon-watching from time to time, but that weird, pallid gray sky made me uncomfortable; it was almost a feeling of claustrophobia. To see only the Moon, the planets, and a few brighter stars, and to be unable to see the summer Milky Way at all, had a demoralizing effect on my desire to observe. After a few attempts – I even had trouble locating Polaris for a while there – I found myself growing reluctant to unpack the telescope at all. There just didn't seem to be any point. Denied the sky as I had known it, the old habit slowly died. Soon I was so out of the habit of star-gazing that on the rare occasion that I found myself out of town at night, I rarely had so much as an old pair of binoculars handy. I would gaze up in wonder, and remembrance, but never did anything to take advantage of those nights. More often than not I would not have been free to do so, being involved with other activities at such times.

When faced with adversity you can respond creatively (as my father did in attempting to establish a business following his lay-off) or otherwise. Sadly, "otherwise" describes the route I followed with regards to amateur astronomy while living in Phoenix. I could not do it the way I had in that small town and could not imagine a way to adapt to the new circumstances. Lack of experience is the only real explanation I have for following the path I did, that and a regrettable lack of understanding regarding the true depth of amateur astronomy. Even with that 60mm refractor there were options available to me as an amateur – lunar observing not the least of these – but I never really considered them. I lacked reliable transportation, and so could not reach dark skies, not that I would have known where to go. There were surely astronomy clubs in the area, but between the distractions of the new way of life and not yet being all that confident socially, it never occurred to me to investigate such an option.

Loss of the dark night sky was complicated by what in some ways was a far more grievous blow, one that really pulled the rug from under me. As an amateur naturalist in Illinois I collected things: minerals, leaves of trees (pressed, mounted, and labeled), and fossils. I also kept the aforementioned journals full of bird lists and observations of the natural world in and around Hickory Creek. A separate set of notebooks held my astronomical observations and the laboriously copied material from Olcott's *Field Book of the Skies*. These were treasures to me, of course, and strong connections to life as it had been. You need such connections when you move through a time of changes. When the time came to unload the moving van, the old wooden box I packed them in was missing, left behind. I've never been clear how or why it happened, but there I was, adrift in an unfamiliar environment, with all those precious links to who and what I'd been nowhere to be found. An attempt to recover the lost material came to nothing in the end.

There was nothing for it, and I could only move on. What followed was both an awkward and a rewarding time in my life. Almost in spite of myself I gathered momentum and a broader understanding of life, in some cases involving things that should have been clear to me in high school. My social awkwardness wore away quickly as I met and interacted with a larger and more diverse population. It was, on a grand scale, what happened to me during my first attempt at college. No one knew me; no one had preconceived notions about who I was (which did not prevent some from making snap judgments, of course). A big change came in the late '70s when I attended a large science fiction convention, and began a long association with the local science fiction fandom crowd in the

Phoenix area. I'd read of such gatherings, and to have a "WorldCon" held in my back yard was a wonderful opportunity, one I seized without hesitation. It all combined to launch me on an ascending curve that took me from something of a misfit to a man capable of moving through life with a measure of confidence. Friendships grew, and some became strong and long lasting. I continued to write, and for a time my rate of success in that field increased.

A sign that something of the person I'd been survived could be seen in the effort I put into the raising of exotic tropical fish and house plants. These interests were surely sublimations of childhood fascinations that managed to follow me west. I felt the lure of nature study any time I made it out of town and into the desert, a habitat that both fascinated and – at first – intimidated me. None of these excursions were frequent enough, or long enough, to allow for the sort of nature study I'd done in my homeland, but were sufficient to remind me that the city did not cover everything.

Astronomy refused to just curl up and die; the interest had grown too deeply into my spirit for that. It became an armchair enthusiasm, a matter of books and magazines. I followed the Pioneer and Voyager space missions avidly, thrilled by the images sent back by those probes. At science fiction conventions, I attended any talk or panel discussion featuring a NASA scientist, or having space exploration as a subject. The television series "Cosmos" came along and blew my mind, leaving me a life-long admirer of Carl Sagan. The few nonfiction books I read – science fiction and fantasy having taken over much of my time and imagination due to my "fannish" involvement – were almost entirely on astronomy and cosmology.

The telescope generally served only to decorate various bachelor pads, but I kept the thing. I was rather protective of it, and so it survived the passage of time in pretty good shape.

I wrote in every spare moment. Short stories, novels (all unsold), and various short essays and articles, many of which *did* sell, though only a handful had a byline. (I also did some ghost writing, which did nothing to move my career forward, but paid a lot of my bills.) For a time I supported myself on a mix of writing, helping the family business (which sadly was failing even then) and a variety of temporary service jobs. It was a hectic, and at times frantic, way of life, one that gradually wore me down. Money was always short, and I grew tired of working without a net. In 1984 a friend mentioned that the bookstore in which she worked had a part-time opening, and that she would be willing to speak on my behalf to her manager. I was oddly reluctant at first – it felt too much like an admission of defeat – but went in for an interview and got the job. Whatever reluctance there might have been at first, I found myself with a dependable if modest source of income, while working in a marvelous environment for a bibliophile. The amount of reading I did went up dramatically, as did the range of materials. Among the tomes to cross my path were the volumes of Burnham's Celestial Handbook, a compilation that both fascinated and depressed me. The fascination came from its marvelous scope and depth, the depression from wishing I'd owned these books many years before, when I could still use them. The black and white pictures in particular brought back sharp reminders of nights alone in the dark with the stars, stars I could no longer see. But that life seemed a distant memory by then, and I don't remember seriously considering the purchase of a set.

The bookstore job accelerated me up that ascending curve, and was ultimately the start of the journey back to the stars. Working there put me in the company of people – both coworkers and customers – representing a range of ideas that might otherwise not have had a direct influence on me. One such relationship led to a bicycle adventure that saw me peddling from Tijuana to Cabo san Lucas, pretty much the length of the Baja California peninsula. On that trip I spent every night for more than three weeks under skies darker than those of my childhood home. I beheld one starry sky, with a waxing Moon, over boojums and cardón cacti growing in a land of huge granite boulders, worn by the wind and weather into great round shapes. The image comes back to me now like something I dreamed, or invented for a tale of fantasy. As impressive as that experience was, however, it was eclipsed by another that had a more profound effect on my life.

In 1985 the famed periodic comet 1P/Halley made its long-predicted return to the inner solar system. The event produced a media feeding frenzy, with just about all the major players in the publishing industry rushing to put out guidebooks to finding and observing Halley's Comet. The book retailers dutifully set up displays of this timely merchandise on tables and racks in the fronts of their stores; the B. Dalton Bookseller at which I was employed was no different.

One evening I struck up a conversation with a customer browsing this material. The woman involved was taller than most women I chatted up, with very long, very blonde hair. She was also a familiar face, having been a regular customer for some time, and had already caught my eye. I'll freely confess that I was interested in seeing if the conversation might lead to something more than a book sale; in this the conversation was no different from any number of other careful flirtations I indulged in while working there. I asked if she had managed to see the comet and she replied that she *thought* she had, using a large pair of binoculars. She wasn't entirely sure. Speaking from hard experience, I pointed out that such an object would be a bit hard to see from within town, with all the city's lights getting in the way.

The conversation took a surprising turn after that statement. When asked if I had seen the comet for myself, I confessed that I had not even tried – at least, not yet. I told her that I had a telescope, but had not been able to get out of town to a darker location, my car being in a constant state of disrepair. Her response was that she had a reliable vehicle, but otherwise wasn't sure of what she was doing while searching the skies. I couldn't help pointing out, mostly in jest, that between the two of us, we had what we needed to see Comet Halley.

Imagine my surprise when this tall, beautiful blonde agreed with me, and took my remark as a suggestion. In the end, we swapped phone numbers for planning purposes and parted company for the moment. My mind was boggled. I barely knew this woman, and had only that evening learned her name, and she was suggesting we drive out together into a remote desert location for a bit of star-gazing. On the heels of a recently ended relationship, this experience held an air of unreality. I had either seen a stunning reversal of bad luck (I was all too well known among my friends for getting mixed up with the wrong girls) or I had simply done it again, this time with a lunatic.

But I couldn't pass up the chance, so on the appointed evening I made the call. We ended up having a long, very pleasant, and interesting conversation. At some point one of us, I can't remember who, finally made the obvious observation that she was making a surprising leap of trust in planning this excursion. She admitted that a friend of hers had made just this point, and insisted on accompanying us, after first having a chance to check me out for herself.

Herself? This just kept getting more and more interesting. Out into the desert on a cold winter night with *two* women I didn't even know? Either my luck had been transformed by outrageous good fortune, or I was being set up big time. The proposed dinner meeting, however, seemed to take some of the risk out of the situation, all around. If I didn't like what I picked up from that, I could blow it all off easily enough. Surely there was nothing to lose by going that far.

I left work on the agreed-upon evening and took a booth at the burger place more or less across the mall from the bookstore. I don't recall waiting long before the blonde object of my current interest appeared, and with her the friend, who turned out to be someone I knew from the science fiction fan scene. This coincidence was greeted with considerable humor and no small amount of teasing from the acquaintance involved. Since she recognized me, the friend found the idea of the three of us driving off into the dark together acceptable. The plan for the trip was set for the following Saturday night.

A week later we drove together out into the desert south of Phoenix, to a large highway rest area part way to Casa Grande. There we parked and walked through a gap in the fence between the lighted area and the darker desert beyond. It was cold, and all three of us stumped along, bundled up against the chill. I lugged that old refractor along in its wooden case, setting it up in the dark as my companions held flashlights. It was a curious experience to say the least. I was setting up the old telescope for actual astronomical use for the first time in ten years and for only the second time with a willing audience. If you'd told me in my teens I would have such an audience – two attractive women – I'd have laughed myself silly.

The look and feel of the telescope was so familiar, and yet there was a rather distressing difference, as years of relocations and disuse showed in the way things went together and moved. It wasn't as tight, and it wasn't as steady.

Of course, clouds rolled in. High, thin clouds of a sort very common in this part of the world in winter, the result of storm systems passing by well to the north, their skirts trailing down over south central Arizona to veil the stars. We tried to find the comet, but it was much too faint to see through that haze. After a while we decided to call it a night, and shivered our way back to the car after I repacked the telescope. The looks we received from travelers as we appeared from the desert with a long wooden case that we shoved into the back of the friend's station wagon were worth the chill, and we were hooting with laughter over the matter as we drove away. A week later my now girlfriend – the blonde one – and I were out there again, this time unchaparoned, surrounded by half-seen cacti and with a clear winter night over our heads. Orion loomed overhead, a bit higher than I remembered. We found the comet, and then held hands as the Geminid meteor shower silently decorated the December sky.

Less than a year and a half later, we were married.

That brief resurrection of the 60mm refractor was only one of several events that could be called near misses in ending the hiatus. My new bride and I shared an interest in the natural world, especially birds. Birdwatching excursions often involved the refractor, which we employed somewhat awkwardly as a spotting scope. When these trips happened to be overnight (or longer) camping excursions, we would take in a few celestial sights. No real observing, though. I was unprepared for such, after so long, and the need to be up at the crack of dawn to chase birds left late-night eyepiece sessions out of the question. Still, while out under the stars in out-of-the-way places, I felt them pulling my eyes skyward, and I remembered former days.

One summer the Perseid meteor shower was predicted to be a grand affair, so we drove out to Lake Pleasant – a reservoir near Phoenix – to see what we could see. We were not the only people out there for the purpose, and each bright shooting star was met by a chorus of shouts and cheers.

While doing volunteer work at a nature preserve near Wickenburg, we found ourselves out on a dark, December night, peering at a new comet (I believe it was comet Bradfield 1987) through a fellow volunteer's eight-inch SCT. I'd never seen such a telescope before and was fascinated. On my income level at the time, however, I was not inclined to rush out and buy one.

One night I set the now rather care-worn refractor up in a field beside the Sunny Flat campground in the Chiricahua Mountains. I had no observing plan; I just scanned the sky, and briefly shared the view with a man and his two young sons. The boys were fascinated, and their interest in the night sky was obviously not a spur-of-the-moment thing. I found myself wondering if I might be seeing the equivalent of my own childhood enthusiasm as it once had seemed to parents and teachers, back in the day. A few days later we were camping in Chiricahua National Monument and went up to Massai Point for the sunset. Two men were setting up a rather large Dobsonian mounted reflector in the parking lot. I did not know what it was called then, but had the sense it was a telescope. I never quite got around to asking them about it. I often wonder – had I done so and shared the view, would the hiatus have ended that night?

But I didn't ask, and the hiatus went on a bit longer.

VI

LIGHT ECHOES

"There is nothing like returning to a place that remains unchanged to find the ways in which you yourself have altered."
- Nelson Mandela

Not long after getting married, the bookstore job went south as the result of a corporate merger. The merger mania of the 1980s struck close to home in another way, as publishing companies found it expedient to cut costs by relying more on in-house work and less on freelancers. My income level dropped sharply just as my wife and I began to build our lives together. Before it became an outright crisis, I managed to switch jobs, taking a position at a community college bookstore. We continued to explore Arizona and New Mexico and to study both the history and natural history of the

Southwest. We became regular volunteers at the Nature Conservancy preserve near Wickenburg, an episode that did more than anything else to re-awaken the natural science fixation of my childhood. We maintained a very successful backyard vegetable garden. Underneath it all, however, was the feeling that I'd hit a dead end. The job I held was proving difficult to sustain physically, involving too much time on my feet, and too much heavy lifting. Most of the writing I did then was fiction, and none of it was selling. Magazine work had dropped from a trickle to the odd essay now and then, adding nothing meaningful to our income. It was time to find another way to live.

To accomplish this required a return to college, something deferred so often and for so long that the option did not occur to me immediately. When it did, the idea, and the specific goal to pursue, came with the force of a revelation. I was all about gardens and plants (in fact, I was planting onions in our garden when the thought came to me) and anything to do with nature and biology at that point, so a course that involved agronomy or botany was the most attractive of the possibilities to suggest themselves. I took aim at a Bachelor of Science degree in plant biology, and this required relocation from Phoenix to Tucson in order to attend classes at the University of Arizona. This we accomplished – more easily said than done, of course, though without blizzards this time – over the summer of 1995. In the end we found ourselves in a new and more congenial environment.

I took the classes and passed them. I did well. I even (finally!) overcame the dreaded math phobia, which did not, I'm happy to say, have its old power over me. I'd endured harder things than math quizzes by then. Oh, I found algebra a tough nut to crack, but I cracked it, and passed those courses as well. In the meantime, my wife and I explored Tucson and its vicinity, and the night sky started to send me more insistent reminders of times past. For one of the first things we noted about Tucson were its darker skies.

Although not a dark sky city by any stretch, Tucson has some pretty effective lighting ordinances, designed to protect the observatories perched atop nearby mountains. Among our numerous day trips during the student phase was a trek out to the Kitt Peak National Observatory. The drive took us across classic Sonoran Desert country and into the Tohono O'odham Nation, and then up a rather steep drive into the rocky Baboquivari Mountains. I'd never visited a real observatory before, and was a bit overwhelmed by the experience. The mountain ridge KPNO calls home is a rocky place, with scrubby oaks and alligator junipers and silk tassel growing, and home to gray-breasted jays and bridled titmice. We checked in at the Visitor's Center, then wandered the self-guided tour available at the time, and gaped at a gigantic image of the sun projected by the solar telescope. We walked the catwalk around the dome of one of the telescopes, taking in the sweeping desert vistas all around. While not the tallest mountain range in the region, the Baboquivari Mountains rise abruptly from the desert, so the view is spectacular. From that catwalk we looked out over a wrinkled mosaic of tan and brown and gold, threaded through with gray-green where desert vegetation crowded washes and dry stream beds. The desert swept out around us until it faded into a dusty gray horizon, out of which rose the pale blue desert sky.

We had a picnic lunch almost in the shadow of a gossamer steel radio telescope dish. Cool breezes sighed through the trees around us as we ate sandwiches and pasta salad, fending off hungry jays and cheeky ground squirrels. When we were done we returned to the Visitor's Center, where items astronomical were for sale, including telescopes. Being where we were, knowing what was going on around us, I felt a tug from that old interest, believe me. But living on student loans and my wife's paycheck, I couldn't even begin to consider such self-indulgence.

The cosmos seemed bound and determined that I heed its call. Comets graced the skies while I was a student: Hyakutake in 1996 and Hale-Bopp in 1997. Hyakutake came first, and because I was so busy with class work, I nearly missed hearing about it. Fortunately, my wife now had a thing for comets, and hearing of this one, brought it to my attention. That spring semester I had an evening lab course, and my wife would come pick me up, rather than letting me take the risk of a night ride on the bike. One evening I found myself at the usual spot, waiting in the chilly dark, matters to do with the transport of ions through a plant replaying themselves in my head. The comet was supposed to be high in the northern sky, and as I waited, I looked up to see whether or not I could spot it. It had been a cloudy late winter, so chances before then had been few. I remember being startled first that I could see it, next by how clearly visible that long, slim apparition turned out to be. Someone standing nearby – it was a popular drop-off and pick-up location on the west side of Old Main – saw me staring and looked puzzled. I told her what I was looking at, and pointed up across the rooftops. A moment later, her puzzled look was replaced by one of amazement. She had just seen a comet for the first time in her life.

Comet Hale-Bopp prompted a trip out of town for a clear view. My wife and I drove out to Catalina State Park one evening, and pulled to the side of the entrance road. We spread a blanket over the still-warm hood of our small pickup truck, and stretched out there, heads propped on the windshield. The sight was spectacular, with or without binoculars, and overall it was a brighter, more compact comet than Hyakutake. The old telescope was stored away somewhere, unavailable, but would have been of little use for the comet in any case. As we reclined there, cars came into the park, pulled off the side of the road, and did as we did. By the time we gave it up, there were a number of other vehicles parked along the road.

In between classes and comets, we discovered that the city of Tucson was for us an excellent fit, and by the time I graduated, we had decided to stay where we were. This was just as well, because obtaining the B.S. had badly strained our resources while leaving us with a significant debt, so for this and a few family-related reasons, the option of going on into a graduate level program was dropped for the time being. Instead we found jobs, bought a house, planted a new garden, and called Tucson home.

Birdwatching remained a strong interest for us both, and Tucson put us in a very good location for such a pursuit. Two years after graduation I found myself in need of new binoculars, and following a recommendation went to a shop with the unusual-sounding name of Starizona. The reason for the business name became obvious as soon as we arrived; there was a very large refractor in the parking lot, pointed at the sun. It was fitted with a hydrogen alpha filter system. The man watching over this solar telescope invited us over, and we both saw the sun in a way we'd never seen it before. This was a first for me, as I had no idea anything except those weighty bits of green glass filter existed. My wife was mesmerized by the sight of prominences curling up and away from the red disk of the sun.

Starizona is, of course, a very well-known telescope and astro-imaging gear retailer. I did not know this before going in, but two steps inside the small showroom took care of that. This was their original, and smaller, location, and the place was just stuffed with telescopes. There were Dobsonian-mounted reflectors and SCTs of various sizes, refractors of impressive aperture (and length), and cases full of the assorted bits and pieces that make it all work. I imagine I stood there a bit goggle-eyed at first. (My wife was still out watching the sun.) I'd never seen such an assembly, and never imagined such a thing as a teenager. I wandered about for a while, trying to catch my breath, and made small talk with whoever was running the show that day. I was tempted, very strongly tempted, standing there in what felt like telescope central. Then I looked at the price tags, and shut it all down. I was paying off student loans and trying to manage my share of a mortgage, and buying a pair of binoculars was already going to be a bit of a stretch. This was not the time to contemplate the much larger expense of a telescope. The binoculars were a more immediate need, and to be technical about it, I already had a telescope – which I was not using.

So I stayed focused on my stated intention for the visit and turned my back on the room full of telescopes. I fell into a conversation with someone I assumed was an employee, who was very knowledgeable and willing to help with the selection process. At some point we got around to introductions, and I discovered that I'd been talking to Thomas Bopp, co-discoverer of comet Hale-Bopp. I do not know why he was there that day – surely not to help people pick out binoculars – but the conversation that followed was memorable, as was the look on my wife's face when I introduced them. (Yes, she had finally found it necessary to come in out of the sun for a while.) I ended up buying the binoculars he suggested, and have been happily watching birds, wildlife, and the stars with them for almost twelve years, as I write these words.

The telescopes arrayed across the tiny sales floor were not by themselves a sufficient temptation, not under the circumstances of that time. I didn't take the step that day, but I certainly wanted to, and I started to remember just how important time at the eyepiece had once been for me. This was in the summer of 2000, and the 21st century was brand new.

Almost exactly two years later, the degree landed me a job in a laboratory on campus, with a higher rate of pay and more promising prospects for the future than I'd seen so far. Adapting to the new type of work took some doing, and I was further distracted by the passing of my mother-in-law. My wife and I started taking long walks on evenings when she was not back in Phoenix to help her father cope with the sudden change in his situation. (That year, 2002, was a bad one all the way 'round for us.) We discussed strategies for dealing with what was going on, and the walks were anything but relaxing strolls. For it seemed obvious that we would need to give up on Tucson and move back to Phoenix for her father's sake. We actually made the decision to do so, and on one of those walks around our still new-to-us neighborhood, we tried to get our heads around what it was going to take to make it happen. It was not a happy conversation, and as my anxiety increased over the idea of moving back to a place I'd never really cared for in the first place, I looked up at the stars and remembered the pale skies of Phoenix. Depression immediately replaced anxiety. A new mortgage meant we had to rent our place rather than sell it, to avoid a significant financial loss. The new garden had just begun to show its promise. I was barely a year into a new line of work. And yet the idea of being under that pale, nearly starless sky again was what unnerved me, and filled me with a familiar sense of loss, even though I hadn't given much thought to such things in more than a quarter of a century.

The crisis passed when her father, realizing the likely costs and troubles of our planned relocation, announced a change of plans. He had been pleased we were coming back; now he was appalled by the thought of what we were about to sacrifice on his behalf. It was a thing he could not let happen, so he announced his intention to move to Tucson instead. We were elated, and then guilt-stricken by that delight. This was a hell of a chore for a man in his seventies, with health problems that required constant monitoring, but he was adamant, and we caved in. We would keep the garden and the somewhat starrier skies of Tucson, and avoid the headaches of being landlords. As it turned out, our guilt proved to be quite unnecessary, for Tucson proved to be a very comfortable fit for him, a better place to be than the larger city to the north. Of course, he has been well looked after, all the while.

Life seemed to pause at that point, and draw a calming breath. I settled into the lab and my wife busied herself with helping her dad search for a new home. Over the summer of 2003 we toured neighborhoods and checked houses, while tomatoes grew wild in the garden. The desert monsoon was fairly generous that year, and we were blessed with thunderstorms that ranged from entertaining to alarming. And talk of Mars began to show up in the news. Mars was coming. The Red Planet was about to pass nearer to Earth than ever before, it was said, or it would ever be again – from the perspective of those of us alive to witness the event. Ridiculous stories of Mars looking the size of the full Moon circulated for the first time.

Working on campus as I did, I was in the habit of reading the college newspaper. One day I found a story about the Flandrau Science Center holding public viewings of the Red Planet, in association with the local astronomy club. As we had done with the comets, we decided to take advantage of this once-in-a-lifetime opportunity, and attended the first of the two scheduled events. Unfortunately, that very same generous monsoon thunderstorm season made Mars viewing a moot point. The participants with their telescopes were set up on the grassy campus mall, but were limited to chasing Mars (and other objects) through gaps in the clouds. We did not observe Mars, we glimpsed it.

I almost didn't care about Mars playing peek-a-boo through the clouds. We wandered the grassy mall on the east side of the University of Arizona campus in the gathering dark, surrounded by telescopes set up by members of the Tucson Amateur Astronomy Association. The people with the telescopes – reflectors and refractors and SCTs of various apertures, and huge binoculars on tripods and parallelogram mounts – all reminded me of someone I'd known, once upon a time. It took a while, in my distracted state, to realize they reminded me of myself, back in the proverbial day. I met and spoke to many telescope owners that night, asking questions and receiving answers from folks ready and willing – eager – to share. I looked at Mars and other sights as sucker holes in the debris clouds drifting over us opened, and then talked some more when the holes slowly closed.

The following Saturday night a second outreach event was held, this time with clear skies. Hoping for better luck – Mars never did show clearly that first time – we gave it another try. This time, the Red Planet was free to exert its full power over me, and I saw it through an assortment of eyepieces and telescopes beyond anything I might have guessed even existed, when I was fourteen years old. The combination of gear and people and Mars sent me home determined to haul out the now old refractor, and see what it could do with Mars hanging in our cosmic back yard. The next night I did so, after cleaning eyepieces and tightening what could be tightened on a well-worn mount. I found myself in the back yard, mesquite trees crowding in on three sides, carefully trying to focus a pale, salmon-orange ball in a once familiar field of view.

And there was Mars, with traces of markings just barely to be seen, but the thin, bright sliver of a polar cap was clear as could be. The image didn't hold a candle to those seen the night before, in much larger telescopes. But it was a good image for that small scope, thanks to the proximity of a cooperative Mars and half decent seeing conditions. I shared that view with my wife, who surely saw what was coming. Afterward, I stared at Mars for a long time, setting it just off one edge of the field of view, then watching it float across to the other, the trick coming back to me without any need to think about it. It was as if I'd never stopped in the first place.

Just like that, the hiatus was over.

VII

THE COSMIC COMEBACK TOUR

"These instruments have play'd me so many tricks that I have at last found them out in many of their humours."
- Sir William Herschel

Even as I started using the old refractor again, I began the process of seeking an upgrade. My income level at that time was such that I could manage the bills and still spend a reasonable – though not a very large – amount of money on something not entirely essential, like a bigger telescope. As soon as I began my search for the telescope of my boyhood dreams, whichever telescope that might turn out to be, I discovered how little I really knew about telescopes in general. So much had changed since I placed that order with the J.C. Penney catalog department!

While I researched the telescope market, using internet tools that had been the stuff of science fiction in my teens, the refractor and I became reacquainted. I went back to Starizona, where I made a modest investment to upgrade the old telescope. I bought a hybrid diagonal and a couple of Plössls. The views through the refractor were enormously improved by those higher quality (and much newer) eyepieces. I revisited what I could remember of old friends in the autumn and winter skies of 2003. I doubt I've ever been *more* enthusiastic about star-gazing than I was in those months. Something lost had been regained, and that was both a deeply satisfying and a really exciting experience. I refreshed my memory of the Moon, looked at double stars I remembered (I was surprised by how many I could recall), and marveled again at the misty sweep of the Great Nebula in Orion. I remember odd and frequent feelings of déjà vu, such as when I accidentally "rediscovered" M41 near the cold bright fire of Sirius. Still, I was painfully aware that I'd forgotten a great deal of what I once knew, and so many things I *did* remember didn't look quite the same to me, in part because of those new eyepieces, but also due to my location. Tucson has much darker skies than Phoenix, to be sure, but the skies into which I gazed using binoculars and the old refractor were (and are) anything *but* dark.

The internet had an immediate and profound influence on my return to amateur astronomy. I was soon in a state of information overload, and my "favorites" folder assigned to astronomy soon held as many links as most of the other collections of links put together. At the same time, this became a shared pursuit, and not merely the backyard obsession of a lone teenage amateur. I discovered discussion groups on amateur astronomy in general, and on just about any equipment angle you could imagine. I joined the still relatively small and new Cloudy Nights forum. Online, I found that each potential telescope option had numerous, vocal proponents, eager to convince me that *their* favorite telescope was also the right one for *me*.

As I rebooted myself as a star-gazer, I immediately renewed my grief over all those lost notebooks. My personal library included books on astronomy, but very few of these – Muirden's *Amateur Astronomer's Handbook* and *Whitney's Star Finder,* among them – dated back to my high school days. The materials that once had actually guided my explorations, the charts copied from Olcott's *Field Book of the Skies*, were long ago lost. I was keenly aware of their absence as I stood there with the old telescope, night after night. The half-remembered star-gazing routine was incomplete; the telescope was there, but the table with the notebook full of charts was missing.

I was already a regular customer of various online used book sources, most notably Alibris, and so must admit to being embarrassed about how long it took for the obvious solution to occur to me. And in the end, it wasn't even my idea. Someone on the Cloudy Nights forum began a discussion about another of Olcott's books, *In*

Starland with a Three Inch Telescope. I recognized the author's name, of course, and joined in the discussion, mentioning at one point that another book by the same author had greatly influenced me. I told in brief of how I duplicated the charts and used them at the eyepiece, and mentioned what a blow it had been to lose that material. The tale of the lost notebooks generated a number of sympathetic responses. Even more gratifying was the fact that no one questioned, much less scoffed at, the long effort of copying the charts! And, of course, along the way someone suggested that I "look online," since copies of the book seemed readily available.

I could never replace those long lost notebooks, but I *could* buy my own copy of *Field Book of the Skies!* I checked Alibris, and immediately found multiple listings for the book, in the correct edition, available in good condition for a reasonable amount of money. I ordered one, and for good measure ordered a copy of *The Sky Observer's Guide* at the same time. It took more than a week for the books to arrive; it's been years since I anticipated the arrival of a parcel in the mail that much. I think it took most of my wife's considerable self-control to keep a straight face the evening I charged into the house with that small box in my hands. I opened it carefully, as if an ancient heirloom or a religious relict had just arrived. *The Sky Observer's Guide* was on top, and holding that little book in my hand again brought memories and feelings back that I had not experienced in years. Then I picked up Olcott's field guide and opened it, saw those charts again, and felt a powerful emotional jolt. Nights under stars, standing in wet grass or cold snow; watching fireflies and hearing mosquitoes; the smell of DEET on a humid summer night with heat lightning on the horizon; afternoons at the library table, with protractor and pencils, with the short fat book open before me and the window air conditioner murmuring behind me. It was all still there in my mind, fragmented by the passing years, but still very much a part of me. Not even the resurrection of the 60mm refractor brought it all back to me as suddenly or as sharply. The feeling of familiarity and of time passed was a physical sensation in its intensity.

In a way, I'd once again found myself in possession of a telescope and in need of guidance. I solved the problem using the very same book.

I used Olcott's field guide for a time much as I had the long ago copied charts. I used his lists for the selection of objects to observe, double stars for the most part. The winter of 2003-2004 was a refresher course in the night sky. I bought a copy of Cherrington's *Exploring the Moon through Binoculars and Small Telescopes* and used it to re-familiarize myself with the Moon, the NGS map from my boyhood having vanished with the notebooks and copied charts. (I still have that old Rand McNally globe of the Moon, though. Somehow, like the telescope and a couple of books, it survived all the changes.) I used my copy of *Field Book of the Skies* by

William Tyler Olcott to relearn the deeper end of the Universe. It was a copy of that same edition from the home town library, and not a set of charts taken from it, which was both different and wonderful.

I continued to study material online, and read reviews of and comments on a host of telescope types and designs. I bought books, *Burnham's Celestial Handbook* to begin with, all three volumes in hardcover, found by chance in a local used bookstore. In my teens I owned maybe half a dozen books on amateur astronomy, and read perhaps as many more in the town library. Before that winter was over I had a shelf full of volumes on many aspects of the hobby, as well as a steadily deepening pile of *Sky & Telescope* magazines. I learned more in those few months than I'd known all through high school, and for all of that, it was obvious that the amount left to learn was more than anyone could take in during a lifetime. It certainly did not hurt the cause that I had a resource base a bit deeper and more stable than a borrowed lawn mower and a few neighbors' lawns!

At the heart of it all was the Old Scope, as it came to be known on the Cloudy Nights forum, but even as I narrowed down the selection of possible telescope purchases, age began to catch up to my old friend. The mount was slowly coming apart, and an attempt to tighten it up backfired, hastening its decline. One cool spring evening in 2004, while taking aim at the Moon, the mount failed completely. Like another long lost telescope, this one took a plunge, toppling that night when the fork component of the mount came loose. Unlike that other, the loss of which led to ownership of the Old Scope in the first place, I was right there, and had better and more experienced reflexes. This time I caught the telescope and there was no damage, but the Old Scope, long-time companion of my youth, was now unusable. It felt like someone had died.

To continue my return to amateur astronomy it was necessary to make a final decision on a telescope and place the order. With one last round of online comparisons, I went to Starizona yet again and did the deed. As spring warmed up in Tucson in May, 2004, I became the delighted owner of an eight-inch, equatorially mounted Newtonian reflector, the SkyView Pro 8 EQ sold by Orion Telescope. My relationship with amateur astronomy was transformed yet again, as I found myself with an instrument that would have left my fourteen-year-old self struck dumb with awe and envy. Dean at Starizona set the thing up the day I took possession, and focused it on the Moon, hanging above his store in the early twilight. I went through the process in a sort of daze, I'm afraid, with the teenager still within me struggling to catch his breath. A thing the boy I used to be saw as hopelessly out of reach was right there, ready to go home with me. I could touch it and make sure it was real. The man I had become handed the good people at Starizona his credit card.

Clouds, of course, prevented the official first light of the telescope from taking place for several days. While waiting, I put the decision of a first light object up to the members of the Cloudy Nights forum community. That turned out to be a good idea, and we all had a bit of fun with it as a list developed, a vote was taken, and of all things *Jupiter* won the contest! No one knew that Old Scope's first light had involved Jupiter in the summer of 1970. And so, on a clear, warm spring evening, with the Moon high and Jupiter blazing, I assumed true ownership of that telescope by looking at the King of Planets, just as I had with the old refractor so long before. To say it was a very different experience would be an understatement. I saw more of old Jove that evening than I'd seen in all my previous, teenage observations put together. Before the evening was over I also had my mind thoroughly blown by the starry mass of M13 in Hercules (second in the vote) and saw the Moon in greater detail than ever before (it came in third). And I did note, at the time, that of all the things I ever observed in years past, it was surely a curious coincidence that these three things topped a list generated by people who did not know my observing history in detail. The Moon, Jupiter, and M13 all played roles in how I came to be doing this thing called amateur astronomy, and now together in one evening, they helped launch the next phase.

A new level of experience and involvement with amateur astronomy began, that night in May of 2004. I'd come all the way back from the hiatus, and then raced on into a future beyond what I'd ever imagined possible. The potential I'd seen in the 60mm refractor, more than thirty years before, had increased by orders of magnitude. I was for a time a bit overwhelmed by the changes, but the learning curve was manageable, and unlike the experience of my teen years, I had plenty of help available. More than aperture increase, access to an online community of kindred spirits utterly changed the way I did astronomy in my back yard. If something puzzled or troubled me, I had only to post the question online and the generous nature of this community saw to it that I was informed, or set straight. Of course, opinions being what they are, there was plenty of chaff and nonsense as well, but it was (and remains) in its way a self-correcting system, and in the end the useful answers always came to the surface.

So many of these people extolled the virtues of their local clubs that I looked up the Tucson Amateur Astronomy Association, the same group responsible, with an assist from Mars, for getting me rolling again under the night sky. Real life, for a wonder, reflected the internet; these people were as varied and eclectic as the ones on the forum, and just as generous with their help and support. Of course, I joined the club. Over the next several years I attended star parties and outreach events, and at some of the star parties had the opportunity to meet face-to-face a few people from Cloudy Nights. Amateur astronomy as a lone teenager in a rural back yard became a distant memory. Amateur astronomy was now a social thing. The impact of this change was greater by far than the significant increase in aperture.

In all the excitement, the now unusable Old Scope was packed up in its battered wooden box and all but forgotten. Newer observing manuals – *The Night Sky Observer's Guide* and O'Meara's *Deep Sky Companions* series, to name a few – up-to-date and aimed at users of modern equipment, took places of prominence on my bookshelves, and in my session planning. And like the Old Scope, *Field Book of the Skies* slipped from its place of prominence when it came to guiding my observation experiences. It was not forgotten, never, but it sat on the shelf unused, just a few months after I'd celebrated its acquisition as a milestone. Even events that change your life for the better can have unintended consequences.

VIII

RETURN OF THE REFRACTOR AND THE SHORT, FAT BOOK

We all have big changes in our lives that are more or less a second chance.
- Harrison Ford

For the next few years astronomy became for me everything I remembered, and then passed beyond into matters previously only imagined. These were rewarding times. If you are as addicted to the pleasure of learning new things as I am, believe me when I say few hobbies can compare with amateur astronomy. If you enjoy the challenge of climbing a learning curve, astronomy will not disappoint you. And I was not disappointed. I read books, magazines, and online postings, with the latter, especially when combined with Phil Harrington's *Star Ware* – giving me an ever improving grasp of matters to do with equipment. As I'd done while deciding on a telescope, I took it slow. Many, if not most, newcomers to amateur astronomy (technically, I wasn't really new, but so much had changed!) make a lot of impulse purchases, then find themselves reselling gear when items either don't actually suit them, or fail to live up to expectations. That sounded like a major pain in the ass to me. To be fair, some seemed to enjoy the eyepiece shuffling and the wheeling and dealing as much as time spent at the eyepiece. I decided not to go there, so I followed discussions most closely that involved folk with similar basic equipment, and who expressed interests and goals that resembled my own. In the process, I slowly built up the kit I use today. Lots of new stuff has come out since my equipment-buying phase faded out, but I remain pleased with what I have and lack any real motivation to seek endless upgrades.

I put it all to the best possible use. I improved my observing and record-keeping skills – especially the sketching of objects observed. Each night I worked at it I became better at hunting down targets, a necessity, since I did not elect to purchase a computer-guided scope. The SVP 8 EQ has drives on the mount to keep objects in view; more than that would have meant buying a smaller telescope to stay within my budget. A computer that could find things for me just didn't seem necessary. Remembering the alt-az nudging of my youth and the desire then for "clock drives," this driven mount was more than adequate.

As my old skills returned and I built on them, and developed a broader knowledge of amateur astronomy in general, I found myself more and more often passing what I'd learned along to beginners who logged on to the CN forum and joined the beginners group of the TAAA. That, more than anything, gave me a feeling of progress being made. Amateur astronomy even led to a modest return to writing, as I shared observing reports, star party experiences, and book reviews. Two of my astronomy essays ended up published in Sky & Telescope.

So I use a bigger telescope, these days, and fancier eyepieces, along with references to match. *The Night Sky Observer's Guide* (among others) provides lists of targets, while the Herald-Bobroff AstroAtlas and charts from *Carte du Ciel* show me the way. I use a table larger than the one I had in Illinois to hold it all. Everything has scaled up from those teenaged nights under the stars. I've become a grown-up amateur astronomer, with more options to explore than I would ever have imagined possible.

At about the time I realized all of this, a feeling of being slightly disconnected from it all made itself felt. As the first decade of the new millennium approached its end, I found myself somewhat blasé about the whole thing. Clear nights that were seized upon just a year or two before passed me by, and often for no good reason. It was almost as if, having arrived, I had no idea where to go from here. As if my attention had wandered, that sort of distracted state in which you're likely to set something aside without paying attention, and then can't remember what you did with it.

One day, not long after the excitement of rediscovering the stars had clearly faded, a teenage amateur astronomer on Cloudy Nights posted a particular leading question. Not a new question, one that others have asked, and others will surely ask again in the future. He wanted to know what brought us, his fellow amateur astronomers and forum members, into this admittedly unusual pastime. People responded freely with many tales of how they started out. I responded that I couldn't actually remember what got me started, but in the process of considering the matter while I formed my response, I *did* start to remember things. Lots of things. That's when I began to understand the nature of my recent malaise. Somewhere in the process of becoming that *grown-up* amateur astronomer, I'd lost the connection with the beginnings of the obsession. Somehow I'd lost the thread, and the youthful motivation to which I was connected by that thread of experience winding through my entire life subsided under the weight of years.

I needed to catch hold of that thread again. Perhaps if I could reconnect past and present, I could renew that old enthusiasm.

Easy enough to simply look back down the length of lifetime and see how the story unfolds. Doing so without letting the golden and often less than honest glow of nostalgia take the truth out of those memories is a bit more difficult. It seemed to me that the best way to go about this would be to seek tangible reminders of what used to be. For the astronomical theme that threads through my life, this was not such an easy thing to do, with so much lost along the way. I looked up at the shelf over the computer, at that globe of the Moon, and remembered illusory shadows on the snow. The memory of winter stars blazing and the smell of bitterly cold air came back for a fleeting instant. Then I looked behind me to the bookcase, seeking a familiar volume, short and fat, black and yellow . . . I didn't see it.

Vexed, I began to rummage around various bookcases in the house. (We have more than a few.) It annoyed me that I might have misplaced that copy of *Field Book of the Skies*. The sad truth is that it had been several years since I'd last picked it up. When I could not turn it up quickly, I moved on to another tangible relict, the Old Scope itself. The wooden case was set upright, on one end, in a corner of the room that also stored cases of newer astronomy gear. Sitting on the end, with a significant amount of dust on top, where *Whitney's StarFinder, The Sky Observer's Guide,* and Olcott's *Field Book of the Skies,* all set aside together, as if waiting.

Relieved to have the book back in hand, I opened the wooden case, which was battered, chipped, and faded with age. The latches sort of stuck, and the hinges no longer opened straight and smooth. The tripod legs were still there on top of the fitted styrofoam blocks, still showing

119

the loss of stain from standing in dew-soaked grass. Beneath were the ruined alt-az mount and the telescope itself, the tube now sporting a few scratches and chips in its paint job. I took it out and held it, trying to remember what it had been like, the day this became my first "real" telescope. It can be a strange thing, being a fifty-something-year-old man, trying to recall the feelings of a fourteen-year-old boy. The feelings were still there, but they somehow seemed to belong to someone else, proof of the disconnect I'd discovered between then and now.

Holding the telescope and thinking of nights long past, I realized that the view through that telescope might, more than anything else, remind me of how it had been. I decided then to see what I could do to restore the Old Scope to its original optical function, in spite of its years. Taking stock, I found that the optical tube assembly was very nearly all that was left of it in a useful state. The focuser worked, though not smoothly. The eyepieces could not be cleaned of whatever fogged them over. The Barlow lens was just plain gone, lost somewhere along the way. And the little finder scope could no longer be adjusted at all. The tale of years. I thought of my bad knees and sciatica, and found it possible to sympathize with a telescope.

The process of restoration unfolded slowly, and in the end I decided that the bottom line had to be the view, eyeball to eyepiece. I'd experienced grander views of things since acquiring the Newtonian on its EQ rig, but these sights could not tell me why it mattered. Such sights were available to me *because* it had mattered, once upon a time. I very much doubt I would ever have spent so much money on a telescope, had not the memories of nights long past left such a deep impression. While it's true that I used the Old Scope for a few months before buying the Newtonian, I wasn't trying to get back to the roots of the matter, and the eyepieces I used during that episode in no way duplicated the original views!

I tracked down replacement 0.965 inch eyepieces to complete the optical configuration of the original kit, one each of the 20mm and 6mm Huygenian eyepiece types that originally came with the telescope. (I was in luck; a simple cleaning of the original prism diagonal restored it to full function.) It proved a good thing I'd settled on the views as the bottom line. The purist in me wanted the thing mounted on a small alt-az system, but that would take money I did not have available at the time. Since I already owned a small EQ mount, purchased for a 'grab 'n go refractor,' I decided to put rings on the Old Scope and put it on that mount, which could be dropped into an alt-az mode easily enough. I eventually told the purist to shut up and quit worrying about having a different mount. After all, there was no way I could duplicate the experience of finding objects as I had back then; I knew the sky too well. I might as well have the Old Scope on a mount that – finally! – did the instrument justice.

Unable to locate a duplicate of the original finder, I ended up replacing it with a simple red dot finder. Considering how restrictive that old finder turned out to be, this did not bother the purist too much, as the only resulting difference would be a trifling difference in magnification.

I soon found myself able to see the stars as I had seen them as a teenager, in the optical sense. Being a different person, after so many years, the true experience of astronomy from a teenage perspective could not be replicated without surgical intervention, and on my budget a lobotomy was out of the question. I'd have to make do with whatever memories were evoked.

And as had been true all those years ago, I needed some source of guidance to lead me back to objects I'd viewed. The answer to that one was already in hand, literally, as I reopened my copy of William Tyler Olcott's *Field Book of the Skies*. I sorted through it, desiring a list of likely targets, objects that when seen through the refractor would make for a reasonably impressive view. It was while making the list I realized, with a bit of astonishment, that I couldn't remember ever actually *reading* the book. I'd read portions, and copied some of it out in that hometown library, but actually read it through, as I've done with the works of Burnham, O'Meara, and French? If I did so, back in the proverbial day, I could not remember it. So while once again using the refractor to make observations, I read the short, fat book that started me out in amateur astronomy. And of course, I read it from the unavoidable perspective of a somewhat more experienced observer.

To the eye of an experienced amateur astronomer today it might not look like much. The star charts for each constellation entry appear almost rudimentary. I certainly didn't look at it that way in the summer of 1970, when I discovered it. I remember being handed the book by the librarian, and then sitting at the long table in the front of the library to examine it. Holding a copy now, it looks just as I remember it, short and thick, with a clunky looking black and yellow cover. The title – *Field Book of the Skies* – is at the top in bold black letters on yellow. An odd bit of art graces the cover, a square of deep blue, star speckled sky over a rural scene, with a blank golden orb that may or may not have been the Moon, and a few streaks of gray clouds. "With Charts, And Special Diagrams" it says beside the picture. Under that, in yellow letters on black, are found the names of the author and the editors of the 4th edition, printed in 1954. Last of all, there's a nutshell description of the book's contents: *"A clear and concise presentation of the main facts of modern astronomy, a brief story of the mythology of the constellations, and a practical field book for the observer of the stars, whether with naked eye, field glasses, or telescope."*

The science of astronomy, as known at the time the book was written (or presumably at the time of revision) is painted in the first part of the book in quick, broad strokes. This is not an Astronomy 101 text; what Mr. Olcott is providing, clearly, is a brief overview. *Field Book of the Skies* reads like a book aimed at casual telescope owners, folk who bought small refractors in the two-to four-inch aperture range so commonly available in the first third of the 20th century. They were almost certainly not mirror grinders and telescope makers, dyed-in-the-wool students of binary star orbits or variable stars; the book does not seem technical enough to appeal to such an audience. And as a matter of fact, Mr. Olcott does describe objects in the field book in terms of what could be seen by users of such modest refractors. He did not specify telescope type, since if you owned such a thing then, it was almost certainly a small refractor. I find myself imagining new telescope owners, in search of a starting point, and a book to guide them. It seems to me that, in the *Field Book of the Skies,* Mr. Olcott wrote one for them. *Field Book of the Skies* could be considered a sort of primer, designed to give readers an introduction without overwhelming them with a welter of details. If I'm correct in this interpretation, it still served well in that capacity more than forty years later when I found a copy.

Scientifically, *Field Book of the Skies* is now terribly out of date. The edition I found at my hometown library was printed in 1954, two years before I was born, and represents the last revision of the book, to the best of my knowledge. It was out of date back when I found it, something that was lost on me at the time since almost all the astronomy books available to me in that library were from the Forties, Fifties, and early Sixties. I simply was not well-enough educated in the astronomy of the late Sixties to realize the book was behind the times. Nor would I have cared. My interest at that time was in learning to find my way around the sky, and to see interesting things up there. The general science in the book was more-or-less correct, if not entirely current, so it was good enough for my purposes.

The nutshell account of astronomical science includes a chapter that is supposed to address how we could possibly know what we know – or thought we knew in 1929 – about the universe. It's an odd little essay, read by modern eyes. I can't think of a single book aimed at casual stargazers or amateur enthusiasts printed in recent years that deals with such a topic. They all discuss what we know, and sometimes go into how we find things out, but it is *assumed* that these things are knowable. This essay seems aimed at proving that we *can* know these things, that the reader can safely take the word of the astronomers and assume that their conclusions are reasonable. Today, we take it for granted that astronomy can indeed discover the nature of objects so distant their light headed our way before humans could build campfires. Apparently, this was not the case in 1929.

I'd have glossed over that stuff, as a teenager. I might not have understood what I was reading, at the time, lacking the necessary frame of reference. It didn't matter. I'd already seen the star charts, the part of the book directly relevant to my needs and with which I was to become so intimately acquainted. There was an immediate and obvious priority involved; I needed star charts, and there they were. The constellations in *Field Book of the Skies* are grouped by season, a convention that is likely as old as the publication of astronomy manuals. Each season is prefaced by a two-page all-sky chart that shows the various constellations relative to each other, along with a page listing the times and dates at which the sky you see will reflect the arrangements on those pages. The individual constellation charts are rather odd little diagrams, when compared to observing guides I use today, showing only the brightest stars and the main asterisms associated with a given constellation. The faintest star plotted is 6th magnitude, but not every star 6th magnitude and brighter is shown. Like one of O'Meara's Deep Sky Companions, this looks like a guide rather than an actual atlas, and would no doubt work best used in conjunction with a star atlas of some sort. Aside from the tiny charts in the back of *The Sky Observer's Guide*, which I found very confusing and difficult to use, this was the first book of its kind to cross my path. I had nothing against which to compare it, and would never have guessed it begged for a real atlas as a companion volume. I didn't even realize, until reading it this time around, that it shows almost nothing of the celestial coordinate system. The grid lines showing right ascension and declination that I take for granted in my current references are nowhere to be seen. Nor do the lists of double stars provide RA and DEC coordinates. Instead we have a "designation" that proves to be an amalgamation of RA and

DEC, though it isn't described as such. Not knowing any better, and lacking an actual atlas, I somehow found my way to enough objects to keep me interested, all the same.

Regarding the objects "of interest to those possessing telescopes," the overwhelming majority are double and multiple stars. The number of double stars listed (though not actually discussed) absolutely dwarfs the list of deep sky objects, most of which are open and globular star clusters, with bright nebulae and planetary nebulae being a minority, and galaxies (still called nebulae in the 4th edition) rarely plotted. Clusters and nebulae (both real nebulae and galaxies) are plotted on the chart and labeled, but are usually not discussed in the accompanying text at all. My assumption that Mr. Olcott had in mind the users of modest refractors is based in part on the objects he lists, since double stars are probably the best of all deep sky targets for such instruments. I suspect there is also a reflection of the science of astronomy in his day to be found here, as well. The great age of binary star observation had not yet passed, and so the emphasis surely is a reflection of the great importance of binary stars to professional astronomers in the time that Mr. Olcott wrote the first edition of *Field Book of the Skies*.

In reading the book now, one thing becomes very clear to me. Because of that emphasis on double stars, I was a devoted double star observer by the end of that first summer of the refractor. I tried for the star clusters and nebulae, and found a few, but the double stars were generally the easiest objects to locate with that small telescope, and the most rewarding to view. I was immediately enchanted by them back then, and not knowing any better, I thought binary stars were the things most amateurs studied when they didn't look at Jupiter or the Moon. It would never have occurred to me that my approach to visual observing was being shaped by an accident of history. Many, though certainly not all, of the doubles plotted in *Field Book of the Skies* could be resolved by my small telescope, and so rather than being frustrated by the limits of aperture, I beheld objects of beauty and fascination, jewels in dark settings, objects well suited to my limited aperture. I couldn't get enough of them; I still can't. Mr. Olcott's short, fat book is responsible for all of this.

The section of charts does not mark the end of the *Field Book of the Skies*, however, and one third of the book remains to be discussed, that dealing with the solar system and some basic aspects of the practice of amateur astronomy. The curious thing about this part of the book, roughly a third of the page count, is how little of it I recall. I recognized the star charts like old friends; this other material was strangely unfamiliar. Much of this surely has to do with the effort I put into copying the star charts. You are most sure to learn things by interacting with the information, and least likely to do so by passively reading the material. I may have read the solar system and practical material, but it's also possible that I never got around to it. Reading this part of the book, more so than the pages at the beginning, had the feel of a new experience. It really is a pity that, as a youngster, I did not yet have enough experience to appreciate the material in the last third of the book. There is a great deal of very useful information there, much of it apparently aimed at readers ready to take a step further down the road than the charts and double star listings alone would take them. That wasn't me, the summer of my fourteenth year.

An account of the Moon is included in that back third of the book, and it is clear Mr. Olcott (or his later editors – it is difficult to pick out from the text where updates and additions occur) placed little emphasis on lunar observing. The section on the Moon contains a small number of what are easily the least useful lunar maps I've ever seen. To the uninitiated, these maps would be terribly confusing. This was one element of *Field Book of the Skies* that had no influence on me as an amateur astronomer.

Another curiosity this book presents the modern reader is the location of information on telescopes and techniques at the *end* of the book. I've found other old astronomy tomes that are arranged in the same fashion, so this was not merely some foible of William Tyler Olcott. Why this might have seemed necessary or useful, I can't say.

In the context of more recent experience, my fond memories of the book have taken on just a bit of tarnish upon this rereading. Even so, they retain most of their potency. It would be tempting to write off these memories as mere nostalgia, but that wouldn't be fair to the book, or to me for that matter. Context makes all the difference. My recent re-examination of this old book for the most part reveals how I've changed and how amateur astronomy has evolved in the years since William Tyler Olcott (and his editors) did their work. And yet, it is surely both understandable and predictable that my fondness for that old book has survived. The adult I am looks back on the boy I was when I first held *Field Book of the Skies*, and understands. This was new stuff. This was the first time. And if the old book falls short as an observing guide when compared to newer works that have lately accumulated on my overburdened bookshelves, it does so only on the basis of somewhat unfair comparisons. Amateur astronomy was a different sort of pastime back then, and Mr. Olcott was not aiming this text at the users of eight-to twelve-inch Dobsonian mounted reflectors, SCTs, or CCD imaging equipment. His book was aimed at folk like me, or the person I was in 1970. The boy I used to be could only be excited and motivated by those little star charts. That short, fat book provided my first look at a deeper universe, and the memories that awaken when I hold the copy I now own are well worth the modest price I paid.

IX

REDISCOVERY

"In youth we learn; in age we understand."
- Marie Ebner von Eschenbach

So there I found myself, with a refurbished relict of childhood and an old book seen in a new light. These two items felt like the key to the process of finding my way back to a firm grasp of the astronomical thread running through my life. With these, I hoped to reconnect with and perhaps to understand what it was that made star-gazing so compelling, and for so long.

In reading *Field Book of the Skies*, I naturally paid attention to objects and double stars that came to mind as things I remembered observing as a teenager. That wasn't as hard to manage as I might have thought: the Pleiades and the Great Nebula in Orion were obvious, as were M13 and M31. Among double stars, Alberio and Mizar/Alcor were sure bets, along with Polaris and Rigel and a handful of others. The Beehive Cluster, along with M41, M6, and M7, stand out in my memory. Out of the host of things I observed, these I can be sure of, after so many years. So I made an effort to re-observe these objects that I came to know first through Mr. Olcott's book and a 60mm refractor. Along with them, I renewed my acquaintance, in a 60mm way, with Jupiter, Saturn, and the Moon. I observed objects from home and at dark sky sites, and I tried to remember how it felt when I first saw such things through the eyepiece.

It took some effort to get past the difference between 203mm of aperture and 60mm. I'd grown accustomed to the view through the EQ mounted reflector (affectionately nicknamed the Three-legged Newt), and so it should come as no surprise that the views through the Old Scope were disappointingly dim. (Using 0.965 inch eyepieces with tight fields of view surely added to the need for adjustment.) The first thing to come of this exercise, then, was to realize why people come up with some of the rationalizations they do regarding the unsuitability of a 60mm refractor for youngsters just starting out. It's easy to be critical of the view when you are accustomed to something more powerful, easy to forget the magic of seeing a star through a telescope for the very first time, even through a small telescope. When I was fourteen years old, the sight of Rigel and its tiny spark of a companion was mind-blowing. Having never seen such a thing through a larger telescope, there was no comparison to be made, and so I was enthused, not disappointed. I suspect this is how it is for many young telescope recipients today, at least those for whom the gift telescope was the result of something deeper than a momentary impulse.

After coming to terms with this necessary change in perspective, I made the Old Scope my instrument of choice for at-home observing sessions. As I became re-accustomed to the views it provided, I discovered that it is a very good telescope for spur of the moment, 'grab 'n go' style observing. It is, in fact, a better telescope for lunar observing than the 102mm, $f/5$ refractor I often pressed into service for such things. (Less chromatic aberration.) The more I used the Old Scope on its spiffy EQ mount – really, the mount it was made for – the more often I chose to use it, and the more I *enjoyed* using it. And in the end, the Old Scope showed me what I needed to see.

However many memories are evoked by renewing your acquaintance with a topic or things from your past, it's true what they say about not being able to go home again. You'd need one hell of a lot of aperture to clearly and honestly see your own past from the here and now. I can't look through the 0.965 inch eyepiece at an image brought to a focus by a 60mm lens the way I did in the summer of 1970. I've seen too much and learned too much, and that stuff just naturally gets in the way. I can remember that, yes, it looked this way, and I was thrilled by it. But it's never more than a memory; I don't literally relive it. I'm the man remembering the boy, and as clear as some of the memories are, they are recollections of the experiences, and not the experiences themselves. That's reality for you.

So I can see what I saw, and remember. I can't see it as I saw it. And yet, in the end, the memories brought to life by using the Old Scope again realized the purpose of taking this trip down memory lane. It came together for me one night at one of the dark sky locations used by the local club. I'd brought the Old Scope along in part to provide alternate views of double stars for people participating in a beginner's double star program. This purpose was soon lost when I discovered how many of those in attendance were distracted by contemplation of times past as they peered through that old refractor, and remembered the small telescopes of their own younger days. I put the Old Scope on Jupiter, and people saw it as they had seen it themselves long ago, just as I had done for first light four decades before. Everyone recalled those early views fondly, and a few shared memories of how things had begun for them. No few expressed open envy that I still had my "first" telescope.

When the group thing was done, I sat there in the dark by myself and went from Jupiter to M31 and back. The common memory, shared by us all that night, was not of the quality of the view, but of the experience of looking. Of being out there in the night, filled with wonder. The desire to enjoy that sense of wonder to the fullest launched me on a journey of sorts, one on which

I lost my way for a time, though I never completely lost sight of where I wanted to be. It was the trip through time and life that took me from a kid with a small telescope to a man with the means and equipment to finally realize the full potential of what that boy had found. It had begun with a sense of wonder.

The thread of astronomy that winds its way from my past self to the present day is once more firmly within my grasp. The connection it provides is to that sense of wonder that took control of my youthful imagination. I cannot relive those long ago observing experiences, but as I learned that night among friends in the dark, the wonder remains the same. It's the wonder felt by my boyhood self I needed to remember, and that turned out not to be so hard to do, after all. Any clear night will do.

And in learning to see it all as a journey, I also understood why things seemed to have cooled off. A journey of sorts has indeed ended. I have the telescope and equipment I wished for back in my teenage years. I have the patience and experience and education necessary to realize the full potential of the stuff I've bought. I have finished the journey from the star-gazer I was years ago to the amateur astronomer I always wanted to be. And when you reach the end of a journey, don't you usually stop for a while? It turned out I was experiencing nothing more than a pause at journey's end. In that pause, I looked back the way I'd come and in so doing renewed my sense of why the journey mattered.

My observing will once again, for a time at least, be guided by William Tyler Olcott's *Field Book of the Skies*. This time I will do so under desert skies, sometimes from the light-polluted suburbs, sometimes under conditions closer to the dark skies of my childhood home. But this time I will do so, constellation by constellation, with a telescope of a size and light-gathering power I could scarcely have imagined I would ever own. The fourteen-year-old I used to be would be thrilled beyond words.

In the meantime, the Old Scope sits proudly on a mount that does its modest Towa optics full justice. With it I return to the Moon from time to time, and with the help of a homemade full-aperture solar filter, I now see sunspots in a brand new – and much safer – way. The Old Scope performs splendidly in these capacities, and is no slouch on wide double stars, either. The Old Scope and Mr. Olcott's *Field Book of the Skies* will not find themselves squirreled away in an odd corner again, forgotten, any time soon. A trip that took years of nights is over. The real adventure, the one this journey made possible, has begun.

About the author . . .

I've been told it's a good idea to put something like this at the end of a book, though it seems a tad redundant in this case. After all, this one is all about the author by its very nature. Still, it's sometimes wise to heed the advice of those who have been there and done that (publishing books, in this case), so I'll add that I am a writer, naturalist, and amateur astronomer delighted to find himself living in Tucson, Arizona. That puts me in an amazing and biologically diverse desert land, and right next door to some very dark skies. When the sun goes down, I mean. And assuming there are no clouds.

www.ingramcontent.com/pod-product-compliance
Lightning Source LLC
Chambersburg PA
CBHW050632110626
46523CB00044B/643

MIDNIGHT

SHARON SALA

sourcebooks
casablanca

Copyright © 2026 by Sharon Sala
Cover and internal design © 2026 by Sourcebooks
Cover design by Ervin Serano
Cover images © Efasein/Shutterstock, Nick N A/Shutterstock

Sourcebooks and the colophon are registered trademarks of Sourcebooks.

All rights reserved. No part of this book may be reproduced in any form or by
any electronic or mechanical means including information storage and retrieval
systems—except in the case of brief quotations embodied in critical articles or
reviews—without permission in writing from its publisher, Sourcebooks.

No part of this book may be used or reproduced in any manner for the
purpose of training artificial intelligence technologies or systems.

The characters and events portrayed in this book are fictitious or
are used fictitiously. Any similarity to real persons, living or dead,
is purely coincidental and not intended by the author.

All brand names and product names used in this book are trademarks,
registered trademarks, or trade names of their respective holders.
Sourcebooks is not associated with any product or vendor in this book.

Published by Sourcebooks Casablanca, an imprint of Sourcebooks
1935 Brookdale RD, Naperville, IL 60563-2773
(630) 961-3900
sourcebooks.com

Cataloging-in-Publication Data is on file with the Library of Congress.

Printed and bound in the United States of America.
VP 10 9 8 7 6 5 4 3 2 1

Chapter 1

THE GROCERY BAGS FULL OF BRENDA KINGSTON'S PUR-chases were in the floorboard of her car. Her elbow was resting on a box of crackers and two liters of pop. Her knees were the cradle between which Pete Brandt was rocking—chasing a brain-busting climax. Between the muffled scream in his ear and the fingernails digging into his back-side, he had her right where he wanted her. And when she finally climaxed, he let go with a shudder and a groan and went with her.

"Baby, baby, you're the best," Pete groaned, then pulled out and sat up, shifted the groceries to allow for his feet, and left Brenda to right herself.

Brenda threw back her head and laughed, both from the blood rush and the high. Pete was a blond hunk of danger. Always good for a quickie, and free rushes from the pills they popped together.

But Pete was suddenly all business. He glanced at his watch. "It's go time, baby. Do you have your two-way?"

Her eyes widened. "Yes."

"Remember, all you have to do is go to the airport park-ing lot, then radio where you are. Don't use your phone to call me. We'll radio you when we enter the airport, and when you see the van, just back out of your parking spot. We'll pull into the empty space. You pop the trunk. I'll trans-fer the money to your car, and we'll meet up at my place. My crew will converge after midnight to split the take."

"What about me?" Brenda asked.

He winked. "We'll go to Mexico and spend the hell out of it."

She hesitated. She didn't care about leaving Jacob, but she'd never thought she and Pete would get past sex in the back seat of the car, and the thought of abandoning her sons made her sick.

"I don't know, Pete. I can't go off and leave my boys. I'll do the airport run for you, but I can't go to Mexico. I can't leave my boys."

Pete shrugged. "Whatever. I'll just spend it on my own."

She nodded. "Thanks for understanding. What if it all goes south?"

"It won't. Just chill out and do what I said."

When the old white service van with Pete's crew arrived, he jumped in with them and they took off downtown, while Brenda headed for the airport. She found a parking place, radioed her location, then settled down to wait.

The day was cool, so she rolled down the window and began eyeing the people coming and going, a little nervous about the occasional security car making sweeps through the lot.

A shuttle bus came through, unloading returning travelers and their luggage, while others were just arriving and waving down a bus to take them to the terminal.

An hour passed, and she was getting antsy. The sky was clouding up and it looked like rain. She rolled the windows up and turned on the radio to a local station, and sat there praying she'd get the nod to just go home. The longer she sat, the more convinced she was that this was a big mistake. The sky was clouding up. It looked like rain was imminent, so she rolled up the windows.

Moments later, the two-way radio crackled. It was Pete.

"We're coming in hot. Start your car so I can see the brake lights."

Her heart began to pound as she started the engine. Even though the car was in Park, she pushed down on the brake to activate the brake lights.

She saw the white van approaching in her rearview mirror, and then saw Pete flash his lights to indicate he'd located her. As soon as he turned down the parking aisle, she backed out and pulled forward just enough for them to swing into the empty space, then popped the trunk and sat there, waiting.

There was a sharp thud in the trunk, a slam of the trunk lid, and then Pete was at the window.

"We had trouble. Ollie is shot. The money's in your trunk. Take it home and hide it. I've got to drive Ollie's car to get him to the hospital. The other guys are already leaving."

Brenda gasped. "No! No! I can't go home with that!"

"Give me the two-way," he said, and when she handed him the radio, he grabbed her by her arm and squeezed it to the point of pain. "Do what I said! I don't have time to argue!" Then he slapped his hand on the top of her car and took off running.

She floored her car and never looked back. Having to stop and pay to get out of the parking lot was a nightmare. She just knew the police would come flying into the airport and arrest them all, but they didn't.

She left Amarillo with a knot in her gut, and didn't breathe easy until she saw the city limit sign at Crossroads. She'd made it home, but with a trunk full of stolen money.

As usual, she drove around to the back of the bar and went into the house, carrying groceries as she went, then peeked into the bar to see what was happening. It was full of customers, and Jacob was tending bar. So she went back into the house, locking the door between the business and their home, then made a mad dash outside. She didn't

know what the money was in, but she had to get it out of the trunk.

When she popped the lid and saw a strongbox, she groaned. What if she couldn't lift it? Fear lent her strength as she grabbed it by the handles, pulled it toward her, then lifted it out and took off up the steps, staggering as she went. She got to the kitchen, opened the door that led down to the full basement, and then went down the steps backward, dragging the box with her, bouncing down one step at a time.

"Help me, Jesus," she muttered, and began dragging it all the way to the back of the basement. She threw a drop cloth over it and shoved a bunch of empty boxes and crates in front of it, then ran back out, shut the trunk, and locked her car.

Her legs were trembling by the time she got back inside the house, but she didn't have time to waste. She put up all the groceries, then ran to the bathroom to wash up, and puked her guts out instead.

When she finally pulled herself together and realized it was almost time for school to be out, she frantically splashed some water on her face, grabbed a bag of chips from the pantry for the boys, and a cold pop from the fridge for herself, and headed back to the car.

She was shaking from the inside out as she drove to the school and got in the pickup line, then took the lid off her bottle of pop and took a big drink. The Coke brought tears to her eyes and burned her throat all the way down. She couldn't think. She couldn't focus, and leaned back against the headrest, choking back the urge to scream.

What have I done? What have I done?

A short while later, the bell rang, and the students began filing out, staying with their classes as the teachers on bus duty began sorting out the kids who were picked up from the ones who were walkers.

Her eyes welled as she saw Asher, her oldest, looking for her nine-year-old, Dylan, and Gunner, her baby. He lived the role of big brother as if he'd been born to lead.

She watched as he found them and began gently herding them to her car. She'd carried them within her body, and brought them into the world with great pain, but they were the spitting image of Jacob. Black-haired, blue-eyed, and already growing so tall for their ages.

All of a sudden, Gunner, her youngest, stumbled and fell, then let out a wail. She was about to get out and go to his rescue when she saw Asher pick him up, dust him off, and carry him the rest of the way.

By the time they were loaded up, the bag of chips she'd brought for them to snack on had cured the crocodile tears on Gunner's cheeks, and Asher was doling them out one at a time.

She took one last drink of her pop and gave it to Asher. "Share with your brothers," she said, and headed home in a daze. For that moment, it felt like every other day of her life, except it wasn't.

The evening went by in a flash. It was Gunner's seventh birthday. She had cake and ice cream for them, and a present for Gunner. Jacob left the bar long enough to watch his youngest son open his presents and eat birthday cake with the family, before he went back to the bar. She oversaw homework while doing the dishes, and with an eye on the clock, gave them a couple of hours to watch TV or play games before bedtime.

The noise from the bar was a constant in their lives, but they were used to it. Finally, she reached the moment of tucking the last of her sons into bed and kissing them good night. Even Asher expected the pat on his shoulder and his mother's fingers combing the hair from his forehead as she kissed him good night.

But on this night, Brenda didn't go to bed. As soon as she knew the boys were sound asleep, and Jacob was knee-deep in customers and serving drinks at the bar, she headed down into the basement on the run. She grabbed a shovel from the rack of tools hanging on the wall, then hurried to the southeast corner of the back wall, moved everything away except the strongbox, and started digging.

It wasn't easy, but she didn't have time to waste. When she hit rock, she got down on her knees with a small pickax and chunked at the dirt around it until it came loose and then dug some more. When it was wide enough and deep enough, she got down on her knees and pushed the box into the hole, then frantically began covering it up, one scoop at a time from the pile of displaced dirt.

She was almost done when she heard footsteps in the house above her, and then Asher calling her name.

"Oh shit, oh shit," she mumbled, and threw the last shovel full of dirt in, tamped it all down with the back of the shovel, then began stacking boxes and crates on top of it, finishing it off with a wooden crate of empty canning jars.

Asher was still calling when she took off running. She hung the shovel back in place and went up the stairs two at a time, coming out into the kitchen just as Asher came back into the kitchen. She could hear Gunner crying down the hall and the murmur of voices.

"What's going on?" she asked as she hurried to the sink to wash the dirt off her arms and hands.

"Gunner just woke up. He and his bed are all bloody. He lost a tooth in his sleep, and we guess he swallowed it. He's crying because he won't have a tooth for the tooth fairy."

"Then we better get him cleaned up," she said, and headed to the big bedroom where the two younger boys slept.

Brenda calmed Gunner down with a promise to write a

note to the tooth fairy and sent Dylan and Asher to bathe the blood off her baby boy, while she stripped the bed and put on clean sheets.

Finally, she had Gunner in clean pajamas and fresh sheets on his bed, and a handwritten note to slip under his pillow for the tooth fairy. He smiled at her, and the little gap where his tooth had been broke her heart. Innocence. She was going to destroy their innocence.

When Dylan and Asher saw her slide the note under the pillow, then lean over and whisper in Gunner's ear, they grinned. Their little brother still believed in Santa Claus, and the Easter Bunny, and the tooth fairy, and they kept up the pretense for him, and for her.

She did the tucking in bed business all over, but this time pausing in the doorway between their adjoining rooms. The rooms were dark but for the little Pokémon nightlight by Dylan's bed.

"I love you guys...so much. Thank you for being my best boys," she said, and then walked away.

Later, she slipped back in, took away the note to the tooth fairy that she'd written, and replaced it with a dollar bill, then took herself to bed. She was pretending to sleep when Jacob finally came to bed. She was too emotionally wrought, and terrified of what yet may come. When Jacob slipped into bed beside her, she heard his weary sigh as he pulled up the covers and turned out the bedside lamp. He was such a good man.

Oh God, oh God... What have I done to this family?

In the bright light of a new day, things didn't seem so awful.

Gunner was crowing about the money under his pillow, and sticking his tongue between the space where his tooth

used to be as they were eating breakfast. She had the TV on in the other room and was listening to the news and weather when she heard the lead-in to the morning news, stopped what she was doing, and took her cup of coffee to the living room.

"...daring robbery of an armored van in front of the downtown bank in Amarillo yesterday. Four gunmen wearing motorcycle helmets, and driving a white van, opened fire on the guards. Two guards were killed. The driver and one other guard are in the hospital, recovering from multiple gunshot wounds. Less than an hour ago, three of the gunmen were arrested and the fourth one, who was shot during the robbery and dropped off at the hospital afterward, was instrumental in naming the others involved. We will be reporting on updates as they occur."

Brenda went numb. She didn't know whether to run now or wait for the other shoe to fall. Then Asher was behind her.

"Mom, we're ready to go," he said.

She turned, saw her sons with their ready smiles and backpacks, set her coffee cup down and kissed each one of them on the forehead, and went to get her purse and keys.

"Did you tell Daddy goodbye?" she asked.

"Daddy's in the shower," Asher said.

She nodded. "Then let's go."

They filed out the back door and into the car. Brenda waited for them all to buckle up and then drove away. There was already a line of cars and kids on the walkway and others going into the building when she pulled up.

"Love you all. Have the best day ever," she said, and blew them all a kiss. They got out on the run and never looked back.

It was the final cut of the cord that bound her to them. She knew before the day was over that federal agents would be coming for her, and the swath of shame and humiliation

she would be leaving for her family to suffer. And all for the sake of a fuck and a high.

Jacob had already opened the bar by the time she got back. She cleaned up the kitchen, then went up front as he was plugging in new kegs and refilling the coolers with his best-selling longnecks and cans. She stood for a few moments, staring at him, wondering what happened to her to make her forget how much she'd wanted him. What she'd done to get him.

He was a tall, broad-shouldered man with sharp, chiseled features and eyes that turned a little icy when he was angry, an emotion he rarely allowed to show up, and even then, it was never with them. Just the occasional unruly customer. All three of their sons were younger, smaller, versions of him.

And then Jacob looked up and caught her staring.

"Morning, honey; did the boys get off okay?" Jacob said.

"Yes. Gunner lost his first tooth in bed last night. He woke up bloody as hell, bawling because he'd swallowed it."

Jacob grinned. "I'm sorry I missed all that."

"He's okay. I wrote an excuse note for the tooth fairy. He was crowing about his dollar this morning."

Jacob winked. "You're a good mama."

She turned away before he could see the flash of her tears. "Not really," she said.

He frowned, but before he could ask her what she meant, customers began coming in. The regulars who played dominoes at the two front tables, and the old cowboy who shot pool alone, so he didn't ever have to say he lost a game. And in the process, he forgot about Brenda's comment until two black SUVs pulled up in front of the Tumbleweed.

Four men entered the bar, flashed their badges, and asked to speak to Brenda Kingston.

Jacob's heart skipped. "She's my wife. What's this all about?"

"Sir, we need to speak to her. Is she here?"

"Our home is attached to the bar. She's back there. Follow me."

Jacob's heart was pounding as he walked them to the door, unlocked it, then walked inside with the federal agents right behind him.

Brenda had been outside when she saw the cars drive up and had raced back into the house. She'd been thinking all morning about what she'd done, and the one thing she couldn't face was having her sons know that their mother was in prison. Her hands were shaking as she emptied the bottle of antidepressants into her hand—all thirty-two of them—and washed them down with a glass of water, then walked back into the living room and sat down to wait.

When she heard the key in the lock, she closed her eyes and took a deep breath, then began whispering the Lord's Prayer in her head. She was right at the "yea though I walk through the valley of the shadow of death" when Jacob spoke her name.

"Brenda? Honey…"

She opened her eyes.

"These men are from the FBI. They want to talk to you."

She nodded.

Jacob's heart skipped. "What have you done?"

She stood up and held out her hands. "I'm sorry," she whispered. "So sorry. For everything."

The special agents were taken aback by her acquiescence as they handcuffed her.

"What has she done?" Jacob shouted.

"Abetted in the armored car robbery resulting in the death of two armed guards and the wounding of two others. One of the robbers who was shot yesterday named all of the participants. According to the confession, Brenda Kingston has been having an affair with Pete Brandt, the man who planned and orchestrated the robbery."

Jacob reeled as if he'd just been shot. "No. I don't believe it. Brenda! Tell them it's a mistake!"

She dropped her head. Her silence said it all.

They walked her out of the bar in full view of everyone inside, and then the regular customers all ran into the house looking for Jacob, who was coming undone before their eyes.

But what the special agents didn't know was that Brenda Kingston was, for all intents and purposes, already dead when they put her in the car and drove away.

When she fell asleep in the back seat, they thought little of it until they reached their destination and found out they hadn't transported her. They'd transported her body.

The shock of her arrest and subsequent suicide left Jacob and his sons prostrate with grief and disbelief, and then following that, the shame that came down upon them. Dylan and Gunner hadn't been told the details, but Asher knew, and it forever changed the child he'd been meant to be.

Jacob began closing the bar at 10:00 p.m. to take care of his boys, and not one customer complained. Asher stepped up and stepped into a man's shoes. He hadn't only lost his mother, but he'd lost the rest of his childhood. He became

the one who helped his brothers with homework, and did the laundry, and when Gunner or Dylan woke up crying for their mother, Asher was the one who took them into his bed and cradled them back to sleep.

Within days, the whole town of Crossroads picked up the rest of the slack in Jacob Kingston's life. A volunteer cadre of people began taking the boys to school, while others picked them up and took them home at the end of the day.

Pete Brandt and his crew got life in prison.

Life went on, and Jacob's boys grew up and moved away.

The Tumbleweed Bar saved Jacob's sanity, and ultimately, forever rooted him in Crossroads, and the missing money became a footnote in history.

Texas State Prison—Twenty-one years later

Mostly, it was the machines hooked up to Pete Brandt's body, and the steady morphine drip going into his veins deadening the pain of his cancer-ridden body, that were still keeping him alive.

The prison warden had notified his next of kin that death was imminent, and the next morning, both of his sons were at the prison asking to see him. It had been a little over five years since they'd been to visit, partly because they'd been incarcerated for their own sins in those years.

Today, as they entered the building, their pasts were just shady enough that even entering a prison made their skin crawl. But when they were escorted into the hospital infirmary and saw what was left of their father, Everett cursed beneath his breath, and Freddie stumbled.

Pete had lost his hair and most of his teeth and was down to skin and bones. They wouldn't have recognized

him on the street. The prison doctor approached, quietly gave them the lowdown on Pete's condition, then pointed out the other patients nearby, and asked them to keep their voices down.

"Is he even conscious?" Freddie asked.

The doctor nodded. "He's not comatose. He's just heavily drugged because of the pain, but he's still cognizant. I'm afraid you'll have to keep your visit short though. Twenty minutes, tops, boys," the doctor said, then pointed to the guards inside the ward. "When you're ready to leave, let them know. One of them will escort you out, so say what you want to say today."

They nodded, and then moved to Pete's bedside as the doctor walked away. Everett, the oldest and a redhead, was a taller, skinnier version of his mother. Freddie, the youngest, was Pete's mini-me, right down to the broad shoulders and blond hair, and the first one to speak.

He leaned over and patted Pete's shoulder. "Hey, Pop. It's me, Freddie."

Everett followed suit and took hold of his dad's hand. "Pop, it's me, Everett. I'm here, too."

Pete's eyes opened, blinking a few times as if trying to focus, and then grinned, revealing the tooth loss from all the cancer treatments.

"Hey, boys... Come to get your old Pops a send-off, have you?"

"Are you in pain?" Everett asked.

"Not much," Pete said. "Good drugs here. I'm glad you came. You need to know that Brenda has the money."

They both looked at each other, thinking it was the drugs and disease already eating up his brain.

"Uh... Dad... Brenda's been dead for twenty-one years."

Pete shook his head as he inhaled, trying to catch his breath enough to speak.

They could hear the death rattle in his chest.

"Hell, I know that, boy. I had nothing else to think about since the day they locked me up. I knew what she thought of her boys. She likely couldn't face the shame. I might as well have put a gun to her head myself."

"You weren't mad at her, then?" Freddie asked.

"For what? She did exactly what I asked her to do. I got her high and talked her into it. She wasn't anywhere near the robbery, but I put the money in the back of her car at the airport and told her to take it home and hide it. I don't know what she did with it, but they came and got her the same day they arrested us, and she killed herself on the way to jail. The location died with her."

"Then what are you saying?" Everett asked.

"That she wouldn't have had much time to hide it, and I told the cops I'm the one who hid it, and that the location would die with me. Only I'm dying now, and I don't know where it is. They said on the news at the time, it was more than a million-dollar heist, and part of it was bearer bonds."

Everett frowned. "That doesn't mean anything. We didn't know her. We don't know where she lived."

Pete moaned and took another rattly breath. "Her old man owned the Tumbleweed Bar in Crossroads. It's south of Amarillo on Highway 86. Their house was attached to the back of the bar. He still owns and works the bar, and still lives there. He didn't know shit about what was going on, and I know she would have hid the fact that she'd had the money from him, so no one would have ever thought to search there, because I said I hid the money, remember?"

Their eyes widened as the truth sank in. "You mean all that money is likely somewhere in the bar or in their house?"

Pete blinked. "Likely."

"But how would we get Kingston out of there long enough to search?" Freddie asked.

"That's for you to figure out," Pete said. "Consider it your inheritance from me." He took another breath, and was slower in talking. "Is your mama doin' okay?"

"She died four years ago, Pop."

Pete frowned. "Why didn't you tell me?"

"We were doin' time," Freddie said. "We didn't make it to the funeral, either."

"Then I reckon I'll be seeing her again before you do," Pete said, and closed his eyes. "I'm tired talking. Y'all go on now."

Thrown off by his instant dismissal, neither of them bothered to even tell him goodbye. Their heads were full of dreams of getting rich, the same way their dad kept trying to get rich. By stealing what didn't belong to them.

They talked about it all the way back home to Amarillo, but before they could act on their plan, Pete Brandt died. They didn't have the money to bury him, and there was no one else left to claim the body. That left Captain Joe Byrd Cemetery, the largest prison graveyard in the United States, as his final resting place.

Pete Brandt's death regained media attention, and as they reported the story, they also resurrected the old crime on the air and in the papers, including the names of the guilty parties and victims with it, and ending their piece with mention of the unrecovered money from the robbery.

Jacob Kingston heard the news live from the television above his head at the bar. He was drawing a beer when he heard the words *Pete Brandt* and *armored car robbery*. Shocked, he turned his back to the customer and upped the volume, and when he did, the whole bar went silent. There wasn't a man among them who didn't know the

history, and when it was over, Jacob lowered the volume and turned back to the customers.

"Took a long time for that son-of-a-bitch to die," he muttered.

Joe Dunn, one of his regulars, tapped his empty shot glass on the counter to break the tension.

"One more for me, Jacob, and then I'd better get home before the phone starts ringing and you have to lie and tell Polly I'm not here again."

Jacob grinned and poured another shot of rye whiskey in Joe's glass while the other men laughed, and the moment passed.

But Jacob wasn't the only one yanked back into the past.

Thirty-two-year-old Asher Kingston heard it through the grapevine at his work as an investigator for the state attorney general's office in Austin, and the first thought he had was for his dad.

Twenty-seven-year-old Gunner Kingston was a homicide detective with the Dallas Police Department. His lieutenant called him into the office to give him a heads-up, and his first thought was for his dad.

Twenty-nine-year-old Dylan Kingston, who owned and operated a general contracting business in Austin, was at work when his fiancée, Angie Trent, who was also his secretary and company accountant, called his cell. When he saw her name pop up on Caller ID, he quickly answered.

"Hey, pretty girl. What's up?" he asked.

"I didn't want you to hear this on the news, but that whole thing about the old, armored car robbery and your mother's part in it is all over the news."

Dylan's gut knotted. "What the hell? Why?"

"Pete Brandt, the leader of the gang who participated in the robbery, just died in prison and the missing money never being found. It stirred everything up, I guess. You know how the media is these days. All about sensationalism. I'm sorry, honey. I just didn't want you to be blindsided at work."

He sighed. "Angie, my love, thank you a thousand times. I'm sure my brothers know, but I'll text them anyway. See you at home."

"Absolutely," Angie said. "T-bones on the grill?"

"Perfect," he said, and hung up.

Within the hour, the brothers were on a three-way conference call, worrying about their dad, but it was Dylan who suggested their older brother be the one to make contact.

"Asher, you be the one to call and check on Dad tonight, okay? If we all do it, it might freak him out and make him think he has something to worry about," Dylan said.

Gunner frowned. "Maybe he does...have something to worry about, I mean. The media now, compared to the media back then, has turned into a Medusa. They'll likely come looking for a scandal to create."

"And Dad will tell them which jackass to ride off on," Asher said. "But I will definitely call him anyway. Are either of you bothered? If this had brought up any bad shit, spit it out now. We don't keep secrets from each other, remember?"

Gunner heard the worry in Asher's voice. "We're good, Ash. I promise. Dylan has Angie to kiss his boo-boos now, and I have so many calluses on my heart from that time, that I have yet to meet a woman I trust. I doubt I'll ever get married. Are you okay?"

"Of course, I'm fine. I chose a long time ago, not to carry the years of resentment with me. It lessens as time passes. You'll figure that out one day on your own."

"Whatever," Gunner said. "Thanks for the call. You and

Dylan aren't just my brothers. You're my best friends." And then he disconnected.

Dylan sighed. "He doesn't do emotion, does he?"

"Not very well," Asher said. "I'm gonna call Dad now before it gets too late. Talk to you soon." And then the conference call ended.

But Asher wasn't as casual about ignoring Gunner's reaction as he let on. He ached for the little boy Gunner had been when it happened. He was barely past being a baby. He lost his first tooth and his mother all on the same day, and took her suicide as a sign that she didn't love them enough to stay. And no number of explanations from Asher or Jacob had ever changed that.

Their baby brother had grown up into a full-grown hardass, and one of the best homicide detectives in the Dallas PD.

Chapter 2

THE NEWS REPORT ABOUT PETE BRANDT'S DEATH HAD resurrected a few old ghosts for Jacob, but he felt no compulsion to relive any of it. What was done was done a lifetime ago. All he remembered from that time was the heartache and betrayal, and having to tell his boys that she was never coming home.

To this day, he credited Asher for stepping into the gap. For giving up the carefree years that had still been ahead of him, to make sure his little brothers knew he had their backs, and that they mattered.

Back then, Asher's high school sweetheart, Nora Borden, had been the anchor in his life. So, when Asher finally called, Jacob wasn't surprised.

It was just after 8:00 p.m. and the Tumbleweed Bar was busy. An impromptu pool tournament was ongoing, and a college football game between Texas A&M and Oklahoma State University was airing live on TV. Between the crack of the balls, the cheers and jeers of the ones watching the game, and the customers coming and going, Jacob was in his element.

Jacob's accountant, Lily Piper, a high school math teacher who moonlighted on the side as an accountant, had been by earlier to pick up last week's receipts, and during a lull in the business, the subject of Pete Brandt's death arose.

"Have you been bothered by any journalists?" she asked.

"Not really. A couple of random phone calls, but I just told them to get lost and hung up," he said.

She shrugged. "I didn't mean to pry, but I had to ask."

"It's fine. Everyone in Crossroads knows our story. It's sure no secret, and thanks for the concern."

Before he could say more, his phone rang. He started to let it go to voicemail, then saw Caller ID.

"Lily, it's Ash. I need to take this," he said and stepped into a hallway so he could hear a little better as she left the bar.

"Hey, son, what's going on?" he said.

Ash chuckled. "Not nearly as much as what's happening there. Lord! Can you hear me over the roar?"

Jacob laughed. "It's Saturday night. College football and a snooker tournament I didn't know was going to happen."

"Ahhh, well that's money in the bank, right?" Ash said.

"Yep. Is everything okay with you?"

"Yes, but I'm calling on behalf of your other sons, too. We assume you heard the news about Pete Brandt dying and all the media outlets digging up the gory details?"

"Yep. We all watched it together in the Tumbleweed, and then went back to business as usual," Jacob said. "I'm fine. There's nothing to talk about and nothing to dwell upon. Is Gunner okay with all that, though?"

Ash sighed. "You know Gunner. Hardcore to the max. If he's bothered by anything, we'll never know it. Don't worry about him, Dad. He's a big boy now. Just don't be surprised if reporters come calling wanting to get a comment from you about Brandt's demise."

"I handled it before when it was messy as hell. This is nothing. Don't worry about me, son. I'm good here." Then there was a big roar back in the bar and Jacob sighed. "I

gotta go. Texas A&M either scored, or they fumbled the ball. Love you. Thanks for calling."

"Sure thing," Ash said as the call ended.

A couple of days later, a news crew from an Amarillo TV station arrived at the Tumbleweed and made a beeline for the man at the bar. The reporter was a woman, and the man with her had a camera on his shoulder.

Jacob looked up, cursed beneath his breath, and three cowboys at the bar turned around, saw what was happening, and got off their stools and stood in front of Jacob, like bodyguards.

"We don't reckon you're welcome here," they said.

"Move aside please," the lady said, and nodded to the man beside her, and when he swung up the camera, Jacob stepped out from behind the bar, tossed a bar towel over the lens, and gently took the mic from her hands and shook his head without saying a word, then pointed at the door.

Out. Now. He mouthed.

She frowned. "But we just—"

The cowboys were already escorting the cameraman out of the door when Jacob interrupted.

"Lady, you're gonna miss your ride home." Then he slipped his hand in the crook of her elbow, walked her to the door, handed the mic back to her, and shut the door behind her.

The three cowboys stayed on the porch until the news van drove away, and then walked back into the bar like they were arriving anew.

"Thanks," Jacob said.

They high-fived each other, and then Jacob.

"We got you, buddy."

The Kingston family wasn't the only family dealing with ghosts.

Nora Borden, Asher's high school sweetheart, had just driven past the Tumbleweed Bar and the Yellow Rose Café with a lump in her throat. Her father, Thomas Borden, had finally passed away from Alzheimer's, and she'd come back to Crossroads to deal with the consequences of what to do with the family home.

It had been vacant ever since she'd moved her dad to a memory care facility in Fort Worth to be near her, and she hadn't been back to Crossroads since. That was over two years ago. She was concerned about the condition of the house.

Coming back to Crossroads was like going back in time. The same people, the same businesses were still here. Nothing changed. If you didn't own land and cattle or horses, you didn't have a lot of options. Crossroads hadn't grown any bigger, but the plus side was that it was still as lively and vital as it always had been. Good people lived here. And that was the blessing of the place.

But coming back resurrected all kinds of emotions for Nora, most of which were tied to Asher Kingston. He'd been her whole world through all four years of high school. But when they graduated, they both knew that their lives were going to go in different directions.

He wanted a life in some form of law enforcement, and she wanted to work in the field of technology. They swore undying love to each other on their last night together and made promises to stay in touch. They made love for the last time, and the next day he got on a bus bound for Austin, and her parents loaded her up and drove her to Dallas.

They faithfully texted and emailed each other for nearly

a year, until the messages became less frequent and less intense, and time finally eroded the connection they'd once had.

After that, every time she'd come home to visit her parents, she never asked about him, because she didn't want to know that he'd fallen for someone else and got married. She wouldn't ask, and they never mentioned him.

Now here she was again, a thirty-one-year-old woman with a great job and a fancy apartment in Fort Worth, and nobody left to wonder or worry about where she was, or what she was doing.

Nora paused as she pulled into the driveway and parked beneath a leafless tree, reluctant to give up the comfort of the warm air from the heater on her feet. But there was no reward for putting off the inevitable, so she took a deep breath and killed the engine.

She knew the utilities were still on, because she'd paid the bills to keep them on. She'd called Pearl two weeks ago to ask who to call to get the place cleaned before her arrival.

Pearl quickly assured her not to worry, that she'd get someone in to do that for her, and she could pay Pearl back when she came home. Nora was in tears, thanking her profusely, then immediately mailed a house key and sent a hundred dollars in advance via Venmo, with a note that if it wasn't enough, she'd settle up with Pearl after her arrival.

Pearl called her the day the key arrived, and that the cleaning would be done before Nora came home, and now she was here, dreading the lingering ghosts within.

A blast of cold air sent a shiver up her spine as she got out and rounded her car to get the suitcases from the trunk, then rolled them up the steps to the front door. But there was still the business of getting inside out of the cold.

There were no tricks to getting in. No security system to disarm. No warm welcome waiting as she turned the key.

She heard the lock click, then reached for the doorknob, and pushed the door inward before pulling the luggage in behind her and shutting out the cold.

The house was warm enough to keep the pipes from freezing, but it was an uncomfortable setting, so she turned up the thermostat as she went down the hall to her old bedroom. Everything was so familiar, but the house had been empty for so long, it had lost the vibrancy of human energy. She left the luggage by the bed to unpack later, and as she turned to leave, caught a glimpse of herself in the full-length mirror on the back of her closet door.

Her long brown hair was tangled and windblown. There were dark shadows beneath her eyes from the stress of the last few months of her father's life, and she knew she'd lost weight. Once he was put in hospice, the days of sitting by his bedside were excruciating. When he finally fell into a coma, she never left his side. Listening to him struggling for every breath had been hell. He'd fought the inevitable for eighteen hours before he managed to exit this world.

But that was over, and she was here, standing in an empty house frowning at her reflection, which accomplished nothing, and left the room. She needed to see what the pantry situation was like and check to see if the fridge needed to be cleared, then go to Belker's supermarket. It would be foolhardy to wait to stock up, then wake up tomorrow morning to bad weather.

Still, she took the time to walk through every room in the house, including the primary bedroom. Her father's clothing had long since been removed when he moved with her to Fort Worth, but the faint scent of pipe tobacco was still there when she opened the door.

"I'm here, Daddy. Wish you were, too, but I wouldn't wish you back the way you were. You were a good man. You

didn't deserve that end-of-life journey. I'm still a little mad at God about it, but that's between Him and me."

She left the door open to air out, and kept moving through the rooms, then back through the living room to the kitchen, turning on lights as she went. Same pale-blue walls and white cabinets. Same white-and-gray quartz countertops. The dining table and chairs had been polished. Whoever Pearl hired to clean had done a good job.

She pulled the curtains open at the sink to let in more light, then thought she saw a maverick flake of snow, which ended her musings. The fridge was empty and there were only a few cans on the pantry shelves, all over three years out of date. They'd go in the garbage later, and there was no need to make a list. She needed a little bit of everything. After a quick trip to the bathroom to freshen up and brush her hair, she grabbed her purse and keys, locked the door behind her as she left, and quickly drove away.

Within ten minutes of entering the store, she'd been greeted and welcomed home by every person there. They all knew her, and the same question followed. "Are you here to stay?" A question for which she had no answer.

Long after she'd been home, fed herself, and had a long soak in a hot bath, she was curled up on the sofa under an old quilt, absently watching some game show and remembering sitting on this same sofa with Ash and watching a movie while her parents were at the kitchen table, playing cards with friends.

Later, after she finally went to bed, she lay curled up beneath the covers she pulled to her chin, listening to the wind and the dry rattle of skeletal tree limbs. She felt isolated from humanity without the sound of the city lulling

her to sleep, yet sleep she did, and woke up to the sound of the central heating coming on.

Another day had dawned, and she was in Crossroads for a reason. There were things to do and people to see, so she got up and dressed, made herself a cup of coffee and some toast, and then set up a little office area in the kitchen, with her printer and laptop. Wi-Fi was strong, and so was her phone signal. If there was a need for her workplace to contact her, she was good to go.

She worked through the first part of the morning on work from her job, then began checking real estate estimates, and making notes of small repairs to the house that needed to be done. There was a loose pane in one of the kitchen windows, because it rattled a little in the wind. She was going to need a handyman for several projects.

When noon rolled around, she shut down the laptop, brushed her hair and grabbed her purse and keys, and paused to zip her coat up against the wind as she left the house. She was going to lunch at the Yellow Rose to thank Pearl in person, but most of all, she didn't want to be alone.

The parking lot was already filling up when she arrived, so she made sure to park where she wouldn't get blocked in and wasted no time getting in out of the cold.

The Rose was warm and lively and full of people talking and eating and having discussions with the people at the tables around them. It was like being at a family reunion, and trying to make sure you caught up on all the new family gossip.

She saw an empty seat at one of the little tables near the corner and sat down. As she glanced up at the wall, her gaze went straight to the painting hanging there. It took her a few moments to realize it was a painting of this very dining room, and of Pearl, and customers in it. And then she saw the artist's signature and gasped. It was a Magnolia Brennen original.

A waitress saw her heading that way and called out, "Be right with you," then delivered the food she was carrying to a table before grabbing a menu and the carafe of coffee and heading for Nora's table. "Cold enough to freeze the hair off a turtle," she said, and then giggled at her own joke. "I'm Darla. What are you drinking today?"

"Coffee, please, and I'll have whatever the special is today," Nora said.

"It's chili beans and cornbread, and a dessert. Your choice," Darla said.

"I'll have that," Nora said, "and tell Pearl that Nora Borden is here. I need to settle up with her for organizing the cleaning crew at my dad's house."

"Will do," Darla said, and went off to turn in the order. "Hey, Pearl, there's a Nora Borden out front. She wants to settle up with you about getting a house cleaned?"

"Oh, great! She got here, then," Pearl said, and turned to her grill cook. "Hey, Davey, I'm going out front a minute. Be right back."

Davey nodded. "I'll catch your orders."

Pearl spotted Nora sitting by herself in the corner the moment she walked out into the diner. *God love her. She looks exhausted*, Pearl thought. But as she started weaving her way through the tables, Nora saw her coming and stood up to greet her.

"Pearl! I know you're busy, but I had to thank you personally for helping me."

Pearl hugged her. "Oh hush, girl. It was nothing. I'm so sorry about Tom, but I know it was a blessed relief. Damn Alzheimer's anyway. Are you okay? You're a little pale."

Nora sighed. "I am tired, but I'll catch up on rest here. I want to settle up with what else I owe you."

"You don't owe me anymore. We're good. I gotta get back to the kitchen, but I expect to be seeing a lot of you

while you're here. You take care and rest up, you hear?" Pearl said.

"Yes, ma'am," Nora said, and sat down.

Moments later, Darla brought her order, and she wasted no time digging in. The food was warm, and filling, and it tasted like home. She ate her way through her lunch and finished it off with a small bowl of peach cobbler.

Darla had already left her ticket on the table, and she was on her way to the register to pay when Pearl carried a to-go order to the cash register. "This is Jacob Kingston's order. Somebody call and let him know it's ready," Pearl said.

"Oh, I'll take it to him," Nora said. "I wanted to say hello to him anyway. This is a good excuse to interrupt his workday. Just add his ticket to mine."

Pearl smiled. She knew how close Nora and Asher, Jacob's oldest, had been when they were in school. "Sure thing. Why not, and that's really sweet of you," Pearl said.

Darla added the second ticket to Nora's meal.

Nora swiped her credit card, then picked up the bag and left the Yellow Rose with a bounce in her step. If the opportunity arose, maybe she'd finally find out what Asher Kingston had done with his life.

The Tumbleweed was nearly empty. Since Jacob didn't serve food, most of the morning clientele went home, and after lunch, the afternoon clientele would show up. It was a win-win for him, and gave him a breather, too. He was sweeping up beneath the seats at the bar when he heard the door open. He turned just as a young woman walked in.

A big smile spread across his face as he propped the broom against the bar and went to meet her.

"Nora, honey! As I live and breathe! What a surprise!" he said, and gave her a big hug.

She was smiling from ear to ear as she handed him the sack she was carrying. "I was just leaving the Rose when Pearl brought your lunch to the register. I volunteered to deliver it, and it's on me."

He took the sack, then took her by the hand and led her to one of the poker tables.

"Can I get you something to drink?"

"No, but thank you. I'm so full of Pearl's chili beans and cornbread I feel like I'm waddling. You sit. Eat while you have a minute."

"Will you stay and talk to me?" he asked.

She grinned. "I hoped you would ask. I'd love to."

They sat, and she watched as Jacob took out a container of chili beans, crumbled some of the cornbread in it, and took his first bite. "Ummm, that Pearl sure can cook," he said. "So, what brings you to Crossroads?"

"Dad passed away three weeks ago. I'm back to deal with the family home," she said.

Immediately, Jacob reached for her hand. "Aw, honey. I'm so sorry to hear that. I knew you'd moved him, but I didn't know where."

"To a memory care unit near where I live in Fort Worth. It was weird coming home last night to that empty house, but I'm here for a while. Not sure what I'm going to do with it."

Jacob nodded. "So, you work in Fort Worth?"

"I work from home, but yes, I live in Fort Worth. I work for an IT company that specializes in troubleshooting for big companies and corporations. That kind of thing. What are your sons doing? Are you a grandpa yet?"

Jacob's eyes narrowed slightly. He knew what she was asking and why. Ash never mentioned her, and he never knew why or what happened.

"None of them are married and no grandchildren, but Dylan is engaged going on over a year. To my knowledge, he's the only one with a girl. Gunner is a homicide detective in Dallas, and Asher is a policeman too, but moved up to being a special investigator for the state attorney general's office in Austin."

Nora's eyes widened. "Wow. Good for him. He knew what he wanted to do from as far back as I can remember, but I never saw Gunner as a policeman. What does Dylan do?"

"He owns a general contracting company, building housing additions, that kind of thing. They're all successful men, which is amazing to me, considering I raised them in the back of a bar."

Nora frowned. "No sir. You raised them in a home. You own and run a bar. You were the best father ever for them. I know. I was in the middle of them and their antics during those years."

He nodded. "I remember. Now I'm going to pry. Do you have a significant other? Or do they have another name for that now? I can't keep up with the rules of polite society."

"No sir, I do not. I used to date some, but my job is very demanding, and honestly... Ash was a hard act to follow. Nobody ever measured up."

He frowned. "It's not my business, and you don't have to answer if you don't want to, but what happened between you two?"

There were tears in her eyes, but she was smiling. "That's the pitiful part. Nothing happened. We used to stay in contact...and then one day I looked up and realized it had been months since our last email, and for no apparent reason other than we didn't put each other first. I haven't spoken to him in years. I didn't even know where he was living or what he was doing."

"And now you do," Jacob said. "They always come home

for Christmas. If you're still here, maybe you can catch him under the mistletoe or something."

She laughed. "I think that ship already sailed, but a nice thought. Anyway... I'll let you finish your lunch before you get busy again."

She stood, and when she did, Jacob stood with her and walked her to the door. "This has been an absolute delight. Don't be a stranger. Women are welcome at the Tumbleweed, too, but you might have to fight off the lonesome cowboys who wander through. They're terrible romantics and always looking for a pretty girl to dance with."

She laughed. "Sounds a little risky, but I'll definitely come see you again." And then she threw her arms around his neck and hugged him.

Jacob watched until she drove out of sight, and then went back to his food, picked up his phone, and sent Asher a text.

You'll never guess who brought me lunch from the Rose today. Nora. Her dad died. Her mother passed four years ago, and now she's in Crossroads trying to figure out what to do with the family home. She is sweet as ever. Turned into a real beauty, but she looks lost...and tired. And she's still single. Crying shame. That's what it is. A crying shame. Anyway... It's cold as blazes here and I'm eating some of Pearl's chili and cornbread. I never could make good cornbread.
Love you, son.
Be safe wherever you are.

Asher was sitting at a red light in downtown Austin when he got the text. He smiled when he saw it was from his dad,

but then he read it, and a wave of longing gut-punched the smile off his face.

Nora.

They'd let time and distance change the paths they'd meant to take. Dad said she'd turned into a real beauty, but he didn't see how she could have gotten any prettier. She'd always been a beauty to him, and he also read between the lines of his dad's text. Crying shame.

"Yes, Dad, I screwed up on that front," he muttered, and then the light turned green, and he drove through the intersection.

There was still time and distance between them, and right now, there was nothing he could do about it, and it was after 8:00 p.m. before he made it home. His feet were dragging as he walked into the house, hung up his Stetson, left his wallet and keys on a silver tray in the foyer, and then went to his bedroom, locked up his gun, and took off his boots.

He sat down on the side of the bed to order DoorDash, then changed into a sweatshirt, sweatpants, and a pair of thick fuzzy socks, and walked back into the living room, plopped down on the sofa, and turned on the TV.

He was tired. So damn tired, but the current investigation he'd been involved in was finally over, which meant a lull in stakeouts and hunting down witnesses who flew the coop before they were meant to testify at trials. By tomorrow, there would likely be a handful of new cases and more facts to confirm, and reluctant witnesses to find, but not tonight. The text from his dad had resurrected old memories, and not all of them were about Nora.

He leaned back and closed his eyes, but when he did, all he saw was the look on his mother's face that last day when she took them to school. It was almost as if she was memorizing their faces.

A whole hour had passed, and he was almost asleep when

his doorbell rang. "DoorDash," he muttered, reminding himself that was still imminent, and got up. A few minutes later, he was downing a chopped brisket sandwich and a double order of onion rings and thinking about what was on the agenda tomorrow. But this was still today, and he was weary to the core.

First food.

Then a shower.

And finally, bed.

But alone. Always alone, except for tonight. Tonight, he took memories of Nora with him and woke up regretting that he'd let her slip through his fingers. At that moment, he rolled out of bed and called into work.

"What's up on the agenda?" he asked his boss.

"Nothing. Our witness turned up in court, thank you very much for your efforts, and we just got some delays on the other cases... Why?"

"Then I'm requesting the next two days off for personal reasons," Ash said.

"Done. Be safe. See you in three."

Ash sighed. "Thank you."

Then he made a call to the hangar where he kept his chopper.

"Rafael, this is Asher Kingston. I need you to fuel up my chopper and do a thorough flight check. I'm flying out this morning."

"Will do, Mr. Kingston. It will be ready," Rafael said.

After that, Asher filed a flight plan, packed an overnight bag, and went to shower and shave.

He ate toast standing up in his kitchen and took a to-go cup of coffee as he headed for the hangar, and called his dad as he drove.

When Jacob answered on the second ring, Asher could hear the surprise in his voice.

"Morning, son! What's up?" Jacob said.

"Just calling to let you know I'm coming to Crossroads this morning in my chopper. Didn't want you to freak out when I land in the open land behind the house."

"That's awesome! What's going on?"

"Nora. I didn't know she lost her mother. I didn't know her dad even had Alzheimer's. I didn't know she was still single. The thought of all she's gone through alone is hard to hear. I'm about to pay my respects. If she runs me out, I'll be spending the night with you. If she doesn't, I'll be there, hoping to talk my way back into her life."

"Finally," Jacob said. "Safe travels. See you later."

"Right, and thanks for the heads up," Asher said, and disconnected.

A little over two hours later, the Tumbleweed Bar was busy and loud. But not too loud to drown out the sound of a chopper overhead.

The crowd suddenly hushed.

"Not a LifeFlight chopper. Just Ash coming to pay a visit."

An old man sitting at the bar frowned. "Sounds like 'Nam," he said, then took a sip of his beer.

They all knew the old cowboy had seen the fall of Saigon, but he rarely talked about it, and now Asher's visit was bringing back unwelcome memories.

"Sorry about that," Jacob said.

The old man shrugged. "Ancient history. Ain't no never mind."

A few minutes later, Asher came into the bar from the house and gave Jacob a hug.

"Want the keys to my truck?" Jacob asked.

"It's just four blocks up the alley. I'll walk," Asher said, and then he was gone.

Chapter 3

NORA WAS SITTING CROSS-LEGGED ON THE LIVING ROOM floor, going through a box of childhood keepsakes she'd pulled out of her closet, knowing that she'd be better off if she chucked them all. She hadn't seen them in years. She didn't even know what was in there, which meant if she hadn't missed them, they didn't matter.

But as she was sorting, she pulled out a program from her junior prom, and when she opened it, found a dried flower from the corsage Asher had given her pressed between the pages. Before she knew it, tears were rolling down her face.

At the same moment, she heard footsteps on the porch, then a knock at the door. She grabbed the tail of her sweatshirt to wipe her eyes as she got up to answer, opened the door, and froze.

It was Asher, and she was struggling to find the boy she remembered in this man on her doorstep. Thick black hair with a slight tendency to curl. Black brows and lashes, and those clear blue eyes—at the moment, slightly wide with the same shock she was feeling.

She could see the evidence of a life in law enforcement in every facet of his face and body. Physically fit. Giving nothing away from his expression. Stoic to the point of stern. And then he started talking, and she couldn't move. Couldn't speak.

"I'm so sorry. I'm so sorry. I didn't know about your mother. I didn't know about your dad. I lost you and then

was afraid to go looking, because I didn't want to see you with another man."

She was trembling. Tears were rolling, and then the sobs came bubbling up, and she was in his arms. He toed the door shut behind him and just held her.

"It's okay, darlin', it's okay. Cry it away. Cry it all away." He was shocked by how light she was when he carried her to the sofa. Too thin. Too weary. So much loss. Too much grief. "I promised you so much and gave you nothing. I let work become my life, and ghosted the only woman I ever loved, and I have no excuse for how it happened. I didn't quit loving you, Nora. I just lost you, and didn't have the guts to go find who you'd become."

Nora was hiccupping on a sob when she crawled out of his lap to grab a handful of tissues. She wiped her eyes and blew her nose, scooted to the far end of the sofa, and then sat staring at the ghost he was, until she calmed down enough to speak.

"You've done this before... Come back to me, I mean. Always in my dreams. Tell me I'm not dreaming," she whispered.

The ache in his heart was physical. The devastation in her eyes was going to haunt him. "You're not dreaming. Do you hate me?"

He watched the shock of his question spread across her face.

"No! My God, no, I don't hate you. I have loved and lived with your ghost so long I don't know how to handle the reality of your presence. But at the same time, the blame is not all yours to own. I didn't go looking for you either, did I? And it was for the same reasons. I couldn't bear the thought of you loving someone besides me. Your dad told me you were single, but that didn't tell me anything other than you weren't married. I was afraid to ask if you had someone

special in your life, and if I didn't ask, then I could pretend you still cared."

This was more than he'd dare hope for, but he wanted more. He wanted her back in his life. "Nora. Darlin'. You have always been my true north. Are you willing to do us again? But not long distance? Would you be open to figuring out how we could do what we do and be together now?"

Her hands were clutched against her breasts to keep them from shaking. "Yes, a thousand times, yes."

He opened his arms, and she crawled into his lap, straddled his legs, and wrapped her arms around his neck.

The kiss that became the promise, became an avalanche. Too many years of separation. Too much loss. Too much sacrifice for all the wrong reasons.

"I want to make love with you," he said.

"Then do it. You know the way to my heart. You know the way to my bed."

His eyes narrowed, and then he was on his feet, her legs still wrapped around his waist as he carried her down the hall. Too many years without her slayed any semblance of caution, any pretense of restraint.

They were out of their shoes and tearing off their clothes and then falling onto the bed in each other's arms. Foreplay was the angst of fourteen years apart. He was hard and aching as he slid between her legs and closed his eyes, remembering this part of her that she'd given only to him.

Nora had made love with the boy he'd been, but never the man he'd become, and the only thing that went through her mind before she lost it was that there was no comparison. Dominated by his size. Cherished in the ways he held her. The words he whispered. The vow he made her. She was finally whole once more.

They lay sprawled upon the covers, wrapped in each other's arms with hearts pounding and pulses racing—waiting for the last of sanity to return.

Nora's hair was tangled in his fists—a last gesture of not wanting to let go.

"I love you still. You know that, don't you?"

"No doubts, Ash. You know I do."

"I can't stay long. I have tonight and then I have to fly home tomorrow."

She frowned. "I don't know why, but I guess I thought you drove here."

"I have a helicopter. I flew here," he said.

"You own a chopper?"

He heard the surprise in her voice and grinned. "I inherited a chopper. That's two different things." He began to explain. "I signed up for flying lessons on my twenty-first birthday, then six years ago, the man who'd been my flight instructor and had become a good friend, died unexpectedly. He had no family, and no heirs to inherit, but he'd left a will, dividing up his property as he saw fit, and that's how I became the owner of a Bell Turbine 206B III helicopter. It's a beauty, and I have used it since for work, as well."

"I am impressed," she said. "And with the land area of Texas being what it is, I would imagine it comes in very handy, as well."

"That, too," he said, and then hugged her. "I didn't have much breakfast, and we seemed to have missed lunch as well. I'd just as soon let Pearl feed us at the Yellow Rose, if you are willing."

"That would be wonderful. I haven't had much of an appetite lately, but I am suddenly hungry for everything," she said.

"We'll have to drive your car. I walked here from the bar."

She raised up on one elbow, tracing the shape of his mouth with the tip of her finger.

"Since you just drove me crazy, I am more than happy to reciprocate. Yes, we will take my car. Is Jacob expecting you to stay the night with him?" she asked.

"Only if you sent me packing," he said.

"Well, that's not happening. You know, we've never slept together. Ever."

He kissed the tip of her nose. "But we made love all over Crossroads for years, so I'll be looking forward to hearing you snore."

She frowned. "I do not snore."

"I wouldn't care if you did. You are perfect in my eyes. Now grab your drawers, woman. There's a burger waiting for us somewhere."

By the time they got to the Rose, it felt like all those years apart had never happened. And for the first time, Nora saw past the routine of her life, to the future she'd hoped for, and walking in together made a good many heads turn, which they tried to ignore. Unfortunately, Asher had already set himself up for interrogation by arriving in a helicopter.

Nora watched and listened with delight as he talked his way through the answers without giving away anything of his personal business. She was witnessing yet another aspect of the man he'd become, and she liked it.

They turned in their orders, but it wasn't until their food came to the table that they were finally left in peace. By the time they finished, they were the last ones in the dining room, and Pearl came out smiling.

"I will say, it's a sight to see you two together again. Hope it sticks," she said, and set a sack on their table. "Pie on the house, and drop one by for Jacob, will you? He likes my pie."

"Thank you!" Nora said. "We'd love to. I know he'll appreciate it."

Pearl gave Asher a look and shook her head. "Flying around in a helicopter. You're as flashy and dangerous as your daddy used to be," she said, and flipped herself back to the kitchen.

Asher blinked. "Dad? Flashy and dangerous?"

Nora grinned. "Apparently, she knows something you don't. Let's go."

They left the Yellow Rose with the pie and drove down the highway to the Tumbleweed.

"Unless you want to go in, I'll deliver Dad's pie," Asher said. "You stay in where it's warm."

"I choose the warm, but give him my love."

"Will do. I won't be long, and since I'm not staying here, I need to get my overnight bag." He took one of the little boxes out of the bag, then went inside.

Just watching him go made her shiver. It was amazing what time had done to the man. He was dynamite on two legs. She turned up the fan on the heater at her feet and leaned back to wait.

He came out carrying a duffel bag, tossed it in the back seat, and then got inside. Nora took them home.

They spent the rest of the afternoon talking about their lives apart and debating the different ways they could live the rest of it together. Finally, Nora ended it with the obvious solution.

"I already told you that my office is in my home, in the apartment where I live. It's all online work alone, or Zoom meetings with corporate bigwigs in other nations. Occasionally, I have to make a trip to Europe or Asia. I'm as much of a liaison as a troubleshooter for the foreign branches, as well as the ones here in the states. One of the big issues is always espionage. Trying to duplicate or steal new technology. I know how to trace the online stuff, and track the thieves trying to sell it online as well."

Asher was in awe.

"Nora, honey, I want you to know how proud I am of you. And how much I admire who you have become. As long as it doesn't make work difficult for you, then that works, because I can't keep my job unless I'm living within the beck and call of the state capitol."

"We'll figure it out," Nora said. "But you fly home tomorrow, and I'm still here sorting out the last bits of my parents' lives. I don't expect it to take long, and at the same time, I'm working from here like I work at home, and packing up what to keep and what to let go."

"Then we make the most of our time here together and deal with what comes next when it's time."

She looked up, startled to realize it was already dark outside. She stood and began drawing curtains and pulling down shades. When she saw Ash watching her, she shrugged it off.

"Prying eyes," she said.

He accepted the answer without commenting, which was a relief. He already knew she lived and worked in a high-rise in Fort Worth, but she was unwilling to ruin their reunion by revealing why she'd climbed an ivory tower and refused to come down. That was for another day.

They made love in the dark, and fell asleep in each other's arms, and he was gone after daylight, leaving her well-loved and at peace, and with the knowledge that he didn't snore.

After their visit to prison, Freddie and Everett Brandt made the decision to abandon the Dallas/Fort Worth area and move to Amarillo. It was a place big enough to get lost in, but close enough to Crossroads to investigate the possibility

of finding their inheritance. They'd bought into that idea really quick, and were already imagining it secreted away in some nook or cranny on the Kingston property.

Freddie's truck was in a shop back in Mansfield. He'd taken it in for repair, then didn't have the money to get it out, and a man Everett knew was in jail, awaiting transport to an area prison, so he took it upon himself to pick the lock at the man's apartment, take the keys to his sports car, and drive it out of the parking lot like he owned it. It was an older model white Mustang, but it ran good, and they needed wheels to get to Amarillo.

They packed up what they could carry from the places they'd been living and abandoned the rest, leaving landlords to clear out the refuse of their lives. Freddie hadn't worked since his last stint in jail, and Everett was drawing disability from an on-the-job accident three years ago. The way he looked at it, he was set for life, until they found out about the money. After that, all he could think about was one million dollars.

A week later, they were holed up in Amarillo, paying rent by the month in a rehabbed motel that had been turned into apartments, and planning the kind of house they were going to buy after they recovered the loot.

But the hitch in the plan was Jacob Kingston. He still owned the bar and lived on the property. There was never going to be easy access. Still, they decided to pay a visit to the bar, see the layout, and feel the old man out about selling it.

The sun was shining, but the day was cold as they set out for Crossroads, but the car was warm, and the tank was full of gas. They had beer money in their pockets, and a plan they'd cooked up the night before. Everett was well aware of Freddie's issues. He didn't always understand, or get things right, and began talking about the plan again as they drove.

"Now Freddie, we have been over this a dozen times, but I want to make sure you remember your role. We'll go in the bar like regular customers, and I'll casually ask Kingston if he's interested in selling the property, right? If he is, then he'll have to let us at least look around to check it out," Everett said. "But we don't call each other by our real names. I'm Joe Wilson and you're my brother Dan."

Freddie frowned. "I don't want to be Dan. I want to be Darren."

Everett rolled his eyes. "Fine, you're Darren. And what's my name?"

"Everett," Freddie said.

"No! I'm Joe. Shit, Freddie. Just let me do the talking or you'll screw this up before we even get started."

Freddie frowned, but he didn't argue. Freddie knew his limits. He knew he was good-looking, but Everett had the brains.

It was a chilly afternoon at the Tumbleweed Bar, but late-October weather in the Texas panhandle was iffy on a good day. The wind had a bite to it, and had there been enough moisture in the air, it might have been cold enough to work up a little snow. But it hadn't happened, and the nip didn't slow down the customers. The Tumbleweed was cozy and warm, and the perfect hideout for every old cowboy and every out-of-work local in Crossroads, not to mention the customers from the constant traffic out front on Highway 86.

Jacob was mopping up a beer spill on the floor and waiting for Billy Jack Woford's wife, Lisa, to come pick him up, because Billy Jack didn't drive anymore. Nobody minded Billy Jack's lapses in memory, or that one beer made him drunk. His wife was just grateful he was still alive.

Once Billy Jack had earned a living as a farrier until he got kicked in the head. He had been in a coma for weeks and woke up thinking he was still in high school, and that his wife was his girlfriend. The kick erased fifteen years of his memory. He drew disability and sometimes forgot how to count the money he owed, but Billy Jack would just smile at his own confusion. He didn't have a care in the world.

Jacob got the spill cleaned up, stored the mop, and was back at the bar serving customers when the door opened. He looked up, thinking it might be Lisa coming for Billy Jack, and saw two strangers, instead. He watched them scoping out the place and thought nothing of it as they meandered toward the bar and sat down at the two stools at the end.

"Afternoon. What'll it be?" Jacob said.

"Two Lone Star Originals," Everett said.

Jacob got the bottles out of the cooler and popped the lids, eyeing the men as he served them. "Enjoy," he said as he set a little bowl of pretzels between them and walked away.

"Now what?" Freddie whispered.

"Drink your beer. Have a pretzel, *Darren*. Relax."

Freddie grinned. It was like being a spy. "Yeah...yeah... right," and took a big swig.

Everett was eyeing Kingston's size and age, trying to decide if he was as imposing as he appeared. He'd expected an old man, not a big, physically fit dude. The only thing that gave away his age was the full head of gray hair and the weathered maturity of his face.

He popped a pretzel in his mouth and crunched it, and when Kingston went to the cash register to make change for a customer, Everett saw the ripple of muscles across his back and frowned.

What Everett didn't know was, at the same moment he frowned, Jacob glanced up in the mirror over the bar and

saw it. *That one's trouble*, he thought, then turned back to his customer.

"Here you go, Waylon. Buy Lorraine some flowers before you go home, and she won't even care that you're late."

Waylon grinned. "I'm always late getting home."

Jacob shook his head. "Doesn't mean she'll always be there when you get back. Buy her flowers, man. Trust me. Don't ever take your woman for granted."

The smile slid off Waylon Morris's face. They all knew what Jacob's wife had done to him and their sons.

"Right," Waylon said, and left the bar as three more customers walked in.

Everett Brandt finished his beer and was pulling out his wallet when Jacob came back to them.

"Ready for another round?" he asked.

Everett flashed a big grin. "Not this time. I'm driving."

"Good call," Jacob said. "Just passing through?"

"In a manner of speaking," Everett said. "I'm Joe Wilson. This is my brother Darren. We've been admiring your setup. This is a nice place. Are you the owner, or..."

"Thanks, and yes, the Tumbleweed is mine," Jacob said.

"Ever think of selling it? We're looking for something like this."

Jacob shook his head. "Sorry. No... Not for sale."

Freddie felt obliged to at least participate. "What would a place like this sell for?" he asked.

Everett resisted the urge to put his fist in his brother's mouth.

Jacob's focus shifted to the big blond-headed man. "You don't look much like your brother."

"I take after Pop and Ev... Uh... Joe takes after Mama."

Jacob caught the hesitation. His suspicions were right. They weren't who they said they were, and they weren't here for beer.

"I can't answer your question about what the bar's worth. When you have exactly what you want in life, no amount of money can tempt you to give that up," Jacob said, then took the money they left on the bar and put it in the register. He glanced up in the mirror again and caught them leaving. They were arguing all the way out the door and still arguing when they got into an older model white car and drove away.

He shrugged them off and forgot about them.

As for the Brandt brothers, their reconnoiter had revealed more than they expected, none of it good.

"You just had to talk," Everett shouted. "Damn it all to hell, Freddie! Whatever Kingston thought about us before, when you sputtered around with which name you were going to call me, we were made. He didn't know what we were about, but he knew we were lying."

"Yeah, I'm sorry, Joe."

"Joe? Joe? Now I'm Joe? Look…the charade is over, Freddie. I'm Everett."

"Right," Freddie said, then glanced out the window at the passing scenery.

Silence settled within the cab and Everett was just driving, wanting to get home before bad weather came in, when Freddie shifted nervously, then glanced at his brother.

"Hey, Everett?"

"Yeah?" Everett said.

"What's a charade?"

Everett sighed. Freddie didn't just look like Pop. He wasn't any smarter than him, either.

"It doesn't matter. Don't worry about it," Everett said.

"Okay," Freddie said, and leaned back in the seat and closed his eyes, while Everett was pondering their next move.

It was midnight in Crossroads one week later, and Jacob had just seen his last customer to the door, locked up behind him, and turned the OPEN sign to CLOSED. He paused, watching taillights of the truck as the man drove away. That particular customer stayed until closing every night he was here, not because he liked to drink. He just didn't have anyone to go home to, and Jacob understood that better than most.

He sighed, then turned around and began going through the bar, straightening up chairs and turning out overhead lights, but always leaving on the nightlights and the neon sign over the bar.

He paused for one last look before digging in his pockets for his house keys, then headed down the hallway separating work from home, thinking about a hot soaking bath as he unlocked the door and stepped across the threshold.

But before he could shut it behind him, he heard running steps on the porch, then breaking glass. And his first thought was, *I'm about to be robbed!*

He dropped the keys and ran toward the bar where he kept his gun. Panic added speed, but they were already inside. Someone tackled him from behind, and he hit the floor belly first, with the man on top of him.

Then, to his horror, he heard a whisper in his ear. "You should have sold out, old man."

And that's all it took. Jacob was down, but he was far from out. He made a quick move that took his assailant off guard, then bucked him off and kicked. He heard the assailant hit the floor cursing, as he kept crawling toward the shelf where the gun was hidden. Then all of a sudden, he heard someone jack a shell into the chamber of a rifle.

He looked over his shoulder, saw the silhouettes of two

men behind him, and then the rifle aimed straight at his chest. He rolled and was reaching for his gun when they fired. He felt a hot, burning pain, and then everything went black.

Freddie Brandt was hysterical!

"You shot him! You weren't supposed to shoot. We said we wouldn't kill no one!" he screamed.

Everett slapped him. "It's your fault. You weren't supposed to talk. We were just gonna blindfold him and gag him and do the search, but you had to go and challenge him about not selling up. Even after we were gone, he would have figured out it was us."

At that moment, a pickup truck turned off the highway into the parking lot, its headlights sweeping across the wall, then in their eyes as it began to make a U-turn, and their first thought was that they'd been made. When the truck suddenly sped away, they immediately assumed they'd gone to call the cops.

"We gotta get outta here!" Everett shouted, and started running for the door, with Freddie right behind him, running through broken glass, and leaving the door ajar. They jumped in the Mustang and gunned it, spinning out on the graveled lot as they drove away.

Pearl Fallon not only owned and operated the Yellow Rose Café, but she also lived in the apartment above it. Every night when she closed down the Rose, she set the security alarm, then went upstairs and locked herself in for the night. It was the sanctuary where she could indulge in a

quiet bubble bath, watch her prerecorded shows, or eat a whole pint of rocky road ice cream if she wanted.

She hadn't planned to live a solitary life, but it's how her journey was turning out. Fate had given her an accidental daughter when she'd taken an abandoned teenager under her wing years earlier, and now her accidental daughter, Magnolia, had married a famous bull rider from the rodeo circuit, and they became the family Pearl never birthed. Having a famous artist for a daughter now, and a world-famous rodeo star for a son-in-law, had enriched Pearl's world. She was about as happy with herself as she'd ever been.

Even though the nights were getting colder, Pearl still liked to sleep with her bedroom windows open. She liked hearing the traffic going by on the highway outside, and she liked sleeping in fresh air, instead of the lingering scent of whatever she'd cooked that day wafting up from the kitchen below.

She'd gone to bed around ten, but was awakened sometime later by the sound of a gunshot. The moment she heard it, she flew out of bed and ran to the window just in time to see a black truck driving past the Rose. It went all the way to the Tumbleweed, then made a U-turn in the parking lot and drove back toward town. But it was the white sports car that shot out of the parking lot seconds later that gave her cause for concern. She watched it heading west at a high rate of speed, and then glanced at the clock.

It was just after midnight. Jacob closed the bar at midnight. Maybe someone tried to rob him? Maybe he took a shot at them? But with no police presence at the Crossroads, people here had learned to look out for each other first and call for help later. She was thinking of Jacob as she grabbed her phone and pulled up the number from her contact list, and called him. When it rang and rang with no answer, she got worried.

She slammed the window shut, pulled the shades, and turned on the lights to get dressed, yanking on blue jeans and a heavy sweatshirt, then socks and shoes, before calling Jacob one more time. When he didn't answer, she grabbed her keys and her phone and took off down the stairs with a flashlight in her hand.

Unsure of what she might be walking into, she took her shotgun from beneath the counter, disarmed her security system, and let herself out the front door, locked it behind her, and took off running down the highway toward the bar.

The air was cold on her face and her heart was pounding as she ran, but when she reached the parking lot and saw the front door ajar, and the glass broken out of the window in it, her heart began hammering even harder.

She ran into the bar, flipping on lights as she went.

"Jacob! Jacob! It's Pearl! Are you okay? Where are you?" she shouted, but he didn't answer.

From where she was standing, she saw the door leading into the house was open, and she began running toward it. That's when she caught a glimpse of a body on the floor behind the bar and skidded to a halt.

It was Jacob, lying in a spreading pool of blood.

"No, no, no," she muttered, and ran to his side, frantically feeling for a pulse. To her undying relief, it was there.

She made a quick call to 911, then laid the phone on the floor and began grabbing clean bar towels from a shelf.

She stuffed a handful beneath his back at the exit wound, and then folded some more into a pack and put it on the entrance wound and pressed down hard, still trying to stop the flow.

She looked at his face, once so dear to her, and began talking, begging, threatening him, hoping he would fight to stay alive.

"Jacob, this is Pearl. I don't know if you can hear me, but help's coming. Stay with me. Just stay with me. Damn it, don't you dare die on me. After all these years, I don't want to lose you again," she said, and swallowed back tears.

The dispatcher was still talking. "Ma'am. Ma'am. Are you still there?"

"Yes, I'm here. I have towels on the wound. I'm applying pressure, but he's going to bleed out. Just hurry. Please hurry."

"We've dispatched Texas Highway Patrol, a LIFESTAR chopper from Amarillo, and the Briscoe County Sheriff's department. Help is coming. Is he conscious? Is he still breathing?"

Pearl kept applying pressure to the makeshift pad. "No, he's not conscious, but yes, he's still breathing. Just tell them to hurry... Please tell them to hurry."

At that same moment Pearl was talking to the dispatcher, Sonny Bluejacket woke and sat straight up in bed. His wife, Maggie, rolled over, saw the look on Sonny's face, and knew he was having a vision, something that he'd begun experiencing after dying twice on the operating table a few years ago. He'd come back from the dead with a gift they no longer ignored.

"Sonny! What's wrong?"

He blinked, then wiped his hands over his face, as if he was trying to remove what he'd seen.

"Somebody shot Jacob Kingston. Pearl's at the bar covered in blood. I don't think it's hers."

Pearl had become the mother to Maggie that she'd never had, and the thought of her in danger was horrifying. "Oh my God, Sonny. I have to go," Maggie said.

"We both go, darlin'. It's cold. Dress warm and hurry."

Within minutes, they were out the door and running toward the truck, then speeding away from the ranch.

Chapter 4

PEARL COULD HEAR THE DISPATCHER STILL TALKING, and she kept answering the same question over and over, saying yes, he was still breathing, but when she finally began to hear the distant sound of sirens coming from both directions, she knew help was actually on the way.

The chopper would be coming by air, so the sirens had to be the law. She didn't know how much time had passed, but Jacob hadn't twitched a muscle, and she was scared to death he was going to die. Her arms were trembling from the pressure she was exerting. Her fingers were aching. She'd already replaced the blood-soaked pad with a fresh one and was almost as bloody as him.

"Hang on, Jacob. I hear sirens. Help is on the way. Don't give up. Stay with me. You can have free lunch forever if you promise you won't die."

She was angry this had happened, and fiercely determined this wasn't going to be the way he died. She kept thinking of his sons. What they would think. How they would feel, having their father murdered, to add to their mother's suicide.

The sirens were a steady scream now, and then they were in the parking lot, red and blue lights flashing, and right behind them, two cruisers from the Briscoe County Sheriff's office.

She could hear shouting, and then patrol cars moving out onto the highway, blocking off both lanes of traffic coming and going to make a landing spot for the inbound chopper.

"It's happening, Jacob! They're here! The LIFESTAR chopper is arriving. I can hear it now. Hang on. Hang on."

Moments later, she heard footsteps on the porch and then people coming inside on the run.

"Here! Behind the bar!" she shouted, and looked up just as Sheriff Reddick appeared.

He grimaced at the sight of them, both covered in blood. "Oh my God, Pearl. What happened?"

"I was asleep at the Rose when I heard a gunshot. I bailed out of bed and ran to the window just as a black truck turned off the highway and made a U-turn in the Tumbleweed parking lot like all the locals do, and then it drove back into town. But moments later, an older model white sports car suddenly shot out of the parking lot, spinning out in the gravel, and headed west, too. I tried to call Jacob, and when I didn't get an answer, I came running."

He saw the shotgun on the floor beside her.

"Is that your shotgun?"

"Yes, I brought it with me from the Rose."

Reddick glanced up. "The chopper is landing. Be right back."

After that, everything became a blur.

Pearl was moved out of the way as paramedics began to work on Jacob, but time was not on their side. They stayed long enough to get an IV started, then began moving him away. There was no time to try and stabilize him first. He was already too close to death.

Pearl was sitting out on the steps of the Tumbleweed when they loaded him into the chopper. After their presence was no longer needed, the highway patrol cars departed, leaving the witness and the crime scene to the sheriff's office.

Between the sirens and the inbound chopper, and the crime scene tape being rolled out, the entire town of

Crossroads was now aware that something dire had happened. When word began to spread that Jacob Kingston had been shot, and Pearl had been the one to find him, it was inevitable that someone would call the Sunset Ranch to notify Magnolia. They didn't know she and Sonny were already on the way.

Nora Borden had heard the sirens and was already out on her porch when she saw the inbound chopper. She grabbed her coat and started running, cutting through the alleys to get to the Yellow Rose, only to find it locked up and dark. Then she saw all the police vehicles at the bar and thought, *Jacob!* and took off running again, but this time down the side of the highway.

The first person she saw was Pearl, sitting on the porch with a shotgun beside her, and the chopper lifting off and turning northbound.

"What happened? What happened?" Nora cried as she ran up to where Pearl was sitting. She was wrapped in a blanket one of the paramedics had put around her, shaking both from the shock and the cold.

"Somebody broke into the bar and shot Jacob. I don't know if he's going to make it," Pearl said.

Nora's first thoughts were for Asher and his brothers. "Oh, my God. Oh honey," she said, then scooted down beside her, wrapped her in her arms and pulled her close.

Moments later, a big red truck turned off the highway and pulled up in the parking lot. When Pearl saw Maggie and Sonny running toward her, she started crying.

Nora looked up. "Who are they?"

"My girl, Magnolia, and her husband, Sonny."

Nora's eyes widened as she recognized their faces. "As in Magnolia Brennen the famous artist, and the bull rider Sonny Bluejacket?"

Pearl nodded. "She's not my blood, but she's my girl."

The moment they got to Pearl, Nora stood. "None of the blood is hers," she said, and stepped aside.

Maggie was crying as she held her. Sonny had embraced them both, but he was looking over their heads at Nora. Their gazes locked, and then Nora heard him speak. "You came home to grief, but it will pass. Someone has come to you with love, and it will be good."

Nora's eyes widened, but she couldn't find the words, and then Maggie reached for Nora's hand.

"You're Nora. Pearl said you were coming home. I'm so sorry about your father," Maggie said. "I used to wait on him when I worked at the Rose. His name was Tom, right?"

The moment Maggie touched her, Sonny turned away, and just like that, the moment was gone.

"Yes, I'm Nora. I just got home a few days ago. I heard the sirens, saw the chopper, and it was so close to the Yellow Rose I thought something had happened there, but when I realized it was farther down the block, I panicked all over again. Jacob is an old and dear friend, and I grew up with Asher, his oldest son. If he lives, it will be all due to Pearl's quick actions." She hunched her shoulders against the wind. "Pearl, honey, now that your family is here, I'll be going home."

Before Sonny could offer her a ride, she started walking up the highway. Within a few steps, she was running, then took a shortcut through another alley and ran all the way home.

The moment she was safely inside, she began to shake. The horror of this night wasn't going to fade any time soon, and she wasn't going to be the one to call Asher. He needed to hear it from the authorities. They would have answers to the questions he would ask. All she had was bad news.

The chopper reached Northwest Texas Hospital less than fifteen minutes after takeoff from the bar. They landed on the heliport, unloaded Jacob, and rushed him straight to the ER.

Immediately, nurses began cutting off his clothes as a doctor was assessing his vitals. A nurse found a medical information card in his wallet denoting his blood type and listing no allergies. They began an emergency transfusion of whole blood and sent him straight to surgery.

It was 3:00 a.m. in Austin, Texas.

Life and death were still happening.

Sirens blared.

Horns honked.

It was the lullaby Asher Kingston took to bed, and the song he woke up to each morning. So, when his phone began to ring, he woke abruptly. Thinking it was probably work related, he rolled over and picked it up, then sat up on the side of the bed to answer.

"This is Kingston."

"Asher, this is Sheriff Reddick from the Briscoe County Sheriff's office. I'm calling to let you know that someone broke into your father's bar just after closing and shot him. He was unconscious when found, and he was still alive when the chopper left with him, but he's in bad shape. A lot of blood loss. He was taken to Northwest Texas Hospital in Amarillo. I just spoke to people at the hospital. He was still alive when they took him into surgery."

Shock, followed by an overwhelming fear, took Ash's breath, and then he swallowed past the sudden lump in his throat.

"Oh my God. Do you have any leads? Any suspicions?"

"Right now, not a clue as to who, but we have one witness who saw a car leaving the parking lot moments after the gunshot. That's all, and there's nothing solid to go on yet, but we're still processing the crime scene. The weird thing is that nothing was stolen. Money still in the till. Jacob's wallet and money still on him."

Ash frowned. "Just a thought. After Pete Brandt died and our family became news all over again, my brothers and I actually discussed the possibility of some kind of ramifications. We didn't expect this, but I wouldn't rule it out. Anyway, thank you for letting me know. I'll call Dylan and Gunner. We will be heading to the hospital, ASAP."

"Understood," Reddick said.

Asher immediately disconnected, then called the hangar where he kept his chopper. He left orders for it to be checked out and fueled up, and that he would be at the hangar by sunrise.

Then he called Dylan.

When Dylan Kingston's cell phone began to ring, he thought he was dreaming it until Angie gave him a nudge.

"Dylan... Honey... Wake up."

He jerked, groaned. "Sorry. I thought I was dreaming it."

The first thing he did was look at the time as he reached to answer. It was just after 4:00 a.m., and Ash's name was on Caller ID. This couldn't be good news.

"What's wrong?" Dylan said.

Asher unloaded the info as abruptly as Dylan had answered the phone.

"Dad's been shot. It happened just after midnight after he closed the bar. He was airlifted to a hospital in Amarillo. He lost a lot of blood. Sheriff Reddick said he's in bad shape.

I've already contacted the hangar. They're getting the chopper ready. Just in case, pack enough clothes for a prolonged stay."

"Oh my God... This is the exact kind of shit we were worried about. Yes, yes, clothes... I'll pack clothes and meet you at the hangar. Does Gunner know?" Dylan asked as he threw back the covers and got up.

Ash swiped a shaky hand across his face. "I'm calling him next. Drive safe. See you soon," and then disconnected.

Angie was already up and pulling a suitcase from the closet before she even knew what was wrong, but when Dylan turned around and she saw his face, she knew it couldn't be good.

"Honey! What happened?"

"Dad's been shot. It happened just after he closed the bar. They airlifted him to a hospital in Amarillo. He lost a lot of blood. It doesn't look good. Ash said pack for a prolonged stay. I need clothes for at least a week, just in case."

She nodded. "You go wash up and pack your shaving stuff. I'll get your clothes. Do you have enough cash on you? I think there's a couple of hundred dollars in my wallet. Take it too, just in case. I'll look after the office. If there are major decisions to be made, I'll let you know."

Dylan hugged her. "Lady, you are my rock. Thank you for this."

"Go!" she said. "I'll get you packed."

Within fifteen minutes, Dylan was dressed and heading to the garage with his suitcase. Angie was right behind him, handing him the cash from her purse.

"Just in case," she said, and jammed it in the pocket of his coat.

One last hug and kiss, and then Dylan was gone. She couldn't help him through this, but she knew his business backward and forward, and she knew everything about the

ongoing projects. That much she could do for him, and with his blessing.

Gunner Kingston was on his way to a crime scene when his cell phone rang. He answered via Bluetooth, to keep both hands on the wheel.

"This is Kingston."

Ash winced. He could hear sirens and radio traffic in the background. Gunner was up and working.

"Gunner, it's me, Ash. Sounds like you have a load on your plate already, but I'm adding more to it. Dad's been shot. Happened just after midnight. He suffered serious blood loss. It's not good. They airlifted him to a hospital in Amarillo. I'm flying Dylan and me out as soon as we get to the hangar. If you can get away, pack clothes for an extended stay. There's no law in Crossroads outside of the county sheriff's office half an hour away. Whether Dad lives or dies, I'm not leaving Crossroads until I find out who did this, and I'm gonna need backup."

Gunner took a sharp turn up a dark alley. "Damn it! Just damn it! I've got to call in to the precinct to get another detective on-site. This has to do with that armored car robbery, doesn't it? Somebody with a grudge and nobody left to blame but Dad."

"I don't know, but I'm damn sure going to find out. But we first need to be there for Dad, like he was there for us when our world crashed," Ash said.

"Agreed, and on it," Gunner said. "Text me the location. I'll get there as soon as I can." Then his voice broke. "If you get to talk to him, just tell him not to die." Gunner disconnected, and then immediately called in to the precinct. After a hasty conversation with his superior, he was

given immediate permission and put on an indefinite leave of absence. The moment he got the okay, he turned around and headed back home, weaving his way through Dallas traffic. Once inside the house, he got online to get the fastest flight to Amarillo, rented an SUV to be picked up at the Amarillo airport, then began packing for an extended stay.

Asher was driving to the hangar when it dawned on him that Nora had to have known. With all the sirens and the helicopter that picked him up in the middle of the night, the whole town would have known. And he knew exactly why she hadn't called. Because she would not have had the answers he so desperately would want. She would have no knowledge of Jacob's condition, or anything to do with the actual scene. Only that it had happened. And he knew she would be torn about not being the one to call.

When he came to a red light, he called her, then put it on Bluetooth as he drove through the intersection. She answered on the second ring, and she was crying.

"You know, don't you?" he said.

"Yes, but I had the good sense not to throw the news in your face with absolutely nothing else to say. I don't know Jacob's condition, or anything about what's going on. I knew the sheriff would gather what he knew before notifying next of kin. I'm so sorry."

"Don't cry, honey. You did the absolute right things."

"I first thought something had happened at the Rose and got dressed and ran down there. But when I saw all of the police cars down at the Tumbleweed, my heart sank. I took off running as the chopper was lifting off. Pearl was sitting on the porch covered in blood. She heard the shot.

She tried to call him, and when he didn't answer, she saved his life. That much I do know."

"Good lord. Good to know," he said. "I'm almost at the hangar. Dylan is meeting me here. We're flying to Amarillo and going straight to the hospital."

"I love you so much, and I'm so sorry. Fly safe, love. When you can, let me know how he is."

"Love you most, and I will. Gotta go. I'm at the hangar now."

The crew at the hangar had pulled the chopper out, refueled it, and gone through all the checkups, but as soon as Ash arrived, he put his luggage inside the cockpit, then did his own preflight checkup again.

Dylan arrived as Asher was going through flight check and ran across the tarmac to the chopper. He tossed his bag inside and climbed into the copilot's seat. They took one look at each other, then Dylan buckled himself in and put on the headphones.

"Did you talk to Gunner?" he asked.

Ash nodded. The rotors were already turning as he began prepping for liftoff. He'd filed a flight plan, so when they lifted off, Ash made a half circle in the sky, as if in acknowledgement to the growing light of the day, then headed north/northwest to Amarillo.

They didn't talk much during the flight.

Asher was focused on flying and Dylan was lost in thought, but they were both fearing their arrival might be too late.

When they finally reached the Amarillo airport and got permission to land, the rush to get a cab became the next leg of their journey.

The sky was gray. The air was cold as they hurried into the terminal then all the way through the concourse to hail a cab. Three other flights had just unloaded and there was

a line of people waiting for transportation, too. When they finally got a cab, they loaded their luggage in the trunk.

"Where to?" the driver asked.

"Northwest Texas Hospital on Coulter Street," Asher said.

Dylan was on his phone, texting Angie to let them know they'd arrived, as the cab carried them through the streets of Amarillo.

Ash was doing the same, reading the sympathy text from his boss, and a one-sentence text from Gunner. Boarding my flight, which he showed to Dylan.

"Good. He'll be here in a couple of hours, then," Dylan said.

"Less than that," Asher said. "Look at the time when he sent the text. He's already halfway here."

Neither of them could find the words to say more. All they wanted was to have someone tell them Jacob was going to survive—that he was going to be okay.

When they arrived at the hospital, they grabbed their bags and headed inside. After a stop at the information desk and a trip up in the elevator, they went straight to the nurses' desk.

The duty nurse glanced up. "Can I help you?"

"Our father, Jacob Kingston, was airlifted here a few hours ago with a gunshot wound. Do you have an update on his status? Is he still in surgery?" Asher asked.

The nurse scanned the current patients list. "His surgery was completed. He's been moved to ICU. It's on this floor. There is a waiting area for visitation. Go down that hall and follow the signs. The nurses there will fill you in on visitation rules, and the timelines when his doctor makes rounds."

"Thank you," Ash said, and picked up his bag.

Dylan was already on the move, and Ash lengthened his stride to catch up.

After checking at yet another nurses' station, they learned that Jacob's doctor was on the floor making rounds, and that they would let him know that his patient's family had arrived. They were also informed of the visitation rules. The usual rules for ICU. No more than two family members at a time, ten minutes on the hour, every hour.

They moved themselves to the waiting room, found a place to sit beneath a window, and shoved their luggage against the wall behind them.

Dylan glanced around the waiting area at the people waiting with them, then stood. "I'm going to get coffee. Do you want anything from the canteen area? Coffee, sweet roll, Pepsi?"

"Coffee, black, and a sweet roll is fine," Ash said.

Dylan took off his coat, hung it on the arm of his chair, and headed for the canteen, while Ash shed his coat, then sent Gunner a text telling him their dad made it through surgery, and which floor they were on, then sent Nora the same information.

Dylan came back with their snacks.

"Thanks," Asher said, and carefully set the coffee aside to cool, while he opened the packaging and took a bite of the roll. It wasn't great, but he'd had worse.

Dylan kept eyeing his brother as they ate. The brothers could read each other like a road map, and Dylan guessed Asher was already in investigation mode, and he was right.

Ash didn't believe it was meant to be a robbery. Not even a botched one. Nothing was taken, not the money in the till, and his dad's wallet was still on him when they found his body. He was holding on to what Nora told him until Gunner arrived to hear it, too.

Jacob wasn't the kind of man to have enemies, but Asher needed to find out if he'd recently had words with a customer, or if someone was holding a grudge. But that was all

for later. Right now, they just needed him to wake up and survive this nightmare, then they could deal with whoever had done this, and make sure nothing like this ever happened again.

Within the hour, Jacob's surgeon walked in, scanned the faces of the people in the waiting room, and then walked straight to where Asher and Dylan were sitting.

"Are you Jacob Kingston's family?" he asked.

They both stood abruptly. "Yes. We're his sons," Asher said.

"I'm Doctor Reading. I operated on your father earlier this morning. He is on the critical list, but his vital signs are holding steady. He was brought in with a single gunshot to the chest. It entered between his heart and upper shoulder and exited a little higher on his back, which means the shot was from someone standing above him, firing from a short distance away. He was severely weakened from the blood loss by the time he got here."

"Did you have to transfuse him?" Asher asked.

"Yes, he had a whole blood transfusion. I expect it to raise his numbers to a stronger level. I just checked his vitals. He's holding his own, and that's positive, but as I'm sure you know, the next twenty-four to forty-eight hours are crucial."

"Did he ever regain consciousness?" Dylan asked.

"Not as of yet," Doctor Reading said. "I'll be checking on him again this evening during rounds. We have him heavily sedated, so don't expect too much from him at this point. He's healing, and right now that's what matters most."

Ash nodded. "We have one more brother due to arrive soon. We are all the family he has, and he's everything to us."

"Understood," Reading said. "I need to finish my rounds, but I will say, what a remarkable resemblance you all have to each other. Like younger versions of your father. Rest

assured, we're doing everything we can for him," he said, and then he was gone.

Dylan shoved a hand through his hair in frustration, then turned and walked to the window.

Asher followed and slid his arm across Dylan's shoulder. Several minutes passed as they stood in silence, just staring out the window. Then all of a sudden, a man walked up behind them, stretched out his long arms, and gave both of them a hug.

"Got room for one more brother?" he said.

They turned. "Gunner!" they said, then hugged him.

The only sign of emotion on his face was a quick muscle jerk at the side of his jaw as he hugged them back.

"Sit," Ash said, and they did. "Are you hungry? Do you want some coffee? Something to eat?"

"Not until I know what you know," Gunner said, and so they began filling him in on everything the doctor told them, with him listening intently until they finished.

"I called Nora on the way to the hangar," Ash said.

They both looked up. "You're talking to Nora?"

"More than talking. After Dad told me that her father had recently died, and her mother had been gone four years, and she'd come home to deal with the family property, I felt the guilt. Then when he told me that she'd visited him, and that she looked like the stress of it all had just about broken her... I couldn't bear the thought of how she'd faced all that alone and went begging. Long story short, she not only forgave me, but I'm flying high on my second chance. When I was driving to the hangar, it dawned on me that she and everybody else in Crossroads would have known about it before we did. I wondered what she knew that Reddick didn't tell. She said Pearl heard the shot. She's the one who found him bleeding and unconscious, and saved his life."

"My God. What are the chances? We owe her big time," Dylan said.

"This kind of shooting isn't the Crossroads we grew up in," Gunner said. "Nothing was stolen. He hadn't received any threats, or we would have known about them. And unless the character of the residents has drastically changed, I'm not going to believe it was a local who did this. Did he ever say anything to either of you about having trouble with someone?"

"Not to me," Dylan said.

"Nor to me," Asher added. "When I called him after we learned about Pete Brandt dying in prison, the bar was full and there was so much laughing and shouting going on, he had to walk into the hallway to talk to me. I asked him if he'd been hassled by reporters, and kind of reminded him that might start happening. He just blew it off and said he had to get back to the bar. Half the clientele was watching a football game, and there was an ongoing snooker tournament as well. He was in great spirits, and then this happened."

Gunner sighed. "That's a whole lot of nothing to go on," he said. "Maybe he'll have something to point us in the right direction when he wakes up." He glanced at the clock on the wall. "I assume it's the usual rules about visiting hours in ICU?"

Dylan nodded. "We go in on the hour, ten-minute time limit, and only two family members at a time."

"It's almost time. Asher, you and Dylan got here first. I'll catch the next visit. Are we staying here through the night, or do you want me to organize a motel room somewhere close?" he asked.

"We don't have a car to drive back and forth. We'd be wasting a lot of time calling cabs and waiting on cabs," Dylan said.

Gunner arched an eyebrow. "You two take the first

visitation. I already rented an SUV. It's here at the hospital. I'll find the nearest hotel. We may be here for days."

Asher glanced at Dylan, then they both gave Gunner the nod. "Good idea. You do your thing. We'll settle with you later on the costs. We can get in several visits before midnight, and if all is well and he's stable, we'll call it a night and be here early in the morning. Maybe catch the doctor making rounds again and get an update on his status."

Dylan tapped Asher on the shoulder and pointed at the exodus of people leaving the waiting area. "It must be time," he said.

"Tell Dad I'm here," Gunner said, and went to get his bag as they walked away, pulled out his laptop, and then over to the little canteen in the corner and got a can of Dr. Pepper and a couple of snacks. Moments later, he was logging in on his laptop and pulling up hotel websites while he ate.

It didn't take long to settle on a hotel called Studio 6 Suites. The rooms looked good on the website, and it was less than a mile from the hospital. He rented three connecting suites with king-size beds. Each suite contained a bath, and a small living and kitchen area. Satisfactory for what they needed. Then he finished off his snacks and went to get a cup of coffee. He'd already been up for almost twenty hours, and it was going to be even longer before they got any rest.

Asher dreaded this first confrontation. Jacob was their anchor. The steadfast man who'd stepped up for them in every way that mattered. Even though they were all as big and tall as him now, they still viewed him as the trustworthy voice in their ear when they needed it most, and knowing he'd been struck down in such a vicious assault was shocking.

When they entered the actual ICU area, the energy shift was palpable, and the silence frightening. All those cubicles. All those desperately ill patients in the beds. And all they heard were beeps from the equipment registering the fluctuation life levels.

And then they saw their dad and moved toward him.

"Jesus," Dylan whispered.

Asher put a hand on Dylan's shoulder. "Dad's as tough as they come and he's still alive. Don't count him out."

They moved to his bedside—Asher on one side, Dylan on the other, and both reached for him at the same time, feeling the warmth of his skin, and eyeing the steady rise and fall of his chest.

"Hey, Dad... It's me, Ash."

"I'm here, too, Dad. It's me, Dylan. Gunner is in the waiting room, but they only let us in two at a time. He'll see you soon."

"I don't know why this happened to you, but we will find out who did this, and we will not leave Crossroads until we put their asses in prison," Asher said.

"You aren't alone in this fight. You saved us when the world blew up in our faces. We've got your back, Dad."

Then they looked at each other across the bed, then down at their dad.

Dylan's voice was shaking. "I have this overwhelming urge to call him daddy."

For a moment, Asher went straight to the past, remembering how many times he'd pulled back the covers so nine-year-old Dylan or seven-year-old Gunner could sleep with him. Sometimes they were all piled into the same bed, crying for what they'd lost.

"I refuse to accept anything but his full recovery. We're not going to lose him this way," Asher muttered, then caught motion from the corner of his eye and realized

visiting time was nearly over. Ten minutes had flown. "Dad, we have to leave now. Visiting time is over, but we'll be back. Rest and heal. You are loved."

Dylan leaned over and gently kissed Jacob's forehead. "Love you, Dad. We'll be back."

They were walking out when Ash suddenly stopped and looked back. The steady beeps throughout the room were no longer eerie. They were signs of life, and in this place, that was enough.

When they re-entered the waiting room, Gunner looked up, gauged the look on their faces, and waited for the verdict.

They sat on either side of him and lowered their voices as they spoke.

"He's pale and motionless, but everything that's supposed to be ticking and beeping is happening, and his breathing is steady," Asher said.

"He's really pale," Dylan added.

"Blood loss," Gunner said. "Seen it dozens of times when questioning hospitalized witnesses and perps. That whole blood transfusion should help."

"Truth," Asher said, and leaned forward. "I want to talk to some of Dad's regular customers. Find out if he'd had trouble with anyone recently. But I don't know who to call."

Dylan stood up. "Is anybody else hungry besides me?"

"There's a cafeteria. I know where it is," Gunner said.

Asher frowned. "Have you been here before?"

"Naw... I asked an orderly who was out in the hall. Wherever I am, I like to know my options," Gunner said.

"Then lead the way," Dylan said.

They stood in unison and headed for the elevator.

Chapter 5

EVERETT AND FREDDIE BRANDT WERE BACK IN AMARILLO, hiding in their rooms with the shades down and the curtains pulled, and their car only yards away from the exit door.

They couldn't look at themselves in the mirror, and wouldn't look at each other. Freddie was afraid to open his mouth and make Everett mad. He would never have guessed that his brother had the balls to kill someone, and now he felt afraid for himself. He was always doing something wrong. What if Everett got fed up and just shot him, too?

Everett was bothered that he'd had to do it, but after Freddie popped off about selling the bar, it became an act of self-preservation. He had no idea that he'd put the fear of God in Freddie, and would have been horrified to know that Freddie was now afraid of him. It had yet to occur to Everett that Freddie had left his DNA all over Jacob Kingston when he tackled him. All he knew was that they bungled what they'd set out to do, and killed a man.

They were sitting in the darkened rooms with the TV on low, waiting for the local news to air. They needed to know if they'd been made, and how far and how fast they should run.

Freddie was hunkered down on one end of the sofa and Everett on the other.

"I wish we'd never gone to see Pop," Freddie muttered.

Everett frowned. "What do you mean?"

"If we hadn't gone, then he would have died without telling us what he did, right? And if we didn't know it, then we wouldn't be in this trouble," Freddie said.

"Just because Pop told us what he did, didn't mean we had to act on it," Everett said.

Freddie's eyes widened. "Then if we didn't have to, why did we do it?"

"It was our inheritance," Everett muttered.

Freddie frowned. "I don't know what that means. Pop stole money and gave it to Brenda. So that makes it hers, right?"

Everett's chin jutted stubbornly. "But she's dead, Freddie. So, by rights, now it's ours."

Freddie sighed. "I don't want it. I just want all this to go away. Can't we just forget about it?"

"Well, we can't just forget about it, can we, Freddie? Because a man is dead, and the cops won't quit looking for us. We're either going to jail, or we're going to die. Depends on who shoots first."

Freddie dropped his head and started bawling. "I don't wanna die."

"I don't suppose Jacob Kingston was planning on dying, either, but he did, didn't he? We don't always get what we want. If we can find that money, we'll have all we need to get out of the country. Live in style in Mexico," Everett said, and upped the volume. It was almost time for the evening news.

When it began airing, as always, it led with a teaser about their biggest story, and to their horror, it was about the break-in and shooting at the Tumbleweed Bar, then went to a commercial.

"Well, we made the news," Everett muttered.

"What do we do?" Freddie asked.

"Nothing yet. They don't know our names. They don't

have any witnesses, beyond whoever was driving that black truck, and I think it was just making a U-turn. Our car wasn't parked out front. We parked on the side, remember? I bet they didn't even know anything was going on."

And so, they sat waiting for the full report.

But they didn't get the full report, because Sheriff Reddick kept key details out of the press, and when the journalist reported that Jacob Kingston was still alive, and in a hospital in Amarillo, they both jumped to their feet.

"He didn't die! He didn't die!" Freddie kept shouting.

"Right, but that means, eventually he'll go home. We'll give it a few days, let everything cool down, and when the time is right, we'll go back to that bar and search for that money without interference," Everett said.

"Right!" Freddie said, and hugged Everett before he remembered he was supposed to be afraid of him. But when Everett didn't shove him away, he took it to mean they were good again.

The Kingston brothers were back from the cafeteria, waiting to be allowed back in ICU, and when the time arrived, there were only a couple of other people in the waiting area besides the brothers.

"I'm sitting this one out," Dylan said.

Gunner stood, then looked at Asher. "You're going in with me, right?"

"Right beside you," he said.

They filed into the unit in silence. Ash led the way, with Gunner matching him step for step, but the moment they got to Jacob's bedside, Gunner paused, taking in all the medical equipment before he let himself look, really look, at his dad.

"This can't be happening. I want this to be a bad dream," he muttered, then leaned over and softly spoke. "Dad, it's me, Gunner. Ash and I are right here with you. We're both damn good at our jobs, and we're going to find the people responsible for this. That's our job. Your job is to rest and heal and get well."

Then he straightened up, took a deep breath, and for the first time, touched his father's face.

"It's tough seeing him like this, but we know what he's made of. I have to believe he's going to pull through," Ash said.

Gunner nodded. "God, I wish he would just open his eyes and tell us everything that happened. Give us a starting point, you know?"

"We'll find something. You know we will. But it's not going to happen overnight," Ash said.

They stood with him for the allotted amount of time, bringing up stories from their youth, and reminding Jacob how much he meant to them in the hopes that, wherever he was, he could hear them.

When time was up, they walked out. As they entered the waiting room again, Ash glanced toward the window, then across the street at a sign flashing the temperature.

"It's getting colder," he said.

Dylan turned around. "How do you know that?"

He pointed. "From the temperature reading on that digital sign across the street."

Dylan grinned. "Oh. For a second there I thought you'd grown psychic in your old age."

"Shut it," Asher said, and grinned.

Gunner was quiet, still riding out the shock of seeing his dad like that.

"Will we get to talk to his doctor?"

"I'll check," Asher said, and went back to the nurse's

desk. "Excuse me, but will Dr. Reading be making evening rounds, or does he only do it in the mornings?"

"He'll make rounds some time, but it's hard to say when. Likely between five and seven," she said.

"Would you mind letting him know that all of Jacob's family has arrived and we would greatly appreciate an update on his status?"

"Of course, I'll do that."

"We'll be in the waiting room," Asher said. When he went back to the waiting room, Gunner was sitting at a table in the canteen area with his laptop open, and Dylan was sitting beneath the window, talking on the phone.

Gunner looked up as Asher approached. "Well?"

"They'll tell him we're here for an update."

Gunner nodded and went back to scrolling.

Asher sat down at the table with him. "What are you doing?"

"Finding out everything I can about Pete Brandt. He's dead, but the dead always leave secrets behind."

"True that," Asher said, then found a chair in a corner, pulled out his phone, and googled the number for the Yellow Rose Café. If there was one person in Crossroads who was up on all the gossip, it was Pearl Fallon, and he wanted to thank her for saving their dad's life.

It was another cold day in Crossroads, but the dining room in the Yellow Rose was as cozy as being rocked in your grandma's lap.

It was warm and bright, belying the gray skies and the bite from air so cold it made your face burn. The aromas coming out of the kitchen were a mixture of sweet and savory, and the coffee was abundant.

Normally, Pearl was in her element there, but the events of last night were still with her. The horror of what had happened to Jacob Kingston had rocked their world. It was the topic of conversation at every table, and while they all knew Pearl's part in the drama, no one questioned her about it. They didn't have to. They could see she was still wrapped in the shock of it.

When the phone rang at the Rose, one of the waitresses answered.

"Yellow Rose Café. This is Cheryl."

"Cheryl, I'm Asher Kingston, Jacob's oldest son. Will you give Pearl a message for me?"

She inhaled softly, then reached for a pen. "Yes, of course."

"Ask her to call me when she has time. We're trying to find a reason for what happened to Dad, and thought she might know something we don't. This is my number," he said, and repeated it for her as she wrote it down.

"Got it," Cheryl said. "Jacob is well-loved and respected here. We're all in shock. Do you have an update we could share?"

"Well, he came through surgery. He's still in critical condition. They are keeping him sedated for healing purposes, and he's in ICU. No visitors at this point except family."

"Got it," she said. "I'll tell her to call you first chance she gets."

"Yes, please do, and thank you," Asher said, and disconnected.

Cheryl tore the note from the pad and raced into the kitchen.

"Pearl, Asher Kingston just called. When you get a chance, you need to call him. Jacob's sons are at the hospital and know little to nothing about what happened other than he'd been shot."

"Well, bless their hearts," Pearl said. "Did you get his number?"

"Yes, ma'am. Right here," Cheryl said, and held it up.

"My hands are a mess. Put it in the pocket of my apron," Pearl said.

Cheryl nodded, folded the paper, and slipped it into the bib pocket of Pearl's apron.

"Did he say anything about Jacob?" Pearl asked.

"Yes, ma'am. I asked. He's out of surgery. Listed in critical condition in ICU, and sedated to aid in healing. No visitors except family allowed."

Pearl absorbed the news as Cheryl went back to the dining room.

At the same time Pearl was getting Asher's message, he was headed for the table where Dylan and Gunner were now sitting.

"I just called the Yellow Rose. I wanted to talk to Pearl because she knows a little bit about everything going on in Crossroads. One of the waitresses answered. I gave her my number, asking Pearl to call me when she could, so we wait for the call."

Gunner leaned forward and lowered his voice. "It makes almost no sense to assume that this was a revenge shooting. To our knowledge, Dad has no enemies. While I was in the airport waiting to board, I decided to check the robbery angle. All of Pete Brandt's known associates are either still in prison, or deceased, like him. I also called the prison warden where Brandt was being held and asked about visitors he might have had. Turns out, he's had no visitors for over five years, until just before he died. It was after the warden notified his next of kin that Brandt was

dying, and gave them permission for an end-of-life visit, so to speak."

"Did anyone show?" Asher asked.

"Yes, his two sons, Everett and Freddie Brandt. The warden gave them thirty minutes. They were at his bedside the entire time until Brandt ended it on his own and sent them away. But that doesn't have to mean anything. Family is always called when a prisoner is dying like that," Gunner said.

Dylan was already lost. "I build houses. My puzzles involve plumbing and electrical issues, and supply issues, so you're going to have to spell all this out for me, because I don't think or speak cop like you two."

"Sorry, brother," Asher said. "It's basically laying out all of the what-ifs, and then eliminating what doesn't fit, or finding the connections. Right now, everything is a theory. We don't have one solid piece of evidence. Maybe after we talk to Pearl, we'll have a starting point."

Gunner nodded. "Everything is a process of elimination, and being able to see through the bullshit in the statements we take."

"Got it. I won't be much help when it comes to all that, but I've got your backs, whatever is going down," Dylan said.

Asher grinned. "We know that. Remember the positions we played in high school football?"

Gunner looked up and almost smiled. "Ash was the quarterback. Dylan was the center, always blocking the opponent, and me...a running back on offense, and the safety on defense."

Dylan laughed. "Fastest little shit on the field I ever saw. Ran forty yards in under five seconds. They were scouting you for college football when you broke a bunch of hearts and went into law enforcement instead."

Gunner shrugged. He had his reasons, most of which pointed to Brenda Kingston's double life. He glanced up at the clock. "Visiting time again."

"I'll sit this out," Dylan said. "You and Asher go in," then went to a vending machine to get a can of pop as they left, and began going through email and took a phone call from Angie about work. A tile order for six houses got back-ordered, so he cancelled the order and told Angie to pick out something comparable and see if the company could put a rush on delivery. Then the brothers returned.

"Any change?" Dylan asked.

"No, and the doctor isn't likely to make rounds before late. Some kind of surgical emergency. I told the nurse we were leaving for the evening but staying nearby. They'll call if there's a need," Asher said.

Dylan repacked his laptop as they retrieved their luggage, then they all headed for the elevator.

Gunner led them to where he'd parked. They loaded their luggage and got into the SUV. Moments later, he drove out of the parking lot and headed down the street to the hotel.

Nora Borden was knee-deep in memories as she continued sorting through what was left of her parents' belongings, and she wasn't making much headway. The figurines that had meant so much to her mother were still in the etagere in the living room. Her dad's pipe and a nearly empty tin of pipe tobacco were lying in an ornate ashtray, on a table next to the sofa. Every time she looked at it, it made her feel like he'd walk in at any moment, ready to shake in a little tobacco, tamp it down with his thumb, then add enough more to fill the bowl before lighting it up.

The "good dishes" were still in the china cabinet in the

dining room, and the kitchen was full of everyday dishes, and all the pots and pans. The curtains were clean, but faded, and hung limply from the rods. She was torn between guilt and necessity, and knew she was going to grieve it, regardless of her final decision.

And now, after what had happened to Jacob, and guessing what Asher and his brothers were going through, she had this overwhelming need to reach out, but at the same time, didn't want to intrude.

Finally, she gave it up for the day and made a quick trip to the Yellow Rose to pick up her to-go order. They'd be closing soon, and she didn't want to cook. Cars in the parking lot were thinning out fast when she got out and ran inside and up to the register.

Darla was already there checking out a customer, so Nora got in line. About that time, Pearl came out of the kitchen carrying two bagged up to-go orders. When she saw Nora, she smiled.

"Good timing, sugar! This one is yours," Pearl said, and set them down on the counter as Darla went to tend to her tables. "How's it going at home?"

Nora shrugged. "Slow. Depressing."

"I can only imagine," Pearl said as Nora paid for her order.

Pearl went back to the kitchen, while Nora got in the car and drove home.

She transferred her food to a plate, made herself a drink, and carried it to the living room to eat, and as soon as she sat down, turned on the TV for the sound of voices.

She hated to eat alone.

By the time the brothers checked into the hotel and got to their rooms, they were ready to unwind. They unlocked the

connecting doors between their rooms, giving each other free rein, and began to unpack.

Eventually, they gathered in the living area of the middle room, which was Asher's. He was sitting on the side of his bed. Dylan was on the other side, and Gunner had pulled the chair away from the desk and was straddling it backward, using the chair back for an arm rest.

"Did either of you get any grief for taking a leave of absence from work?" Dylan asked.

"I didn't," Ash said. "I'd just finished up on a case when I got the call from Reddick. It was just a matter of letting them know what happened, and then I was off."

"I was en route to a murder scene when I got Ash's call. I called into the precinct, told them I needed to take a leave of absence, and why, and they sent another detective to the scene and told me to take all the time I needed to sort it out," Gunner said.

"Is Angie coping okay with you gone?" Asher asked.

Dylan rolled his eyes. "She knows as much about the business as I do, and the men on my crews respect her. Besides, before they're hired, I put the fear of God in them about messing with her. They know she's to be viewed as the manager when I'm gone, and they damn well better respect her."

"In other words, they're scared of you," Gunner said.

Dylan shrugged. "Six crews of twelve men each, besides all the subcontractors we work with… They need to be just scared enough not to lie to me, not to steal from me, and not to piss me off. I'm a fair boss, and they get paid well."

Gunner threw a wad of paper at him. "I'm not scared of you," he said.

Dylan laughed. "That's fine, baby brother, because we're not scared of you, either. So, stop ruffling your tail feathers at us and help us decide what we're going to do for dinner.

We could order from any restaurant via DoorDash, or go out to eat somewhere."

They all started talking at once when Asher's phone rang. He glanced at it and then held up his hand.

"Hush it! It's Pearl. I'm going to put her on Speaker."

They silenced immediately. Gunner turned around to get a pen and paper from the desk behind him, as Asher answered.

"Hello. Pearl?"

"Yes, it's me, honey. Sorry it took so long to get back to you. It's been a hectic day, and I had to wait until we'd closed."

"That's okay. I appreciate you returning my call. My brothers are right here with me, and I have you on Speaker. We were told you're the one who saved Dad's life, and the only witness."

"Well, I kept him from bleeding out, but I'd reckon that doctor who patched him up is the one who saved his life," Pearl said.

"We beg to differ, but we have so many questions and know very little about what happened," Asher said. "Sheriff Reddick only told me Dad had been shot and was airlifted to Amarillo. We don't know anything about the incident, and didn't know anything about your part in it until Nora told us. Would you walk us through it? How did you even know what happened?"

"Sure," Pearl said, and began with the mention of her open window and hearing the shot. Then seeing a black truck make a U-turn in the empty parking lot like the locals do, and her calling Jacob and getting no answer.

"It was only after that white sports car shot out of the parking lot and took off west slinging gravel and burning rubber, that I feared he'd been robbed. I tried calling him again, and when I didn't get an answer, I got dressed, took

my shotgun, and ran down the highway to the bar. The door was open. There was broken glass on the floor as I walked in. I began turning on lights as I went, thinking he might be in the living quarters, because I could see the door open into the house. But as I was running that way calling his name, I saw his body behind the bar. I called 911, and then put pressure pads on the entrance and exit wound to slow down the flow of blood and told him not to die."

"Damn," Asher muttered. "We will never be able to thank you enough. You put your own life at risk for him and we know it."

Pearl was teary all over again. "He's been my friend for a very long time. He would have done the same for me."

"Pearl, this is Gunner. I have a question about the white sports car. Can you describe it for me?"

"I'm not good with makes and models of cars. I'm way better with pickup trucks, but if I had to guess, I might say an older Mustang."

"Got it," Gunner said. "Can you remember if it was just a two-seat style, or if there would have been room for a back seat?"

"Not sure, but it was definitely a two-door, not a four-door," she said.

"That's great, honey. Thank you. I made note of all that. You're way better than most of the witnesses I deal with," Gunner said.

"How is Jacob doing?" Pearl asked.

"He's holding his own," Ash said. "Thank you for calling me back."

"You're going after them, aren't you? Whoever shot your dad. You're going after them," Pearl said.

"Let's just say, we're not leaving Crossroads until who-ever did this is behind bars," he said. "We'll see you soon."

The call ended.

Gunner looked up. "First lead. We just need a name to link it to."

"God knows how we'll find that out," Dylan muttered.

"Oh, we'll find them," Asher said.

"Where do you even start?" Dylan asked.

Asher frowned. "I can't stop thinking that it's somehow linked to the robbery. And since we were kids when all that happened, I think we start at the beginning. We'll get background on all of the conspirators and go from there," Asher said.

"So, do we go out, or do we order in?" Dylan asked.

"Tonight, I vote for DoorDash," Ash said. "We all need sleep, and I'm not in the mood to get back out in the cold tonight."

"I second that," Gunner said.

Ash opened his laptop, pulled up his app, and began scanning restaurants. In the end, they went with Chinese, and ordered a varied assortment of dishes to cover all the bases. After they finished, they turned on the TV in Ash's room and settled down to wait.

Dylan and Ash were sprawled out on the bed, and Gunner was on the love seat beneath the window.

While they were waiting, Ash's phone rang again. It was Nora.

"I'm going to take this in the other room," he said.

"Tell Nora we said hello," Dylan said, and threw a wad of paper at him.

Ash ignored the teasing as he sat down on Gunner's bed to answer.

"Hey, darlin'. Good to hear your voice."

"I hope I'm not intruding, but I wanted you guys to know how much you all mean to me, Jacob included."

He closed his eyes and swallowed past a lump in his throat. "No, you are not intruding or bothering. I haven't been mad at you even once since I first set eyes on you."

"I wondered if it would be okay to come see all of you, and let you know you're not in this alone. The whole town of Crossroads is rooting for Jacob and his boys," she said.

"Then come see us. We're staying at the Studio 6 Suites near the hospital, but we're only here at night. Right now, we're spending most of the day in the ICU waiting room, waiting on the ten minutes per hour that we can see him."

"So, it would be okay if I came to the hospital some time tomorrow morning?" she asked.

"It would be very okay. And Nora…"

"Yes?"

"Love you, baby."

"Love you, too," she said.

He went back to join the others just as someone knocked on the door.

"That'll be DoorDash," Asher said and reached for his wallet as he went to the door. The delivery guy had a big bag at his feet and was holding another one in his hand.

"Order for Kingston?" he said.

"Yes," Ash said, and handed him an extra tip, picked up the bags, and closed the door. "Buffet on the counter?"

"Works for me," Dylan said, then got up and began helping Asher set out the containers.

"Are there plates and flatware in that cabinet?" Gunner asked.

Asher looked. "Only two."

"I'll bring some from my room," he said, and went into his suite to get another plate and a chair.

Within a few minutes they had food on their plates and were eating in comfortable silence, commenting mostly on the food they were eating.

"Either of you like sushi?" Dylan asked.

Asher shrugged. "I can take it or leave it, but it wouldn't be my first food choice."

Gunner shook his head. "Don't eat raw meat. Don't even want it rare, and there's not enough hot sauce in Texas to make raw fish rolled up in rice and seaweed edible."

They both burst out laughing. "Hey, Dylan, I don't think Gunner likes sushi," Asher said.

Dylan was still chuckling. "Heard that loud and clear."

Gunner grinned. "Never ask a question if you don't want an answer."

Nora was asleep when the clock in the hall began to strike. She pulled the covers up a little closer and listened, counting the gongs until it stopped.

Midnight.

She sighed and rolled over, nestling back beneath the covers. There used to be a time when that clock struck all hours of the day and night, and it was background noise that never registered. Now it was startling.

She'd been gone too long.

When she woke again, it was morning. She got out of bed to turn up the thermostat, ran to the kitchen to start coffee, then peeked through the curtains to check the weather. Cold but clear skies. She could work with that, but not just yet. Still shivering, she ran back to bed until the house warmed up, and the scent of coffee was a big enough draw to get up again, get dressed, and head for the kitchen.

A bowl of cold cereal and a cup of coffee later, all she could think about was Ash. The fact that he was within a thirty-minute drive made her feel like a little girl again. Like she was about to make a wish and then blow out birthday candles, and get him for her wish.

She got up from the table, rinsed her bowl and cup and put them in the sink, then made a call to the Rose to order

three pieces of cherry pie to go. She wasn't going into that waiting room empty-handed, and face three Kingston men all giving her the once-over. Pie was always a good diversion.

A few minutes later, she was in her car and on the way to the café.

The parking lot was full of breakfast customers when she pulled in, and the wind was cold enough to make her eyes water. She got out on the run. By now, she knew the waitresses by name, and when they saw her walking up to the register, Cheryl headed that way.

"Morning, Nora. Your to-go order is right here, with forks and napkins included. That will be $12.95."

Nora swiped her card through the machine, signed the printout, and picked up the sack. "Thanks a bunch," she said, and went back to the car.

It was twenty minutes after ten. Barring any traffic delays, she would be there before eleven.

Chapter 6

DOCTOR HOYT, WHO HAD TAKEN OVER JACOB'S CARE, was making rounds when the Kingston brothers arrived. Hoyt saw them walking into the waiting room and stopped to give them an update.

"Good morning," he said. "I'm Doctor Hoyt. I'll be taking care of your father from now on. Jacob's vitals are good. His numbers are up, and they've had no issues out of the norm," he said.

"Is it the sedation that's keeping him from waking up?" Asher asked.

Hoyt nodded. "It has been, but I ordered a reduction in the dosage last night. It could take as much as another day or so before we see a change in his awareness. Again, don't worry. Just talk softly to him when you visit. Familiar voices are good. We always find out after patients wake up, that they were more aware of what was going on around them than we knew."

"Thanks. We're just anxious to hear what he saw, and what he remembers, because until he wakes up, we have no idea why any of this happened," Ash said.

Hoyt frowned. "I thought it was a robbery."

"Nothing was taken. Not even the money from his wallet," Gunner said. "He was just shot and left for dead."

"Oh… I see," Hoyt said. "Then I understand the urgency."

It was frustrating that their dad's condition hadn't

changed, but they had to be satisfied with the fact that it hadn't worsened. And today, they'd brought work with them to pass the time.

All three found a spot out of the way and opened their laptops.

Dylan immediately logged in and began checking messages, and sending answers to the questions Angie had sent.

Asher was on the phone, checking in with Sheriff Reddick.

"How's Jacob? Has he regained consciousness yet?" Reddick asked.

"No, but his condition is holding, and his vitals are steady. I was wondering if the crime scene crew is finished at the bar?" Asher asked.

"They will be sometime today," Reddick said. "A local tacked some plywood over the broken window on the door. They've been told to leave the keys with Pearl after they've locked up and left."

"Do you have any inkling of who might have done this?" Asher asked.

"Not yet. We're still running a search on how many white mustangs there are in Texas. We're up into the thousands and the search is still running, and a large portion of them are listed as having been stolen, so I don't think this is going to help until we get more information."

"Damn it," Asher muttered. "Look, I'm going to be honest with you. Gunner and I have taken a leave of absence from our jobs, and we're going to be investigating from our end, too. We will gladly share info with you as we go along, because ultimately this is your case. But he's our dad, and we are both cops. We can't let this slide into someone else's lap."

"I don't have a problem with any of that, and completely understand," Reddick said. "And by the same

token, if there's anything we can help you with, just ask. Jacob is a friend. An old friend. And this pisses me off big-time."

"Crossroads is a sitting duck for crime. It's a wonder stuff like this doesn't happen more often, since everybody knows there's no local law enforcement in the town."

"I completely agree, but Crossroads doesn't have the finances to support that," Reddick said.

"Yes, I know how it works," Asher said. "So, to verify... We'll be free to come and go from our home after today?"

"Yes. And I assume the bar will stay closed?" Reddick asked.

"For the time being, yes. That's Dad's baby. And when he's better, he'll make those decisions. Thanks again," Asher said, then hung up and headed for the vending machine to get coffee.

Gunner had just sent a request to the FBI for access to the files from the armored car robbery. Of all the brothers, he'd known the least about what happened, and had the least interest in finding out how deeply involved their mother had been. He just didn't want to know. But the shooting changed everything.

Having this happen on the heels of Pete Brandt's death was more than coincidence, and even though it was now a cold case, they needed to know what info the Feds had accumulated.

Asher and Gunner had been the first to go into ICU together, and now this visit, Ash stayed behind while the other two went in. He was sitting at the far end of the waiting room, trying not to dwell on how pale and small his dad looked in that hospital bed, when he heard footsteps and looked up and saw Nora walking in, wearing jeans and boots, and a gray coat with a fur-lined hood. Her hair was wind-tossed and wild around her face. Her eyes still had

shadows under them, and he could see she'd already chewed off her lipstick. Something she'd always done when she was bothered.

He went to meet her, and got a kiss and a hug for the trip before he led her back to where they were sitting and helped her off with her coat. Ignoring the curious eyes of the other people in the room, he took her hands in his and rubbed them until they were warm.

"How's Jacob? Any change?" she asked.

"Not yet, but he's not any worse."

She saw the fear in his eyes and knew how scared they must be. And then to her horror, tears welled.

Asher's heart sank. "Nora... Sweetheart... Don't cry."

"Sorry. So sorry. My emotions are all over the place anyway. I've been crying my way through sorting stuff at Mom and Dad's house, and then this happening to Jacob, and seeing you again and... It all feels surreal," she said, and started digging in her purse for a tissue.

He reached for her hand. "No apologizing. You've had the weight of the world on your shoulders for years, and I didn't even know it. It breaks my heart for you."

"I'm just an emotional wreck. I'll be fine."

Moments later, they heard footsteps in the hall, and then people were walking past the waiting room.

"Visiting time is over," Asher said, and kissed her hands before letting her go. "Hold that thought. Brothers approaching. I can hear them arguing from here."

———

Dylan was standing on one side of their dad's bed, holding his hand and talking to him about Angie, and when they were planning on getting married, and Gunner was speaking quietly to a nurse when Dylan felt movement in Jacob's

fingers. At first, he thought it was just a muscle twitch, but then he leaned down and whispered in Jacob's ear.

"Dad… Daddy… It's Dylan. Can you hear me?"

Seconds later, Jacob's fingers tightened just enough that Dylan felt the grip. He gasped, then called out to the nurse, who hurried over with Gunner beside her.

"I think he's trying to wake up. I was talking to him and holding his hand and felt his fingers twitch. Then I leaned down and asked him if he could hear me, and he actually gripped my hand."

The nurse began checking the blood pressure readings and the heart monitor, and then quickly took his pulse and checked the pupils in his eyes. "I'm going to contact Dr. Reading," she said, and headed for the nurses' station to deliver the message as Gunner moved closer.

"Dad, it's me, Gunner. Asher is here, too. Keep fighting. We love you."

"He squeezed my hand again," Dylan said.

Gunner looked up at his brother with tears in his eyes. "Thank the Lord."

On the heels of their revelation, visiting hours ended.

"Dad, we have to leave now. Visiting hours are over. But we'll be back. Just keep getting better," Dylan said.

They walked away, eager to tell Asher the news, and then walked into the waiting room and saw their visitor. They paused, then started grinning and headed toward her with a single intent.

"Brace yourself," Ash said as she stood to greet them, and then once again, she was engulfed in a group hug.

"How wonderful to see you," Dylan said. "Thanks for coming. It means a lot to all of us."

"Really great to see you," Gunner said. "And very sorry to hear about your parents. Life has dealt you quite a hand."

She forced a smile as she was blinking back tears.

"Adulting is not as much fun as we thought it would be, is it?" she said, and then changed the subject by opening the bag she'd brought with her. "Three giant pieces of Pearl's cherry pie. Forks included," she said.

"Oh man, thank you!" Dylan said, and began doling out the containers. "Wait. You didn't bring one for yourself. Now how do we eat this in front of you without feeling like pigs?"

"I'll share my piece with her," Ash said. "She ate off my plate for years."

"Oh, look, there are four forks in the sack," Gunner said, and handed one to her, as they all moved to one of the tables in the canteen to eat.

A man entered the waiting room, and a few moments later, other visitors began trickling in.

Nora was eyeing the people's faces, empathizing with their worry and sorrow, understanding that tragedy had brought them here.

"It's like this all day long," Ash said as he opened the box holding his piece of pie. "You get first bite for bringing the treat."

"Nora, honey, do you want coffee or a soft drink?" Dylan asked.

"Coffee, please. I can't seem to stay warm," she said.

He got up to get the drinks as they began to eat. Nora didn't take more than a couple of bites before she put her fork down.

"You can't quit this soon," Asher said.

She shrugged. "I don't have much of an appetite these days."

"Well, we have news," Dylan said. "Seeing you distracted us a bit, but while we were in visiting Dad just now, he responded." And then he related the events.

"This is the best news," Ash said. "He's going to keep getting better, and when he wakes up, maybe we'll finally find

out what happened. Hopefully, he'll know who did it. Or at least give us a starting point."

Gunner glanced at Nora. "You're our good luck charm. You brought good juju with this pie."

"I sincerely doubt the veracity of that would ever stand up in court," she said, and poked his shoulder.

He laughed, and both brothers stared at Gunner in disbelief. Laughter like that from him was rare.

Asher kept watching her changing expressions, and the light in her eyes, and thought maybe being with him and his brothers was good for her, too. She'd been the only guard at the family gate for too long.

The camaraderie of their conversation became easier as the time kept passing, and the stories of "remember when" were all after they were on their own with their dad. But it was an eye-opener for Asher. He had memories of his mother that were good, until they weren't, but his two younger brothers had either blocked them, or forgotten them. Either they had not had her in their lives long enough, or the brutal betrayal of what Brenda Kingston did had destroyed any memories of the family they thought they were.

Nora loved listening to them bickering and teasing, and it even reminded her of times when she'd been with them, and the joy and innocence of those years, but she was conscious of not wanting to overstay her welcome.

She was still there when visitation time came again, and she was about to gather up her things and leave when Ash glanced up at the clock and saw the time.

"Nora, if you want to go see Dad with me, you can. He doesn't look terrible, or anything like that, but if it's too soon after spending so much time with your own father, then I understand."

To his surprise, she didn't hesitate. "Yes, I would like to

see him. The last time I saw him was when I dropped off his to-go order from the Rose. I sat with him while he ate. We had such a good visit. I would like to think he might hear my voice and know I came."

"Yes, you go, Nora. We've both been in and out countless times," Dylan said.

"Is it time now?" she asked.

Asher stood and held out his hand.

"Is it okay if I leave my coat here?" she asked.

"You can even leave your purse if you want," Gunner said. "I'm good at surveillance. I'll watch them for you."

She grinned. "Then, I will and thank you," she said, slipped her purse beneath her coat, and took Asher's hand as they left the room.

The brothers looked at each other and grinned. "He's still got it bad," Dylan said.

"She isn't fighting him off, either," Gunner said, then as promised, went over to where Nora left her things, and sat down in the chair beside them.

Despite Nora's claim that this visit wouldn't be a trigger, when they first walked up to Jacob's bedside, the memory of sitting in a place not unlike this watching her father taking his last breath was all too real. And then Asher reached for his dad's hand.

"Hey, Dad, it's me, Asher. Nora is here with me."

"Jacob, it's me, Nora. Pearl is the one who found you and saved your life. She sends her love, as does everyone in Crossroads. We're all praying for you, honey. We miss you. Get well soon so you can come home."

Within seconds, Asher jumped. "He just squeezed my hand. He heard you. He knows we're here. Dad, you're doing great. Stay strong. We need you to wake up and tell us

what happened, and who did this. We'll find them, but we don't know where to start."

Jacob's eyelashes fluttered, and then he stilled.

"He'll wake up on his own time," Nora said, and then moved to the foot of the bed and slipped her hands beneath the covers. "His feet are cold. I'm going to ask a nurse for another blanket," she said, and walked away, leaving Asher speechless.

They'd never even thought to check for discomfort, but she had, because she'd just gone through several years of palliative care for her dad.

A few moments later, a nurse returned carrying a heated blanket, put it over Jacob's legs and feet, and then slipped her hand beneath the sheets and nodded.

"You were right," she said. "His feet are cold. We'll get some socks on his feet shortly, but this will help. I'll make a note of it on his chart for future reference," then walked away.

Ash kissed her on the cheek. "Thank you, darling. Thank you for thinking of his comfort in that way."

She shrugged. "It's weird what you take for granted, like getting more covers when you're cold. Or getting a drink when you want one. I used to do all that and more every day for my father, when he could no longer speak up for himself."

"You've just taught me to pay attention, and I thank you for that," he said, then put his arm around her shoulder. "Visiting time is over. After you, darlin.'"

"As soon as I make a quick pit stop, I'll be out of your hair," Nora said as they were walking back to the waiting room.

"When you're ready, I'm walking you to your car," Asher said.

She was reluctant to say goodbye, and as soon as they entered the waiting room, she headed for the restroom.

"How did it go?" Gunner asked.

"Good. He recognized her voice. He squeezed my hand," Asher said.

"Progress," Gunner said.

"One of the first things Nora did after talking to Dad, was move to the end of the bed and slip her hands under the covers. She said his feet were cold and went to get a nurse to bring another blanket. We never thought of any of that. And it was the first thing she did," Asher said, and then slipped his hands in his pockets. "I'm going to walk her down to her car."

The brothers were still absorbing the enormity of what she'd done for him, and they'd never thought. He would have had to wake up and ask for covers before they would have known he was cold, and she'd had the foresight to check it for him.

"It's what she did for her dad," Asher added as he put on his coat.

When she came back, Gunner hugged her.

She smiled and patted his cheek. "What's that for?"

"For cold feet," Gunner said. "We missed you. You're the best. Don't lose us again."

"That's not going to happen," Asher said, and helped her put on her coat.

When he held out his hand, she slung her purse over her shoulder and clasped it without thought. They rode the elevator down in silence, both of them struggling with what to say because Jacob's life still hung in the balance. But as they exited the lobby, they were hit with a blast of cold air.

"Good lord," Asher muttered, and used his body to block the wind from her as they crossed the parking lot to her car.

Nora unlocked it with the remote, then turned around to tell him goodbye. Instead, he cupped her face and leaned forward until their foreheads were touching.

Nora's heart was pounding, but before she could think, she was in his arms. His breath was warm on her face and then the chill of his lips melted into a kiss that took her breath, and the last ounce of her hesitation.

When he finally let her go, it was with a groan and a sigh. "When you get home, promise you'll text me to let me know you arrived safely."

Nora nodded. "I promise. And you will keep me updated on your dad's progress, okay?"

"Absolutely," Asher said, then opened the door. "You need to get in out of this cold. I'll call you tonight, okay?"

She nodded. "See you when I see you," she said, then got in and began to buckle up.

He leaned in for one last kiss, and then stepped back as she started the engine, then flashed him a smile before driving away.

He didn't move until she drove out of sight, then on his way in, he met his brothers coming out.

"What's going on?" he asked.

"We're not having canteen food all day. We're going somewhere to get a steak," Dylan said.

"Works for me," Asher said, then jammed his hands in his coat pockets as they headed for the SUV.

Nora was shivering as she drove, still reeling from that kiss as she drove away from Amarillo. She thought of her apartment in Fort Worth, and the work from her office that she had waiting for her on her laptop. Thankfully, she could catch up with what was left of this day and start anew on the house business tomorrow.

Elated over her and Asher's reconciliation, she was soon on Highway I-27 southbound, dodging the occasional

tumbleweed blowing across the highway, while keeping an eye on the weather. After she came to the Highway 86/I-27 junction and turned east on 86 toward Crossroads, she began to relax.

Less than fifteen minutes later, she was back in town. She drove straight to Belker's Grocery and parked, sent Asher a text, and then got out and hurried inside.

The Kingston brothers were just finishing up their meal when Asher's phone signaled a text. It was from Nora.

I'm in Crossroads. About to go into Belker's and then home.
First love. Only love. Forever love.
Nora

He swallowed past the lump in his throat and sent a message.

Thank you for not quitting on me.
Love you more.
Ash.

Then he dropped the phone back in his pocket.

"Everything okay?" Gunner asked.

"Yeah, just Nora letting me know she got home okay."

"What are you going to do about her?" Dylan asked.

"Live the rest of my life with her," he said.

Gunner frowned. "What does she say about that?"

Asher reached for the check, glanced at it, then laid down his credit card.

"She gave me a second chance to do it right, and the

steaks are on me. Let's get back to the hospital. I have a feeling Dad's going be waking up and talking within the next twenty-four hours, and I want to be there when it happens."

Nora spent the rest of the afternoon working through the backlog of her job, finishing up details, and one long-distance fix of a computer glitch at a high school in Peoria, Illinois. She was good at her job, and her tech skills made her indispensable to the company she worked for.

But working in her childhood home made her realize how isolated her life really was in Fort Worth.

It had happened because of a stalker, and now she lived and worked in her high-rise apartment, and referred to it the ivory tower. She rarely went out. Ordered food and groceries in. Her only times away for the last two years had been to spend time with her father at the nearby memory care facility. He had not known who she was, and wouldn't have missed her, but she knew, and she cared, and then he died.

Coming home to Crossroads felt like a pilgrimage. She had needed this. To remind herself that she would never be a stranger here. That she was safe here. And Asher was the promise of all things better.

By the time she finally put the fires out at work, and had answered all of the emails, she was mentally and physically exhausted and still needed to eat something. But it was late, and cooking after 10:00 p.m. wasn't happening. So, she fell back on a childhood favorite, heated a can of chicken noodle soup, and opened a sleeve of crackers and sat down at the table to eat.

The house was silent, but the ever-present west Texas

wind was not. It was whistling around the corners of the house like the big bad wolf from the childhood story, huffing and puffing, trying to blow it all down. She could have turned on the TV while she ate, but she didn't have the energy left to get up and do it.

When she finished, she took the dishes to the sink, rinsed them and put them in the dishwasher with the other dishes waiting to be washed, dropped a packet of soap into the dispenser, and started it up.

She was just about to turn around when she got a whiff of her mother's perfume. She stilled, took a deep breath and closed her eyes, accepting the visit as the gift that was being given.

"Oh, Mama... I want to open my eyes and turn around and see you, but I know that's not going to happen. I miss you and Daddy so much, but I'm okay. I promise. You know what's going on. If you have any sway with the angels, tell them that Jacob Kingston's sons need him to wake up." Moments later, the scent faded, and Nora knew she was gone.

With feet dragging, she left the kitchen, turning out lights as she went, finally headed to bed. The thought of a long soak in a hot bath was enticing, but then her phone rang. When she saw Asher's name pop up, she sat down on the side of her bed to answer.

"Hey, you."

Asher smiled. Nora had always answered his phone calls this way.

"Hey, sweet lady. We just got back to the hotel. Hope I didn't wake you."

"No, but you did interrupt a date I have with a long soak in a hot bath. I worked through a backlog of work after I got home. How's your dad?"

"Lord, thanks for planting that thought in my head. You in

a tub of bubbles is an image to sleep on. As for Dad, he's sort of conscious, and sort of not, and for brief periods of time. We're hoping to get some answers tomorrow. Once we do, we'll be headed to Crossroads. The forensics team is through at the crime scene, so we're free to resume residence."

"I know you and Gunner are going to begin investigating, but I'm hoping for a few fly bys while you're here. The grown-up version of you is still a little intimidating. I think I just need a little acclimatizing."

He laughed, and the sound filled every sad, empty place within her.

"I'm not a storm front, darlin'. Just a bigger, older version of me."

"I was just teasing a little. I always felt safe with you. I still do. But it's almost like starting over, isn't it?"

"Not starting over, honey. We just needed a jump start to get us back on track and we're already good to go. Now, you go run that bath and relax. We'll talk tomorrow, okay?"

"Okay. And Ash… I'm glad you called. I needed to hear your voice."

He heard the loneliness in her words, and it broke his heart.

"I love you, Nora. I promise. We're not lost anymore."

"Lost isn't always geographical, Ash. Sometimes people just lose themselves."

The call ended.

Nora held the phone against her ear for a few seconds more, reluctant to give up the connection, then laid it on the bed and began stripping off her clothes.

Asher sat with the phone in his hand, staring down at the floor and listening to the sounds of his brothers' voices, while knowing he was too many miles away to comfort her.

Everett and Freddie Brandt were still holed up in their Amarillo apartment, watching every newscast, praying there would be some mention of Kingston's death.

Everett was pissed. Kingston needed to be dead. He should have been dead. He still didn't understand how he'd survived. He would have bled out in minutes. How was he found that fast? What were they missing? There weren't any vehicles nearby. The residential part of Crossroads was well off the highway that fronted it, and the weather was damn cold. Windows would have been closed.

Freddie was asleep in the other room, and they were out of beer and nearly out of food. Everett's disability check was by direct deposit, and it was due to show up in his account by tomorrow. They had to get out and get groceries. Maybe show up at a pool hall and drink a beer. Maybe play some pool.

As soon as the late-night news was over without so much as a mention about the shooting in the Tumbleweed Bar, Everett turned off the TV and went to his room. Ignoring the ashtray full of cigarette butts and a trashcan full of empty beer cans, he shoved the dirty clothes off his bed and stretched out on his belly on top of the covers.

He heard what sounded like the lid of a trashcan hitting the pavement. Or maybe it was a hubcap. Damn wind. In this part of the state, if it wasn't tied down, then it was rolling, like the ever-present tumbleweeds.

He rolled over onto his side, grabbed what he thought were the covers, and pulled them up around his neck. The wind was just a lullaby he'd heard all his life. He fell asleep within minutes, covered with what was left of his SpongeBob sleeping bag from childhood.

Jacob Kingston had been hearing something beep for a while now. It sounded like the same beep the refrigerator made when someone left the door open too long. He kept trying to wake up enough to get out of bed and go shut it before everything spoiled. He tried to call out for his boys. It was probably one of them that had left the door ajar. He was saying their names in his head, but they didn't answer, and the door was still beeping as he slipped away into the shadows again.

It was just before sunrise. The nurses were changing shifts. The night nurses had checked out and were going home, and the day nurses were starting their day as always by checking the vitals on every patient.

The nurse at Jacob Kingston's bedside had just replaced a bag on his IV drip, and was checking the dosage when she heard him groan. It was the first audible sound he'd made since his arrival. And when she saw his pulse rate rising, and his eyelids fluttering, she quickly alerted the nurses' station.

Asher had just finished shaving and showering and was already half dressed when his cell phone rang. When he saw the name pop up on Caller ID, his heart skipped. And then he grabbed it.

"Hello, this is Asher."

"Mr. Kingston, your father is waking up. He keeps asking for his boys."

"Thank you! We'll be there soon," he said, and then glanced at the time as he headed for Dylan's room. It was

just after 6:00 a.m. when he knocked on Dylan's door, then walked inside. When he heard the shower running, he loped across the room and flung the bathroom door open.

"Dylan! Dad's awake and asking for us. Get dressed!" and then ran back through his room and knocked on Gunner's door, then walked in.

Gunner was already dressed and working at his laptop when Asher burst in.

"What?"

"Dad's awake and asking for us," Asher said.

"Hot damn," Gunner said, logged out of his laptop, and put it in his messenger bag.

Within minutes, they were out of the hotel and hurrying toward the SUV.

"Crap, it's cold," Gunner said as he got into the driver's seat.

"I'll take the back seat," Dylan said, leaving the passenger seat for Asher.

They buckled up and sped out of the parking lot.

"Will they let us visit Dad even though it's not visitation time?" Gunner asked.

"I doubt they would have called us if they weren't going to let us in," Asher said. "Besides, I know there's a notation in his chart that law enforcement will be notified as soon as he's able to talk, and we're law enforcement."

"If they won't let all of us in, then you and Gunner have to go," Dylan said. "You're the cops. You need to hear whatever he has to say firsthand."

"We're in this together. Just because Gunner and I have the authority to act on information, doesn't mean your input doesn't matter. We discuss everything with each other, okay?"

"Yes, okay," Dylan said.

Gunner pulled into the hospital parking lot, parked as close as he could get to the entrance, and then they grabbed the bags with their laptops and took off running.

Jacob knew his sons were coming. A nurse said they were on the way. His eyes were closed, but he was conscious of every sound around him. He could easily slip back into the oblivion his pain meds offered, but he was waiting. There were things he needed to tell them, and he didn't know if he was going to survive this.

Then all of a sudden, he heard footsteps. Not the soft-soled shoes the nurses wore, but the long stride of boot-shod men. Tears welled. His sons were here.

"Dad, it's me, Asher. Gunner and Dylan are here, too. Can you hear us?"

Jacob opened his eyes, blinking through tears. His voice was weak, but his grip on Asher's arm was not.

"I drift in and out. I need to tell you. Two men. It was dark. One behind...took me down. You should have sold the bar, he said. I kicked him off, and other one shot me."

Gunner frowned. "Should have sold the bar? What does that mean? Did you have it up for sale?"

Jacob shook his head slightly, closing his eyes briefly to gather his strength.

"Two men in the bar...a week ago. Didn't know them. Asked if it was for sale. I said no."

Gunner was taking notes of everything Jacob said, and Dylan was recording the audio on his phone.

"Did they give you names?" Asher asked.

Jacob blinked and slowly nodded. "Joe and Darren Wilson. Fake for sure."

"What did they look like?" Asher asked.

Jacob was sliding backward fast. Their faces were fading. "One tall and thin. Red hair. One big blond. When I said not for sale, they left."

"That day, did you see what they were driving?" Asher asked.

Jacob's eyes closed. His voice was softer, growing weaker. "Car. Not a truck. Maybe white. Why am I still alive? Did they rob me?"

"No robbery. Pearl Fallon heard the shot. She tried to call you. Thought you had been robbed. When you didn't answer, she took herself and that famous shotgun of hers and took off running toward the bar. She saved your life," Asher said. "Dad... We're going to go home. We need to see the scene of the crime. We aren't leaving you. We're just going to find out who did this."

"Yes... Knew you would. Pearl... My God. Should have married her instead of Brenda..." and then he was out.

Chapter 7

THE BROTHERS WERE STILL REELING FROM HIS LAST comment when the nurse escorted them out, and they immediately headed for the waiting room to discuss what they'd just learned.

"I'll get the coffee," Asher muttered, and turned toward the vending machines in the waiting area.

"I'll get some breakfast sandwiches," Dylan offered, and followed.

Gunner grabbed napkins and then headed for a table.

As soon as they were gathered, they looked at each other in disbelief.

"That last comment. What the hell?" Gunner said.

Dylan shrugged. "Don't look at me. I have no idea."

Ash cupped his hands around the warmth of the coffee cup, staring down into the dark-brown liquid.

"That's a cup of coffee, not a crystal ball," Gunner said. "What do you know that we don't?"

"I know Mom didn't like Pearl, but I never knew why. Maybe once upon a time, Pearl was in the running for Dad's affections before Mom showed up. But right now, we need to talk about what he said before that. Two men attacked him in the bar. High possibility that it was the same two men who'd come a week earlier asking if the bar was for sale."

"I'll run a search on those two names, but if Dad thought they were fake, then it may come to nothing," Gunner said.

"The car they were driving matches the description of the one Pearl saw driving away that night, so I'm saying it was the same two men," Asher said.

"Likely with the fake names," Dylan said.

Gunner nodded.

"The big question is, why would someone want the Tumbleweed bad enough to kill for it? And why would they assume that killing Dad would even give them access to it afterward? We're still in the loop of ownership," Dylan asked.

Asher's eyes narrowed. "What if they didn't know about us? And why would they want access to the place? I think their identities will give us answers. We all worried about what might happen to Dad after Pete Brandt's death resurrected the big story about the missing money. Who is still living that has a grudge to settle?"

Gunner nodded. "Give me a few minutes to write up my notes on what Dad said, and I'll email them to your laptop. Then you can send it to Reddick as Dad's first statement."

Asher nodded. "Yes...but breakfast first, before the coffee and the microwaved sandwiches get any colder."

"Then what?" Dylan asked as they began opening their sandwich packets.

Ash frowned. "I think we need to go home and get busy. It's hard to investigate something long-distance. The scene of the crime is always the best place to start."

"Is it safe to leave Dad alone?" Dylan asked.

Gunner frowned. "As long as he's in ICU, I'd say he's fine. We leave word no one visits him but us."

"Yes, okay," Dylan said. "But I'll be the one coming back every day to check on him. He might remember more as he becomes more alert, and I'll be there to hear it and pass it on."

Asher looked up and grinned. "Good thinking, Dylan. You would have made a good cop, too."

"Oh hell, no," Dylan said. "I'll stick with hammers and nails, not the bad guys and guns. Besides, I've got Angie to go home to. She makes my world go 'round."

"Okay then. Check-out time at the hotel and then home," Asher said.

"I'll keep my room just in case," Dylan said. "The weather is iffy this time of year, and the roads might become impassable for a time. I'd rather be snowed in with Dad, instead of knowing he was on his own."

"Then when we get back to Crossroads, you keep the SUV to drive back and forth," Gunner said. "We've got Dad's truck to use if we need wheels."

"Finish up eating," Asher said, pointing to their food. "I have some people to talk to here first, and then we're gone. I want in that bar. I need to see where it happened."

A short while later Asher and Gunner had checked out, leaving Dylan's room active. They loaded up their bags and headed home.

"It's going to be weird going home without Dad there," Dylan said.

"And we have some housecleaning to do before it's safe to bring him home," Asher added.

Dylan's phone rang, ending their conversation. It was Angie, needing verification on a decision she was about to make, so Asher took the opportunity to text Nora.

Dad woke up. He's continuing to improve. We have new info and we're all on the way home. Hope you had a good night's sleep. Wish I could be with you and help you finish up at your house, but we have some serious issues to solve here before my life is my own

again. Call or text me any time. I will be at your doorstep if you need me.

We're keeping Dad's progress under wraps for now. It
has to do with keeping him safe. If the shooter thinks
Dad has yet to wake up, he won't be inclined to try
and finish the job.

Nora was in the hardware store, picking up some small
hinge screws. Fixing loose hinges and recaulking window-
panes weren't part of her skill set, but she was getting there.
Her phone signaled a text as she was heading to the check-
out counter. When she saw it was from Ash, she went ahead
and checked out, then got into the car before she stopped
to read it.

Finding out that they were coming home was both exciting and worrisome. From the tone of the message and their
previous conversation, she understood what wasn't being
said. They were going to begin a serious investigation into
the attempted murder, which may or may not become risky
to them, as well. But just knowing they were going to be
residing only a few blocks apart made her heart skip. She
sent back a response, and then headed home.

Best news ever! Understand the seriousness of what
comes next. My lips are sealed. Looking forward to
random visits. You know where to find me.

Asher smiled when he got her response, but said nothing. Discussing her with his brothers wasn't going to
happen. He didn't want their input, and he didn't want the
teasing that would ensue. They were grown-ass men until

they got together, and somehow, they always reverted to the old childhood ranking of him in charge and being the referee for them.

Nora went home with her purchases, unloaded them on the counter and quickly replaced the screws in the cabinet doors she'd found missing, then went outside to reapply caulking to the window she'd heard rattling. She had just finished and was turning around, when she tripped on the edge of a brick border around an old flower bed long devoid of flowers.

The tube of caulking went flying, and there was nothing to grab hold of to break the fall. She hit knees first, then hands down to keep from face-planting.

Within a heartbeat of impact, she felt a sharp, burning pain in the palm of her left hand and screamed as she jerked it back. Even as she was scrambling to her feet, she saw the piece of glass embedded in her palm, and the blood oozing out around it and groaned.

"Oh. My. God. What next?"

She started to pull out the shard and then guessed it would exacerbate the bleeding. So, she made a run for the back door, then into the kitchen and grabbed a couple of kitchen towels and lightly wrapped them around her hand. "Purse, I need my purse," she mumbled, then ran to get her purse and car keys. She didn't stop to lock the door, and she didn't even have her phone. She just got in the car and headed for the ER, driving as fast as she dared.

By the time she arrived, she was in tears. The shock of the accident was passing, but this felt like the last volley from a long-fought war. She grabbed her purse and ran inside, but the towels were as blood-soaked as her clothes, which startled the ER nurses to come running.

"Nora! What happened?" Peggy asked.

"Tripped in the back yard and fell. When I got up, this was in my hand."

"Dr. Sherrod is on-site today. Let's get you back in an exam room and clean this up," Joan added.

As they were walking her down the hall to an exam room, Nora began seeing spots before her eyes and felt her legs getting weak. "I think I'm going to pass out."

"We've got you, honey. Take deep breaths and relax. You're going into shock. Forget the chair. Let's get her on the bed," Joan said, and then pulled up the guard rails while Peggy went to get the doctor.

Joan had a pan of water and antiseptic, and was washing off the blood and dirt from Nora's hands and fingers when Dr. Sherrod walked in.

"Peggy tells me your name is Nora. I'm Dr. Sherrod. You've had quite a nasty fall. Let's see what we can do about fixing you up, okay?"

Nora couldn't stop the tears, and was afraid to open her mouth for fear she'd choke on the sobs she was suppressing, so she just closed her eyes and nodded.

She felt the burn when they removed the glass, and heard the warning that the shots to numb her hand might hurt. She shut her mind to what they were doing and saying, and kept telling herself it would soon be over, and thought about Asher.

The man he'd become was intimidating. A beautiful face of planes and angles. Eyes long since adapted to squinting against the sun's glare, the wind, and the heat. Tall enough to see what was coming, and hard-headed enough to face it head-on. And when they made love, it was like flying and falling, and still wanting more.

The Kingstons were West Texas born, like her and her people. They were used to the hardscape of High Plains

living. Never quite enough grass and water. Sunsets unlike any place else on earth. Blizzards that killed men and cattle alike. Snakes in the grass, and snakes wearing boots. Few stayed by choice, and only the hardiest survived.

This little cut on her hand was nothing to the scars life had left on her heart. She kept telling herself she needed to stop crying. That this was ridiculous. But this was one unexpected pain too many to let go.

It was nearing noon by the time the brothers got to the Tumbleweed Bar. Seeing the parking lot empty at this time of day was weird, but seeing the piece of plywood nailed over the front door where the window used to be made them sick. As usual, they drove around to the back to park, then grabbed their bags as they got out.

"I've got my key," Asher said, unlocked the back door, and entered the house and into the kitchen with his brothers behind him.

Clearly, the forensic team had been through here, but nothing had been broken, and things were mostly still in place. He quickly turned up the thermostat to take off the chill.

"You two take the extra bedrooms. We're all too big to sleep together anymore. I'll sleep in Dad's bed for the duration," Ash said, and dumped his stuff in Jacob's room, while his brothers went further down the hall to leave their bags, then met up in the living room.

"You ready to do this?" he asked, and when they nodded, Ash opened the door leading into the hall between the residence and the bar.

The first thing they saw was the plywood over the missing window in the door, but as they moved into the bar,

their eyes immediately went to the bloodstained floor behind the bar.

"Ah, God," Gunner muttered. "Hell of a thing for Dad to walk in on when he re-opens."

"I can get some stuff to take that up and replace the glass," Dylan said.

Asher walked all the way to the front door, taking care not to crush any more glass shards into the floor, and then turned around and looked back at the crime scene.

"They came in fast. If Dad made it into the house, then by the time he heard the glass break and came running back for the gun, they were already inside and set up to take him down," Ash said. "But there's something off. If he was already in the hall, they would have seen his silhouette from the glow of the nightlights. Right? He was a big target in their sights. Why wait to shoot him until he was back in the bar?"

Gunner's eyes narrowed. "Good eye, Ash. Maybe they never planned on encountering him? Everyone knows he lives in the attached house."

Asher frowned. "Then why make all that noise coming in?"

"Stupid thieves?" Dylan offered. "We get break-ins at job sites all the time. They see the security cameras. They see the posted signs if there are guard dogs on the premises at night, and still try it anyway."

Asher turned around, opened the front door, then looked at Dylan, who was still standing at the bar.

"From where you're standing, what do you see?" he asked.

"The parking lot," Dylan said.

"The truck that made a U-turn!" Gunner said. "That's what spooked them! They were already inside. They'd already shot Dad for whatever reason, but they didn't take

anything, because the headlights from any car making a U-turn would have swept through the bar like a searchlight."

Asher nodded. "It's a theory, but it's the only one that makes sense with the little we know. If we could only find out who was driving that truck, maybe they saw something and didn't realize what they saw meant anything."

"But how do we do that?" Gunner muttered. "Go door to door?"

Dylan frowned. "No. Go to the Rose. Talk to Pearl. She's the witness. Ask her what the black truck looked like, too? What? Don't look at me like that."

Ash grinned. "We weren't looking at you like anything... Just proud of you for seeing the obvious when we were still looking at maybes."

Dylan shrugged. "Happy to be of assistance. And if it's okay with you two, while you are sleuthing about, I'm gonna make a quick run to Lowe's Hardware downtown and see if they can cut me a piece of glass for the front door. It's too damn cold for the patch job they've done. I just need to get a tape measure. I know where Dad keeps the tools."

Gunner tossed him the keys. "You're the boss man when it comes to all that," then pulled out a couple of twenties and handed it to Dylan.

Asher handed him a couple more.

"Thanks," Dylan said. "I shouldn't be long. And didn't Sheriff Reddick tell us the forensic team was leaving Dad's keys with Pearl when they left?"

"Yes, he did," Asher said. "How about we meet there for lunch? You text us when you're at the Rose and we'll meet you there. I know where Dad keeps the extra set of keys to the truck. You do your thing. We'll be in the house."

Dylan nodded and went to get a tape measure. As soon as he had the measurements needed to replace the window glass, he locked the door and headed uptown.

"I need to send Dad's statement to the sheriff's office," Ash said.

"I'll make some coffee," Gunner offered, and they quickly retreated to the warmth and comfort of the family home.

Ash unpacked and hung up his clothes, then got his laptop and went into the living room to work where it was warm.

The first thing Everett Brandt did when he woke up was to check his account. He grunted in satisfaction when he saw the disability deposit had come through in his Direct Expense account, which meant his allotment card was loaded with money again. He stomped his feet into his boots and went to the bathroom. It was too cold to shower, and he didn't have any clean clothes because they'd didn't have laundry soap, so what did it matter?

He could tell by the scent of fresh brewing coffee that Freddie was up. Likely downing all the toast, but whatever. Today was for groceries and washing clothes, and hoping old man Kingston quit breathing.

Freddie looked up and smiled as Everett entered the kitchen.

"I saved you toast!" he said.

Surprised, Everett smiled. "Thanks, Freddie. We're going grocery shopping this morning."

"Can we get Twinkies?" Freddie asked.

"We can get Twinkies," Everett said, grabbed a piece of cold toast, poured himself a cup of coffee, then dunked the toast in the bitter brew and chomped.

Sheriff Matt Reddick was in a mood. Forensics just informed him that so far, they had pulled DNA from over twenty different people off of Jacob Kingston's clothes, and they still weren't finished—the result of having a victim be the owner, wait staff, bartender, and janitor of a very busy bar who'd been rolled all over said floor by his assailants before they shot him. It wasn't going to point the finger of guilt at anyone, due to the constant contact of customers coming and going. And from a period longer than just that one day. Trying to identify the DNA on his clothes from the floors alone was about to cause a walk-out in forensics. It was turning into a no-go as far as good clues went.

And then Reddick received the email from Asher Kingston, and the first thing that stood out to him was the request to not publicize the fact that Jacob had awakened and told them what he knew. He understood why, and hated that this was happening. But knowing what Jacob had seen...what he remembered...was more than they'd had five minutes ago.

So...now Reddick knew that two men had approached Jacob a week before the shooting to ask if the bar was for sale. Two men had been involved in the shooting. One of the attackers told him he should have sold the bar, and then they shot him. What didn't make sense was why nothing was taken, and why they ran after they'd done the deed. That sounded more like a revenge shooting than a botched robbery. But why? And if it did have anything to do with the old, armored car robbery, why now?

He sent a reply saying Message Received.

A few minutes later, the sheriff's office received a 911 call from a teenager, saying his dad was beating his mother for gambling away their rent money. At that point, the Kingston shooting was put on the back burner as the sheriff and two deputies headed to a small cattle ranch on the outskirts of

Silverton to save a man from himself, and a woman from dying for her sins.

―――――

Dylan had just loaded up a piece of tempered glass for the door into the back of the SUV. The glass had been cut to size and safely taped between two pieces of cardboard. He also had putty, some caulking points, and a new putty knife in the bag he was carrying, and some stain remover for hardwood floors.

As he was getting into the car, he saw Nora walking out of the ER with a bandage on her hand. She looked like she'd been crying, and he immediately sent Asher a text.

> Headed to the Yellow Rose. Just saw Nora coming out of the ER with a bandage on her hand. Go get her and bring her to eat lunch with us. She walks like she's carrying the weight of the world, and she's been crying. But drop Gunner off first. No woman wants an audience when she's crying.

―――――

When Ash's phone signaled a text, he shut down his laptop to read it, guessing it was probably Dylan. And then he opened it, read it, and bolted to his feet.

"Gunner! Time to go." He grabbed his coat and the keys to Jacob's truck and headed for the back door with Gunner behind him.

"What's the hurry?" Gunner asked as he slid into the passenger seat.

"I'm dropping you off at the Rose, then going to check on Nora. Dylan saw her coming out of Urgent Care with a bandage on her hand."

"Hope it's not something bad," Gunner said.

"At this point, a hangnail would probably be her last straw," Asher said as he drove out to the highway and gunned it up to the Rose. He let Gunner out and then drove to Nora's house, pulled up behind her car, went up the porch steps two at a time, and knocked.

A few seconds later, he heard footsteps coming to the door, and then it swung inward. There was a mop in her hand, and the shirt she was wearing was stained with blood, he assumed from the bandaged hand she was holding up between her breasts. Tears were rolling and her chin was trembling.

He felt like he'd just been stabbed, as he stepped over the threshold and opened his arms. She fell into them as he kicked the door shut behind him.

"Nora... Sweetheart, what happened? Dylan saw you coming out of the ER."

"I'm not crying because I hurt myself. I'm crying because I'm mad, tired, and frustrated. I tripped over a loose brick in the backyard, fell and cut my hand on a piece of glass half buried in the dirt. I didn't even see it," she sobbed. "I have four stitches in the palm of my hand and I'm mopping up blood I strung all over the house. I want my family back. I want my life back. I don't have a rudder anymore. I'm afloat, but drifting."

"You still have me," he said, then led her to the sofa, sat down beside her, and held her while she cried. "You're breaking my heart. Life drop-kicked you big time. Our reunion has resurrected a multitude of emotions, and you were already dealing with too many responsibilities and grief before this. Did they give you anything for pain?"

"Yes. They're going to deliver it."

He grabbed a handful of tissues from the box on the coffee table and handed them to her. "Is it hurting bad right now?"

"It's still numb from the shots to deaden it."

"Then we're going to go pick it up, and then we're going to the Yellow Rose, and you're going to eat lunch with me and my brothers. I will feed you myself, and you can soak up the sympathy and kind words from the other diners and get free pie from Pearl. You have been alone too long. I will either take you home after or bring you home with me and put you to bed there, while we fix a window. Okay?"

She wiped her eyes and blew her nose, and then laughed through the tears. "I don't know as I've ever had an offer like that before, but it's one I don't want to pass up. Even if my eyes are all red from crying."

"They'll be fine by the time I get a pain pill in you," he said.

She wrapped her good arm around his neck and hugged him. "You were my best friend before you were my lover. I missed you, Ash. I missed you so very much."

"I missed you, too, love. I missed you, and I missed this." He brushed his mouth across her lips, then went back for more, until their hearts were pounding, and they were waffling between sex or soup. "I can't go anywhere in these bloody clothes, though."

"I've stripped you before. I remember how it goes. You lead the way and pick out what you want to wear. I'll help with the rest. And pack an overnight bag, too. You're staying the night with me and the boys. I wouldn't sleep a wink thinking of you alone and hurting."

"What if they don't want—"

He rolled his eyes. "Nora... Honey... They love you. They always have. Now let's get this over with, and I'm sorry ahead of time if I hurt you."

She nodded, and when he began, she kept thinking, this was Ash. He'd always taken care of her, even when she hadn't needed the help, she'd understood his need to matter

to her. To take care of someone he loved, and this was no different.

He pulled her bloody jeans down to her knees first. "Now sit down on the bed, and I'll get your boots and pants off, then we'll do the shirt."

Within minutes, he had the bloody clothes off and her clean clothes on, and with her standing by him with instructions, put the bloody clothes into the wash.

"With laundry soap and on cold, right?" he asked.

She nodded, then laid her head against his shoulder as he did as he'd been told.

"Okay…we've got your overnight bag packed. Go rest a minute while I finish mopping up the blood. I called Belker's and told them we were coming by to pick up your meds."

She sighed. "You think of everything."

"On-the-job training," he said, and winked.

A few minutes later, they walked out, locking the door behind them. He had one hand under her elbow, helping her down the steps, and was carrying her bag with the other.

He put her bag in the back seat and buckled her in before closing the door.

Nora sat, thinking his sheepskin coat made his shoulders look even wider, then watching the way he walked into the wind with his head down just enough to keep the wind from catching his Stetson as he got into truck. Before he could start the engine, Dylan called, and the first words out of his mouth were, "Is she okay?"

Ash turned his head, looking at the sheen of tears in her big brown eyes, and the beautiful shape of her, then answered.

"She will be. We have to stop at the pharmacy, then we'll be right there."

By the time they got to the Rose, Nora knew Ash had been right. She needed to feel normal again. To soak up the hometown welcome and be with people who knew her for the girl she'd been, and were not impressed with the high-powered world in which she now lived and worked.

Dylan had chairs waiting at their table, and when she walked in, and they saw her and Asher together again, and the fresh bandage on her hand, she became the object of much teasing and much sympathy.

One man they'd grown up with shouted out at Asher.

"Dang, Ash. Did you have to twist her hand that hard just to get her back?"

"Hush it, Roger. Everybody in town knows Nora Borden doesn't do anything she doesn't want to."

That comment brought up countless stories from friends at the Rose, about their high school years. About Nora at fourteen, refusing to play basketball just because she was tall, and the fit the athletic coach had when she said no. And the time Nora proved to the computer science teacher that there was a flaw in the program he was teaching from, then fixed it for him on the spot.

Nora sat listening, surprised so many people remembered anything about her, and that she'd been admired for standing up for herself, when she'd felt like the nerdy girl who always made perfect scores and ruined the grading curve for everyone. Now, it was funny, and she could see that they were laughing with her, not at her, and all the sad, empty places inside her began to fade.

Pearl even made a quick trip out of the kitchen to give her a hug, and as she did, Gunner took it upon himself to ask about the black truck that made a U-turn the night of the shooting.

"Miss Pearl, did you recognize that truck, or see who was driving it?" he asked.

She frowned slightly, trying to picture it in her mind. "I know for certain that it was an extended-cab truck with big dually wheels, a ladder sticking out of the back, and one broken taillight. I didn't see the driver. But I know he had nothing to do with shooting Jacob, because I heard the gunshot first and ran to the window. Then, I saw the black truck pass by the Rose and watched it go down the highway and make a U-turn in the parking lot and come back into town. I was calling Jacob by then, and still watching out the window when I saw the white sports car come flying out from the bar parking lot and go west. At that point I got dressed and ran to check on Jacob's welfare. That's about all I know. I need to get back in the kitchen before Davey messes with my chi."

They were smiling as she left, trying to imagine what Pearl's punishment to her grill cook might be for interfering with the setup in her kitchen.

"Black extended-cab truck. Dually wheels. Ladder in the back. One broken taillight," Gunner repeated, and at that moment, Nora interrupted.

"That sounds like Miles Terrell's truck. He works at Lowe's. I was just in there earlier today and saw him leave in it to make a delivery. No ladder in the back but it had all of the other features."

"Can't beat the grapevine of small-town living," Gunner said as he wrote down the name. "If this is him, then he may have more information for us. Many thanks, Nora."

Ash winked at her, and Dylan gave her a quick pat on the arm.

"You are officially part of the investigation," Ash said, "and here comes our food. Did you take a pain pill yet?" he asked.

She nodded.

He leaned over and kissed her cheek, then winked when she blushed.

"Outrageous man," she said.

"No shame within him," Gunner added.

Ash shrugged. "I'm not ashamed of anything. Didn't you see the way those two truckers have been staring at her? I just posted my own version of a No Trespassing sign."

Nora glanced up at him and winked. "Like I said...such an outrageous man, but since he did offer, I plan to keep him."

After that, they began eating, but still talking among themselves.

"I'll go run down Miles and see what he has to say," Gunner said.

"After I tuck Nora in Dad's bed, I'll help Dylan install the new glass in the front door," Ash said.

"You don't have to do that," Nora said. "I'll be fine on my own."

Ash shook his head. "But I won't be fine knowing you are worn out, half sick and hurting, and doing it alone. If you were operating on what's left of your emotions, I'd say you're about one pothole away from having a wreck."

Nora grinned. "Such a sweet-talking man. You always were a charmer. Pothole, indeed."

Dylan laughed as Ash reached for the check.

"I can't eat my pie. I'm too full," Nora said.

"We'll take it back to the house. I'll eat it for you later," Ash said.

And this time, it was Nora who laughed.

"That will be another thing about you that hasn't changed, but I'll gladly give up pie for the pleasure of your company," she said.

At that point, Gunner stood. "I'm taking the truck. You

two can ride home with Dylan. See you later, hopefully with more info," and then he was gone.

Nora could almost see the chip on his shoulder as she watched him walking out.

"Gunner holds a grudge better than anyone I ever knew," she said.

Ash nodded. "Yes, he does, but he's damn good at his job. You go on ahead with Dylan. Get in the front seat with him. I'll be out as soon as I pay up."

Dylan winked and held out his arm. "Come on, darlin'. The Kingstons will always have your back," then he helped her on with her coat and zipped it up for her, before escorting her out of the Rose.

Asher glanced back, satisfied that his brother was on the job, and waited for someone to get to the register so he could pay.

Finally, he threw down a couple of twenties on the counter on top of his ticket, and waved Darla down.

"Keep the change. I need to get Nora home."

Darla rang up the money paid, pocketed the eight dollars in change, then watched him walk out of the Rose.

"That is one fine man," she muttered, then reminded herself she already had one, and two kids to boot, and went to bus a table as they drove away.

"Remember, as soon as we get the door fixed, I'm heading back to Amarillo to keep an eye on Dad," Dylan said.

Ash nodded. "Is this interfering with your work?" he asked.

"If it wasn't for Angie, it would be, but we've managed to keep everything running smoothly with phone calls and texts, and I'm still communicating with the crews via texts and video calls."

Nora smiled. "Isn't technology amazing? We couldn't have done anything like this when we were growing up

here. There was nobody and nothing for miles and miles, and no way to communicate beyond phone calls. Now I have Zoom meetings with people in London, and China, and LA, all at one time."

Dylan's eyes widened. "Dang, girl. I had no idea. I don't know what I thought a job in technology meant, but I didn't think worldwide when I thought it."

"I'm going to have to readjust my schedules now because of this stupid injury. My typing will be ridiculously slow until the bandage comes off," she said.

Ash frowned. "When did they say you could do that?"

"I'm not to get it wet for forty-eight hours, and then take the bandage off and let it heal without it. If all is well, they'll take the stitches out in about a week. It's not the end of the world, but it sure slowed my world down."

Dylan pulled up to the front of the bar, then turned around and backed up to the front door.

"I've got keys," Ash said. "Let me get Nora settled in the house, and then I'll be right back."

"No hurry," Dylan said. "I have to remove the trim and what's left of the old glass before we can put in a new piece."

"I'm sure glad you know what you're doing," Ash said.

Dylan grinned. "I'm glad I know what I'm doing, too. You get Nora inside where it's warm, and Nora honey, I'll say goodbye now, in case you're asleep when I leave. Glad to have you back in the family."

"I'm glad to be back," she said, and went up the steps with Ash, then through the bar to the house.

Then the moment she walked into the living room, she had a sensation of déjà vu. In all the years that had passed, nothing much had changed.

"You know where everything is," Ash said. "I've been sleeping in Dad's bed until he gets back." He hung up her coat, then picked up her bag. "I'm going to put this in his

room with my stuff. Do you want to watch TV, or would you rather lie down a while?"

"Lie down, please. I feel like I've been up a week, and the day is only half over."

"Then follow me," he said, and led the way down the hall and into the big room. "There's an en suite attached. Let me help you get your boots off. Can you manage your jeans? I mean…getting them down and back up again?"

"Probably not. Just help me get them off and I'll sleep in my sweater and underwear," she said.

So, he did, then waited until she came out of the bathroom and eased her down on the bed, covered her with a blanket, and kissed her.

"Rest, darlin'. Ignore the ensuing noise. You're safe here."

She rolled over and closed her eyes so he wouldn't see the tears. She hadn't been tucked into bed in years, and the thought of feeling safe again made her weep.

She heard Asher walking out of the room, then closing the door behind him. Her hand was sore, but the pain pill was working. She was so tired, and the pillow smelled of Ash's aftershave. She'd never slept with Ash before. They'd only ever made love. The bed was soft, and the blanket so warm. It was as close to sleeping with him as she'd ever been. Within minutes, she was out.

Chapter 8

Gunner went straight to Lowe's Hardware, but when he didn't see the truck Nora described, he circled the building to the employee parking lot. It was there, and exactly as Pearl had described it. He circled back around the building to park and went inside to look for Miles Terrell. Even though Miles was Asher's age, he remembered him, and headed for the lady at the checkout register.

"Afternoon," she said. "Are you looking for something in particular?"

"Yes, Miles Terrell. I'm Gunner Kingston. I need to talk to him."

"Oh, you're one of Jacob's boys. We're praying for him. Miles is stocking shelves on aisle nine, I think."

"Thanks," Gunner said, wondering who the woman was as he headed toward the far side of the building. When he saw the stocky, brown-haired man in blue jeans and a plaid flannel shirt about halfway down aisle nine, he knew he'd found his man. He walked past bins full of knobs and drawer pulls, and boxes and boxes of different-size screws, to where Miles was working. "Hey, Miles, got a minute?"

Miles turned and smiled in surprise. "Gunner Kingston! Man, it's been a while. How's Jacob? We all heard he made it through surgery."

"He did, and holding his own. Still in ICU though. Listen, is there somewhere private we could talk...just for a few minutes? I wouldn't want to get you in trouble with your boss."

"Sure, follow me," Miles said, and led him to their break room, and motioned toward a long table with benches on both sides. "Have a seat," Miles said.

As soon as they had settled, Gunner lowered his voice and leaned forward. "You know I'm a homicide detective with the Dallas PD, and that Asher is a special investigator with the attorney general's office, right?"

"Yeah, yeah, I do. Jacob is always talking about all three of you," Miles said.

"So, we're helping Sheriff Reddick with the shooting at the bar."

"Not surprised," Miles said. "Pearl saved his life, didn't she?"

"That she did," Gunner said, "and that's why I'm here, trying to verify the timeline of what she saw and heard."

"Okay, but I don't know how I can help with that," he said.

"Maybe you can and just don't know it," Gunner said. "By any chance, were you driving your truck in Crossroads around midnight when the shooting occurred?"

Miles frowned, thinking back. "I was driving home from Tulia just before midnight. I'd been visiting a girl I date there. Her name is Patsy Adams. I left later than I should have, and was driving back down the 86, and thinking about what was on the agenda at work the next day, and didn't know I'd missed the turnoff into Crossroads until I realized I was passing the Yellow Rose, so I slowed down and made a U-turn in the Tumbleweed parking lot and backtracked."

"That's perfect, Miles. You just verified Pearl's timeline. By that time, she'd already heard the gunshot and gotten out of bed. She was looking out the window overlooking the highway when she said she saw a black pickup make a U-turn at the Tumbleweed, and then drive back toward town. So... my question to you is, did you see anything in the parking

lot or around the bar when you turned around? Did you see the open door? Did you see another vehicle? Anything?"

"I didn't even look toward the bar, but as I was turning, I saw the front end of a white sports car parked on the east side of the bar, the back half was in the shadows. I wouldn't bet my life on it, but I thought it was an older model Mustang. I didn't think anything of it other than probably a customer was too drunk to drive, and Jacob told him to leave it there. That happens from time to time."

Gunner nodded. "Thanks a lot, Miles. This was a big help, and we'd appreciate it if you wouldn't mention we'd talked about this, okay?"

"Sure thing, and just so you all know, we're all praying for your dad."

"We appreciate that," Gunner said. "I'd better let you get back to work."

They walked out of the break room together and then parted company.

Gunner hurried back to the SUV and was about to drive home when he remembered there was little to no food in the house, and headed to Belker's.

Dylan had already poured Blood Buster stain remover on the stain behind the bar, and was letting it work before mopping it up.

He had taken the door off the hinges and made sawhorses out of two bar tables to lay it on and was working quickly, because the cold north air was blowing straight into the bar. He'd already removed the plywood that had been tacked over it, as well as the trim and the rest of the broken glass. He was cleaning out the old putty from around the opening when Ash returned.

"Wow…it's cold in here."

"I noticed," Dylan said, and then grinned. "Get one of those putty knives and help me clean this out," he said, and soon the brothers were working head-to-head, until Dylan called a halt. "That's good. Now for the new glass."

"Where is it?" Ash said.

"On the bar, sandwiched between those two pieces of cardboard. Help me carry it over here, and I'll finish it off. Then you can help me hang the door back on the hinges. It's heavy."

A short while later, Dylan stepped back to eye his work. "Looks good to me. Let's get this door hung and shut out that north wind."

Dylan took one side and Asher the other as they carried the door back to the entrance. They stood it up, slipped the hinges in place, and then while Ash held the door, Dylan tapped the bolts back into place. After that, they closed and locked the front door.

"Great work," Asher said.

Dylan shrugged. "It's missing the gold lettering that was on it before, but Dad can have that done at a later date. I'll clean up the mess I made before I head back to Amarillo, and then wipe up the stain remover from behind the bar. You go check on your girl. She has been dealing with the stress of elder care alone, for a long time. Look at the mess we're in now, but there's three of us. She is in serious need of TLC."

Before Ash could answer, he got a text from Gunner.

Miles saw a white sports car parked on the east side of the bar. He thought it was an older model Mustang and assumed someone had left it behind for being too drunk to drive. I'm at Belker's getting groceries. Be back soon.

He showed Dylan the message. "That's going to be an affirmative for me, if two witnesses both saw a white, older model Mustang there that night. I'll update the sheriff later. You go get your stuff and get on the road. I can clean up. You still have to drive back, and it'll get dark early."

"Thanks," Dylan said. "Keep me in the loop about what's going on. I'll make sure Dad knows you're investigating the shooting. And if you need me for anything, I can be here in less than an hour, okay?"

"Absolutely," Ash said. "Go on. Gunner and I will set up office on the kitchen table and take care of business here."

Dylan left the bar and went into the house, while Ash got the broom and dustpan and began cleaning up and putting the bar tables back into place. Then after reading the instructions on the bottle of stain remover, proceeded to clean that up, as well.

He was putting the CLOSED sign back on the front door when he saw Dylan driving away, and Gunner arriving, then turned up the thermostat in the bar before retreating to the house to help Gunner.

"Nora still asleep?" Gunner said as he came in with his arms full of sacks and put them all on the kitchen counter.

Asher nodded as he got out two packages of ham steaks Gunner just brought home. "How good are you at cooking?" Ash asked.

"Good enough on basics. What do you need?" Gunner asked.

"Preheat the oven to 450. Wash three of those baking potatoes, wrap them in foil, and put them in the oven."

Gunner grinned. "That, I can do. Just like old times, right, Ash? Big brother making our lunches for school, cooking our dinner before ball games, making breakfast. After the fall of the house of Brenda, you became our second dad. Pretty sure I never said thank you."

Ash threw a potholder at him. "I didn't need thanks. You guys were my brothers. I just wanted you to grow up enough to quit peeing the bed."

Gunner grinned, then turned on the oven to preheat and went to get potatoes.

Nora woke to the smell of ham frying in a skillet, and for a few moments before she opened her eyes, could have almost convinced herself that she was home, and her mom was making supper. But when she rolled over on her bandaged hand, the pain was all it took to remind her of where she was, and what had happened.

She'd often dreamed of what a reunion with Ash would be like. Sometimes she dreamed she'd be in an airport, and she'd see him walking toward her up the concourse. Other times she imagined she would be coming out of a store somewhere and run into him, like in the movies. There would be this moment of shock between them, and then immediate vows of undying love. But she'd never imagined they'd come together again because her whole family was dead, and someone had tried to murder his father. And yet here they were. She was in his bed with stitches, and a very awkward bandage on her hand.

She groaned as she got up, made a quick trip to the bathroom, ran a hairbrush through the tangles in her hair, and dug a pair of sweatpants out of her overnight bag. It took a few minutes to get them on, and then she left the room.

She could hear Asher and Gunner talking as she came up the hall. The cadence of their speech was alike, but Ash's voice was deeper. It was the only way she could tell who was talking, and the sound of his voice made her shiver

in the very best way. But the second she walked into the kitchen, Ash dropped the spoon in his hand and rushed toward her.

"Sweetheart... You're awake. Did you rest... Are you hurting? You can have another pain pill if you are. We cooked."

She stopped. "I know. Yes, I did. Yes, I am. I believe I do. It smells good."

He grinned. "You sorted through all that as quickly as you used to find the mistakes in my math homework. Come sit. Supper is almost ready."

Gunner was shuffling papers aside and moving laptops to make room for her and the food. "You slept a long time, and I was getting hungry enough to consider checking you for a pulse," he said.

Nora laughed. "You didn't have to wait. I would be happy with leftovers."

"That's just it," Asher said. "The Kingstons don't leave leftovers. I'll make your plate if you'll allow me, and cut up the ham for you, too. The rest of it is easy to manage."

"Feel free," Nora said.

"We're having baked potatoes. I made them," Gunner said.

"Yes, you did, little brother. You turned on the oven and rolled them in foil, then forgot to set the timer. I saved them from incineration, and we are all grateful for your assistance."

Gunner shrugged. "Oh. Well. I'm better at my job, I assure you. Butter *and* sour cream, Nora?"

"Yes, please, and salt and pepper," she added, then watched them working together and knew this was how they'd grown up. Without a mother, they'd learned to do everything together.

When they finally sat down to eat, the first bites of food

delayed the need for conversation, but when Nora realized Dylan was gone, she spoke up.

"Did Dylan go back to Amarillo?"

Ash nodded. "Yes, right after we got the door fixed."

"What were you doing when you cut your hand?" Gunner asked.

"Re-caulking a loose windowpane on the back of the house. I'm getting it ready to sell. I can't live here and do my job, and I don't want to be a long-distance landlord."

"Where do you live in Fort Worth?" Ash asked. "I mean...house or apartment?"

"A very tall apartment building I call my ivory tower. Since I work mostly from home, I don't get out much," she said.

"Ash has a really cool house," Gunner said. "Lots of room. Multiple bedrooms and stuff."

Nora refused to respond, because she and Asher had already discussed all that.

Ash glanced at her and winked. "She already knows I live in a house now. I did the apartment thing when I was younger, but soon figured out I need privacy and space. Product of all this wide-open space we grew up in, I suppose."

"And I, a single woman on my own, chose the high-rise for the safety features," Nora said. "A doorman. Twenty-four-hour building security. Covered parking garage. Taser. Pepper spray, and I live on the fourteenth floor and have three locks on my door and there are security cameras in the halls on every floor. That leaves two points of escape for any perp. Elevators, which are traditionally slow, or fourteen flights of stairs. It's a serious deterrent."

Ash paled, and Gunner's shock was evident.

"All of those are prerequisites for renting an apartment? Are you serious?" Asher asked.

Nora shrugged. "No, but it's the optimal choices. All women live with the knowledge that anywhere, at any moment, they can become a victim of a mugging, a rape, or a murder. And, lord love a duck, don't forget the stalkers. I'm just fortunate enough to afford the extra perks. Most women aren't. They become the victims you two deal with. I don't want to become a statistic."

"I may never let you out of my sight again," Ash muttered.

Nora frowned. "And yet I have managed to survive the cold, ugly world all on my own for years and years without a keeper." She held up her bandaged hand. "This is just an awkward thing I did to myself. It hurts now, but it will heal a lot faster than the injuries I incurred from a stalker."

All the expression on Ash's face disappeared. "You were stalked?"

She nodded. "Right after I moved to Fort Worth. It was a man where I worked. He thought he was going to scare me into submission. Left threatening messages beneath my door after I turned him down, sent pictures of me walking down the streets to let me know he was following me. So, I hired a private investigator to follow my stalker who was following me... and take pictures of him while he was doing it."

Asher was in shock, imagining all she'd gone through alone, but it was Gunner who asked.

"So, what happened? Did you turn him in to the police?"

"Of course I did. Nothing happened, because he hadn't physically harmed me, and my boss looked at me like it was my fault. So, I got a protective order against him and bought a Taser. He thought he'd skated home free, cornered me in a covered parking lot and hit me in the face with his fist. That hurt way worse than this cut on my hand. He busted my lip and broke a bone in my cheek, and didn't expect me to fight back. But he got the message when I Tasered him

in the crotch and put him on the ground. Then I called the police again."

Gunner's face was flushed in anger. "You better be telling me they jailed him this time."

Nora nodded. "Oh, yes. He's in prison somewhere now. I sued the company I worked for over their refusal to respond to the danger I was in which created a dangerous workplace environment, and I won. Then I took myself to a different company, rented a nice apartment in my ivory tower with the expectation of living happily ever after, and you both know that didn't go as planned."

There were tears running down Ash's face, but he didn't know it. He wanted to say something, but the words wouldn't come.

Nora saw his shock and reached for his hand across the table.

"Don't, Ash. I didn't tell this for sympathy, or to make anyone feel bad. It's just a part of what happened to me after I left Crossroads. You weren't responsible for me. You weren't my designated bodyguard. You were the boy from home who I loved, and clearly, still love."

Gunner stood up and walked out. They needed to talk, and he wanted to check on Dylan and make sure he got back to Amarillo okay, so he sat down in the living room, turned on the TV to drown out their conversation, then made the call.

Dylan drove straight to the hospital, arriving in time to get an update on his dad's condition before he went in to visit, and was relieved to learn he was continuing to improve. There was a nurse checking Jacob's vitals and the drip in his IV when he walked up to his bed.

"How's he doing?" Dylan asked.

Jacob opened his eyes. "He's still ticking," he said.

Dylan smiled. "And making jokes, thank the Lord."

The nurse smiled. "Jacob is a good patient. We're going to miss him when they move him into a regular room."

"Really? When is that happening?" Dylan asked.

"Doctor will make that decision tomorrow after rounds," she said. "I'll leave you to visit. Ten minutes go fast."

Dylan reached for his dad's hand. "You scared the hell out of us, Dad."

"Scared myself pretty good, too," Jacob said. "Did I dream it, or were your brothers here, too?"

"Yes. You talked to them. Do you remember what you said?" Dylan asked.

"Did I mention the two men who wanted to buy the bar?"

Dylan nodded. "You also told us two men broke into the bar right after you'd closed. That one of them took you down, told you that you should have sold the bar, and then another one shot you. Is that still how you remember it?"

"Yes. Did you tell me it was Pearl who saved me?"

"Yes, we did. She was sleeping with her bedroom window open. The gunshot woke her. She tried to call you, and when you didn't answer, she got dressed, grabbed that shotgun of hers, and took off running toward the bar. She found you bleeding out behind the bar, called 911 and then applied pressure bandages until help came."

A tear rolled down the side of Jacob's face and onto the pillow.

"I owe her, big-time," he said.

Dylan nodded. "When we told you that the first time, you made a rather surprising comment. You said that you should have married her, instead."

Jacob didn't respond and Dylan was afraid he'd said something he shouldn't have, and then Jacob sighed.

"We were a couple for nearly a year, then we had a falling out because of Brenda. She told Pearl a lie about me that I knew nothing about, and it broke her heart. I didn't know why she quit me until long after I'd married your mom. Brenda was always a little wild, but I didn't know the depths of her deception until she got drunk one New Year's Eve and told what she'd done for a laugh." Then Jacob went into detail about the lies, and shook his head. "I'll admit, it was a shock, but it was in the past. Asher was two years old and as they say... I'd already made my bed."

"Oh man. Did Pearl ever know this?"

"I doubt it. And I was sad that she'd been hurt like that. Water under the bridge," Jacob said.

"Ash and Gunner send their love. They're already in investigation mode and determined to figure out why this happened and who did it. I'm staying in Amarillo to be with you," Dylan said.

"You don't need to do that, son."

"Yes, sir, I do need to do this. You were the best dad that three little boys could have, and this is our chance to give back to you. Now, I'm getting the nod that visiting time is over. I'm staying in a hotel just down the street. I'll be back in the morning to see what your doctor has to say. Just rest and get stronger." Then he leaned over and gave Jacob a gentle hug. "Love you, Dad."

"Love you, too," Jacob said, then shifted slightly and closed his eyes.

Dylan's head was spinning when he left the hospital. Finding out what Brenda had done to break up Pearl and Jacob had

been shocking. But like Jacob said, "water under the bridge." He drove past his hotel to a fast-food drive-through, and then headed back to the hotel.

The sky had been gray all day, which meant no elaborate sunset, and the bite from the wind was getting colder as the day was coming to an end. Dylan parked near the entrance and hurried inside, then took the elevator up to his room. It wasn't home, but it was warm and clean and quiet. He shed his coat, washed up, then sat down in front of the TV with his food and called Angie, talking as he ate, while she updated him on all the projects. Then he began filling her in on everything they'd learned.

"Are you three in any danger?" she asked.

"I don't see how or why we would be, but we're definitely on alert, and I have two hard-nosed cops for brothers. Don't worry about us. I'm just sorry I've dumped all the work on you, but so grateful to you. You are my world. I know you know that, but I don't say it enough. I love you, lady."

"Love you more," Angie said, and hung up.

Dylan finished his food, then cleaned up the refuse and put it in the trash. He was stripping down to shower and shave when Gunner called. He smiled. They were already checking on him.

"Hey, Gunner. Yes, I'm fine. Dad was awake and talking. He's getting stronger and they're considering moving him out of ICU into a regular room. I'll find out more tomorrow."

"Oh, good news," Gunner said.

"How's Nora?" Dylan asked.

"She's okay. Hurting some, but she is a continuing revelation," and then he proceeded to tell Dylan about Nora's stalker incident. "I'm going out on a limb and say it's also the reason she chose a job that she could work from home. That workplace stalker did a number on her, even if she won't admit it."

Dylan was stunned. "Good lord. Poor kid."

"I know. Take care. Call if you need us," Gunner said.

"Same to you," Dylan said, and then headed for the shower.

Gunner fell asleep on the sofa watching TV, and Asher covered him over with a blanket and left him there. He was a big boy. If he woke up later, he'd take himself to bed.

Nora was already in bed, but Asher needed to make one last sweep through the bar before he joined her. He felt the warmth as he opened the door between and started up the hall.

The security light lit up the parking lot, and the lights beside the door were on. The door was locked, and there was no sight of an unattended vehicle anywhere. But as an added deterrent, he jammed the back of a chair beneath the doorknob, then put a bowl of balls from one of the pool tables on the chair seat. It wouldn't stop someone from coming inside, but it would make a hell of a noise when they did it, and that's all the warning he would need.

Satisfied that all was well in the front, he went back into the house and locked the door between, then made one last sweep through the house, making sure the back door was locked, and the porch lights were on. As he walked through the kitchen, he glanced at the door leading down into the basement and on impulse, turned the lock on it, too, but when he walked into the bedroom and saw Nora lying in the bed, curled up on her side with her bandaged hand resting on a pillow, it turned on every protective instinct he had. He was never going to get over what she'd gone through alone.

He stripped, left his clothes on a chair, and headed for the shower. Minutes later, he came out freshly shaved, with a towel wrapped around his waist. The covers had slipped

from her shoulder, revealing the T-shirt she was sleeping in. He frowned, and moved closer for a better look, then froze. It was his old high school football jersey. She'd kept it all these years! Sleeping in it.

Shaken by the revelation, he removed the towel from around his waist and hung it back up in the bathroom, and ever so quietly, eased himself into bed behind her, pulled the covers up over both of them, and laid there listening to the sound of her breathing, and fell asleep.

It was just before 5:00 a.m. when Nora woke. She rolled over on her back, saw Asher sleeping in the bed beside her. Her hand was throbbing, and she needed to pee. She eased out of bed, tiptoed into the bathroom, and closed the door. When she was through, she took a pain pill from the bottle on the counter, ran a little water in the glass, and downed it.

She combed her fingers through her hair, then turned out the light before opening the door so she wouldn't wake Ash, but he was already awake.

"Are you okay?" he asked.

"Potty break and a pain pill," she said, and slipped back into bed.

He pulled up the covers, then leaned over and brushed a kiss across her lips. "You still have my old football jersey."

"I sleep in it. It was as close as I could get to being in your arms," she said.

He groaned. "I regret being the coward. For not being man enough to call and ask your mom how to contact you. Here you are still sleeping in my old jersey and every year on your birthday, I stick a candle in a piece of carrot cake, then light it and make a wish for you."

Nora's eyes welled with sudden tears. "Why did we let this happen?"

"I don't know, but having been given a second chance, there's no way in hell I'm losing you again. If you weren't hurt, you'd be naked right now. Keep that in mind, okay?"

"Okay."

He slid his arm beneath her neck and pulled her close. "It's too early to get up, darlin'. We can sleep, or we can talk. I don't care which, but I don't want to give up this bed with you in it."

"I'm hurting too much to sleep. Maybe we could talk until the pill kicks in?"

"Then I have something I wanted to ask you the entire length of our senior year. Nora Borden, will you marry me?"

"Yes. Anywhere. Anytime. In a heartbeat."

"Thank you for the second chance," he said, then kissed her again, and again, until kisses weren't enough.

Nora reached for him then, holding on to him with one hand and every ounce of her will. "Make love to me, Ash. You aren't going to hurt me. Just help me out of this shirt."

The covers flew back.

Nora sat up as Asher rose from the bed, lifted the shirt over her head, and carefully hung it on the bedpost.

In the dawning light, his silhouette momentarily blocked the window. Nora's heart was pounding as he came back to her, then he was above her. The moment he slid inside the wet heat of her, she sighed and then closed her eyes. It was just like always. One slow stroke, and she was his.

Asher's concentration was off the chart, trying not to give in to the ecstasy of her too soon, but it was good, so good, and it felt so right. He was watching every nuance of her face—every flutter of her eyelashes as the minutes passed, until he could feel her tightening from the blood rush.

At that point, he knew within moments that she was

going to wrap her legs around his waist and pull him deeper, wanting it harder, wanting more. So, he gave her what she wanted. Heard the moan, and then the catch in her breath as the climax rolled right through her, then pleased himself by letting go.

He was still inside her, even though the last ripples of their lovemaking were beginning to fade, when he propped himself up on both elbows and brushed a kiss across her lips. "We're still the perfect fit."

Nora cupped the side of his face with her good hand. "Love always fills the awkward corners of a life. Love you most. And today, because I love you, you are going to take me home. I'll be fine. Belker's delivers from the pharmacy and from the grocery. I can still do my job with one hand, while you are going to devote every waking hour to the investigation with Gunner. We have the rest of our lives. You need to get those people out of circulation before Jacob is well enough to come home. Okay?"

He knew she was right, but didn't like it. "Yes, okay."

"If you'll put a plastic bag over my hand, I would love a shower."

He looked up, saw the expectation in her eyes, and grinned. "I suppose you're going to want someone to scrub your back, too?"

Nora smiled. "You have the most beautiful blue eyes."

"Is that a yes?" he asked.

She nodded.

"You still know how to tie me in knots," he said.

He got up, wrapped a towel around his waist, and headed for the kitchen to get a plastic bag and a roll of masking tape from the junk drawer, then hurried back down the hall.

Moments later, he had the bag taped around her wrist and the water running in the shower. She'd gathered all her

long hair into one thick twist and pulled it up to the top of her head, then handed Ash a big banana clip.

"I remember how this works," he said, and deftly clipped her hair up off her neck. "The tub is slippery. Let me get in first, and then I'll steady you, darlin."

With the two of them in the shower, it was like trying to bathe a big wiggly dog in a very small tub. They managed to sling soap and water on everything but the bathroom floor. The mirror was fogged. There was steam hovering on the ceiling above their heads like a rain cloud trying to form.

He'd washed every inch of her body twice, which led her to laughingly accuse him of feeling her up for the fun of it. And to his credit, he did not deny a thing. It was just the first of many good memories to come.

When they finally got out, he dried her off first, then removed the plastic bag from her hand.

"Clean and shiny," he said.

She grinned. "Unlike the bathroom we just demolished."

He gave her backside a little swat as she walked past, and while she got dressed, he stayed behind to dry himself.

A short while later, they were in the kitchen making coffee to go with their bowls of dry cereal, when they heard Gunner shout out in the hall.

"What the hell? There's no hot water!"

They looked at each other, and then burst out laughing.

Chapter 9

ASHER RECOGNIZED THE WISDOM OF NORA'S REQUEST. They had nothing in the way of evidence that pointed to anyone, or a reason for why it had happened. Time was not on their side, so it was with reluctance that he took her home.

He carried her bag into the house, then followed her down the hall to her bedroom.

"Just leave it on the bed, love. I'll deal with it all later," she said, then wrapped her arms around his neck and kissed him until he groaned.

"Will you promise to text me now and then just to reassure me that you are okay?" he asked.

"I promise. Go find the bad guys, and keep me in the loop with Jacob's progress," she said, then walked him to the door.

As soon as he walked out, she locked the door, then stood at the window, watching him drive away before she retrieved her laptop and settled down to work.

By the time Asher got home, Gunner was dressed and in the kitchen, working on his second bowl of cereal.

"Morning, bro," Asher said.

"Take off your coat and sit," Gunner said. "Dylan unloaded some interesting info this morning while you were draining the hot water tank."

"About the case?" Asher asked.

"It's about that bombshell comment Dad made regarding Pearl," Gunner said. "It is not going to endear you any further to Brenda, but it's an eye-opener as to her moral fiber."

Asher frowned. "She already darkened her own memory for all of us, but enlighten me, anyway."

"I'll hit the high points. Brenda and Pearl were friends. Dad and Pearl were in a serious relationship. Brenda wanted Dad, so she told Pearl some horrific lie about him, and they broke up. Dad was crushed but never knew why she quit him. Then Brenda makes a play for him months later, and over time I guess Dad gives up on Pearl, and he and Brenda marry. When Asher is two, Brenda gets drunk on New Year's Eve and blurts out the whole story. Dad is horrified, but like he told Dylan, it was too late…water under the bridge. He never said anything to Pearl, and to his knowledge, she never knew the truth."

Asher shook his head in disgust. "What a bitch. And at the same time, she didn't fall short on motherhood because I know she loved us… Just not enough to give up her wild ways."

"She was the worm in the apple of my life, and FYI, the files I requested from the FBI regarding the armed car robbery arrived in my email. We're going to be doing a whole lot of reading for a while."

"Great," Asher said. "Remind me… What was it you found out from the prison warden where Pete Brandt died?"

"He rarely had visitors. None the last five years until the warden notified next of kin that he didn't have long to live. At that point, his two sons showed up. They visited briefly and Brandt was the one to end the visit and send them away."

Asher nodded. "Okay. I have seen files on the robbery

before, and if I remember, Brandt said in his statement that he'd been the one to hide the money, and he wasn't talking. Double-check that for me when you're going through the files."

"Will do. What are you gonna do?" Gunner asked.

"Run background on Brandt's sons. Maybe something will pop."

Satisfied that they had the beginnings of their investigations mapped out, they settled down to work.

Everett Brandt woke up in a mood. His neck was on the line here, and he still didn't know anything more about Kingston other than he'd survived the surgery and was in ICU. It was clearly old news because there was nothing more being reported about him or the investigation.

Freddie had already eaten his way through half the groceries they'd brought home, which aggravated him even more. Added to that, there was a storm front heading this way with temps below freezing. He was still antsy about Kingston, and made a knee-jerk decision to call the hospital, but he wasn't going to use his cell phone. He had a burner with some minutes still on it, and went to his bedroom where it was quieter to make the call.

The call went straight to the switchboard, and a woman answered.

"Northwest Texas Hospital. How may I direct your call?"

"I'm inquiring about a patient's status. Would that be registration?" he asked.

"Yes," she said. "One moment please."

A few seconds later, another female answered. "NTH, Abby speaking. How can I help you?"

"I was calling for an update on the status of a patient. His

name is Jacob Kingston. Is he still in ICU or has he been moved to a regular room?"

"I can't give specifics, but he's still in ICU."

"Right… Sure… I understand. Thank you for this much," he said, and disconnected. "So, if he's still in ICU, he's not improving," Everett muttered. "I'll take that as a plus."

He tucked the burner into the back of a drawer beneath his socks, and turned up the thermostat on his way back to the living room.

What he didn't know was that Asher had left word at the front desk not to give out any information about his father's welfare, and to notify him if there were calls. While Everett was patting himself on the back for his bit of detective work, the receptionist was calling a real detective.

The two Kingston brothers were ensconced within the warmth of their kitchen as they worked. The room was mostly silent, but for a clock ticking on the wall. A second pot of coffee was brewing as they sat making notes from the background searches, and the requested FBI files.

Finally, Asher looked up. "Brandt was married at the time of the robbery and the only member of that gang who had kids. One other man, who is now deceased, was married at the time. That wife has since divorced him and moved to Florida. They had no children. One gang member is still alive and in prison. He's the one who was shot during the robbery and ratted out the rest of the gang while he was in the hospital. No next of kin."

Gunner frowned. "It could be coincidence that this happened to Dad on the heels of Brandt's death, but it doesn't feel like it. There is nothing random about choosing to kill

a man who owns a bar, in a little town, in the middle of nowhere. No thief would assume there were any large sums of money in any of these businesses. I know the lack of law in Crossroads would be tempting, but why the kill shot when you're only intent on robbery?"

"And yet there was no robbery attempt," Asher said, and then his phone rang. He glanced at Caller ID and frowned. "It's the hospital. I'm putting it on Speaker," he said, then answered. "Asher Kingston speaking."

"Mr. Kingston, this is Carla, the receptionist at the information desk at NTH. You asked me to notify you if anyone called for information about your father."

Asher glanced at Gunner. "Yes! Are you saying someone called?"

"Yes, sir, about five minutes ago. It was a man. He didn't give me a name. He just asked if Jacob Kingston was still in ICU or if he'd been moved to a room."

"What did you tell him?" Asher asked.

"That he was still in ICU, as you requested."

"Thank you, Carla. I know there's a chance he'll be moved out soon, but we don't want that known until we've arrested the people responsible for trying to kill him, so letting the public believe he's still in ICU is the best protection he can have at the moment. Let me know if you get any further calls."

"Yes sir, I will," Carla said, and hung up.

"Well now," Gunner said.

Asher nodded. "That call didn't come from a concerned friend of Dad's, because everybody here in town goes to Pearl for information, or asks us when we're out and about. They wouldn't cold-call the hospital. Somebody is antsy about him still being alive."

Gunner reached for his laptop and logged into the police database. "What are the names of Pete Brandt's sons?"

Asher read back through his notes. "Everett and Freddie, both last names Brandt."

Gunner nodded, typed in the names. "They both have priors. Last known address on Everett is Fort Worth. Last known address on Freddie is Mansfield, which is a suburb of Dallas. We have their mug shots. What if Dylan showed those mug shots to Dad?"

"We have nothing to lose. Do it," Asher said. "While you're sending those to Dylan, I'm going to check the DMV to see if they own cars or trucks, and what kind."

Dylan was at the hospital, standing in the hall outside his dad's new room, waiting for the nurses to get him settled. Moving him out of ICU was a relief, because it meant he was getting better. And, that he was no longer limited to ten-minute visits once an hour.

He wondered what was happening back in Austin, and if the crews were all showing up on time, and how many orders had been delayed or back-ordered. Building a house was one thing, but constructing whole housing additions took an assembly-line mindset, with attention to fine details and good work crews. And his business would be going to hell right now were it not for Angie. He missed her like crazy, but he couldn't not be here. Their dad was everything to them, and there had to be a reckoning with this atrocity.

He was still standing in the hall when his phone signaled a text. It was from Gunner.

These mug shots are of Pete Brandt's sons. Show them to Dad, but don't tell him who they are. We want to know if he recognizes them. If he doesn't, then that

means we're looking in the wrong direction for the
shooters. Let me know yea or nay ASAP.

Looking at the faces of those men made Dylan's skin
crawl, then he sent a response.

They've moved Dad into a private room. I'm waiting in
the hall for them to get him settled. Let you know as
soon as possible.

A short while later, the last nurse exited Jacob's new
room, and Dylan went in, closing the door behind him.

Jacob was exhausted by all of the relocating, and it
showed.

"Dad, are you okay?"

Jacob nodded. "Just trying to find a comfortable spot,
and waiting for the pain shot to kick in."

"Gunner just sent me a couple of mug shots he wants
you to look at. If they look familiar, or if you know who they
are, we need to let him know. They're just going through a
process of elimination, I think. Are you up for it?"

"Of course. Show me," Jacob said.

Dylan pulled up the first mug shot and watched his dad's
face.

"Show me the other one," Jacob asked.

Dylan swiped the phone for the next photo to appear
and showed it to Jacob. "Do you know them?" he asked.

"Those are the two men who tried to buy the bar. Joe
and Darren Wilson were the names they gave me. Who are
they?"

"Pete Brandt's sons. Everett and Freddie."

Jacob paled. "Son of a bitch. Then it does have something
to do with that damned robbery. But what's the motive?
What do they have to gain by killing me?"

"Could you recognize them as the men who shot you?" Dylan asked.

"I never saw their faces. The only thing that could link them was one of them telling me I should have sold the bar. But that's just my word against theirs, isn't it?"

Dylan nodded. "For now, yes, but this will be a huge help to Ash and Gunner. They'll know what to do next. Give me a sec. I need to call them and let them know."

The revelation was enough to silence Jacob, and the pain meds were kicking in. When Dylan saw his dad drifting, he walked into the bathroom and shut the door to call them.

Gunner answered on the first ring and put his phone on Speaker so Asher could hear. "What did Dad say?"

"They were definitely the two men who came in asking about buying the bar, who called themselves Joe and Darren Wilson. But he could not identify them as the men who shot him. He asked who they were, and I told him. He's pretty rattled about the why. As he said, why would they have a grudge against him? He had nothing to do with anything. What would be their motive?"

"We'll figure that out," Gunner said. "It's just good to know our instincts were on the right track. It all has to do with something about the robbery. Give Dad our love. Tell him not to worry. We'll figure it out."

"Looks like it could snow," Dylan said. "Stay warm."

The call ended.

"Okay...so now we have suspects. However, we don't know where they are. They no longer reside at their last known addresses. Freddie Brandt owns a truck that is being held at a garage for collateral because he couldn't pay for the repairs, and there is no car registered to Everett. Texas is huge, and they could be anywhere, hiding out thinking the driver of that black truck made them," Ash said.

"Well, we do know that they are aware that the man they tried to kill is still alive," Gunner said.

"I'll let Dylan know about the call, and we need to decide now, what we do with what we know."

"You make the calls. I'm going to run a background check on Brenda," Gunner muttered. "There may be a buttload of stuff that we know nothing about. Stuff that Dad might not have even known. This is good. We're farther ahead now than we were when we woke up."

"I'm not going to call Reddick. I'm going to type up a report and send it to him. He can put it in his file as part of the investigation."

Nora spent the rest of the day online, and when possible, opted for some face time rather than texts and emails, to ease having to use her bandaged hand. Her boss was sympathetic, while praising her for keeping up with the job in the middle of all her personal turmoil. She had a Zoom meeting scheduled with a branch of the company in Japan, and had double-checked time zones to make sure she would still catch them at the office, and had everything she needed to refer to printed off for easy access.

Now all she had to do was dress the part. She changed her sweatshirt for a more professional top, then brushed her hair, added a slash of lipstick, and returned to the little office space she'd set up in her kitchen and waited for the others to log on. Within minutes, all five of the officers were online, with her leading the discussion, explaining what she'd found, the new firewalls she'd installed, and advised they limit access to certain areas of the factory, and limit the number of people they let in. She was back in her element, doing what she did best.

It was a quarter after four when Ash glanced up and saw the time. He and Gunner had been sitting and working almost the entire day, and were getting nowhere on locating the Brandt brothers, but after that phone call to the hospital asking about their dad's progress, they began worrying about Jacob's welfare when Dylan went to his hotel room for the night.

After a brief discussion between them, they opted to hire security for their dad, leaving Dylan free to go back to his hotel room to get some rest, then they called Dylan to tell them what they'd done. They sent him photos of the two security officers they'd hired, verifying that it was not two pictures of the same man, but identical twins.

Dylan sent a thumbs-up emoji, and an LOL.

At that point, they shut down for the night.

"I'm in no mood for cooking. I'm going to the Rose to get supper. Do you have a request, or do you want a surprise?" Ash asked.

Gunner frowned. "I'm too pissed and worn out to make another decision today. I'll take the surprise. Say hello to Nora for me."

Asher ignored the dig. "I said I was going to the Rose."

"Via the Borden detour. Take your time. I'm going to run a tub of hot water, and take a beer with me to the bath, and I'm not getting out until the water gets cold."

Ash saw the shadows in his brother's eyes. It was that background search he was running on Brenda. "Just because Mom screwed herself up, doesn't mean we have to own that, too. Don't hate. She didn't do that shit because she hated us. She hated herself. We were the collateral damage, and we survived it, and we have succeeded in spite of it. Okay?"

Gunner sighed. For a moment, he was the little boy again, absorbing his big brother's wisdom.

"Message received," he said. "Don't forget to bring me some pie." He walked out of the kitchen.

Asher frowned as he put on his coat, pocketed his phone, and picked up the tuck keys on his way out the back door, taking care to lock it behind him.

A tiny flake of snow landed on the windshield as he was driving away. As soon as he got to the parking lot at the Rose, he parked, then called Nora.

She answered on the second ring.

"Hey, you," she said. "How's it going?"

"Good enough, darlin'. I'm parked at the Rose, about to go in and order food for me and Gunner. Nobody wants to cook tonight. Can I bring something by for you, too?"

"That would be wonderful. I've been all over the world via Zoom meetings today and I'm exhausted."

"What sounds good to you?" he asked.

"Anything I don't have to eat with two hands, and I love you for thinking of me."

"Always. See you soon. Love you," he said.

"Love you biggest," she said, and hung up.

He was still grinning when he got out of the truck and went inside.

The place was busy with diners coming and going. As he approached the register, he heard a loud bang that sounded like a dozen skillets had just fallen off a rack, and then an "Oh, for pity's sake!" shout from Pearl.

Moments later, Pearl stepped into the dining room. "Sorry for the racket. That was just the diamond falling out of my ring," she said, and bustled back into the kitchen, leaving the diners laughing.

Ash grinned. Somebody was going to catch hell after she closed up shop. Pearl was little, but she was mighty, and nobody wanted to be on her bad side.

He read the menu, and saw the special written on the

chalkboard, and when Darla showed up to take his order, he was ready.

"Evening, Darla. I need two orders of beef stew and cornbread, with peach cobbler, then another order of beef stew and cornbread with apple pie in a separate order. I'm dropping one off at Nora's house and taking the others home with me."

"Got it," Darla said, and hurried back to the kitchen to deliver the order.

Ash sat down on a little bench to wait, and began reading faces, something he'd developed on the job. Two of the three men at one table were angry, but he couldn't tell if they were angry with each other, or a situation. The other man was ignoring both of them and eating his food.

A mother was feeding a toddler from her plate and trying to have a conversation with her husband at the same time. She looked weary, but she was smiling, obviously happy with her lot in life, and while she was feeding the baby, her husband was feeding her bites from his own plate.

Their obvious devotion to each other was noted. He tried to remember if Brenda had been like that. He remembered she always had good food cooked, and helped them with their homework, and made sure they had clean clothes, and went to all of their school events, and tucked them in at night. But he didn't remember her playing with them. Maybe because there were three of them, she expected them to play with each other.

He shrugged off the thought and looked away. He hadn't thought of her like this in years, until the shooting. Now every memory he'd had of her was creeping back into his consciousness, and he didn't like it.

A short while later, Darla came back with his orders. He noticed as he was driving away that the predicted storm front was approaching. The sky was already dark, and the

wind was rising. He drove straight to Nora's house and got out on the run. Before he could knock, she opened the door.

"Come into this house," she said, then closed the door behind him.

"Storm's approaching," he said. "Is everything tied down that you don't want to blow away?"

She laughed. "I'm good, unless the house gives up the ghost, too."

He set her food on the table and then wrapped his arms around her. "You smell good. You feel good in my arms. I may perish for lack of your loving before this investigation ends."

"We did without each other for a really long time. As long as I know I am attached to you again, I will take whatever time allows. Now kiss me senseless and take yourself home before the storm hits."

His face was cold, but his lips were warm. The kiss was both a hello and a goodbye, as she melted into his embrace, but it was the wind that ended their reverie.

"Good lord, Ash. That was a blast. Go home with your food. Call me whenever."

He sighed. "I'm going as soon as I get your food out of the bag." He carefully lifted the hot container of beef stew, the cornbread wrapped in foil, and the little box with her apple pie, loosened the seal on the bowl of stew, then wiped his hands. "I think you can manage from here. Love you, baby. Enjoy."

"Thank you so much, and I will."

She followed him to the door, turned on the porch light as he drove away, then locked the door and pulled the shades. She could still feel his kiss as she sat down to eat. The food was good, but the love that came with it warmed her heart and her belly. And as she ate, the day turned to night. The wind howled, and the tumbleweeds rolled.

At 5:00 p.m. sharp, a giant of a man named Bill Eldredge showed up at Jacob Kingston's room armed and in uniform, flashed his identification and introduced himself to Jacob and Dylan.

"Bill Eldrege. Starpoint Security—retired military reporting for duty. My twin brother Phil will be taking the day shift. We're identical, so don't assume that's me doing twenty-four-hour shifts."

Dylan grinned. He liked the man on sight. He was Reacher-sized and armed. "My brother sent me a photo of you for verification. We can't be too careful right now."

Eldredge nodded. "Understood. I know Asher Kingston. Got quite the reputation and all good. I know of Gunner. Homicide hotshot, they call him. Asher is methodical. Gunner is persistent. They'll get their man. Rest assured that Starpoint Security is here for your father."

"Much appreciated," Dylan said, and left the hospital, relieved beyond words that the security aspect had been taken out of his hands.

He was tired, worried about the Brandt connection to the shooting, and hungry as he headed to his hotel. Once he was in the room, he ordered Thai food from DoorDash, took off his boots, stretched out on the bed to wait for it to arrive, and fell asleep.

He woke an hour later to a knock at the door, then rolled off the bed to retrieve his food. He ate his solitary meal with the TV for company, while missing home and Angie. He knew she was going to a birthday party for a friend of theirs this evening, and he was waiting for her text to let him know she was home safe before he laid his head down again.

Sunup came to West Texas, bringing with it another blustery, cold day without the threat of snow.

Nora was puttering around the kitchen while her coffee was brewing, learning how to manage with her bandaged hand. The pain pills were keeping the worst of her misery at bay.

When her phone rang, she knew before she picked it up it was going to be Ash, and it was.

"Hey, you. I'm fine. I love you," she said.

Ash laughed, and the sound of his voice made her ache for him.

"Love you more, and I have a technical question. Neither Gunner nor I are proficient in tech problems, but I have a question. Right after he logged in on his laptop, the screen froze. He tried to turn it off and on again, but as Coach Teters used to say when I got a wild hair to call a play on my own, 'Boy, that ain't happenin.'"

Nora burst out laughing. "Is Gunner there?"

"Yes."

"Then put your phone on Speaker so he can hear me, and I'll walk him through it. There are a couple of things we can do before you need to panic. Sometimes a simple power surge can cause something like that. Are you ready, Gunner?"

"I'm listening."

"I'm assuming you've already tried to turn it off and nothing is happening."

"Yes, I did try that," he said.

"Then we're going to try Control/Escape. Press down on the Ctrl button and the Esc button at the same time. Hold them down and see if the screen reacts. If it does, release the keys, then tell me what the prompt says."

"Holding, holding, holding, hold... Oh! Yes, hot damn, girl, you're the best. It tells me it didn't shut down properly and is giving me prompts."

"Can you follow those prompts without confusion?" she asked.

"Yes, yep, doing it now. Oh man, okay... It's rebooting," Gunner said.

"Then you should be good to go. If you have any other problems, just give me a call. I'll come over and check it out more thoroughly," she said.

"Just think... When you and Ash get married, we'll have our own tech genius. Can't beat a deal like that," he said. "Okay... it's up and running like normal now. Thank you so much."

Ash was laughing as he took the phone off Speaker. "Well, now you know where you stand in this family," he said.

Nora was grinning. "Being indispensable is job protection. Stay warm. Love you."

"Love you more. I'll see you sometime today, if that's okay with you?"

She smiled. "Totally okay, just come prepared."

"Prepared for what?" he asked.

"For me. You turned on all the want I'd stored away, and now I can't think of anything else."

"Lord," he muttered.

"Don't ask Him for help. It's you I want to see walkin' in my door."

Ash was still laughing when she disconnected.

Dylan was dressed for the weather as he got in the SUV, but when he turned the key to start the engine, noticed he was low on fuel. So instead of the hospital, he headed for the nearest gas station and pulled in at an open pump, pocketed a credit card and the keys as he got out, then started refueling.

He was standing with his back to the wind and waiting for the pump to kick off when he happened to look up and saw two men coming out of a store across the street. One was a tall, thin redhead. The other a big, stocky blond. When they headed for the white Mustang parked at the curb, he couldn't believe what he was seeing, and immediately grabbed his phone and started taking picture after picture after picture, making sure he got the tag number on the car, as well. If it hadn't been for the gas still pumping in his car, he would have given chase. There was no way to know where they were holed up, but he had proof that the Brandt brothers were in Amarillo. The moment he screwed the gas cap back on, he got in the car and began sending picture after picture to Asher's phone.

They're in Amarillo. I was fueling up when I saw them. They were gone before I could get loose from the pump. But now we know that they're here.

Chapter 10

ASHER WAS FRYING BACON WHEN HE GOT DYLAN'S TEXT.

"It's Dylan," he said, then pulled up the message. "No way! What are the odds," he said, and handed his phone to Gunner. "Take a look at this!"

"Oh crap! They're in Amarillo! I'm running that tag right now," Gunner said.

Asher sent a big smiley emoji to Dylan and a two-word response.

You rock!

Then he remembered the bacon, took the strips out of the skillet, and set it off the burner to cool a bit before he fried the eggs. The urge to dance was strong, but he was saving his urges for Nora.

He finished making breakfast, and they talked as they ate, while waiting for the info on that car tag to come up.

"I have to let Sheriff Reddick know the Brandt brothers are in Amarillo, but at an unknown address. And we still can't pin the shooting on them without valid evidence," Asher said.

Gunner nodded. "Pearl didn't get a tag number. She didn't see if there were two men in the car. Reddick has a DNA nightmare in progress because of too many people in the bar before the shooting. I can't believe how much DNA was on Dad's clothing."

"Because he was crawling all over the floor trying to get his gun," Asher said. "Makes me sick just thinking about it. How scared he must have been. And how helpless he must have felt. And there's still no freaking motive."

Gunner agreed. "We really don't want Reddick trying to pick them up for questioning and have nothing concrete to link them beyond a conversation that would be Dad's word against theirs. All that would do would be to make them run, then Dad would come home to nothing being resolved."

"I'll talk to the sheriff. He'll likely agree with us," Asher said, and began clearing off the table and loading the dishwasher. "I'm going over to see Nora sometime today, but if you need the truck, I'll wait until you're back to go."

Gunner stowed the butter and jelly in the refrigerator. "I have no need to get my ass out into the cold, but I do need to do laundry. If you want anything washed, toss it out in the hall. I'll throw it in with my load."

"Yeah, I will, and thanks," Asher said, then dried his hands and went to sort it out.

Dylan was walking up the hall to Jacob's room when he saw their guard sitting in a chair outside the door.

"Morning," he said. "I'm Dylan Kingston. Are you still Bill, or is Phil on duty now?"

The man stood. "I'm Phil. Nothing untoward to report, and I'm told your father is doing well."

"Awesome," Dylan said. "And, I have something to show you." He pulled up the pictures he'd just taken and showed them to Phil. "These are the two men we suspect of the shooting. We don't have enough proof for an arrest, but knowing what the enemy looks like is always a good thing."

Phil eyed the photos, then nodded. "If you would be so

kind as to send a couple of these to my phone, I will share them with Bill," he said, then gave his phone number to Dylan.

"Will do," Dylan said, picked out two pictures to send, and then went into Jacob's room. He'd already made the decision not to say anything to Jacob. He didn't need the stress. "Morning, Dad! How goes your world today?"

Jacob smiled. "It goes well, considering. Everything okay at the bar?"

"Yep. Asher and I replaced the broken glass in the front door of the bar. It will need new lettering on the front, but that could happen later. They're deep into the investigation, and that's about all the news I know. Oh...nearly forgot. Asher and Nora have made peace and renewed their relationship. You might wind up with two daughters-in-law after all."

"That's the best news I've had in weeks," Jacob said.

"Have you had breakfast yet?" Dylan asked.

"Yes, I've been fed and bathed, and feel like a baby just waiting to be burped."

Dylan grinned. "It would take a pretty big person to put you over their shoulder." Then he brushed Jacob's hair away from his forehead and sat down beside him. "When I was little, I thought you were a superhero."

Jacob's eyes widened. "Did you really? Why?"

Dylan shrugged. "You were so tall, and all muscled up. And you looked like a version of Superman to me. You had black hair and blue eyes, and that strong, sharp cut to your jaw. You looked invincible, even before I knew what that meant."

Jacob gave his son's hand a squeeze. "And yet I wasn't any kind of a superhero. Just a man who made mistakes, and lived life, and has three of the best sons a man could lay claim to."

"Well, the other two are unraveling all kinds of stuff, and all of us have been thrown back into the past, whether we like it or not. You've never talked about any of it, but we're grown now, and I'm curious. What do you remember about the day of the robbery?"

Jacob frowned. "Not a lot... Mostly because I didn't know about any robbery until we heard it on the morning news the next day. And I didn't associate your mother with any of it, so it wasn't a remarkable event to me until after the fall. The FBI interrogated me as a possible accomplice until they finally accepted that Brenda's affair and association with Brandt would not have included me in their plans."

"Lord, Dad. That must have been horrible."

"It was," Jacob said. "But you boys were the most important. You were devastated that she was gone and didn't understand why. Asher was the only one old enough to realize what a slur she'd left on our name."

"So, what, if anything, do you remember about that day?"

"Well, it was Gunner's seventh birthday. She told me she was going to Amarillo to pick up presents and groceries and a birthday cake. She was gone all morning and well past noon before I saw her drive up. I didn't think any more about it, because as soon as she unloaded groceries, she took off to school to pick you all up. The evening was normal. I popped in long enough to watch Gunner open presents and eat a piece of his cake, told him happy birthday, and went back to the bar. Your mom cleaned up supper stuff and put you all to bed."

"She didn't seem weird in any way when you went to bed?"

"I remember she told me about Gunner losing a tooth, and all the bleeding and crying. And that she wrote a letter to the tooth fairy to please excuse Gunner for swallowing his tooth. Then she put a dollar under his pillow later and

took away the note. I told her she was a good mother. I don't remember anything after that."

"And that's it?"

Jacob shrugged. "The next morning, we heard the news report about the robbery, and that the wounded gang member ratted everyone out. I suppose she knew then that her days were numbered. She took you boys to school, then came home. She was in the house when the Feds showed up. She was just sitting on the sofa, like she'd been waiting for them. Told me she was sorry as they led her out in handcuffs. Nobody knew she'd already swallowed most of a full prescription of anti-depression meds. And you know the rest."

"Not really. I guess I blocked out every good thing I would have remembered about her, and as you know, Gunner believed that she killed herself because she didn't love him. He's a grown-ass man and still holds that grudge against her."

"I know, but I have faith that one day he's going to find a woman who will heal every broken piece of him. Like you did. And like Ash did."

A few minutes later, a nurse came in and interrupted the visit. "Mr. Kingston, we're going to go for a little walk down the hall and back. It's time to start building up your strength."

Dylan stood. "Then I'll take myself out of the way of good works. I'll be back this afternoon, Dad. Is there anything you want? Maybe something to read?"

"My reading glasses are at home. I'm okay," he said.

"Okay then. See you later."

He heard the nurse talking to Jacob as he was walking out.

"Your son looks a lot like you," she said.

"I have three sons. They all wound up with a double dose of my DNA."

Dylan thought about that all the way to the elevator. They'd made him proud, and now they had to keep him alive.

Asher typed up yet another report on the Brandt brothers and included multiple photos of them that Dylan had taken, and sent it to Reddick at the Briscoe County Sheriff's office, along with the opinion that picking them up at this point for interrogation would go nowhere until they had actual proof and a motive for doing it, then hit Send.

He was still reading through FBI files when Gunner sat down at the table and opened his laptop. "The info came back on the owner of that white Mustang. It belongs to a man named Carl Lee Sherman, presently a resident of a Texas prison. It was reported stolen after his incarceration. And here's the connection. He was a resident of Fort Worth, as was Everett Brandt. That's how they came to be driving that car. They stole it!" Then he frowned. "But we don't want them picked up for car theft."

Ash frowned. "No, we don't, but Reddick might. Sit on this for a bit and let him do his own digging. They have the photos now. They can run their own search. It'll give us a little more time."

"Agreed," Gunner said, and saved the info in his work file. "I don't know about you, but I need a break. All of the info we've gathered isn't getting us to where we need to go."

"We skipped lunch. Wanna go to the Rose?" Asher asked.

"Yes, please! But we can't do fun stuff without your girl. Call her. Tell her to pack her sleepover bag and we're picking her up."

Ash paused. "Thank you, Gunner. You like her, don't you?"

He shrugged. "When you were dating her, she felt like a

sister. I was sorry for the both of you when you lost touch, and knowing she'll be part of our family now is good."

"I'll call her," Ash said.

Nora was curled up in the middle of her bed, going through a pile of old photos when her phone rang. She saw Caller ID and smiled.

"Hey, you," she said.

"Slight change of plans if you're amenable to it. Gunner and I are both calling a halt for the day. Pack your sleepover bag. We're coming to get you to eat early supper with us, then home we go."

She started smiling. "My sleepover bag. I love that. Give me a few and I'll be ready, and I love the invitation."

"See you in a few. Love you."

She was still smiling when she disconnected, then rolled off the bed and went to the closet to get a duffel bag and began packing, taking care to throw in the bottle of pain pills. The stitches were beginning to draw, making it harder for her to flex her fingers.

As soon as she had her bag ready, she slipped off the old sweatshirt she was wearing and put on a pink sweater, and hurried across the room in her sock feet to get a pair of slip-on shoes. She caught a glimpse of herself in a mirror and paused. Her eyes were bright. Her cheeks were flushed. She hadn't seen herself like this in years, and it was all due to having Asher back in her life.

When she heard the knock at her door, she abandoned her reverie. The cavalry had arrived!

"It's unlocked! Come in!" she shouted, then put on her coat, dropped her phone in the pocket, and was reaching for her purse when Asher walked into her room, laughing.

"Woman… What do you mean…it's unlocked?" he said, and wrapped his arms around her.

She laughed. "I knew you were on the way. Stop fussing and kiss me," so he did. Deeply. Longingly, and reluctantly let her go. "Gunner's keeping your seat warm," he said. "Is this the bag you're taking?"

"Yes."

He ran a finger down the side of her cheek. "Got your nightie?"

"Don't make fun of my sleepwear," she said. "Besides, you know you're just going to take it off."

He was still smiling as he picked up the bag and led the way out of the house. Nora paused to turn on the porch light, then locked the door and followed Ash to the truck.

Gunner winked at her as Ash helped her up into the seat, then buckled her in.

"Hey, Lefty, how's it going?" he asked.

She held up her bandaged hand. "Still hanging on. Shifting subject matter on you guys now. How's the investigation going?"

"All kinds of puzzle pieces, but we're missing that corner piece. The one that makes everything else fit," Asher said.

"We'll get there. We just need to refuel ourselves, thus the trip to the Yellow Rose," Gunner said.

"Well, thanks for including me in the party," Nora said as Asher backed out of her driveway. He put the car in Drive, then reached across the seat and clasped her hand as he drove away.

The parking lot was over half full when they arrived, and entering the Yellow Rose was like visiting family. The warmth of enticing scents and the faces of people

they knew greeted them as they headed toward an empty table.

"Nora! What are you doing with those two outlaws?" someone called out.

"None of your business!" she said, which made Asher smile.

They shed their coats, leaving them on the empty chair at the table as they sat.

Menus were on the table, as were coffee cups and flatware.

Nora saw Cheryl coming with a full carafe of coffee and noticed Cheryl had gone from a blond to a redhead since the last time she'd seen her.

"Coffee?" Cheryl asked.

"Yes, please," Nora said. "And I love what you've done with your hair. It suits you."

Cheryl beamed. "Freaked my kids out, but my better half likes it."

She filled all their cups and moved on as they were reaching for the menus. Again, Nora was limited by choices because of the bandage, then saw fried catfish and hush puppies were the daily special and that ended her indecision.

"I'm having the special," she said, then leaned back with her hands in her lap, while the men were still deliberating, remembering the times she'd spent here with her family, and with Asher and his brothers. The only times he'd left them behind was when they were on a real date, then let go of the memories when Cheryl came back to take their orders.

Asher had been keeping a casual eye on Nora, and when he saw her staring out the windows, he knew she'd gone somewhere else. Somewhere too far away for him to reach.

He was still considering the wisdom of interfering with her muse, or letting her be where she needed to be, when a man staggered in with a boy not yet in his teens behind

him. He paused at the doorway as he looked for a place to sit, and then stumbled across the dining area to the empty table behind where they were seated.

Gunner eyed him as they passed, then gave Asher a look. "Jasper Henry. Drunk as a skunk," he muttered.

Asher nodded.

Within seconds, Jasper shouted, "Anybody waitin' tables in here? Leroy wants a burger!"

Before either waitress could turn around, Pearl appeared. "Whoever is yelling in here, this isn't a bar. Keep it down."

But Jasper was too drunk to get the message, and chose to argue, instead.

"Yeah, and if the damned bar wasn't closed, that's where I would be," he shouted.

Before Nora knew what was happening, Ash and Gunner had come up out of their chairs and were standing at Jasper Henry's table.

"What the hell? Get outta my face! Why ain't you runnin' the bar for your daddy? A man needs a drink now and then."

"It appears you have found a whole lot of liquor on your own, and without our daddy's help," Asher said. "You need not to be shouting at Pearl and disrupting the diners."

"I can do whatever I want, when I want," Jasper shouted, and started to stand up.

Gunner leaned over, looked Jasper square in the eye, and said, "No sir, you cannot. It's called disturbing the peace."

And then they pulled their badges out in unison. "Asher Kingston, special investigator for the attorney general's office."

"Gunner Kingston, homicide detective with the Dallas PD. You are setting a bad example for your son."

The mention of his son shifted Jasper's focus. He saw a mixture of fear and shame in his little boy's eyes and wilted. "I didn't mean nothing by it," Jasper mumbled.

Asher sighed. "You already know why the bar is closed. You know somebody tried to kill our father, and that's why we're here. We're not leaving Crossroads until the guilty party is behind bars. Was it you?"

Jasper Henry's eyes widened in sudden horror. "No, no, hell no, I didn't kill no one. I'm sorry for what I said. Me and the boy will be leavin'. My apologies to Miss Pearl."

"Unfortunately for you, you aren't driving anywhere," Gunner said.

Ash saw the fallen look on the little boy's face. "Hey, Leroy, it's okay. You're not in trouble, and neither is your daddy. He's just had too much to drink, hasn't he?"

Leroy nodded.

"Is your mama at home?" Asher asked.

"Yes sir."

"Does she have a car to drive?"

Leroy nodded.

Gunner knew where his brother was going with this. "Jasper, I'm gonna be needing your wife's phone number."

Jasper groaned. "She'll have my hide."

"You should have thought of that before you decided to get pie-faced drunk with your son in the car. Give me her number," Gunner said.

The dining room was silent, the diners watching as the drama unfolded.

As for Pearl, the moment she saw Ash and Gunner step into the uproar, she went back to the kitchen, satisfied they had it under control.

Jasper pulled up his wife's number.

Gunner called it, then stood waiting until she answered. "Hello?"

"Mrs. Henry, this is Gunner Kingston. Your husband is at the Yellow Rose, too drunk to drive, and your son Leroy is with him. They are unharmed, but they need a ride home.

You can lock Jasper's car, take the keys, and make sure he does not retrieve his vehicle until sometime tomorrow when he's cold sober."

"Oh, my God," she muttered. "You're one of Jacob's boys, aren't you?"

"Yes, ma'am, I am."

"I'll be right there. Thank you for calling," she said.

While all of that was happening, Nora's heart had gone out to the little boy. She slipped up to the front desk and was now waiting for Darla to finish sacking up six of Pearl's cowboy cookies. They were giant oatmeal chocolate chip cookies that she sold individually wrapped. Leroy wasn't going to get his burger, but maybe these would help, and as soon as Darla gave her the bag, Nora headed back.

Ash and Gunner were holding Jasper up to keep him from falling as they walked him out of the Rose. Leroy was behind them, his head down, his eyes blurred with tears, when Nora stopped him.

"Leroy, honey, these are for you and your mama," she whispered. "None of this is your fault. You are a good son for trying to take care of your daddy, okay?"

Leroy looked in the sack, blinking back tears. "Thank you, lady."

"You're welcome, sweetheart. Go on now, and don't be scared of the big guys. They're really, really nice men."

Just as they reached the door to go out, Ash realized Leroy wasn't behind them. He looked back and saw Nora talking to him, then giving him a little sack and a pat on the back, right before he bolted for the door.

Nora was smiling as she watched Leroy run to catch up, and at that moment, she saw Asher watching her and winked, then went back to their table.

As soon as Leroy caught up, they walked Jasper out, with Leroy at their heels.

"She gave me cookies for taking good care of my daddy!" Leroy said, clutching the white sack against his chest like the treasure it was.

"She's a really nice lady," Asher said.

The little boy beamed. "She's pretty."

Asher smiled. "She's that, too."

By the time Jasper's wife arrived, the cold wind and the shame had gone a long way to sobering him up. But, when he started to get in the front seat, his wife stopped him.

"You sit in the back seat. Leroy rides with me," she said, and loaded him into the front seat, leaving Jasper to get himself into the rear.

"That's one pissed-off woman," Gunner said.

Ash nodded. "With good reason," he said, and led the way back inside.

Cheryl had just delivered their food to the table as they sat.

"I waited...almost," Nora said, pointing to the bite she'd taken out of one of her hush puppies.

Ash leaned over and kissed her on the cheek. "You pulled the stinger out of that little boy's heart. You are the best."

Gunner nodded. "Not gonna get an argument out of me about that. Let's eat. I'm all fired up to get back to work. All I needed was a confrontation to stir the brain cells."

Pearl came to their table with three desserts on a tray.

"Bouncer pay and one for Nora," she said, and flipped back to the kitchen.

The night sky was clear. The sky was full of stars, but it was too cold for stargazing and too early to go to bed, so the current residents of Jacob Kingston's house had gathered in the living room to watch a movie. They let Gunner pick. He chose *The Bourne Legacy*.

"Why do you always choose this one?" Ash asked.

"Jeremy Renner. He's a badass in that movie, and a badass in real life. Anybody who survives being run over with a snowplow is a badass."

Nora glanced at the brothers but said nothing, guessing it likely had something to do with their family history, as much as the movie.

Two hours later, they had moved into the kitchen and were playing Train with a set of dominoes.

"You can't put that double six there," Ash said.

Gunner grinned. "I didn't think you were paying attention."

"I'm out," Nora said, and got up to refill her drink. When she sat back down, they were still going at it. "Can I ask questions about the investigation? You already know you can trust me, and I'll match my security clearance and your security clearance and raise you," she said.

The mere mention of security clearance got their attention, and the game of Train slid to a halt.

"You have security clearance?" Asher asked.

"I'm in IT. I consult worldwide. Yes, I have security clearance. You both said you have information. You also said the pieces don't fit with your theory. I'm a troubleshooter...of sorts. I'm here. I already know about the white Mustang. I know you are trying to connect it with Pete Brandt's death. I understand the timing could just be coincidence, but I doubt it, and I think you both do, too."

The men looked at each other. Gunner shrugged. "Fine by me."

Ash leaned back in the chair, eyeing the intent expression on her face, and then he began.

"We had nowhere to go with the investigation until Dad woke up. He told us that a week before the shooting, two men came to the bar, and asked him if he was interested

in selling it. They said their names were Joe and Darren Wilson, and even then, he knew they'd given him fake names and told them he wasn't interested in selling. They left. About a week later, the shooting happened. It was two men. He couldn't see their faces. Didn't recognize their voices, but the one who took him down from behind whispered in his ear, 'you should have sold the bar, old man,' and then the other one shot him."

Nora was leaning forward now, resting her arms on the table, intent on every word.

After that, Ash began to lay out the rest. About the avalanche of DNA from the bar, and the background research they did on every gang member, and about Brandt's sons visiting him at the prison on his deathbed.

Then Gunner filled her in on the FBI files they'd accessed about the armored car robbery, and Pete Brandt's statement that he'd hidden the money and was going to take the location with him to the grave. He told her about learning of Brandt's sons visiting him in prison. That after he and Asher ran background checks on both Everett and Freddie Brandt and learned they both had priors.

Asher picked up the story, explaining how Jacob identified them from their mug shots as being the men who asked about buying the bar. But he could not identify either of the men who shot him.

"So now we knew that much. But neither of Brandt's sons was at his last known address. One in Fort Worth, one in Mansfield, a suburb of Dallas, and neither of them owned, or had ever owned a white Mustang. Then yesterday morning, Dylan was at a gas station refueling before going to see Dad, and who does he see coming out of a store across the street, but both of Brandt's sons, getting into an older white Mustang. He was caught at the pumps and couldn't get free in time to follow them, but he took a

good dozen pictures, including several with a good shot of the car tag."

"I ran the tag," Gunner said. "It came back reported stolen. It was stolen after the owner was imprisoned for a crime. Everett Brandt was living in Fort Worth at the time. Apparently, he knew the owner was in prison, so he stole it. And that's where we are."

Ash nodded. "We now know they're somewhere in Amarillo, but we don't want them picked up just for car theft, and we have zero motive for why they would want Dad dead. We also have hired around-the-clock security on Dad's room."

Nora had been silent through the entire scenario they'd laid out, but for her, there was one huge omission.

"I already see a glaring hole in all of it, but if we're going to discuss this, it needs to be all of you hearing it and answering questions for me. Would it be possible to call Dylan, then put the phone on Speaker so he could be a part of it?"

Asher nodded, then made the call and was waiting for an answer.

Dylan picked up on the fourth ring. "Hey, Ash, what's up?"

"Nora is here. Long story, but we've been having a gathering of evidence meeting, and as we laid out what we knew, she found a gap...something we hadn't even thought of, but she didn't want to start discussing it without including you. Are you free to be in on this right now?"

"Absolutely," he said.

"Okay, I'm going to put you on Speaker so you can hear everything we're about to hear." He set the phone down on the table in front of Nora.

"Dylan, this is Nora, can you hear me okay?"

"Yes, ma'am. Fire away."

"This is for all of you. I'm going to ask questions for

you to think about, and if you know the answers, speak up, okay?"

"Okay," they echoed, and so she began.

"Pete Brandt told the Feds he hid the money, and that he was taking the location to his grave, and they took that as gospel. Am I right?"

"It's a written statement in their files," Asher said.

"And his sons were called to his bedside only hours before he died?" she said.

"The warden notified them what was happening with their father, and they came," Asher said.

"This is pure conjecture, but what if Pete Brandt told his boys where the money was buried?" Nora said. "And if he did, then why would their next port of call be your father's bar?"

Gunner stilled. Asher paled, and Dylan was in shock, too stunned to comment.

"Okay…don't answer that," Nora said. "Just think about it. Now I'm going to switch gears a bit. You're all too close to this to see the hole in the investigation, but it's big as Dallas to me."

"We're listening," Asher said. "Ask."

"What was happening in your world…in your house… the day of the robbery? Jacob isn't here, so I can't ask him, and I know at this time, you're all three still kids. What do you remember?"

"It was my birthday," Gunner said. "I turned seven. We were having cake and presents after school."

"I needed a permission slip signed, and mom couldn't find a pen. She signed it with a crayon," Dylan said.

"Mom took us to school like always. She told me she was going to Amarillo to get presents and a birthday cake. This was before Belker's had the deli. She said she'd be home in time to pick us up from school," Asher said.

Nora nodded. "Okay then, so whatever part she took in the robbery is unknown, right?"

Asher reeled as if he'd just been slapped. "My God, you're right."

"Wait... What?" Gunner said.

Dylan's heart was pounding. "I don't get it. What does that mean?"

"It means that there was no official statement ever taken, because she killed herself before they could interrogate her," Nora said. "Nobody knows what she was doing, only that she'd been 'in on it', and that was according to the gang member who was shot and gave them all up."

Asher already saw where this was going. It was like watching an avalanche coming straight at him, without the ability to move away.

"So, school is out now," Nora said. "Who picked you up?"

"Mom did," Asher said. "She brought us a bag of chips and a cold drink to share, when she picked us up."

"Then what? How was the party?" she asked.

"It was like always. Dad came from the bar long enough to eat cake and watch Gunner open presents. Mom was licking icing off her fingers. We had hot dogs and chips for supper because that's what Gunner wanted. We watched a Disney movie. We went to bed," Ash said, but his heart was pounding. "I don't know anything after that until Gunner woke up bawling, covered in blood."

"We slept together, Gunner and me... I had to change my pajamas, too, because some of his blood was on me," Dylan said.

Gunner's face was white. "I had a loose tooth. I swallowed it in my sleep and woke up to all the blood. I was upset about no tooth for the tooth fairy."

Nora could hear the panic in their voices and hated being

the reason it was there, but she couldn't stop. It wouldn't show them what they needed to see. What they'd known all along.

"Then what happened?" she asked.

Asher couldn't look at her—at the sympathy on her face. "Gunner was hysterical, and when Mom didn't show up, I got out of bed and went to see what all the crying was about. When I went in the boys' room and saw all the blood, then figured out Gunner was mad, not dying, I went looking for Mom, but she wasn't in the house. I got a clean washcloth and handed it to Gunner to stop the bleeding, then made a second sweep through the house, calling for her and..." he hesitated, frowning...trying to remember the order of it all. "She was in the kitchen then, and her hands were dirty, so she washed up at the sink and followed me back to the boys' room, calmed Gunner down, cleaned him up and put clean sheets on the bed, then wrote a note to the tooth fairy to excuse his missing tooth and all was well. We went back to bed."

Nora's heart skipped. "Her hands were dirty? How were they dirty, Ash? What was on them?"

He closed his eyes, trying to recall the details of that moment. "Dirt. It was dirt... On her hands...and on the knees of her jeans." And then he stood abruptly. "Shit... Oh shit... She was coming up from the basement. She didn't hear me the first time because she was down in the basement."

Dylan was flat on his back, staring at the ceiling, while his brothers were miles away, staring at the basement door.

"Do you store tools down there? Yard tools? Like rakes and shovels?" Nora asked.

"Yes," Dylan said. "I was the kid who loved tools. I knew where every tool was, and where it belonged on the board where Dad hung them."

"When you couldn't find her the first time, she could have been outside burying the box, or in the cellar, burying a box," Nora said. "And when you came looking for her the second time, she could have already come back into the house and was putting up a shovel, or coming up from the basement after using it down there. And again…it's just a theory. But it does make all of your random facts fit, doesn't it?"

Gunner's face was frozen in a grimace of disbelief, and Asher was staring at the kitchen clock above the stove. Dylan was trying to absorb the fact that the basement that had once been his best place to play, could have been hiding such a secret.

Nora couldn't bear it for them anymore. "I can only imagine what you're all going through, and I'm so sorry. But you want to make the world safe for Jacob again, and being the ones to find that money first, removes every aspect of the danger it put Jacob in. Forgive me if I've hurt you. Please don't hate me for it."

"No hate for you ever," Dylan said, but they could hear the tears in his voice.

Asher reached for her hand. "Nobody hates you. You're freaking good at what you saw that we didn't. And you're right. We were too close to see the obvious."

"No hate for you ever," Gunner said. "But answer me this? Why would Brandt lie and say he hid it?"

Nora paused before answering, carefully measuring her words.

"Again, this is supposition, but if Brandt already knew your mother was dead before he was officially interrogated, and if he said he'd given it to her to hide, the Feds would have tracked the timeline and eventually found it for sure. But since Brandt knew your dad was completely oblivious to their affair, if he stayed quiet, he knew Jacob would never

even think it was on his property. Nobody would ever think to look for it here."

Gunner got up. "You know we have to go down there. Let's get it over with."

"And you also know we're not going see a damn thing, because all three of us played in that dirt, and it wasn't covered with bricks until my senior year of high school. And we've stomped all over that place countless times in the years since, carrying stuff up and down the stairs for Dad," Ash said.

"Hell, I played down there, and I didn't see anything. I was in and out of that place all through high school because I'm the one who kept Dad's old truck running, until he finally traded for a new one," Dylan said.

"I'm still going down there. Are you coming?" Gunner asked.

"We'll all go," Nora said.

Asher unlocked the door. It swung back into the kitchen as he reached inside the stairwell and flipped on the lights, instantly flooding the entire interior.

"I'm going down first. Gunner, you follow Nora."

Chapter 11

LIKE ASHER SAID, THERE WAS NOTHING OBVIOUS TO BE seen that they hadn't seen a thousand times before.

"This place is huge," Nora said. "I don't think I've been down here before."

"It's the entire footprint of the house above us. It had a hard-packed dirt floor for years, but every time we went down and came up, we tracked in dust. Mom hated it. Dad kept promising to finish it off with a pour of concrete, but then she was gone, and nothing mattered anymore," Asher said.

"So, how did you come by all these bricks?" Nora asked.

"I remember," Gunner said. "I was about twelve... maybe thirteen. They were tearing down an old brick building in Silverton. Anybody who wanted bricks could come to the site and load up what they wanted. Ash measured the area of the cellar, the size of the bricks, and figured out how many we'd need to cover the floor. It was a surprise for Dad's birthday. We did it Ash's senior year of high school during spring break."

"That's quite an engineering feat for a kid still in high school," Nora said.

"I wasn't all that. I asked my math teacher how to figure it," Asher said.

She slipped her arm around his waist. "You are all that, and a piece of cake," she said. "All three of you are amazing. You, Dylan, and Gunner. Jacob did good."

"Asher helped. He stepped into Brenda's shoes," Gunner said.

"Right down to giving us the talk about the birds and the bees," Dylan added.

"Okay, we've seen it and up we go," Asher said, and led the way.

"Dylan, are you still with us?" Nora said.

"Still listening, lady," he said.

"Twenty-one years buried is a long time. You all have a new theory to work with, and to solve it, you need a metal detector. If it's okay with you two, I'm going to exit this meeting, take a pain pill, and a shower. I have one request to make of all of you. Under no circumstances mention that I helped you. You did not inform me of any of your research. I have no knowledge of FBI files, or police files, or the rap sheets. I did not know about Joe and Darren Wilson. I do not know who Everett and Freddie Brandt are. I had no part in pointing out the obvious omission of Brenda's statement. Two of you are cops. You're the ones who figured it out."

"Understood," Asher said, and the other two echoed his comment.

"Gunner, I promise not to use up all the hot water. Asher, when you come to bed, I promise not to fall asleep in the middle of it. Dylan should be able to rent a metal detector somewhere in Amarillo. All three of you became part of the fallout. You should be together when you put an end to it."

"Nora's right, Dylan," Asher said. "The security detail will cover Dad's safety, although now that we have this new theory, the fact that Dad is up there might be right where the Brandts want him. If the bar is closed, they may try to make another run at it, and it's likely they don't know that we're here. We only have a short timeline to see if this plays out. Find a metal detector and come home."

"First thing tomorrow," Dylan said. "See you soon," he said, and hung up.

As Nora stood up, Asher got up with her. "Nora, honey, do you want me to put a plastic bag over your hand again?"

"No thanks. The bandage has served its purpose. It's coming off." Then she kissed Asher on the cheek and left the room.

Gunner got up and began putting the dominoes back in their box. "Do you feel like as big a fool as I do?"

"Probably bigger," Ash said. "We never once thought of what Mom's part in the robbery would have been. Just that she cheated on Dad and killed herself."

"Nora was right. We were too close to it all. We lost our objectivity," Gunner said. "I wonder what the hell her job actually entails?"

"Best we don't ask," Asher said. "We don't talk about our cases with the public. If there's something she wants us to know, she'll tell it." He gave the basement door a last glance, and then opened the fridge. "I need something to wash away the bad taste of all this," and he chose a can of Pepsi. "Want one?"

"Are there any Cokes?" he asked.

Asher handed one to him. They heard the shower come on, then went into the living room and turned on the TV, while Gunner reached for his phone and went through his emails.

Thirty minutes later, Gunner still wasn't watching the show and was still staring at his phone. "Tomorrow is the first of November. The temps are in the mid-thirties. If it's buried outside, it's gonna be hard digging in frozen ground," he said.

"Don't borrow trouble," Ash said. "If she's the one who hid it, I'd bet good money it's in the basement. I don't think she would have chanced digging outside where anyone could have seen her."

"Hope you're right on all counts," Gunner said. "I'm ready to go back to Dallas and chase down killers there. I don't like to think that all this happened here. Crossroads always felt safe."

"What made you choose law enforcement?" Asher asked. "I know why I did it. It's what I'd always wanted to do, but you turned down athletic scholarships. You had free rides to two colleges, and you turned them down. Why?"

He shrugged. "The only thing I was naturally good at was running, but I had no goals beyond playing sports. What would I have done afterward? You're viewed as too old for professional sports past the age of thirty-five. It just didn't feel right...not having purpose. I decided I'd rather run down criminals than chase after football players on a field of fake grass."

"I would have been proud of whatever you chose, but I like knowing what you've become. You're good, Gunner. Real good at what you do. You go on ahead and shower. I'm going to take a quick walk through the bar to make sure everything is undisturbed, then lock up before I quit this day."

Gunner nodded, and then he was gone.

Asher unlocked the door into the hallway between their house and the bar and made a quick sweep.

The front door was firmly locked.

Remnants of the crime scene tape were still tied to a light pole in the parking lot.

The blood stain behind the bar was gone.

There was nothing out of place except the fact that Jacob Kingston was not on the premises, but that would soon be rectified.

Before Nora got in the shower, she removed the bandage from her hand, eyed the stitches in her palm, and decided they didn't look as bad as she expected. The tiny little black bits of thread in each stitch, with the snipped ends sticking up, looked like antennae and spikes on a furry caterpillar. It was a little dicey using her hand, but not as painful as she'd expected. Once she showered and dried off, she pulled her football jersey over her head, then eyed the palm of her hand. She didn't like what she was seeing, and without second-guessing her decision, got a black ink pen from her purse and put two tiny dots at the end of the stitches for caterpillar eyes. Satisfied that she'd turned something ugly into whimsy, she took a pain pill and crawled into bed, weary to the bone. She would go home tomorrow before the search began. She'd done her part. The rest was up to them.

Asher was the last to shower, and the last to go to bed. He didn't know how to feel about what tomorrow might bring. He didn't know how they were going to tell their dad if it was true. And if they did find the money, they still had to find a way to tie the Brandt brothers to the shooting.

When he finally slipped into bed beside Nora, she was lying on her back with her left arm over her head, and the football jersey she was wearing, clearly visible. She was always animated, and seeing her like this was like looking at a painting of her face in a way he rarely saw it.

Her lashes became shadows below her eyes. Her lips were slightly parted, as if waiting for a chance to speak. The high cheekbones and the shape of her face—an exquisite work of art. The inhale and exhale of each breath was almost too soft to hear.

The bandage was gone, the stitches plainly visible. But as

he looked closer and saw what she'd done, turning a wound and a row of stitches into a caterpillar with little round black eyes, it made him smile. She'd turned something painful into something to smile about.

That she still loved him like this was his gift.

She had been everything he'd ever wanted from the first time they'd made love, and nothing had changed that feeling.

When he pulled up the covers over her, she stirred. "Ash?"

"It's me, love. Go back to sleep. I just need to hold you."

"Love..." she mumbled, and rolled over on her side.

Moments later, she was tucked into the curve of his body.

He closed his eyes and dreamed of digging for treasure, and finding Brenda instead, sitting in a hole crying, and saying "I'm sorry, I'm sorry."

The first rays of the morning sun were coming through the curtains when he opened his eyes.

She was watching him, and without saying a word, she reached for him.

He needed no urging.

They made love in silence.

Slow, deep strokes into the warm, wet heat of her.

Watching her face. Waiting for that moment when she closed her eyes.

Chasing that moment when consciousness lapsed into a blood-rush frenzy.

It was so good.

Nora was dressed and at the table drinking coffee when Gunner walked into the kitchen.

"Where's Ash?" he asked.

"Living room talking to Dylan, I think."

He nodded, poured himself a cup of coffee, and sat down at the table.

"Your bandage is off. Can I see?" he asked.

She held out her hand, and smiled when she saw the delight on his face.

"Cute worm," he said.

She glanced at her palm and frowned. "It's a caterpillar, thank you."

He was laughing when Asher walked in.

"What did I miss?" he asked as he refilled the cup he was carrying.

"I dissed her worm," Gunner said.

"Caterpillar," Nora muttered.

Asher grinned. The banter felt good. It took his mind off the nightmare he'd had, and the day ahead of them.

"On another note, Dylan is on the way with a metal detector. Dad's good. He's in PT every day and when they walk him up and down the hall, the security guard is right behind them. I imagine it's quite the sight. The nurses will be glad to see the back of us when he's released."

"I'm packed," Nora said. "If you'll run me back to the house before he gets here, then I'll be out of your hair."

"You haven't eaten anything yet," he said.

She shook her head. "I'll get something at home."

Ash was already feeling her absence, but understood the need. "I'll get your things."

Gunner was stirring sugar into his coffee. "Nora, I have something to say before you leave. Thank you for the honesty and the help, and for taking the scab off of a sore I've been nursing for the last twenty years. I don't know why

Brenda was the way she was, and I've been so bitter, and so angry at her. At the age of seven, all I felt was rejection. I kept thinking that if she'd loved us, she wouldn't have done what she did." He took a deep breath. "Then last night in my sleep, I remembered the note from the tooth fairy. Oh… I knew the story of it, because I'd heard it repeated, but I didn't actually remember it on my own. Until the dream. I remembered that after she slid it under the pillow, she leaned over and whispered in my ear, 'Love you forever.' Asking us to remember that day and that night, and the last time we saw her alive, unlocked that memory. I don't know why she did what she did to Dad, or why she got caught up in Brandt's world, but it wasn't because she didn't love us, was it, Ash?"

Asher shook his head. "No, buddy, it wasn't because of that."

Tears were rolling down Nora's face. "It's going to be okay, honey. It's all going to be okay."

Gunner nodded. "I'll get your stuff," he said, and walked out of the room.

Asher picked up a dish towel and began wiping away the tears. "You're the best thing that's ever happened in my life."

"I think we'll call it even. Get your coat, big man, and take me home."

Gunner came back with her things, and then they were gone, driving away from the bar and up a side street on the way to her house.

Dylan didn't tell Angie what was happening other than Jacob was on the road to a full recovery and he was going home for a couple of days to help out there. But for the first time in days, he felt hopeful that this was going to end

the cloud of suspicion and speculation under which they'd lived.

He was pushing the speed limit, full of anxiety and expectation, but when he saw the familiar sign of the Yellow Rose Café in the distance, he began to relax. He was almost home.

A few minutes later, he passed the café, then the gas station, then took the turn into the driveway leading to their house behind the bar. Even as he was pulling up to park, he was wondering if what they were looking for was buried somewhere out there.

He was circling the SUV to get his things when Ash and Gunner came out to greet him.

"Good to see you. I'll get your bag," Gunner said, then carried it inside.

"That's the metal detector," Dylan said, pointing to the box.

"I've got it. Come in out of this cold," Asher said.

Dylan paused as they were passing through the kitchen and looked at the basement door. "It'll be a hell of a thing if it's down there after all this time, won't it?"

Asher nodded. "I hope it is. We need this over with."

"Okay. Just let me get my stuff put up and we'll get this party started," Dylan said.

Ash was already reaching for his pocketknife to start opening the box. "I'll unpack the detector. We can figure out how to use it afterward."

"I know how," Dylan said. "I've used them on job sites before. Fairly handy in locating where old plumbing lines run beyond housing sites."

"Awesome, then you're going to be our dowser. Only we're trying to find a money box, not a water source," Ash said.

A few minutes later, the brothers were gathered in the

kitchen. They had the metal detector assembled and had just begun charging the battery in it.

"It will take a good two hours at least to fully charge this," Dylan said. "Is there anything to eat here? I've had one cup of coffee and no breakfast. I'll settle for anything," he said.

"I could do with breakfast, too," Gunner said.

Asher knew the day ahead was going to be tough for all of them. Might as well begin it with good food in their bellies.

"Then let's go see Pearl about biscuits and gravy, then swing by Belker's for groceries before we go home."

The Brandt brothers' intent on making a second run at the Tumbleweed stalled when Freddie came down with the flu, then Everett caught it, too. They were both running fevers, aching from head to toe, and huddled up beneath the covers.

Freddie had decided somewhere around midnight last night that his life was in peril. The room was spinning, and his fever had spiked. He got up and staggered down the hall to his brother's room.

"Everett! I'm sick. I'm bad sick," he moaned.

Everett groaned. "Well, damn it, Freddie, so am I. Take something for the fever. Drink lots of water, and get back under the covers."

Freddie headed for the kitchen. Everett had been smoking weed there and the scent made his head spin. He got a glass of water, staggered back to the table. His vision kept blurring, and he had to hang on to the back of the chair to keep from falling as he sorted through the pharmaceuticals spread out before him.

Unfortunately for Freddie, when he reached for the acetaminophen, he picked up one of Everett's party drugs

instead. He made it back to his bed, pulled up the covers, and then laid there waiting for a measure of relief, but what he got was a waking nightmare.

Birds that morphed into bats began flying across his line of vision. A naked woman with green skin was sitting on his feet and fire was dancing across his bed. He was convinced that he was dying in hell.

He started crying and screaming. "Everett! Everything is on fire. I think I'm dying. I'm dying in hell. Save me, brother! I don't want to die!"

It was the "everything is on fire," comment that made Everett ignore his raging fever, throw back the covers, and run faster than he thought possible, considering the floor undulating beneath his feet.

But when he got into Freddie's room and saw nothing but the blown pupils in Freddie's eyes, he cursed.

"Damn it, Freddie! You're not dying. You're high. What the hell did you take?"

"Meds for fever," Freddie said, and pulled the covers over his head to keep away the dive-bombing bats.

"Like hell," Everett muttered and went to the kitchen to investigate. A bottle of acetaminophen was sitting beside a glass of water, but there were only three of the four Ayas he dumped there last night before he put their clothes in the laundry. Freddie was riding an ayahuasca high. Hallucinating at the max, and now Everett didn't dare go back to bed for fear of what Freddie might do to himself before it was over.

Frustrated beyond words, he ran the last three Aya pills through the garbage disposal, pulled the quilts off his bed and headed for Freddie's room, only to find an empty bed. He looked under it, then in the closet, then heard water running in the bathroom, dropped his quilts, and ran.

Freddie was standing under the shower in his pajamas and picking at a loose tile on the shower wall.

"Bugs crawling in my hair. Someone in the wall trying to tell me something."

Everett rolled his eyes. "Don't pick at the walls. You'll let the bad guys in. Don't forget to use soap in your hair," then walked out into the hall and turned up the thermostat. Their inheritance was farther away now than ever. This was going to be a long-ass day.

It was nearing eleven o'clock when the Kingstons headed down the basement stairs with the metal detector. Never had the basement looked as huge as it did at that moment. It was like standing before an enemy they weren't sure they could defeat.

"Do we start at the back and work forward, or start where we stand?" Dylan asked.

Asher turned around and pointed. "We start beneath the stairs, and keep our sweep path four bricks wide, from east to west. We know it won't be beneath the shelves, because they're only six inches above the ground. She could never have dug beneath that. We'll move the stuff stacked on the floor as we go."

"Got it," Dylan said, then walked beneath the open stairwell and began the sweep.

Ash and Gunner were responsible for clearing the pathways, moving crates of Jacob's special whiskey orders. Moving boxes of Christmas décor, remnants of Jacob Kingston's life. There was even a box of their old toys.

It was heavy work and slow going. Nearly two hours later, they were nearing the back third of the basement when Asher called a momentary halt.

"I hear something going on outside. I need to make sure it has nothing to do with the Tumbleweed," he said, and bolted up the stairs with his brothers behind him.

Asher ran into the bar and immediately saw the issue. Someone had sideswiped a truck pulling a bull hauler, and there were longhorn bulls about the size of yearlings running in every direction.

Some were in the Tumbleweed parking lot. A couple of them had cleared out the people at the gas pumps, and some were already running past the Yellow Rose, across the highway, and out into the land on the north side of Highway 86.

One man was sitting in the open doorway of the truck cab holding his head. The hood was up on the car that sideswiped the hauler, with steam spewing out of the radiator. There were people coming out of the Rose, and from the gas station, trying to help round up the runaways.

"What a mess," Asher said. "Grab your coats. They're going to need all the help they can get."

Chapter 12

A COUPLE OF MINUTES LATER, THEY CAME OUT THE front door of the bar, locking it behind them. Someone had opened a gate to the fenced-off area across the highway, and they were trying to herd the runaways into the enclosure.

Ash and Dylan took off east, blocking the escape of a pair of runaways, while Gunner took off after a solitary bull, hoping to at least get it off the highway before it was hit by oncoming traffic.

Before long, traffic was blocked from both directions, while the echoing sound of sirens warned of a highway patrol car approaching from one direction, and an ambulance coming from the other.

But what soon became apparent to the people caught in the traffic jam, was the race between Gunner and the longhorn he was chasing. The young bull was in panic mode as it darted in and out between the vehicles, but it was the man chasing after it who caught their attention.

A trucker stopped on the highway, got out of the cab, and began filming the race, and a pair of teenagers abandoned their truck for the truck bed for a better view, watching the tall, long-legged man chasing after that runaway. What was shocking to the onlookers was that he was gaining on it.

It was midafternoon.

Nora was sitting within the silence of her house, going through another box of old photos, when she heard a loud boom, followed by a screeching of brakes. She'd heard that too many times in Fort Worth not to recognize the sounds.

Someone had just had a wreck!

She ran to the window, saw smoke rising above the rooftops, heard a lot of shouting, then the sound of cattle bawling. She put on her coat, then grabbed her phone and keys and locked the door on her way out. She ran down the steps and then into an alley that came out onto the highway between the gas station and the Yellow Rose Café.

What she saw was chaos. The front end of a semi was crushed and smoking. The trailer of the bull hauler it was pulling had broken away from the cab, and the young longhorns they'd been hauling were out, and running in every direction.

She caught a glimpse of Asher running across the highway with Dylan right behind him, and then saw Gunner go flying past the gas station running west. She could tell the bulls were young, likely yearlings. But they were already bigger than she was, and sporting horns nearly as long as her arm.

Chasing longhorns was not on her agenda, and now that she knew what had happened, she turned around and took herself home.

Gunner was aware of people shouting as he sped past the vehicles, but his focus was on the back end of that bull, and the length of the horns. He didn't have a rope. He didn't know what he was going to do with it if he caught up with it, but he'd never quit a race in his life, and he wasn't starting now.

No sooner than he'd thought of rope, than someone in a pickup truck held a coiled lariat out of the window as he flew past. He grabbed it on the run.

He had never had a desire to rodeo, but like every little boy in the rural part of West Texas, he had grown up knowing how to throw a rope. Now he had the rope. All there was left to do was corner the critter and put a loop around its neck.

The air was cold, but he was sweating beneath his coat. He was in the rhythm of the run, aware of the number of steps he was taking between breaths, wondering where this was going to end, when he caught sight of a crowd of bystanders forming a line across the highway, intent on turning the bull's escape. He saw his chance and extended his kick.

The moment the young bull saw the blockade, it veered to the left, went down into a ditch, and was beginning a climb up the other side when Gunner caught up. He'd already shaken out a big loop on the lariat and was circling it over his head. He was only going to get one chance before it bolted, so he let it fly.

The loop sailed out across the ditch, then over the steer's head just as it was coming up on the other side. Gunner gave the rope a hard jerk as it settled around the yearling's neck, and before he ran out of rope, ran to the nearest truck, and began wrapping it around the trailer hitch, then held on and waited for the bull to run out of rope.

The moment it happened, it yanked the bull backward, landing it on its back with its feet in the air.

The race was over.

The little bull was down.

All of its flight and fight was gone, and the trucker was still filming when Gunner unwrapped the rope from the trailer hitch and let out enough length for the bull to stand up.

Still dazed from the hard landing, with sides heaving from the run, the yearling yielded to Gunner's tug on the rope and climbed back up the ditch, then onto the highway.

Looking back at how far they'd come, Gunner guessed they'd run a good quarter of a mile, and he still wasn't winded. He was in better shape than he thought. He gave the rope another tug, and this time, the young bull followed.

People were laughing and pointing as they passed by the vehicles. Gunner just took it in stride, talking to the weary steer as they went.

"Come on, hot shot. Nope. Don't hook that horn at me. You're already missing the party. Where did you think you were going, anyway?"

Ash and Dylan were back at the crash site. The runaways had been herded into the pasture. They didn't know where Gunner was until they began hearing whoops and whistles, and people clapping, and turned to see what the commotion was all about, and saw him walking back through the line of cars, leading one of the runaways.

"What's all that about?" Dylan asked.

Asher shrugged as a cowboy walked up beside them, grinning from ear to ear. "Did you see that?" he asked.

"See what?" Asher asked.

"That dude ran down one of those yearlings and threw the cleanest loop you ever saw, then threw a knot around someone's trailer hitch and let the bull yank its own ass down. Never saw anyone that fast before."

Dylan started grinning and Asher laughed. "That's our brother."

The cowboy frowned. "What do y'all call him? Roadrunner?"

"His name is Gunner Kingston. He's a homicide cop with the Dallas PD."

The cowboy paused, then looked at them again.

"Kingston, you said? Any relation to Jacob Kingston?"

"He's our father."

The cowboy shook his head. "I heard about what happened to Jacob. I'm a regular at the Weed. I think a lot of that man. You tell him Beau Rangely sends him good wishes."

"I will do that," Asher said.

"Gunner Kingston. I'm gonna remember that name," Rangely said. "Nice to meet you," and walked off.

Unaware he'd been the subject of a conversation, Gunner kept walking toward the crash site, looking for someone to take the bull, when a couple of wranglers came running.

"Good catch," they said, and led the bull out into the pasture with the rest of the herd while Gunner jogged up to rejoin his brothers.

"Did you really run down a longhorn?" Dylan asked.

Gunner grinned. "I kinda did, but he'd still be running if someone hadn't tossed me a rope as I ran past their truck. Anyway, all I need is a good drink of water and I'm ready to get back to work."

"I'm right there with you," Asher said. "I'm not going to bed until we've gone over that whole floor. And if it's not there, we start on the outside tomorrow."

The spurt of adrenaline from chasing longhorns ended as they descended the cellar steps again. Gunner was silent, and Dylan's shoulders were slumped in defeat.

For a few seconds, Asher saw them as children again, with dread on their faces.

"Damn it, boys. We're not digging up a grave, and we know it has to be here somewhere, or Brandt's sons would have never set foot on the property. Dylan, fire up your magic wand. We have work to do."

And just like that, they picked up the rhythm again, trusting Dylan to be the judge of the hits they were getting. So far, he'd identified the sounds as likely old coin or nails, or things like metal belt buckles from centuries past. The little pings that indicated deep in the ground, and the louder pings, indicating just beneath the surface. But they weren't getting anything to indicate something large, something metal, like the missing strongbox, and they were running out of floor to search.

They had one last area left before going outside, but there were things to be moved.

Dylan came to a halt, waiting for the brothers to begin shifting the stacks.

"This stuff needs to be hauled off," Asher said. "It's all wooden crates full of old canning jars, and a full bundle of asphalt shingles from the last time the roof was repaired."

"Not going to argue that," Dylan said.

Finally they had the area cleared, and within moments of Dylan's first sweep, the beep he got was loud and startling. He swept across the area from every direction until he had a fairly clear picture in his head of the size.

"It's metal. It's big. And there's likely less than a foot of dirt over whatever it is," Dylan said.

"Then we start moving bricks. Where does Dad keep his work gloves?" Asher said.

"I saw some in that big bucket we moved up near the stairs," Gunner said.

"Grab some for us, will you buddy? I'll get a pry bar for the bricks. They're not mortared in, but the years have wedged them in tight," Asher said.

The thought of what might lie beneath their feet shifted all of them into high gear. Dylan put the detector aside and gloved up with his brothers as they got down on their knees.

Asher was prying up the bricks and Dylan and Gunner

were stacking them aside, working quickly and in unison, anxious to put a shovel in the earth below.

When they'd cleared a large enough area, Asher stood, took a shovel off the wall where it was hanging. He stabbed it in the dirt, lifted out the first scoop, and dumped it in a wheelbarrow. The ground was hard and full of gravel-size rocks, but he kept shoving it into the ground, pushing it deeper with his foot, then lifting it out, over and over until the shovel clanged against something hard. Something metal.

He shifted where he was standing and began taking out dirt from around the object, scraped away the top layer of what was covering it until the whole lid of the strongbox was revealed.

It was a gut-punch, and a relief. The truth was right in front of them.

"What do we do now?" Dylan asked.

"We leave it. We don't touch it. We don't open it. Grab a drop cloth and cover it up, then stack some boxes in front of where we've been digging. I'm calling the FBI. It's theirs to claim and recover."

They stood, staring at each other, uncertain how to react, and then Asher broke the shock and hugged them in celebration.

"We did it, all of us...together. We'll have to stand up to public scrutiny again when the media finds out it was Brenda who hid it, and right beneath our feet. But to hell with all of them. We have nothing to be ashamed of, and we're the ones who solved a twenty-one-year-old cold case."

"Gunner and I will cover it up," Dylan said.

Asher nodded. "I'll try getting in contact with the Feds, but it's late. Gunner, were there any contact numbers on the files you requested from them?"

"I think so. I'll check as soon as we finish here," he said.

"Lock the basement door after you come up. The next people to go down there will be the Feds. We don't tell anyone, and we ask them not to reveal the recovery until we've got the Brandt brothers for the shooting."

"How are we going to do that?" Dylan asked.

"That's something we still have to figure out," Gunner said.

"I'm going to make a food run," Asher said. "Are you picky, or do you want me to just bring it home?"

"Whatever you get, I'll eat," Dylan said.

"Same," Gunner added.

"Be back soon," Asher said, then headed up the stairs.

Minutes later, he was driving away in his dad's truck. It was too late to dump a big order on Pearl, so the deli in Belker's Grocery was the next choice.

He grabbed a shopping cart as he went in and headed straight for the deli counter, eyed the choices, and opted for an assortment of sliced deli meats and cheeses, potato salad, pasta salad, and put a small carrot cake in the basket before heading to the bread and condiment aisles. Instead of sliced bread, he got hoagie rolls, pickles, a jar of wholegrain mustard and a jar of mayo, a head of lettuce and a couple of tomatoes, and headed to checkout, fielding questions about Jacob, and laughing when he found out that Gunner was the most recent local hero for running down a longhorn, which put him on a pedestal with Sonny Bluejacket, who once caught three men robbing Belker's pharmacy by putting a skunk in their car.

He was still grinning when he exited the store, but instead of going straight back, he made a quick detour to Nora. Got out on the run, took the steps up two at a time, and knocked.

He heard her footsteps as she came into the living room, and the moment she opened the door, he swept her off her

feet and into his arms, kicking the door shut behind him as he entered.

She saw the look on his face and started smiling.

"You found it. Don't tell me. But I can see it in your eyes. My God, Ash... All those years."

"I don't have the words to say how much I love you. Thank you is not enough. I have a phone call to make, and we'll be out of pocket until it's out of our hands. We still have to connect the Brandts to the shooting, but when this mess is over, it's you and me, darlin'. Together forever."

Nora frowned. "Do you think the Brandts will try again?"

"We can't be sure, but greed always changes the odds. We know they're in Amarillo, but that changes nothing. We still need them to make another move."

"You need bait. Who do you know connected with the Amarillo news affiliates? If they would interview the sheriff to air an update on the shooting and the victim, then have Reddick mention Kingston's recovery time is unknown, and the bar has been closed indefinitely, that might give the Brandts the impetus to try again...but both parties would have to agree to do that."

Asher's eyes widened. "While we lay low and wait for them to show!"

"If the universe aligns, it might work," she said.

"You are going to be the best secret weapon a special investigator would ever want, and I have to go. The guys are waiting on me to bring food. God, I love you," he said, and kissed her one last time before walking out the door.

Nora turned the lock, but when she turned to look around at the room in which she was standing, still filled with all of the furniture and photos, instead of the angst and grief that had brought her here, she felt nothing but a sense of duty to see it through. It was the first signal of healing. Being able to see the future, without the need to hang on to the past.

Asher's thoughts were a jumble of what-ifs and maybes as he drove back to the house. Dylan came out to help carry in bags. As soon as he was back inside, everything went on lockdown. Shades down. Curtains pulled.

Gunner had the information Asher wanted pulled up on his laptop and set it aside as they began opening packages and laying out the food.

"Awesome choices," Dylan said. "Submarine sandwiches with all the fixings, and cake. I like the way you cook."

"You like everything," Asher said. "I can't remember you ever turning down food."

"Yes, he did," Gunner said. "I know, because he gave what he wouldn't eat to me. Told me it would make me a man, and not to tell Dad."

Asher grinned. "What was that?"

"Mountain oysters. He just said it was meat," Gunner said.

Dylan burst out laughing. "And when you found out what it was, you blacked my eye, remember?"

Gunner frowned. "Hell yes, I remember. I haven't gotten over it, either."

Asher was grinning from ear to ear. "So, you don't like sushi, and you don't eat…"

"Don't even say the word," Gunner said. "I don't want to spoil my appetite here. This all looks good."

Asher got out plates and flatware and stood back while they built their own subs, then made his after they'd taken a seat. In that moment, life was good, but it would be even better once they exorcised the ghost in the basement.

It was just after 6:00 p.m. when Asher was finally able to contact the federal agent in charge of cold cases, and when he began laying out the whole story, it left the man scrambling for words.

"Your mother? That certainly came out of left field! Of course, that would have been an option for us to explore if we had been able to interrogate her, if she had not killed herself," he said.

Hearing the agent quickly shifting blame to a dead woman ticked Asher off. "That happened in your custody," he said.

"Yes, of course. That had to be rough for your family," he said.

"The whole debacle was a nightmare. She'd already destroyed the image we'd had of her when it happened. We were kids. Dad was humiliated. It was years of hell and finger-pointing, and the rumors he had to live down would have ruined a lesser man. But that will be cleared up now in due time. However, we have a request that you do not reveal the recovery of the money until we get the Brandt brothers arrested. After they are, you will also make it known that it was Jacob's sons who solved the cold case after his attempted murder, or we will make our own public statement to that effect. It will go a long way in clearing our family name. Keeping it quiet is imperative right now. If the Brandts realize the money is no longer within their reach, they'll walk, because we don't have enough evidence to convict them."

"We can make that happen. How long are we talking here?"

"Within the next few days, for sure. We have a plan."

"Then consider it done," he said. "We'll be sending agents to take possession tomorrow morning. They'll arrive at daybreak when most people are still asleep. There will be

three armored SUVs with multiple agents. A lead car. The car that will transport the lock box, and a third car to protect the transport. There will be a chopper flying overhead, strictly for the agents' extra security. It will not be landing. They will ask you to sign off when they take possession, and that will be the end of your participation. We will take an official statement from you at later date, after you have apprehended your men."

"You can always contact me through the Texas state attorney general's office—Department of Special Investigations. My brother, Gunner Kingston, is a homicide detective with the Dallas PD, and my middle brother, Dylan, is a general contractor and lives in Austin, near me. We'll be waiting for your arrival. Tell your men to take the driveway on the west side of the bar and circle behind it. The house is attached to the south side of the bar. If you do, it's unlikely their vehicles will even be seen."

"Will do," the agent said. "And may I say, you three are very remarkable men."

Asher didn't respond. He just hung up.

Saying nice words now didn't take away the sting of how their dad had been treated after Brenda died on their watch. The Feds' passive-aggressive questioning of Jacob had been a feeble attempt to point blame anywhere but at themselves, and even at the age of twelve, Asher knew it.

He dropped the phone in his pocket and then went back to update the brothers, but he was keeping Nora's suggestion about setting a trap for the Brandts to himself until the Feds had come and gone.

Dylan and Gunner were in the kitchen, having carrot cake and coffee.

"We saved the last piece for you," Dylan said.

Asher eyed the measly sliver lying among the crumbs. "Your generosity is overwhelming," he said, then picked up

a fork and ate it off the cake board it had been sold on. "The Feds will be here by daybreak. We do not all sleep at the same time tonight. I'll stand first watch. Dylan can do the midnight to 3:00 a.m. and Gunner can do the 3:00 a.m. to daybreak, at which time we will all be up and ready, understood?"

"Are we arming ourselves?" Gunner asked.

"Considering the fact that Dad couldn't get to his in time, I'd say it's a good decision, wouldn't you?" Asher said.

"I don't have a gun," Dylan said.

"I don't intend to sleep with mine. I'll leave it with you," he said.

"I sleep with mine," Gunner said.

They both looked at him in surprise. "The hell you say!" Dylan muttered.

Gunner shrugged. "I always had a sleep buddy. Just traded Leopard for a Glock."

"I remember Leopard!" Dylan said. "Raggedy little stuffy that you dragged around by the tail. I wonder whatever happened to that thing?"

"I threw it away after Brenda. Asher found it and kept it. He gave it back to me the year he graduated high school. Told me it was bad luck to give away a gift." Then he glanced up at Asher. "Big brother always could talk me into believing just about anything."

"I was ready to take on the world, but I hated leaving you two behind, and saying goodbye to Nora. The little critter was yours to keep," Ash said.

"Where is it now?" Dylan asked.

"In a shoebox in my closet. Just in case I get tired of sleeping with the Glock."

They laughed, and the moment passed. "Go on, both of you," Ash said. "Get some sleep. I'll wake Dylan when it's time." Then he began cleaning the kitchen, loading cups and flatware in the dishwasher before starting it up.

He made a fresh pot of coffee, got his handgun out of the bag in his room, popped in a clip, and took it with him to the living room, turning out lights as he went. He muted the TV, then used the light from the screen as a beacon when he made his first sweep through the bar, then back into the house, locking the door between. Last checkpoint was the back door and the basement door to reassure himself everything was secure.

It was going to be a long-ass night.

The Kingstons weren't the only ones battling their demons. Everett was still sick. Freddie's Aya crash was as miserable as the high had been crazy. He had the worst drug hangover he'd ever experienced, and was still sick with the flu. Amarillo at night was lit up like a Christmas tree. Lots of stuff going on, and they weren't a part of it.

Freddie was stark naked under his covers, listening to the hum of the clothes dryer, and waiting for his pajamas to dry, wishing they'd never gone to the prison to visit their dad, wishing he'd never told them about that damn money. Wishing Everett hadn't shot that man. Wishing he was still in jail with three squares a day and sleeping in a bed he didn't have to pay for.

When he heard Everett get up and then later, heard the toilet flush, he called out.

"Hey, Everett?"

He heard Everett stop out in the hall, then walk to the doorway of his room. "What?"

"Are we still going to try getting into the Tumbleweed again?"

"Hell yes, we're going back, just as soon as we get over this crap. If we don't do it before Kingston gets out of the hospital, then it will be too late."

"How will we know if it's safe?" Freddie asked.

"Shut up, Freddie. Just shut up and go to sleep. Safety is not part of our lifestyle."

"Yeah, all right, Everett. I was just asking, but can I ask one more thing?"

Everett sighed. "What is it?"

"Do you reckon my pajamas might be dry? I can't get warm."

"Damn it, Freddie. You fried your brain, not your legs. Why don't you get up and see if they're dry on your own? I'm going back to bed. I'm still sick, too."

Freddie was even more worried now as Everett walked away.

His brother wasn't going to give up on the money.

They could get themselves killed.

He was going to have to abandon the warm spot in his bed in hopes his pajamas were dry.

That Dallas jail cell was looking better every minute.

Asher was kicked back on the sofa with his laptop. He'd been running online searches on both Everett and Freddie Brandt's names, looking for any kind of rental records in Amarillo that would tell him where they were now, but found nothing, until he began searching city utility records for new accounts, and found a new account under the name Everett Brandt.

"Score," he said, snapped a photo of the address on his laptop, and exited the search, then opened another window in Zillow and typed in the address. He got a photo of the renovated motel that had been turned into apartments, and a map of Amarillo, showing him where it was located.

They were in business.

Just when he was about to go wake up Dylan, he began hearing a calf bawling, and it sounded like it was nearby. His first thought was that the runaways had found a way out of their pen, and he quickly went through the bar to look outside.

It was another longhorn yearling, clearly highlighted beneath a three-quarter moon, standing in the highway, bawling loud and long, trying to find the herd.

As Asher unlocked the door and walked out, he began hearing the ones they'd penned in the nearby pasture beginning to bawl back. That was all the little bull needed to hear. He watched it dart across the highway and clear the ditch before trotting off toward the fence line. Satisfied that since it had found the herd, it wouldn't go anywhere, and the owners could pick up the little runaway when they came to get the rest. After one last look around the area, he went back inside, then down the hall to where Dylan was sleeping, and gave him a tap on the shoulder.

"Hey, Dylan, your turn to stand watch," he said.

Dylan threw back the covers and sat up, rubbing sleep from his eyes, then put his boots back on and stood up.

"Anything I need to know?" he asked.

"Just one runaway bull we missed rounding up. It was bawling for the herd. When they began to answer, it ran across the highway toward the pasture they're in. Nothing more... Oh... I found where the Brandt brothers are living, but that's info for another day."

"I'd hate to try hiding anything from you or Gunner. Had you been living in that time, you two would have found Jimmy Hoffa," Dylan said.

Ash shrugged. "Part of the job. There's fresh coffee in the pot. I'm going to catch a couple of hours sleep before the party starts. Wake Gunner up around three. Oh...and here's my gun. Don't shoot yourself."

Dylan grinned. "I've shot plenty of nail guns. I think I'm good."

Asher shook his head and went across the hall to his bedroom, kicked off his boots, and went belly down across the bed without bothering to turn back the covers.

Chapter 13

THE DOOR BETWEEN THE HOUSE AND THE BAR WAS OPEN when both brothers walked into the living room the next morning. Gunner was standing at the front windows overlooking the highway when he heard them coming up behind him.

"Gut feeling says they're just minutes out," he muttered.

"So, you have become psychic overnight?" Dylan asked.

He pointed up. "A chopper has been circling. Ash said there would be a chopper. I am not psychic, but I am observant."

Asher walked up between them. "It's go time, brothers."

"What will they do?" Dylan asked.

"Likely take photos of the site as it is, then video the removal. It will be verification that it wasn't recently buried. I doubt they'll be able to pull Brenda's fingerprints off the box, but I could be wrong."

"They didn't book her into jail. How would they have her prints?" Dylan asked.

"Autopsy," Asher said, then just as Gunner predicted, they saw three black SUVs coming up Highway 86 from the east. "There they come."

As they were pulling off the highway, the chopper was circling.

Asher rolled his eyes. "Coming in at daybreak to allay suspicion, in a little town that only experiences LIFESTAR choppers. Everybody will be on their phones, or standing

on their porches, waiting to hear who's hurt or dying before we even get to the basement."

The brothers made a quick pivot and headed into the house to greet their guests. They opened the back door as the agents were coming up the steps. As predicted, one was carrying a video camera and a tripod, and there were two carrying what looked like forensic cases.

Asher pointed up. "Unless you want all 2,500 residents of Crossroads in our front parking lot banging on the door to see who's hurt, or who else just got shot here, you might want to tell them to do their backup farther away and higher up."

One of the agents looked a little wild-eyed and grabbed a radio, while the rest filed in. As soon as the last one entered the house, Dylan locked the door, and Asher and Gunner promptly flashed their badges.

"Asher Kingston. Special investigator for the Texas state attorney general's office. Gunner Kingston, Homicide detective with the Dallas Police Department. Dylan Kingston, general contractor out of Austin. Gentlemen, may we see some identification?"

Twelve agents blinked in unison, then promptly displayed their badges.

"Thank you," Asher said. "Can't be too careful these days. The shit we found in our basement is what nearly got our dad killed. Who's in charge?"

A sandy-haired man with a scar across his forehead stepped forward. "That would be me, Special Agent Alex Worth."

"Gunner, lead them down," Asher said. "My brother and I will follow."

"Is there room enough?" Alex asked.

"The basement is the same size as the footprint of the house. We used to play down there when we were kids. Didn't know we were harboring a secret."

Gunner unlocked the door and turned on the light as he went down, with the agents following, one by one. Asher was the last.

The agents were eyeing the jumble of boxes strung out along the walls and on the shelves, waiting to be led to the find.

The brothers moved through the crowd to the far end of the basement, pulled the drop cloth away, and moved the boxes they'd put up to hide the hole and what was in it.

"We used a metal detector to find it. Dylan was our expert there. As you can see, there was less than a foot of dirt covering it, and as soon as he realized it was what we'd been looking for, we stopped digging. Except for the blade of my shovel, no one has touched it since Brenda put it there. And since it's apparent from your clothing that none of you planned to do any excavating, we will dig for you, with your directions. Do you plan to video, or are we doing stills?" Asher asked.

Agent Worthy grinned. So far, they had been very politely chided three times. The chopper. The delay in identifying themselves. And now improper dress. In any other circumstances, he and this dude would be friends.

"Video, and we appreciate your assistance," he said, then eyed the agent behind the camera. "Roll it, Conrad," then for the record, identified himself, the names of the agents on site, and all three of the Kingstons. "Asher, would you please repeat for the camera, how you located it here. We already have your statement regarding the reason you began the search. It was during the investigation of your father's shooting that you discovered an omission from the federal investigation. Now, please proceed."

At that point, Asher repeated it for the camera, then at Worthy's direction, he and Gunner got back down on their knees at the site, and dug the rest of the dirt away from the

sides until the dirt had been completely removed from around the box and the handles were revealed. They were about to lift it out together when Dylan stopped them.

"Let me, brothers."

Asher and Gunner stood up and stepped back, watching as Dylan leaned over, flexing the strong muscles across his back and shoulders as he grabbed the box by the handles, and with one last yank to loosen it from the bottom, lifted it up and out like he was picking up a sack of groceries.

"Where do you want it?" he asked.

Special Agent Worthy eyed the man's massive chest and pointed. "Just there away from the hole, will be fine. Thank you."

Dylan's head was down. His eyes were glazed with tears as he stepped back against the wall, but his brothers knew why. Their mother had been the last person to touch it, and for that moment, when he gripped the handles, he'd been holding her hands.

Worthy was speaking again. "For the camera, it is obvious this lock has not been disturbed. It still has the seal from the armored car company intact. We are going to break the seal now and view the contents before we remove the strongbox from the property. We have statements from the armored car company at that time of the robbery, as to what is supposed to be inside."

Gunner took a bolt cutter from the wall above the workbench and handed it to them. When the lock was cut, it snapped and banged against the metal like a gunshot.

Worthy removed the broken lock and bagged it as evidence, but when he tried to lift the lid, it was stuck. Dylan handed him a small hammer.

"A little tap around the edges should do it… It's probably dirt wedged in the crack." And he was right.

A few quick taps and the lid came up in Worthy's hands.

Bundles and bundles of one-hundred-dollar bills were visible beneath an enormous stack of bearer bonds.

"This is it," Worthy said. "A full accounting of the amount will be made as it's logged into evidence, but at the time it was stolen, it was reported that the bearer bonds alone were in excess of a million dollars."

"Damn sure not worth what it cost," Asher said.

Worthy closed the lid, then replaced the lock they'd cut off with another one that would need a number code to remove, and ended the video. They rehung the borrowed tools, shook hands with all three brothers, and then followed them up and out, carrying the box now covered with the drop cloth, and quickly loaded it into one of the armored SUVs, and then the remaining agents loaded up as well.

The chopper was suddenly visible again, as Worthy turned to say his goodbyes.

"The director will be in touch. I am to thank you men profusely on behalf of the department, for closing this cold case. Our sympathies to your family. I hope you soon have the perps you're after behind bars."

And then they were gone, driving out in the same order in which they'd arrived, and heading back east on 86 with the chopper flying above them.

The money was gone, but the brothers still had work to do. They filed back down the stairs in silence, filled up the hole they'd dug, replaced the bricks they'd removed, and then stared at each other.

"That damn hole felt like a grave," Dylan said.

"But it wasn't, and now it's as if the money was never there. We will come down here again many times, but without the ghost of her with us," Asher said, and wrapped his arms around his brothers. "It's done, and we did good."

"Nora needs to be in on this hug," Gunner said. "We

couldn't have done this without her. It's gonna be good having two sisters-in-law. Takes the heat off of me."

Asher laughed. "Nope. It's going to be worse. Your two sisters will be constantly trying to hook you up. Happy women are matchmakers. Your journey has just begun."

"True that," Dylan said. "But don't fight it, man. Finding the lady who loves you as is and always has your back will be your treasure."

"Whatever," Gunner said. "But right now, I don't know whether I'm hungrier or sleepier."

"Figure it out, because I don't serve breakfast in bed," Asher said.

After the last twenty-four hours, the ensuing laughter felt good.

"I'll make some pancakes," Asher said, "if you'll call Dad to say hello from all of us, and tell him we're fine, and keeping Dylan here for a little longer."

"I can do that," Gunner said, and took off down the hall to make the call and shower and change before they began the day.

It was during the pancake breakfast when Asher brought up the idea of how to bait the Brandts into making a second try. After explaining it in detail, they both agreed.

"So, if you can pull this off, then after it airs, we will basically have to hole up in the house, giving off the perception that we're gone, and lie in wait for them to make a move," Gunner said.

"That's a lot of ifs and maybes," Dylan said.

"That's police work," Asher said. "All I want is to watch that back door opening, and when they get inside the house, slam the door behind them and turn on the lights. I want them to see our faces. I want them to know who we are. I want them to be sorry for the rest of their lives that they ever laid a hand on Jacob Kingston."

"Then set it in motion," Gunner said. "We'll always have your back."

Asher picked up his laptop and cell phone and went into the bar—the quietest place on the property.

His first call was to Reddick. There was a lot to tell, and a chance the sheriff would not be willing to deceive the public. He had to convince him that omitting certain facts in a press conference was just an update without giving away info in a case as yet unsolved. He had all of the updates pulled up on his laptop. There was nothing left to do but make the call.

"Briscoe County Sheriff's office. How may I direct your call?"

"This is Asher Kingston. I need to speak to Sheriff Reddick."

"One moment please."

Asher was staring out the window at the traffic going by when Reddick picked up.

"Asher. Good to hear from you. How can I help you?"

"I have information, and I have a request. Starting with information. You have seen the photos Dylan took of the Brandt brothers, and agreed that we didn't want them arrested on a stolen car when you're trying to get them for attempted murder, right?"

"Yes, and rightly so," Reddick said.

"Gunner and I found the motive. We know exactly why they tried to kill Dad. They visited their dad in prison before he died. We asked ourselves, what if he told them where the money was buried? And if he had, why did they come straight to the Tumbleweed? Then we discovered that the Feds never had a chance to question or interrogate Brenda for anything. They just knew she was in on it in some way and then she was dead. And Brandt said he hid it. Long story short, it wasn't Brandt. It was Brenda who

buried the money, and Gunner and Dylan and I found it. It's already been turned over to the FBI under secrecy. We don't want the Brandts to know that. They won't come back for a second look, and they'll also get away with attempted murder."

Matt Reddick was in shock. "My God... All these years."

"Yes, and Dad still doesn't know any of this, and you can't talk about anything until the Feds have released the news themselves."

"Of course, of course," Reddick said.

"What my brothers and I want to do next is set a trap, but we need to bait it, and that's where you come in. If you were willing to hold a press conference to update the public about your ongoing case, and mention that you are still working leads...and Jacob Kingston, the victim, is still alive, but you have no further information on his condition or when he will be released...and that the Tumbleweed Bar will remain closed until he has recovered, we believe that news will spur the Brandts to come back for another try. A million dollars in bearer bonds is untraceable."

"I can and will gladly do this," Reddick said. "I'll take it from here and contact the TV stations in Amarillo, then hold a press conference on the courthouse steps. Hopefully, our perps will be watching one of the stations when it airs. Now, I have a question. What are your plans to catch them?"

"We already have it in place. There will be no signs that we are there. We're moving the rental car we've been using to a friend's house. Dad's old truck will be parked out back as always, and we're going into stakeout mode inside our own home and wait for the perps to come to us. Shades pulled. Windows down. No indications of life inside. But we'll see them coming and take them by surprise."

"And call me when it's done," Reddick said.

"Yes, sir. They're solely your perps to lock up, and your

case to clear. This has nothing to do with our status as law enforcement. We just want justice for Dad," Asher said.

"Then we're good to go. However, know that I wouldn't be this amenable if you weren't the law officers you already are. That means I trust you not to let your anger influence your treatment of the men you capture."

"We don't beat up the perps we arrest, but we also cannot be worried about a bloody lip or nose if we take one down from behind. These men are big. If they try to make a run for it, it'll take all three of us to bring them down and get them in handcuffs."

"Understood," Reddick said. "Let me make some calls. I'll text you when the press conference happens, and you can watch the stations for yourself when it airs."

"Much appreciated, and thank you, sir."

"No. Thank you. I don't have the manpower or the time to devote that you and your brothers have spent working on this case. I'll be in touch."

As the call ended, Asher leaned back with a sigh of relief. It was happening, and he had a gut feeling that this was going to be the trigger to bringing them down.

He left the bar and went back into the house. "It's done," he said. "Reddick has agreed to all of it. Press conference. The whole thing. And he's setting it up and will let us know details later."

"Hot damn," Gunner said. "I feel good about this."

"I want this over," Dylan said.

"We all do, Dylan. But this is the dirty work it took to make Dad's world safe again, and you were right in there with us. You broke the case when you got their pictures. Knowing what the enemy looks like, and knowing where they hide, is everything to a cop."

Gunner nodded. "Ash is right. You turned a big corner for us. We're all ready to go home."

"And Dad coming home is the last item on our agenda. We can't stay and be his healthcare workers without putting our livelihoods at risk. I'll contact a home healthcare center later, to make sure he has daily visits and help with everything until he is fully healed," Asher said. "And for now, this time is ours. Catch up on rest. Kick back and relax. I'm going to make one last run to Belker's to ensure we don't have a need for anything during the time we're on lockdown. And I'm going to go see Nora. I'm not sure when she's planning to leave."

"Back to Fort Worth?" Dylan asked.

"For the time being, until I can get home. After that, she's moving to Austin with me," Asher said.

"Give her a hug from us," Dylan said. "She is the one who solved the mystery."

"But remember, that's known only to us," Asher said.

He put on his coat and his Stetson, pocketed his phone and the keys to the SUV, and headed out the door.

It was daybreak.

Nora was nose deep beneath her covers when she began hearing the abrupt whap, whap of rotor blades and thought, *helicopter!*

Her first thought was someone was hurt until she realized there were no accompanying sirens, then remembered Ash telling her he was notifying the FBI. If that was them, then she guessed that was an escort, and the Feds had just arrived.

She rolled over and pulled up the covers again, thinking of what they must be going through, then remembered they'd experienced far worse and at a much younger age, and tried to go back to sleep, but it was no use.

"I'd feel a whole lot better about this morning if Asher Kingston was snuggled up behind me," she muttered, then got up and made her bed before she was tempted to get back in it.

She turned up the thermostat on her way to the kitchen, pushed back the curtains over the sink, searching the sky for clouds that weren't there, then started a pot of coffee. It was awkward with only one hand, but she finally got everything filled and hit Start, then turned around and bumped her sore hand.

"Oh lord! Oh crap, that hurt!" she moaned, cradling her hand against her chest until the pain subsided, then gave the caterpillar stitches a quick look.

The eyes she'd drawn on her palm had washed off. It was just as well. She was looking forward to the stitches coming out, and she could hardly wait. She went back to her room to dress, taking the scent of fresh-brewing coffee with her to speed up the process.

Her clothing choices were limited to what she'd brought with her. The house was warm. Yet the sound of cold wind whipping around outside the house made her shiver, which led to pink sweatpants and a matching sweatshirt for the day. She had no video or Zoom meeting scheduled, so the choice went to comfort instead of class. After that, loose fuzzy socks and slip-on shoes were the last to go on.

She was eating a bowl of cereal and on her second cup of coffee, absently wondering how long it took to load up a strongbox full of money, when her cell phone rang. She glanced at Caller ID and frowned. Who did she know from Thomas Realty?

"Hello, this is Nora."

"Nora, it's me, Patty Shreves. Patty Thomas now."

"Patty from high school?" Nora asked.

Patty laughed. "Yes. Mom and Dad still live in Crossroads,

but I'm in Amarillo now. I had dinner with them the other night and found out that your daddy had passed, and you'd come home to 'deal with the house.' Sorry. That was how Mama put it. My deepest sympathies for your loss. You were a good daughter, caring for him for so long."

"His passing was his blessing. He suffered a long time without knowing who he was, or why stuff was happening. I've been here a while, but I'm going to have to get back to Fort Worth soon. It's where I live and work."

"If you decide to rent or sell, I'd be happy to list it for you. I know it's hard to be a long-distance landlord. I handle a lot of rentals."

"I have decided to sell, but I have a houseful of furniture to get rid of first, and I now have stitches in my hand, so work has come to a halt."

"I'm so sorry. When it rains, it pours, right? I won't pressure you, but I wanted to touch base just in case."

"No, no, actually, this is a timely call," Nora said. "Why don't you come and evaluate the property, tell me what to list it for, and get it up for sale?"

"That would be wonderful!" Patty said. "I can come tomorrow morning…around ten? I'll bring my photographer with me. Good pictures for the website sell houses faster, and since the furniture is still there, I'll do a little tweaking for staging, get the photos, and sign the contract. I'll bring comps for the area, and help you decide on a good sale price."

"That would be great. I'll see you then," and the moment Nora disconnected, she felt even more of her burden lifting. One last thing to mark off her to-do list and she'd be leaving.

But leaving Asher up to his neck with bad guys, and Jacob still in the hospital, felt like an act of abandonment. All she could do was hope the sheriff and the media would cooperate with him, and the Brandts would take the bait.

But now that this was happening, she needed to pack up the last of her keepsakes so they'd be out of sight when Patty came tomorrow, and then make one last sweep through the rooms to make sure all the family pictures either had been taken down or were already boxed up for her to take with her.

The business of living began with a birth certificate, kind of like a proof-of-purchase receipt. Death was far more complicated. Letting the world know you were gone required the distribution of multiple death certificates, cancelling policies, ending memberships, and paying taxes even after the last breath had been taken, and Nora was weary of it all.

Asher Kingston didn't thrive in disorder. He needed to know what was happening, what his part in it was, and what needed to happen next, and he hadn't had one solid day of order since the phone call from his dad, telling him about Nora. At that moment, every carefully planned aspect of his life blew up in his face.

It was Brenda's fault. She'd disrupted all of their lives when she ended hers. But it was also the wakeup call that he'd needed, and now he couldn't imagine any aspect of his life without Nora in it.

Finding out about her stalker had been a shock. Learning how she'd saved herself, then found a retreat in her ivory tower that gave her the safety and space to continue her work without giving up what she loved, turned on every protective instinct he had.

He knew she wasn't helpless. Far from it, but he wanted to be there for her when she needed it. To make that happen, they first had to put the Brandt brothers in prison, and that was uppermost in his mind as he came out of Belker's with a bouquet of flowers.

Three minutes later, he was pulling up into Nora's driveway.

He loved her. He wanted her. Every part of him ached to take her to bed. He was saying it with flowers, but if she was slow to get the message, he was willing to strip naked and let her see it for herself.

He traded his Stetson for the flowers and left it in the front seat. Then he was out the door and running up the steps with the wind at his back.

He knocked, waiting for the sound of her footsteps, then all of sudden, the door swung inward and there she stood. A vision in pink wearing fuzzy socks and slippers. The smile on her face was all it took to pull him over the threshold. He shut the door and laid the flowers in her arms.

"Asher! I love them. I never get flowers. They're beautiful."

"Like you," he said. "Go put them in water so I can kiss you."

She laughed. "Come help. I'm still making messes with this one," she said, waving the hand with the stitches.

He shed his coat on the sofa and followed, got a vase from the etagere, filled it half full of water for her, then watched her put them in the water and arrange them.

"The fall colors in this are just perfect. I love them, and they'll make a nice focal point on the dining table. I'm signing a contract with a realtor tomorrow and she's using the existing furniture for staging."

As soon as she finished the arrangement, he carried it to the dining table for her, and as he turned, he caught a wistful expression on her face.

"Are you sad, darlin'... About selling the house, I mean?"

She shrugged. "A little, but realistic about it, too. It's not the same with them gone, you know? I keep thinking about the us we resurrected. That's where my hopes are. They're already with you."

The look in her eyes. The words she'd just said. Like turning a cog and watching it fall into place. With her there was no discord, only peace. He brushed a kiss across her lips, then cupped her face, feeling the softness of her skin against his palms.

"You are my touchstone. You always were. You always will be. I will always love and protect you."

"My darling, Ash. Through no fault of your own, you are the one who was left in charge, but you're also the one who needs to be cared for, and tended to, and loved harder... loved more. Let me be that person for you, too. I know you still have to clear the deck for your dad, but spare me enough time for this. Come to bed with me. It's going to take the rest of our lives to catch up with what we lost. Now is as good a time as any to start refilling the well. Make love now. Make babies with me later."

Then she was in his arms, moving through the shadowed halls, and once again, into her bedroom.

Inhibitions came off with their clothes.

They were as frantic for the joining as they had been when they were young and crazy wild for each other, but old enough now to savor the sweet heat of building a slow fire. One that engulfed, instead of flashed.

Asher was stretched out beside her, tracing the shape of her cheek, to the shallow beneath her throat, to the weight of her breasts in his hand. Watching her eyelids flutter as he rolled her nipple between his fingers. Hearing the catch in her breath when he slid his hands between her legs, then leaving a trail of kisses from her chin to her belly button.

Nora's heart was racing as he moved over her, then in her. It was the beginning, and she already wanted more.

She knew what turned him on. It was her.

Sex between them had always been magic. A quickening of souls as well as bodies, and this time as he began, she

wrapped her legs around his waist and pulled him deeper. It was ecstasy, and a kind of agony as he began to move. One minute, then another and another, and she could feel it building—wanting it to go on forever, then suddenly desperate for a release.

It came without warning. Shattering focus and concentration as the blood rush hit. They lay in each other's arms until there was nothing left of the ride but the intermittent ripple of aftershocks.

Asher buried his face in the thick fall of her hair, groaning softly at the thought of having to move.

"God, Nora, you destroy me."

Nora looked up into his face, at the high cheekbones and stubborn chin. A mouth for laughter, and kissing. And the clear-blue color of his eyes.

"I will lose sleep thinking about this, and doing without you…without this wild madness you turn on inside me, but you are so very worth the wait. I love you. And I also know you haven't finished what you came to do."

He rolled over, taking her with him, and pulled her close as she pillowed her head upon his chest. "Yes, we do, and there's still work to do. Reddick agreed to the press conference. Once it airs, we go on lockdown. The Tumbleweed will appear to be vacant, and we'll be on stakeout inside. If they come, it will be at night. There will be no lights, and only Dad's truck parked out back like always. We don't know how long it will take, but we're hoping for no longer than a day or two, and I have a request. Will it be okay if I park the rental car in front of your house during that time?"

"Park it in the driveway, Ash. It's wide enough for two cars and it will keep it off the street," she said.

"Thank you, honey. If they air the press conference tomorrow, I'll bring the car up before dark, and then go home through the alley like I used to," he said.

He kissed her one last time, and then got up, grabbing his clothes as he headed for the bathroom, leaving Nora free to eye his beautiful body as he was walking away.

"Mine, all mine," she sighed, then picked up her clothes and headed across the hall to the en suite in her parents' room.

All too soon, they were at the door and saying goodbye.

"Asher, please don't get yourself killed. You're all I have left to love in this world."

He hugged her. "We're going to be fine. You go about your days and nights like normal. You already know more about what's happening than it's safe for you to know. Can't have you becoming someone else's target, understood?"

"Understood," Nora said.

"Good luck tomorrow with your realtor. Love you." Then he walked out into the cold and drove away.

Asher ordered food to go from Pearl's, then made one more trip through Belker's before stopping at the Rose to pick it up. He was in and out within minutes, and headed home.

Dylan came out to meet him and carried in the groceries, while Asher brought the food from Pearl's.

"Anyone know when trash is picked up here?" Asher asked.

"Tuesday and Friday for businesses. Tomorrow is Tuesday," Gunner said.

"Then after we eat, we need to get all of our refuse into the dumpster out front so that it gets hauled off before all this goes down. Considering how long Dad's been in the hospital, extra bags of trash might give us away," Asher added.

They got the groceries put away, then sat down at the table as Ash began distributing the to-go meals he'd picked up.

"What are we having tonight?" Gunner asked.

"Meatloaf with two sides, biscuits and peach cobbler. It was the daily special," Asher said. He was about to remove the lid from his order when his cell signaled a text. "Sheriff's office," he said, and scanned the text. "Good news. Reddick scheduled his press conference for tomorrow morning at 10:00 a.m. They'll air it live as a news bulletin, then air the taped version again on the evening news." He sent a thumbs-up emoji back, and disconnected. "This is it, my brothers. Let's hope it works and we close the case."

"Amen to that," Dylan said.

Gunner nodded. He was already fork deep in meatloaf and gravy. "What's going on with our secret weapon?"

Asher looked up. "You mean Nora? She has a realtor coming tomorrow. She's decided to sell the house. I asked if we could park the SUV in her driveway when we go on lockdown. That way the only vehicle left on the property is dad's truck, which would be expected, and she said yes."

"I hope the weather holds," Dylan said. "Cold is one thing, but snow is another. No way for a thief to hide footprints in the snow."

"It's going to work out because Brandt's sons aren't any smarter than he was. The only thing in their heads is that untraceable money. They tried to kill for it once. They're not done."

Chapter 14

THE KINGSTON BROTHERS WERE IN THE LIVING ROOM OF their family home, waiting for the press conference to begin. The local stations had just interrupted programming, and Rachelle Morgan, an on-site reporter, was already setting the stage for what was to come.

News crews from three different TV affiliates out of Amarillo were in Silverton, set up at the steps of the Briscoe County Courthouse, waiting for Sheriff Matt Reddick to appear. Local residents had seen the news crews, and the small gathering around the news vans was a result of curiosity.

As the Kingstons watched in silence, the doors to the courthouse opened just as Rachelle's commentary was in full swing. The tone of her voice shifted to a higher note, and she began talking faster, wanting to get it all said before Reddick took the mic.

"And... Sheriff Reddick has just come out of the courthouse. All we know is this has to do with the attempted assassination of Jacob Kingston, a respected and well-known businessman in Crossroads, Texas. You may remember the Kingston name from some years past, when, unknown to Jacob, his wife Brenda was involved with Pete Brandt, the leader of an armed robbery in Amarillo some twenty-plus years back. Brenda Kingston committed suicide on the day of her arrest, and just recently, the gang leader, Pete Brandt, passed away in prison. There has been

supposition that it could be connected, but we have had no confirmation on that. We're hoping Sheriff Reddick will have some answers."

Asher's eyes narrowed as Reddick paused above the steps for a moment of posterity. Framed by the grand white pillars of the courthouse that stood above the fan of descending steps, all eyes turned toward him.

Good. He has their attention.

And when he started down the steps with an inscrutable expression, the crowd hushed. The silver star of a Texas sheriff's badge was pinned on the sheepskin coat he was wearing against the chill, and the grey Stetson firmly settled on his head was to shade his eyes against the morning sun.

Reddick knew a lot depended on saying the right things, without saying too much. He wanted the perps jailed who'd done this, and the case closed, so when he approached the mic bank, he wasted no time.

"I'm Sheriff Matt Reddick of the Briscoe County Sheriff's department. The reason for this press conference is twofold. It is a plea for help on an open case regarding the attempted murder of Jacob Kingston, of Crossroads, Texas. Apparently, the media has already created its own version of motive, but that's all conjecture. The truth is, at this time, we do not know the shooter's identity, intent, or how many there were. We have received one report of a vehicle speeding away from the bar, but it was midnight. No identification of the driver or the tag number. Forensics is plowing through a mountain of DNA that, so far, tells us nothing except who liked to drink beer at the Tumbleweed Bar. This is a public plea for information. If you know anything that would lead us to the perpetrators,

call the Briscoe County Sheriff's department. The number will be running in a crawl on the bottom of your screen. And a fair warning to those who file false claims, or purposefully point the blame at someone you're mad at as a means of revenge. Rest assured we do not take lightly to people wasting precious man-hours and money running down false leads, and you will face fines and possible jail time if you do it." Reddick cleared his throat, then looked straight into the cameras for full effect. "At last update, we know Jacob Kingston is still in the hospital. We have no information to share regarding his prognosis. All we do know is that, for the time being, the Tumbleweed Bar in Crossroads, Texas, is officially closed, and we have no timeline as to when it might reopen."

Hands were going up and reporters were clamoring for attention as Asher lowered the volume, then looked at his brothers and smiled.

"That was good. Damn good. They'll air this again tonight. Now all we can do is hope the Brandts saw it. I'll get the SUV to Nora's later today, then we're inside until it's over, and I just had a thought as I was watching. What do you guys think about pulling the security detail off of dad's room, and putting them on stakeout at the place where the Brandts are staying, instead?"

Gunner had been slouched in a chair while watching the press conference, but this was a focus shift he liked.

"Yes! Now that you found out where they're staying, security would know if they were venturing toward the hospital, and even better, they would know if they left Amarillo. We'd have a major jump on them if we knew they were headed this way," he said.

Dylan nodded. "But they wouldn't actually follow them all the way here, right?"

"Right," Ash said. "If they follow them through traffic and see for sure that they take the highway I-27 south toward Tulia, then we could safely assume they are making another move. At that point, we tell them to stand by until we have them in handcuffs."

"I say yes," Gunner said. "Get them on it now!"

"Leaving all that to the cops in the family," Dylan said. "I'm just ready to thump some heads."

"I promised Reddick we would not rough up his prisoners," Asher said.

"I hope you left a little leeway, just in case," Gunner said.

"We have leeway, not carte blanche," Asher said. "I'm going to contact Bill Eldridge now. He and his brother can keep the same schedule. It's the location that will be changed. They know what the Brandts look like, and what they're driving, because I shared Dylan's pictures."

"Should I call Dad and let him know why his guard is disappearing?" Gunner asked.

"He'll want to know why," Dylan said.

"Maybe… Maybe not. I think he'll trust us without question, but if he does, just tell him the guards are still on the job, and hopefully it'll be over within the next couple of days. Just give me time to contact the security company, then you can call him."

"Then if I'm not needed for the moment, I'm going to catch up on email, and call Angie."

"Anything wrong?" Asher asked.

"No. I miss her. I just want to hear the sound of her voice. I'll know if she's not okay," Dylan said, and left the living room.

Gunner stood.

Asher was on the phone.

Dylan was on the phone.

So he went into the bar, and began eyeing the layout, making mental notes as to where they should hide if the Brandts came in the front door again. And then he went back into the house, and eyeing the same setup, were they to come into the house first, instead.

Nora watched the whole press conference.

In her opinion, it was an open invitation to the Brandts, but only time would tell if it worked. It all hinged on the possibility they would see it, then decide if they wanted to chance another search, and there was no guarantee any of that would happen. It was all a gamble.

But since Asher warned her to stay out of it for her own safety, she let go of what she couldn't control. She had a house to sell, and Patty Thomas just pulled up into her driveway.

She turned off the television, and as she was getting up to let Patty in, shifted to her work persona—all smiles and courtesy without revealing an iota of what she was thinking.

She opened the door as Patty and a stocky man with a baby face and a receding hairline came up the steps.

"Good morning," Nora said, and stepped aside to let them enter, then closed the door to the cold.

Patty was all smiles. "Morning, Nora. This is my husband Lee Thomas, who does the photography for my listings. Lee, this is Nora Borden."

"A pleasure," Lee said. "Patty speaks of you highly, and my sympathies on your recent loss."

"Thank you," Nora said. "There's a coat closet in the hall. We'll get your coats hung up, so they won't be in the way for the photos you want to take. Why don't you two walk

the rooms on your own, tweak whatever you want for your pictures, and if there are things you need to ask, I'm here."

"Perfect," Patty said. "We'll start in the bedrooms and work our way back through the rest of the house."

Nora nodded. "If you have a copy of your contract, I can be reading it while you're doing your sweep," she said.

Patty hesitated, then realized Nora wasn't going to be someone who needed explanations about the verbiage.

"Of course," she said, pulled a contract out of her briefcase and handed it over.

"Thanks," Nora said, and sat down in a chair by the fireplace, turned on the floor lamp beside the chair, and began to read as Lee and Patty left the room.

She could hear them talking, then soon tuned out the words. She already knew where the flaws were in this house. Hearing them bandied about would have made it feel like a moral judgment, rather than the simple fact that what was here was out of style. This house was where she began her life. Where she grew to adulthood. And when she was honest with herself, the same one she abandoned for a big wide world she'd never seen.

It was the same thing she and Asher had done to each other. Abandoning first love without intention, then letting go instead of trying to keep it alive. She was losing this house but getting Asher back in return, and well aware it was the better deal.

She read all the way through the contract twice, then set it aside. It was a standard contract, without any hidden clauses or fees. She heard Lee and Patty coming out of her parents' room, coming up the hall and into the kitchen and utility area, then heard the back door open and close, and was glad she'd fixed that loose windowpane.

When they came back into the kitchen and began checking water pressure, and the condition of the cabinets and

built-ins, she had no concerns about any of it. The appliances were installed new, less than a month before her mother's death, and the countertops had been replaced at the same time. Nora loved them and hoped the new owners would, too.

The Realtors were back in the living room and smiling as they sat down with her.

"Nora, this house is delightful. It has such a warmth and welcoming vibe," Patty said. "I have a couple of questions. Are you taking the furniture with you, or do you plan to sell it?" Patty asked.

"I won't be taking it. Before I leave, I will have given away every piece of furniture in this house to any of the residents of Crossroads who want it."

Patty blinked. "You don't want to hold an auction?"

Nora shrugged. "It's like putting my parents on the auction block and waiting to see what people think of them. How high will they bid? How low does it go? I'd rather know someone has it who wants or needs it."

Patty stared long and hard at Nora for a good five seconds, and then leaned forward. "What do you do for a living?"

"I'm in IT," Nora said. "Will I need to hire an assessor to put a monetary value on the property?"

"That's part of Lee's side of Thomas Realty. He's licensed and everything," Patty said.

Nora shifted focus to him. "I'll base my decision on an asking price relevant to the assessment value, so let me know as soon as possible as to your decision. Nobody will be fighting for this property. There will be no bidding wars. There is no reason to buy a house in the middle of nowhere, unless you already know what's here. Few amenities. No law. A small school system, basic businesses, and an ER that operates with two nurses on duty and a doctor who shows

up once a week. Fully capable, of course," she said, and held up her hand with the visible stitches for proof.

Patty sighed. "Yes, I know all too well, which is why I left."

"I'll do some figuring today and get back to you," Lee said.

"And I'll get some comps for the area to help you decide…if you still want us to represent you," Patty said.

"That will be fine," Nora said. "And yes, I do, and the contract is agreeable. Shall we adjourn to the dining table to finish this up?" and then got up and led the way.

A short while later, they were gone, and there was a big red-and-white Thomas Realty sign in the front yard, announcing the finality of her decision. FOR SALE.

It wasn't a death notice, but it felt a little like it to Nora as she paused in the hall beside the grandfather clock.

"I'm sorry. But I'll find someone who'll love you as much as Mama and Dad and I did. You won't be empty anymore. I promise."

Everett Brandt's fever finally broke during the night, and by daylight, he was up, his bed stripped of sheets and in the laundry along with what he slept in. When Freddie woke up to the sound of laundry and the scent of coffee, he knew Everett was up; he thought he'd test himself and see if being upright still made the room spin.

To his relief, it did not, and he went in search of a cup of coffee, too.

"Everett! We're better, aren't we?" Freddie said as he entered the kitchen.

"Feels like it. Not taking any chances though. Toast and coffee first just to see if it sets okay on our stomachs," he said.

Freddie poured himself a cup and sat down before reaching for a piece of dry toast. Without butter, it didn't look very appetizing, so he dunked a corner of it in his coffee and took a bite.

"Why are we doing laundry so early?" Freddie asked as he was chewing.

"Washing the sheets I've been sleeping on to get rid of all the germs. Soon as you finish eating, strip your bed and I'll wash yours, too. And your pajamas."

Freddie nodded, swallowed the last of his toast, and reached for another.

The television was on in the other room. Freddie wasn't listening, but Everett was, and all of a sudden, he bolted from the table and ran for the remote to turn up the volume.

Freddie followed. "What's happening?" he asked.

"They just announced the Briscoe County Sheriff is holding a press conference this morning, about the shooting at the Tumbleweed Bar. It starts after the commercial. Sit down and listen. We need to know what they know. Understand?"

"Everett, are we going to jail?" Freddie whispered.

"If they knew who they were looking for, we'd already be there, and why are you whispering? There's nobody here but us," Everett muttered.

"Right," Freddie said.

As soon as the commercial ended, they went live to the site. The reporter was talking, and Everett was riveted with every word she uttered. And then they saw the sheriff descending the courthouse steps, and he held his breath as the man began to speak.

The more the sheriff said, the better Everett felt about everything. Kingston's prognosis didn't sound good, and there was no timeline on when he might be released. They didn't have any leads or witnesses and were asking for the

public's help. And then the icing on the cake was hearing that the Tumbleweed Bar was closed until further notice.

"Did you hear that, Freddie? The bar is closed. Nobody is running it. It's shut until further notice."

"Guess we won't be having any more beers from there then, will we?" Freddie said.

Everett turned his head and stared at his brother like he was looking at a stranger. He would like to believe Freddie was still suffering from the aftereffects of his Aya high, but the truth was, Freddie came this way, and nothing was ever going to change him. He sighed.

"You're right. No more beers, but now we can go back and look for our inheritance without anyone bothering us. They won't even know we're there," Everett said.

Freddie frowned. "I don't want to go back, Everett. I don't really want the money."

"I need you to help. You're stronger than me. And when we get it, I can take care of you real good for the rest of our lives," Everett said.

"You take care of me just fine right now," Freddie said.

"Yes, I do. But who's taking care of me? We're living off my disability and using it up before the end of the month every time." Everett was frustrated and angry, and still felt like shit. "We're going after that money tonight, and I don't want to hear any more about it. Understand?"

"I understand," Freddie said. "Are we gonna be Joe and Darren again?"

"Damn it all to hell, Freddie. No. We're gonna be us, and we're gonna go find a treasure. We need to make a quick trip to the hardware store. We need a shovel and a pry bar to take with us."

Freddie made a U-turn and left the room. Everett was yelling again. Freddie was resigned. Like it or not, they were going back to the Tumbleweed.

Bill Eldredge got the call from Asher just before noon, and without a word to Jacob Kingston, headed for his vehicle on the run. He drove straight to the address he'd been given, then began looking for the white Mustang from the photo.

It didn't take long to locate it. Next step was finding a place to park among the other vehicles that would still give him a line of sight to the car. And when he did, he sent his twin a message about the change of plans and settled in to wait.

It was just before 1:00 p.m. when Eldredge saw two men exit the building who matched the men from the photos he'd been given. Then when they got into the same car, it verified their identities.

He waited until they were on the move, then slowly moved into traffic behind them, and followed them all the way to a hardware store. He parked when they parked, then waited for them to come back.

When they came out carrying a shovel and a pry bar and put it in the trunk of the car, he took photos from his phone, then followed them back to their apartment and guessed it was going to be a long wait.

He sent a text back to Asher, along with the photos.

Somebody's going digging for something.
Phil will be on stakeout after 6:00 p.m.
He knows the score.

The for sale sign at the Borden house was a little shocking. Ash couldn't begin to guess how this made her feel. And, as

he was pulling up into the driveway, the obvious absence of her car made him wonder where she might be, then let it go as he locked up the SUV and headed down the street and into the alley.

The temps were in the high thirties. Not quite freezing weather, but in a land with few windbreaks, it felt much colder. He was walking with his hands in his coat pockets and his shoulders hunched against the cold, with all manner of scenarios tumbling through his thoughts. He came out of the alley at the gas station, then headed toward the Tumbleweed and jogged all the way to the back door of the house. He paused before going in to gauge the appearance of the house.

The shades were down. The curtains had been pulled shut at every window. His dad's truck was parked on the east side of the house, out of sight for anyone coming from the west. If he hadn't known better, he would have assumed no one was home.

Satisfied, he let himself in, locking the door behind him, and then went to his room to hang up his coat. The clip in his gun was full, and his handcuffs were on the bed, ready to grab at a moment's notice.

The door to Dylan's room was open, but when Asher checked, he found him asleep on his bed. It was pure instinct that made him shake out the blanket at the foot of the bed and cover him up, just as he'd done when they were little. The door to Gunner's room was closed, and so he passed it by on his way to the kitchen.

He was making himself a sandwich when he got Eldredge's text, and the moment he read it, he guessed the Brandts had seen the press conference and were preparing to make a night run back to Jacob's bar. So far, so good.

He finished making the sandwich, added a handful of chips, grabbed a can of Pepsi, and went into the living room. He kept the volume on the TV low as he ate, and

then once again, his mind wandered back to Nora, so he sent her a text.

Dropped off the SUV.
Love the warrior you are.
Stay safe for me.
Can't wait to begin our life together.
Ash

———————

After meeting with the realtor, Nora felt unsettled.

The for sale sign in the front yard made her decision so final. Even when she knew it was for the best, it was like going through one more death, and it hurt her heart. She needed food and perspective, and for that, she drove down to the Yellow Rose.

The dining room was nearly full, but she found a seat at a small table by the window, hung her coat on the back of her chair, and glanced up at the chalkboard to read the Daily Special before looking at the menu. When she saw chicken and dumplings, the thought of comfort food settled her choice.

Darla swung by to fill her coffee cup and take her order, then Nora settled in to wait.

———————

Pearl had already heard through the Crossroads gossip train that the Borden property was for sale, and when she found out Nora was in the dining room, she peeked around the corner and saw her sitting alone, and made a quick call to her girl, Maggie, at the Sunset Ranch.

Maggie picked up on the second ring.

"Hello, my sweet Pearlie. What's going on with you today?"

Pearl grinned. Her almost-daughter had recently given her a nickname, and she loved it.

"Quick question," Pearl said. "About your foreman, Chris Jackson... Are he and his wife still looking to move out of my old place for a bigger place of their own?"

"They want to, but I think the bank turned them down for a loan, why?"

"Nora Borden's family home has a For Sale sign in the front yard. I heard she'd be willing to sell the furnishings along with the house. Don't know what she's asking, but it's a little jewel, and much bigger than my little two-bedroom, one-bath house."

"Really? Sonny and I haven't approached Chris about it yet, but we were thinking about buying a property, letting their rent go toward ownership, and not charging them interest. Sonny doesn't want to lose him as foreman. Is Nora still in Crossroads? Do you think we could see it? Or would we have to go through the Realtor?"

"She's sitting in my dining room at this moment. If you want, I'll give her your number and you two can go from there," Pearl said.

"Yes! Please do," Maggie said, and bolted outside to talk to Sonny.

Pearl hung up, smiling, and went into the dining room to talk to Nora.

"Nora, honey. Maggie and Sonny are interested in buying your house. If I give you Maggie's number, would you be willing to call them about it?"

Nora's heart skipped. *Already?* "Why, yes, that would be fine. Are they moving into town?"

"No, they thrive on that ranch, but their foreman recently

married, and he and his new bride don't have room where they are now. They've been looking for a property to buy for him on a rent-to-own basis."

"How generous of them!" Nora said. "I would be happy to talk to them."

Pearl nodded and pulled up Maggie's number on her phone. "Here's her number, and there comes Darla with your food. Good luck."

For the first time in ages, Nora felt optimistic. She didn't wait until after her lunch. She made the call where she was sitting.

It rang three times, and then Maggie Bluejacket answered.

"Hello. Nora? It's so kind of you to call. I hope this isn't interrupting your lunch."

"Not at all. It's still a bit hot and needs to cool. So, you're interested in my family home as a residence for your foreman?"

"Yes. We would love to see it. Has a price been set?" Maggie asked.

"It's been set with the house and land. But the furnishings are available to be left with the property if the buyer so wishes, otherwise, I plan to give them away. I have all of the information at the house, and as soon as I finish lunch, I'm going home."

"Would you be there in about an hour and a half?" Maggie asked.

"For sure," Nora said. "It's the only house on Bluebell Street that has a For Sale sign in the front yard."

"Wonderful. We'll see you soon," Maggie said.

Nora was smiling as she put the phone back in her pocket, then picked up her soup spoon and took her first bite. It was warm, and savory, with light-as-air dumplings, and tender bites of stewed chicken.

She ate all the way to the bottom of the bowl and took a piece of coconut cream pie home for dessert. As soon as she was home, she put her pie in the fridge, and for ambiance, turned on the gas log fireplace at the end of the living room, and all the lights in the house. It was her gift to the old girl, making her look as pretty as possible for the prospective buyers.

Without anything to do but wait, she googled the address of Asher's home in Austin. Even though it wasn't for sale, the exterior and interior pictures were still on Zillow.

What she hadn't expected was the size of it, or the Spanish architecture. It was big and it was gorgeous. With a four-bedroom home, she was fairly certain that she could claim one of them for an office. That was her future, and she was sitting in her past. It was time to let it go.

Maggie and Sonny were changing clothes, getting ready to go into town when Sonny stopped, and turned around.

"Maggie, honey, I think we need to talk to Chris and Ellen about this. They are the ones who need to okay the house. I wouldn't want them to feel obligated to agree to living there, if they didn't like it," Sonny said.

Maggie sighed. "As usual, you're right. You know me, always wanting to fix the world. Definitely talk to Chris. See if he and Ellen will go with us."

"He's unloading feed. I'll go talk to him now," Sonny said, and then stopped and kissed her. "Don't ever stop caring for the world. I'll be happy with whatever you have left," then he put on his last boot and went to find Chris.

Chris Jackson wasn't as skinny as he'd been when he came to work for the Sunset Ranch. Good food and a place to call home had turned the tide. His hair was always about a month past needing a haircut. He'd broken his nose twice in his life, and the last time, it healed just the tiniest bit crooked. His skin was perennially bronzed for all his years in the sun, but when he smiled, his whole face lit up, and that's what had attracted Ellen Hardy to the man she'd married.

Chris had been thanking his lucky stars ever since that day at the Crossroads gas station when he stood at the pumps counting his money to see if he had enough to pay for fuel. He was wondering where he was next going to lay his head, when Maggie Bluejacket walked up to him, said her husband wanted to hire him, and then handed him her phone.

The years since felt nothing short of a miracle, and meeting his Ellen and then marrying her felt like he'd won the lottery. He was unloading the last few bags of cubes for the horses when he heard Sonny calling.

"In here, boss!" Chris said, and stepped out of the breezeway to wave Sonny down, then took the last two bags into a granary and fastened the door on the way out as Sonny walked in. "What's up?"

"You know I don't meddle in your business, don't you?" Sonny said.

Chris frowned. "Of course, I know that. Why?"

Sonny sighed. "Unfortunately, I do not speak for my wife, nor am I ever able to change her mind when she's got a plan, and a grand plan it is, this time. We think the world of you and Ellen. And we knew you were trying to get a bank loan to buy a house, but didn't qualify. And we also know that two people living in Pearl's little house has to be hard."

Chris shrugged. "It's okay. We're managing."

"What if Maggie and I could manage something a little better for you?"

He frowned. "Like what?"

"A really nice house just came up for sale in Crossroads. And Maggie had this idea that if we bought it, then you and Ellen could move in there and start a home of your own. Your rent would be interest free and would go toward ownership of the property. Technically, we're just doing what the bank wouldn't do, without all the fuss."

Chris was stunned. "Oh my God! I don't know what to say."

"We're getting ready to go view the property, and we think you and Ellen should go with us. If you don't like the house, then we won't buy it. But if you do, it will become your new home. Oh…and it comes fully furnished… If you are okay with the furnishings in it."

Chris took off his hat and looked away.

Sonny knew he'd just made a grown man cry. "You go home and put on a pair of boots without horse poop on them, and load up your pretty little wife. The house is on Bluebell Street. It will be the only one with a For Sale sign in the yard. We'll go in together, okay?"

Chris turned. His chin was up. His eyes were shining from unshed tears.

"Yes sir, boss. On the way," he said, and headed for his truck. He was out of the driveway and already on the blacktop before Sonny got back in the house.

Maggie was holding her breath. "Did he just quit from being insulted by the offer, or is he going to get his wife?"

Sonny laughed. "He's going to get Ellen. We need to hustle, or he'll beat us there."

Maggie blew him a kiss and ran to get her purse and coat.

Sonny picked up the keys to his truck, and as soon as Maggie returned, they were out the door and gone.

When Chris came running into the house, Ellen thought something was wrong.

"Chris, honey! What happened? Are you alright?"

Chris picked her up and swung her around in the middle of the living room floor, kissed her soundly, then began pulling off his dirty boots.

"We're going to look at a house that's for sale. Sonny and Maggie said they'll buy it for us if we like it, then we can pay them back on a rent-to-own basis, interest free. The house comes furnished. They want us to go with them. If we don't like it, they don't buy it."

Ellen gasped. "You're kidding. Nobody does stuff like that."

"Sonny and Magnolia Bluejacket aren't nobodies. They're somebodies."

"I can't go looking like this," she said.

"Then change your clothes, and make it quick. We're meeting them at the property, and they were right behind me."

The Kingstons had been alerted to Bill Eldrege's message and immediately formed two plans of action. If the Brandts came back, they would either come in from the bar, or in from the back. But since the bar was closed, any vehicle parked in the lot now would be suspect. And since no one was home, hiding their car in the back, and coming in through that door seemed the most logical, although attributing logic to Everett and Freddie Brandt seemed a bit of a stretch.

The trash truck had emptied the dumpster at the bar.

The only light in the bar was one nightlight. And, once it got dark, there would be no lights turned on in the house. Asher had even turned off the back porch light to give the thieves an illusion of security.

The Kingstons were in the living room with the TV on mute, using the closed-captioning to read what was going on. They were as ready as they could be without knowing when or if the thieves would even show.

"Gunner, what did Dad say when you called?" Dylan asked.

Gunner shrugged. "Very little about what was happening here. He just said that we knew what we were doing, and not to get ourselves killed."

Asher was kicked back in the recliner, watching his brothers' banter and thinking how alike they looked and how different they were. They all had their dad's black hair and blue eyes. They all had varying degrees of his facial features. They were all angles and planes, along with the stubborn jut of Jacob's jaw. Brenda had left no visible evidence of her DNA with any of them. And after her exit from their lives, the only thing she'd left behind was a reputation they had to live down.

For Asher, it was Nora's entrance into his world that turned everything around when he was young, and their reunion had turned him upside down. Instead of being able to celebrate the fact, he was after killers, and she was still going through all the sad, bad days on her own. He knew she understood. He knew she was okay with the status quo at this moment, but he wasn't.

He just wanted this mess to be over.

Nora was sitting in a chair by the fireplace, which gave her a

direct sight line to the street in front of her house. Between the warmth from the fire, and the silence of the house, she was fighting the urge to sleep when she saw two trucks pulling up in front of her house, and then two couples getting out.

She recognized Sonny and Maggie and was wondering who the second couple might be when it dawned on her. The foreman and his wife. The two people who would be living here if they bought the house. That made it all the more important for Nora that they liked what they saw. She waited for them to knock before going to the door, then took a deep breath and opened it wide.

"Welcome! Come inside where it's warm," she said.

"It's really kind of you to do this for us," Sonny said. "Chris and Ellen, this is Nora Borden. I am told this house has been in her family for years. Nora, this is my foreman, Chris Jackson, and his wife Ellen. Maggie and I didn't feel like it was fair to make the decision for them, so we asked them to accompany us. Hope you don't mind."

Nora smiled directly at Chris and Ellen. "Of course I don't mind. I could take you on a tour, but if it was me, I'd want to do the first look on my own, so all of you feel free to look the place over. Open closets. Bang cabinets. Flush toilets for water pressure. If you want to start with the living room, I'll step into the kitchen out of your way, and when you're finished in here, I'll move myself back here and leave the rest of the house to you. Okay? Also, know that I'm willing to leave all of the furnishings, even the grandfather clock, if you wish. When I was little, I always thought of it as the guard up the hall from my room, rather than a time-piece. Hearing it strike the hour was like an all's-well signal. Oh, for the innocence of the imagination of a child, right?"

Chapter 15

SONNY FELT EVERY ASPECT OF HER SADNESS, AND SAW the depths of Nora's secrets. She was a warrior in her own right. The man she chose was her equal. He liked the spirit in this house. It was good.

As they moved through the house, he could hear the excitement in Ellen's voice and witnessed the continuing disbelief on Chris's face. He knew exactly what this felt like. The same way he'd felt when he found out Ellis Cooper had willed him an entire ranch. This was Sonny's way of giving back, and Maggie was right in the middle of their delight, exclaiming over the dark-wood trims and the beauty of the original floors.

"So, what do you think?" Sonny asked as they were viewing the last bedroom at the end of the hall.

"We love it," Chris said. "It's so grand compared to where we are. Not sure we can afford the rent."

Sonny laughed. "Cowboy, you haven't been paying attention. If I own it outright, then I set the rent, and whatever you've been paying Pearl will be fine with us."

Chris blinked in disbelief. "I know you're my boss and all, but I have an overwhelming urge to hug you until you're squeaking for air."

Sonny grinned. "No need for all that, so it's a done deal. We'll get the ball rolling with the realtor. Do you want the furnishings left?"

"Lord, yes," Ellen said. "We have nothing, and these are beautiful. It will feel like home in no time."

Sonny nodded. "Duly noted. Let's go tell Nora."

Nora was standing at the kitchen window, remembering where her swing set used to be, and eyeing the dug cellar out back, when she heard them coming up the hall, and went to meet them.

"What's the verdict?" she asked.

"It's a yes from all of us, with the furnishings," Sonny said.

Nora was beaming. "The comps in this area are great for a buyer. The asking price, with furniture included, is $160,000. Is that okay with you?"

"More than okay," Sonny said, and held out his hand.

Nora shook it gladly.

"Wonderful, Sonny. The phone number for the realty company is on the sign in the front yard. Ask for Patty when you give them a call. I'll notify her tonight that a full offer has been made, so she won't schedule any appointments to view." Then she smiled at Chris and Kelly. "I'll likely be long gone before all the paperwork goes through, but I wish you a long and happy life together here."

"Thank you so much for offering the furnishings along with the house. They will be treasured," Ellen said.

Nora walked them to the door, waved as they drove away, then closed the door and cried. It felt a little like pulling the plug on life support, but she was also glad that it was over. Then she glanced at the time, wiped her eyes and blew her nose, and made a call to the realty office.

A man answered. "Thomas Realty. How may I direct your call?"

"Nora Borden calling for Patty Thomas."

"One moment while I transfer your call," he said.

A few seconds later, Patty picked up. "This is Patty."

"Patty, this is Nora Borden. Good news. I just got a full offer for the house with furnishings included. The buyer is Sonny Bluejacket. He'll be in touch."

"Is he that rodeo guy? Mom and Dad said he was living out on Ellis Cooper's old place."

"He owns it. It is a very large, very well-established training facility for rodeo horses."

"Well, that's just wonderful, but of course we'll have to wait for approval from his bank," Patty said.

"No. He's paying cash, so there will be no need for a property appraisal, however, the inspector will still need to go through the property to identify repair issues," Nora said.

"I guess I didn't know he was that well-off," Patty muttered.

Nora laughed. "Those cowboys pay tens of thousands for well-trained horses, and that's what he does... Train them for any or all rodeo events. However, it's apparent that you don't know who he's married to."

Now Patty was beyond curious. "I don't believe I do. Do tell."

"Ever hear of an artist by the name of Magnolia Brennen?"

"Well, yes! Lee and I attended one of her showings in a big art studio in Santa Fe."

"That's his wife. She used to wait tables at the Yellow Rose. They're buying this property for their ranch foreman and his new bride. Anyway... Just wanted to give you a heads up. He's rodeo royalty and she's the reigning new discovery in the art world. And they're my friends. I know you'll be wonderful with them. I'll probably be leaving Crossroads before the paperwork is ready to be signed, but we'll figure that out down the road."

Patty was still trying to wrap her head around what Nora was saying when she tuned in to "figure that out down the road."

"So, you're heading back to Fort Worth," Patty said.

"Only for a brief time. Asher's job needs to stay in

Austin, and all of my work is online. IT stuff, you know. So, I'm going back to Fort Worth just long enough to get out of my penthouse lease, and then it's Austin and Asher, all the way."

The first thing that went through Patty's mind was *penthouse?* And then Austin and Asher, and thought, *no way.* Still, she had to ask.

"Asher as in Kingston...from high school?"

"Yep. Still my best guy," Nora said.

Now Patty was just the teeniest bit jealous. "Well, that's just wonderful. I'm so happy for both of you. Out of curiosity, what does he do for a living?"

"Oh, he's always been in law enforcement, and for the last few years, a special investigator for the attorney general's office in Austin."

Patty sucked up every snotty thing she wanted to say, and smiled instead, hoping it transferred to the tone of her voice.

"Well, honey, I couldn't be any happier for the both of you. Now, you don't worry yourself further. I've got the sale end of this covered, and we can do a remote closing on signing day."

"Sounds perfect," Nora said. "Thank you so much for contacting me when you did. It's helped everything fall into place, and my best to Lee, as well."

The call ended, and so did Nora's patience. She'd heard the snip in Patty's voice and rolled her eyes. Some people never get past high school drama. And she was tired and wanted nothing more than a long soak in a hot bath. Maybe Asher would call her and maybe he wouldn't. She knew what was at stake for them, and all she could do was pray.

It was just after 6:00 p.m. on a cold, cloudless day. Sunset had already happened, and Bill Eldredge was filling his brother in on their new targets.

"Except for that trip to the hardware store, they've been inside since. If they leave, you are to follow, and if they take I-27 south leading to Tulia, that's where your tracking ends, and immediately let Asher Kingston know."

"Got it," Phil said. "So, are we off guarding Jacob or what?"

"If the Brandts make another attempt and they catch them, then we'll be done. But Kingston will let us know. For now, it's proceed as usual. If the Brandts come back, then we're still on them."

"Got it," Phil said. "Get some food and rest. I've got this."

Bill drove away, more than ready for both, while Phil settled in, keeping his eye on the door the Brandts would exit, and on their car, which had been conveniently parked beneath one of the only working lights in the parking lot.

Phil was trying to learn Spanish and had his earbuds in, listening as he kept watch, repeating the words as instructed.

It was just past eleven o'clock when he saw two men exit the building and walk straight to the white Mustang. When the red brake lights came on, he yanked the earbuds out and started his car. As soon as they began driving toward the street, he followed a distance behind, then became part of the traffic the Brandts were in. He followed them all the way through Amarillo, and when he saw them take Highway I-27 south, he pulled over and sent Asher Kingston a text.

Asher was in the living room with the door open between the house and the bar. Dylan was in the back

of the house. Gunner was in the bar. They were trying to cover all of the points of entrance and exit when Asher's phone signaled a text. He was on his feet within seconds of reading it.

"Phil Eldredge just texted us. The Brandts are heading southbound on I-27 at this moment. It's going to happen tonight. We all know our places, right?"

"Right," they echoed.

"And we're ready to end this," Asher said.

"Hell, yes," they echoed again.

Asher's adrenaline was pumping. He kept picturing that god-awful pool of their dad's blood that had soaked into the floor behind the bar, and he was ready for a takedown.

"We're looking at fifteen or twenty minutes until they show. Gunner gives us the signal as to which way they're coming. We'll be in place before they get out of the car, and then they have to break in. Just stay calm and trust each other. There's three of us, and two of them."

"It's all good, Ash. We've got your back," Dylan said.

At that point, the TV was turned off, and they resumed their positions to wait for Gunner's warning.

———————

Everett was speeding through the night, his gaze fixed on the highway before him bathed in headlights coming and going. Freddie was quiet, which was worrisome, and Everett consoled himself by the thought that Freddie still wasn't a hundred percent from the flu they'd both suffered.

For the past few days, he'd been going through what happened before. The fact that the bar was closed and there was no one in the building to deal with made all the difference.

But…since it was closed, parking in the front parking lot would only bring attention to their presence. He knew

there was a private drive that led around to the back, and his plan was to get out of sight of the highway, and they'd have the whole place to themselves for hours.

When they reached the intersection of Highway 86 and I-27, he took eastbound 86 and headed to Crossroads.

"It's not long now," Everett said. "Another ten or fifteen minutes and we're in business, right, Freddie?"

"You're not gonna shoot anyone this time, are you?" Freddie asked.

Everett frowned. "No shooting needed because there's no one there. It's empty, Freddie, okay?"

Freddie shrugged. "You said you weren't gonna shoot anyone before, and you tried to kill a man."

"And if you had done what I asked you to do, that wouldn't have happened, right?" Everett said.

Freddie frowned. "You never said, don't talk. You didn't say that, Everett. You never said, 'Freddie don't talk.'"

"Fine. Fine. Just let it go, damn it. You're right. I never said don't talk. I never said be quiet. And we're almost there, so calm down, damn it. I need to concentrate."

Satisfied that he'd made his point, Freddie had nothing left to say, and all too soon they were driving past a quick stop, then past the Yellow Rose, past the big gas station, and into the parking lot at the bar.

Everett braked just long enough to get his eye on the drive leading to the back of the bar, then turned off the headlights, and using the light from the streetlights, slowly drove behind the bar.

Gunner saw the car slowing down.

"They're here…and they're heading to the back," he said, then took off running.

Dylan was in the utility room, waiting for them to come in through the back door.

Gunner and Asher were crouched down in the kitchen, hidden by walls and furniture. Waiting.

Everett opened the trunk, handed the shovel to Freddie, then took his flashlight and the pry bar, and headed up the porch steps, pausing at the door long enough to jimmy the lock, then slip inside.

Everett was leading the way, sweeping the LED flashlight from right to left as they moved into the kitchen.

"Everett, I can't see," Freddie said.

At that moment, Dylan flipped on the lights behind them, illuminating the utility room and the kitchen.

Everett gasped and spun around, saw the big man standing between them and the exit, and shouted. "Son of a bitch! Get him, Freddie!"

Dylan was braced for impact when Asher and Gunner bolted, hitting them with the full weight of their bodies, and taking them down from behind.

The Brandt brothers hit the floor belly first, knocking the breath out of their lungs. As they were struggling to catch their breath, Asher and Gunner handcuffed them and rolled them over on their backs.

The first word out of Everett's mouth was a curse until he saw the guns aimed at them, and he shut his trap.

Freddie saw the guns and started crying. "Don't shoot. Don't shoot. I don't wanna die."

"Neither did our father, but you tried to kill him anyway," Asher said.

Everett's shock was visible. "Father? Kingston is your old man?"

"All of us are his sons. You picked the wrong man to mess with," Gunner said.

"We came for what was ours by right," Everett said.

"You mean the money your dad stole, and our mother buried?" Asher said, and then grinned at the stunned look on their faces as he and Gunner flashed their badges. "Once Dad identified you two as the men wanting to buy the bar, we ran background checks on all of you. It was just a matter of working backward. After we figured out what you were after, we did a little digging of our own. We found the strongbox buried in the basement and turned it over to the FBI two days ago. You're going back to prison for attempted murder, and the money is back where it belongs."

Then he handed his gun to Dylan. "You and Gunner just shoot them if they move. I'm going to call the sheriff."

Gunner kicked the toe of Everett's boots. "I'm gonna shoot you if you even open your mouth."

"I'd just as soon shoot them anyway. I'm a general contractor. I can bury them in so much cement on a job site that their bodies will never be found," Dylan said.

Freddie peed his pants, and Everett actually shuddered. Prison was looking better by the minute.

Asher was leaning against the wall as he made the call, and was waiting for the answer.

"Briscoe County Sheriff's office. What is your emergency?"

"This is Asher Kingston. We're at the Tumbleweed Bar in Crossroads. My brothers and I have the two men who tried to kill Jacob Kingston in cuffs. We need officers and transport assistance, ASAP."

"Do you need an ambulance?" the dispatcher asked.

"Not yet," Asher said, and disconnected. Then he took the gun back from Dylan. "Brother, if you don't mind, would you please turn on all the lights in the bar, and watch for the sheriff?"

"With pleasure," Dylan said, and began turning on lights all through the house as he went.

As usual, Pearl was sleeping with her window open and was one of the first to hear the sirens. She got up and ran to the window, and when she saw lights flashing, and all of the vehicles pulling in at the Tumbleweed Bar, but with no ambulances following, she guessed the Kingston brothers had called the police for a reason.

The night air was cold, but she kept watching until she saw the officers bringing two men out in handcuffs, and the Kingston brothers walking out into the parking lot behind them, and guessed it had something to do with Jacob being shot. Whatever it was, they clearly had everything under control.

"Lord, those boys are something," she said, and took herself back to bed, snuggling deep beneath the covers.

Four blocks south, Nora was awakened by the strident sounds of sirens.

"Oh my God, it happened!" she said, and flew out of bed.

She needed to know if Asher was okay, if the brothers were okay. But whatever was going on, they didn't need her crashing the party.

She kept telling herself this is what being married to a cop was going to be like. Knowing his job always carried that measure of danger. Trusting that he knew exactly how to take care of himself, and that he'd always be coming home to her.

But sleep now was impossible. Still in Asher's old football

jersey, she slipped on a pair of sweatpants and stepped into her fuzzy slippers, and went straight to the living room with her phone. Then she turned on the gas fireplace, curled up in the chair beside it, and waited for him to call.

As soon as the perps were turned over to the sheriff, Asher sent a text back to Phil Eldredge, the night security guard.

> Perps are in custody. You are officially off of guard duty for the Kingston family. Many thanks for your service.

Eldredge saw the text, sent back a thumbs-up emoji, then notified his brother and the main office, and went home.

Matt Reddick was on the scene in the parking lot of the bar, eyeing the suspects as they were brought out in handcuffs, with the Kingstons right behind them.

"No bloody noses. No bruises. I am impressed," he said.

Asher didn't comment, but Freddie had plenty to say.

"Them two was gonna shoot us, and that one was gonna bury us in cement," Freddie wailed.

"Them two, as you put it, are officers of the law. If you tried to escape, they would have had every right to do so," Reddick said.

Dylan shrugged. "Mine was more of a promise than a threat, but only if they moved. The complainant did pee his pants, but I didn't count that against him."

Reddick knew what this meant to Jacob's sons, and he was more than slightly surprised by their restraint.

"At any rate, good job, all three of you. I'll need written statements regarding the arrest, but strictly for the files."

"If it hadn't been for your cooperation, and agreeing to the press conference, this wouldn't have happened," Asher said. "We owe you."

"We'll call it even," Reddick said. "Go mop up the pee and get some sleep. Give Jacob my best," he said, then got in his cruiser and followed the deputies who were transporting the prisoners.

And just like that, the law was gone, and the sirens were fading as they drove farther and farther away.

"I'll mop up the pee," Gunner said.

"I'm going to call Angie," Dylan said.

"See you in the morning," Asher said.

His brothers smiled. "Tell Nora we said hello."

Asher just kept walking.

Staring out the darkened windows was like staring into an abyss.

"He's okay, he's okay. I know he's okay. I just need to hear the sound of his voice," Nora kept saying, repeating it over and over like a prayer.

And then her phone rang. When Asher's name came up on Caller ID, she was so anxious she dropped the phone, then dropped to her knees, scrambling to pick it up.

"Hello. Asher? I'm up. Are you okay?"

He took a deep breath. "It's over. We caught them. No one's hurt. Sheriff Reddick has them and I'm walking to your house. Put a light in the window, darlin', and unlock the door."

The line went dead. Nora flung the phone onto the couch and ran.

Asher had just come out of the alley and headed for her house when he saw her porch light come on.

He started running.

Nora swung the door wide as he came up the steps, and then she was in his arms. He kicked the door shut, turned the lock, then started down the hall, carrying her in his arms.

The covers of her bed were all jumbled from her hasty exit, but sleep wasn't on their minds.

"Naked," Asher whispered, and began taking off his boots and then his clothes, as Nora stripped down to bare skin.

"On the bed," he said, and followed her as she lay down, then he buried his face against the curve of her neck and held her. "Love you, Nora, with every beat of my heart."

And before she could answer he was kissing her, and then inside her, and nothing else mattered but that mad chase to ecstasy.

They fell asleep together, and made love again before daylight, and were basking in the aftershocks, when Nora delivered her news.

"I sold the house yesterday to Sonny and Maggie Bluejacket. They bought it furnishings and all for their foreman and his new bride."

Asher's eyes narrowed as he ran his finger down the side of her face. "Good for you, and we just gave it a really good send-off. But does that mean you're leaving town now?"

She hugged him tighter. "Yes, and I'm already trying to wrap my head around the distance between us once again."

He raised up on one elbow, smoothing away the sleepy tangles off her forehead.

"Darlin', that's just temporary. As soon as we get Dad home, which is either today or tomorrow, the only thing I have left to do is organize home healthcare for him until he's completely healed. We're not staying, either. I'll fly in and drive you back to Austin with your things."

"We'll figure all that out after we're both back in our homes. All I need is a place to hang my clothes and a room for an office and I'm in business."

"What about your furniture? Your special things?"

Her eyes welled. "I just sold my special things to Sonny Bluejacket."

He brushed a kiss across her lips. "Then we'll make other special things, and they will be ours," he said. "We'll be going to Amarillo sometime today. We all need to tell Dad in person about Mom and the money, and why he was shot. It's going to be a jolt. Not sure how he's going to take it."

"And I have to clean out the food in the refrigerator, then pack. Let this be our goodbye until Austin. I can't keep saying goodbye. I need the next time to be welcome home," Nora said.

"Then it will be. Promise to call me when you get there, so I'll know you arrived safely," he said.

"I will. You're flying home in the chopper, right?" she said.

"Yes, and I'll let you know the moment we land. Once we're sleeping under the same roof every night, is when the rest of our lives begins. Stay under the covers where it's warm. I'll turn the lock before I let myself out."

She nodded, too overwhelmed to say more, and watched him dressing, then blowing her a kiss as he walked out the door. She closed her eyes, following the sound of his footsteps, until she heard the door open and close, and wished she could just will herself home, without the long hours of driving to get there.

She heard the SUV start, and then heard him driving away.

Until we meet again.

Then she got up, stripped the sheets and put them in to wash so that everything would be clean and fresh when Chris and Ellen moved in.

She made coffee one last time. Ate a bowl of cereal, using the last of the milk, then washed the dishes by hand, dried them, and put them up in the cupboard.

After emptying all of the food in the refrigerator, and dumping it into the garbage bin, Nora pulled it to the curb, then ran back in out of the cold.

The washer had stopped, so she put the wet sheets in the dryer and went to finish packing. By the time the dryer went off, she had everything she intended to take with her loaded up in the back of her car.

The sheets were soft and warm, and smelled faintly of lilac from the scented dryer sheet she'd used. She remade the bed, carefully plumping the pillow shams before giving the room a last look, then turned out the light.

As she was walking up the hall, the grandfather clock was striking the hour.

Nine a.m.

She would not hear that in this place again.

Her coat was on a chair by the door, as were her purse and keys. She'd planned to stop at the Rose and say goodbye to Pearl, but she didn't want to cry again, so she sent her a text, instead.

Thank you for everything. For your help and your love, and for being a friend when I needed one most. I'm going home today. See you next time around.
Nora

She slipped into her coat, grabbed her purse and keys, and walked out, locking the door behind her.

After stopping at the gas station to fill up, she drove out of the lot, past the flapping crime scene tape on the front of the Tumbleweed Bar, and didn't look back.

Dylan had just finished shaving when Asher walked in. He started to say something, then saw the look on his face and went for aftershave, instead.

"If you'll give me a couple of minutes to notify the Feds that we caught our guys, I'll be ready to go."

"If you want to shave, we can…"

"I don't," Asher said.

"Let me guess. Nora is gone," Gunner said.

Asher frowned. "Not forever, and setting our personal issues aside, we still need to organize a home health aide for Dad until he gets some strength. We can't stay forever. We need to get back to our own lives. So back me if he gives me hell when I suggest it."

They nodded in agreement and had the good sense to leave Asher alone to make the call. The phone rang three times before he got an answer.

"Special Agent Worth speaking."

"Agent Worth, this is Asher Kingston. We caught our perps last night. You are now free to release the recovery of the missing money. The fact that it was found on our property is going to stir up a lot of shit for our dad, and he's yet to be released from the hospital. Don't forget what I said. You give Jacob's sons the credit for solving the cold case and finding the money during their investigation into the attempted murder. I better hear a good spin on all that, or we'll hold our own press conference. Dad is the one we intend to protect."

"No worry. We will certainly give all three of you the credit. We were just the recovery team. The announcement has already been written. We were just waiting for the okay. You can expect it to hit local and national news by tonight. Our best wishes for your father."

"Thank you," Asher said, and disconnected.

Chapter 16

THE KINGSTONS LEFT TOWN IN THE SUV WITH GUNNER driving, Dylan in the seat beside him, and Asher in back nursing a cup of coffee. The ride was mostly quiet, which suited Asher.

Saying goodbye to Nora this morning felt like the first time, all over again—when they were so young and so in love—full of excitement for what was to come. They'd never planned to ghost each other. They just drifted apart.

Then the reunion happened, and as a grown-ass man, he fell even harder for the woman she'd become. Despite the turmoil they'd both been in, their reasons for coming back to Crossroads had also been their blessing. Knowing she wouldn't be there when they came back today was hard. Waiting again was harder. Getting her moved was going to be his quest. He was not going to be satisfied until she was sleeping under his roof, in his arms, with a ring on her finger.

And they still had to unload this nightmare onto Jacob's shoulders. The media would do what they do, stirring enough lies into a truth to create a headline. They didn't care what damage the lies left behind. But Asher did, for him. When they arrived at the hospital, they parked and went inside, then went up to Jacob's room.

Jacob was sitting up in his bed watching the morning news when his sons walked into the room.

"Wow! All of you together! This is wonderful. Come sit. Talk to me. Tell me, what's been happening?"

They were all smiles and careful hugs and then they settled around him like they'd always done when looking to him for advice.

"We have a story to tell you, so bear with us," Asher said. "Ever since our arrival, we have been actively looking for your shooters. And once you identified the Brandt brothers, everything else began falling in place. We finally knew who did it, but we had no physical proof to back us up."

"Dad, since I was the one with zero sleuthing ability, I asked to be the one to stay with you," Dylan said. "We still had no motive for why it happened, and all three of us feared they would try it again. That's why you had the security guards at your door."

Jacob nodded. "I guessed that much. Truthfully, it made sleep a lot easier."

Gunner picked up the story. "I ran most of the background checks while Asher was researching facts and sifting through new information. He was an awesome partner to work with, and still a not-so-bad brother, to boot. Little by little, things began popping up that began to make sense, but we couldn't put our finger on what was missing until the night we all finally admitted to ourselves that we were overlooking the obvious. We rarely talk about Brenda, not even to each other, but when we opened that door..." Gunner paused. "You finish it, Ash. You're the one who remembered."

Jacob's heart skipped when they mentioned Brenda's name. What the hell else had she done?

"We were working around a theory. We knew Pete Brandt's sons visited him only hours before he died. We

also knew that it was only a week or so afterward that they showed up at the bar. Then when they came back and shot you, we still had no motive, and it was driving us crazy. So, one night, we were all home, sitting around the kitchen table, and we started talking about the day of Gunner's birthday, and each of us told what we remembered from that day. And the last thing I remembered was Gunner waking up all bloody from losing a tooth, and howling to the moon about swallowing it."

Jacob smiled, and patted Gunner's hand. "I remember that day. You had your seventh birthday."

Asher nodded. "All the crying woke me, and I kept expecting Mom to go see to it, but she didn't, and I went to see what was wrong. When I saw all the blood, I went to look for her. I knew there would be sheets to strip, and Gunner would need a bath. I went all through the house calling for her, but she wasn't there. I went back to the boys' room long enough to give Gunner a cloth to pack in the bleeding gum, then made another sweep through the house, calling her name over and over. I was in the kitchen, thinking she might be outside, when she came out of the basement. I remembered the dirt on the knees of her jeans, and all over her hands, because she had to wash them before she went to tend to Gunner. And that's when it hit us. What if Pete Brandt lied about hiding the money. What if he gave it to Mom to hide? And what if she buried it in the dirt floor of that basement? And what if that's what Pete Brandt told his sons, and that was the reason they came to the bar, then came back and shot you? If they knew it was there, then that would be their motive for shooting you."

Jacob went pale. His eyes welled. "Oh my God. Oh my God. Was it there?"

Dylan and Gunner reached for his hands.

Asher nodded. "We found it with a metal detector. Dug

it up and turned it over to the FBI three days ago, and asked them not to announce the recovery until we got the men who shot you, to which they agreed."

"All these years. God… The nightmare is going to start again. Everyone is going to think I knew it was there," Jacob said.

"No, Dad. It's exactly the reverse. Part of the Feds' announcement will be that the discovery was entirely due to your sons' investigation of the attempted murder. And that the exact location was unknown to everyone, because Brandt told her to hide it, and she did, but then the truth and the location died with her. We would never have known it was there, had Pete's sons not come looking. During the Feds' original investigation, they'd overlooked considering her part in the robbery. It was enough that she'd died on their watch. Asher didn't trust them not to put a spin on the recovery to make themselves look better. He said if they did, he would hold a press conference of his own."

"It won't happen to you again, Dad. One lie from the media and I slap them with a lawsuit for slander so fast it'll make their heads spin. Don't worry. We've got your back. All we want is for you to get well enough to go home."

Tears were rolling down Jacob's face. He just kept shaking his head and clutching their hands until he finally pulled himself together.

"I am so proud of all of you. I don't have the words to express what this means to me."

"It's okay, Dad," Asher said. "I saw. I remember what you went through before. It won't happen again."

"And they're in custody?" Jacob asked.

"As of midnight, last night," Dylan said.

"Where? How?" Jacob asked.

And then they explained the trap they'd laid with Sheriff Reddick's help, and how it all went down.

Jacob shook his head in disbelief. "I will never look at my kitchen in the same way. A treasure was buried in the floor beneath it, and you took down the men who tried to kill me where I eat my breakfast every day."

"It was our home, too, Dad. You made it the best place to grow up," Gunner said.

"Speaking of the kitchen and home, has your doctor given you any indication of when you might be released?"

Jacob nodded. "Probably tomorrow, but once I'm there, you boys do not need to play nursemaid. I can do for myself just fine."

"Maybe so, but until you are well enough to reopen the bar, you will have daily home healthcare," Asher said. "It's the only way we'll feel safe enough to leave you on your own."

Jacob frowned.

"No, Dad. No frowning," Dylan said. "Ash is right."

"He is definitely right, and I am incapable of giving my own father a bath," Gunner said.

They all burst out laughing, and at that point, Jacob agreed.

Asher was still smiling as he got up. "I'm going to the nurses' station for some info on home healthcare. You two feel free to update Dad as to the recent developments of my love life. I'll be back shortly."

The trip back to Crossroads felt shorter—the mood lighter. They were hoping to get home in time to catch a news bulletin about the recovered money. Asher wasn't going to assume the Feds had kept their word until he heard it for himself.

He glanced at the time, wondering how far Nora had

driven, and how many hours she had to go. It was at least a five-hour drive—too early to expect an arrival text, but he was feeling off balance. Thief that she was, she'd left town with his heart.

Once Nora left Highway 86 for southbound US 287, the distance between her and Asher became a reality. The nearer she got to home, meant an increasing distance from him. The next few weeks were going to be challenging. Getting back into the full routine of her job. Notifying her employer of the upcoming move, dispatching her furniture in the ivory tower, before the freedom to move to Austin. The upheaval of her old life had yet to settle.

She knew dithering would not be a wise move. If she didn't get there soon, Asher would come get her, lay waste to whatever barriers she'd made for herself, and what was left behind would go begging. A quick ache of longing washed through her, but she put wishing aside for the reality of what was.

He loved her. He cherished her.

Making love to him made her crazy.

She would never take the love he'd given her for granted again.

Back in Crossroads, the Kingston brothers had just walked into the Yellow Rose for lunch when the breaking news bulletin about the recovery of the missing money, along with the end of Brenda Kingston's story, hit every major news outlet. It was airing in sports bars, businesses, airports, and people's homes, and it was live on the TV hanging behind the register at the Yellow Rose Café.

Pearl saw Jacob's sons walking in, and as always, the thought they could have been her sons came and went. And then Asher was pointing at the TV and asking her to turn up the volume.

The sudden blast of the news alert silenced the entire dining room. They turned where they sat, saw Jacob's sons, and then one by one, got up from their seats and moved closer to hear what was being said.

Asher felt Dylan and Gunner moving up behind him.

When Special Agent Alex Worth appeared on screen, they tensed. But the moment he began, they knew he was good for his word. The first words out of his mouth were about the recovery of the missing money, and then the story of how it came to be found. He stated vehemently that had someone not tried to murder Jacob Kingston, and had his sons, two of whom were officers of the law in their own lives, not joined together to work with the local authorities in an effort to find who tried to kill their father, the money would not have been found. He lauded the sons for solving a twenty-one-year-old cold case, as well as catching the attempted murderers and turning them over to the local authorities. He also included the moral strength and honor it must have taken for Jacob's sons, in realizing the depth of their mother's involvement and still wanting the truth revealed.

The show returned to normal programming, but the room full of diners was silent, in awe of what they'd heard, but not sure how to react. It wasn't until Asher and his brothers high-fived each other that the room erupted in cheers, then the brothers swooped Pearl up into their arms and carried her through the dining room on their shoulders like the heroine she was.

"Pearl is the heroine! She's the one who saved Dad's life. We just butt-kicked the perps who tried to kill him," Gunner said.

Pearl was laughing and crying and whopping all three of them on the head. "Something's burning in the kitchen. Put me down!" she cried.

Davey the grill cook came running. "It was me, Pearl. It was me. It's out. It's okay," then darted back into the kitchen.

More laughter erupted as they were putting her down. She was red-faced and giggling as she hurried back into the kitchen. Diners returned to their seats, and the brothers seated themselves at an empty table.

Asher looked out across the room at the faces of the diners, most of whom they'd known all their lives. Today had ended the last ugly whisper of gossip about them and their dad. It had been a long time coming, but the justice was sweet.

He wished with all his heart that Nora had been here to celebrate with him, but it gave him a sense of peace, knowing the family they made together would never be painted with a brush of suspicion.

As they ate the food that they'd ordered, Jacob Kingston was celebrating on his own. He, too, had been watching TV, hoping to catch the bulletin, but he was alone when it began airing, and it was just as well. He watched the entire press conference with tears rolling down his face.

For the first time since the day the Feds took Brenda away in cuffs, he felt clean again—no longer a shadowy suspect in the eyes of the public. No more ugly gossip. He owed Pearl for saving his life, and he owed his sons for tracking down his killers, and for saving his reputation. He wasn't sure how the rest of his life would play out, but there wasn't going to be another day he lived without gratitude for still breathing.

After the brothers got back to the house, they sat down at the kitchen table for one last meeting, totaled up shared costs, and Venmoed their share of cost to each brother they owed, right down to Gunner's rental car that they'd all been using.

"Okay, we're square with each other on money, but there are still a couple of things we need to do here. If Dad's coming home tomorrow, then we need to clean house, shop for groceries for him, not what we've been eating, do the laundry, and basically give him his house back."

"I'll clean," Dylan said.

"I'll shop for the groceries," Gunner said.

Asher nodded. "Then I'll do all the laundry. Also, if you two want to go home, get online and find flights that will get you home tomorrow. I can drop both of you off at the airport before I pick Dad up, and once I get him home and settled, and the home health nurse shows up, then I'll return the car rental and fly home in the chopper."

"I predict Dad is going to have a string of visitors once he gets home. He won't be lonely, and after he's well enough to open the bar again, he'll have all kinds of company," Dylan said.

"Get your flights figured out first, then we start in here," Asher said. "I have the name and number of the home health nurse who will be coming. I'm going to call him to make sure he has the right schedule. Remember to put everything we dragged out back where you found it, so Dad doesn't have to go looking for what he needs."

"The nurse is a guy?" Gunner said.

Asher shrugged. "It seemed like a choice that would make Dad more comfortable in his own home."

"Good call," Gunner said.

"I know one thing he needs," Dylan said. "He didn't get to winterize the place before this happened. I'll get

the covers put on all of the outside faucets, and put up the storm shutters on the windows in the spare rooms. It will keep the house warmer when snowstorms hit."

"I'll take his truck when I go get groceries," Gunner said. "That way I can take it by the garage, refill the fuel and get the oil changed, and make sure the antifreeze level is safe."

Satisfied with their decisions, Dylan and Gunner got online to book their flights, while Asher went in another room to call the nurse. Everything was finally falling back into place.

The Brandt brothers were in a different situation.

Everett and Freddie were in separate cells, with separate court-ordered lawyers, and Freddie, being Freddie, didn't know enough to lie about even one aspect of what they'd done. It soon became clear that his limited ability to understand and his devotion to his brother was what put him where he was.

And Everett, knowing Freddie, was prepared for the attempted murder charge he saw looming, and mentally preparing himself for the guilt of knowing, by his absence alone, he'd just thrown Freddie to the wolves.

As he was staring through the bars of the holding cell and waiting for his arraignment, he had to admit Freddie had been right about one thing. They should never have gone looking for that money.

Nora's shoulders were tired from the long drive, and her hand with the stitches was throbbing from gripping the steering wheel for so long.

The good news was, she was more or less home. She still had to weave her way through the massive infrastructure of the streets and bypasses of the Dallas/Fort Worth area, but she knew where she was, and how to get where she needed to be, even though that would take at least another hour.

As she'd been driving, a thought about the house she'd just sold occurred to her. Without a bank involved, and with Sonny and Maggie buying the place as is, and once the contract was signed, there was no reason to delay Chris and Ellen Jackson's move. The sooner they could get into the property before hard winter set in, the better for everyone all around.

She made a mental note to call Patty and tell her, and then give Sonny a heads-up that his offer was accepted. It was also a reminder about getting herself relocated for the same reason.

Even the thought of the ivory tower was enticing right now. She was going for a bath in her Jacuzzi with jasmine-scented bath salts, and DoorDash for sustenance. Whatever she'd left in her refrigerator was ready to be tossed, and buying up a bunch of groceries would defeat her plan to exit to Austin ASAP.

She had a running list in her head of things to do, and the first was letting Ash know she was home. The second was notifying her boss she was back on the job full-time and would be moving residence to Austin within the month. The third was getting out of her lease and setting a moving date with Asher, then selling her furniture to a staging company. They were always on the lookout for nice things to stage homes for sale. It was exciting, and nerve-wracking, and every damn bit worth it just to be Asher Kingston's wife.

And when she finally pulled off the city street into the attached parking garage to her high-rise, she was exhausted. She pulled into her private parking space and killed the

engine, then leaned her forehead for a few moments out of relief.

A security guard recognized her car, and when he saw her, came knocking on her window.

"Miss Borden, Miss Borden, are you okay?"

Nora looked up, then nodded and opened the door. "I'm fine, Howie. Just exhausted from a very long drive."

"Can I help you get your luggage out of the car?" he asked.

"Yes, with gratitude," she said, and unlocked the doors for him to get her luggage from the back seat, while she gathered up the things from the front.

"I'll pull it to the elevator for you. I heard of your father's passing. I'm sorry for your loss," he said as they were walking.

"Thank you, but as you know, it was also his blessing. Alzheimer's is a cruel, cruel way to die."

"Yes, ma'am," Howie said, and when they reached the elevator, he pressed the button for her, then rolled her suitcases inside before stepping out of the car. "Welcome home."

The doors slid shut. She pressed the button to her floor, knowing it would take her straight to the penthouse floor without stopping, and when the doors opened again, the long walk down the hallway to her door awaited her.

She began unlocking the first of three locks, then slipped in fast enough to disarm security before it began to sound, but she was home.

Almost immediately the difference between the ivory tower and her childhood home was like a slap in the face. She hadn't been living up here. She'd just been existing. There were no friends, no community feeling, no place to be, no one to see. Just her and the walls and windows of cold luxury.

Asher Kingston would suffocate in a place like this. And now that she'd breathed the air of childhood, this place

stifled. She turned up the thermostat, then rolled her suitcase to her bedroom, sat down on the side of the bed, and sent Asher a text.

> I'm in my ivory tower once more, and never has it felt this sterile or unwelcoming. I miss you madly. Call me when you can. I await the day you tell me to come home to you.
> Love you forever,
> Me

Hitting Send was the same thing as watching him walk out the door. Until he responded, he was still gone.

She hung up her coat, started the water running in her Jacuzzi tub, added a liberal sprinkling of the jasmine bath salts, then began unpacking.

When the tub was full, she stripped and climbed in, easing down into the steamy depths of heat and feeling the stress of the drive slipping away, before turning on the jets. The instant surge of water from all directions was like a deep-tissue massage as she leaned back into the force and closed her eyes.

Asher contacted the home health nurse—a man named Benny Armstrong, who lived in Tulia. It was the perfect solution for Jacob's situation. A man who wouldn't ruffle Jacob's feathers, lived close enough to be timely, and was strong enough to help Jacob up and down until his legs were stronger. The timeline was set, and Asher was satisfied. He decided to only wash the sheets on his dad's bed, and sleep on the spare bed in Dylan's room, then strip all the beds later after the brothers were gone.

Then he gathered up all the bath and kitchen towels and headed for the laundry, as Dylan came in from outside.

"I got everything outside winterized," Dylan said. "I'm going to start cleaning in the living room," and went to get the feather duster and the dust mop. Mopping floors would be the last thing he did before going to bed, so that they would still be clean when they left tomorrow.

Asher put the first load of towels in the washer, added detergent, set the water temp, and hit Start. Before he could turn around, his phone signaled a text. It was Nora!

He read the text with a lump in his throat, and then went to the quiet of his bedroom to call her.

When Nora's phone began to ring, her heart skipped. That had to be Ash. She turned off the jets and dried her hands before answering.

"Hey, you," she said.

He grinned. "Hey, baby. Am I to assume you are safely home?"

"Yes, and in a tub of jasmine-scented bubbles that are rapidly popping. I already miss you," she said.

He groaned. "Wish I was there."

She laughed. "Is everything okay with Jacob?"

"Yes, he's coming home tomorrow. I have a nurse named Benny Armstrong who will be with him daily until he's officially healed. Dylan and Gunner are flying home in the morning, and after I get Dad settled, I'm flying home tomorrow afternoon."

"The helicopter, right?"

"Can't push it home. Too far. The only way to get it back where it belongs is to fly it there," he said.

"Funny guy. Now it's going to be up to you to let me

know when you get back to Austin. I need to at least know you're back on the ground."

"Yes, ma'am. As for moving in with me, you tell me the day and I will come get you."

"I'll get myself there," Nora said. "What I need to know is if you have a spare room that I can use as an office. A lot of my work is sensitive, and I need space and quiet for the times we have video conferences and Zoom meetings."

"Darlin', there are four bedrooms in my house, besides my office. You can have your pick, as long as you sleep with me."

She sighed. "That's a given. I already miss coming apart in your arms. So, as soon as I get signed out of my lease and my furniture sold, I'll let you know."

"Works for me," he said. "Marriage license, rings, wedding day."

"Um, Ash… About the wedding…"

He heard sadness in her voice again. "I know, baby. I know. They're all gone, aren't they, and it wouldn't be the same. I'll be just as happy with a justice of the peace, if it gets me you."

Tears were rolling down her face. "You read me like a book. Thank you for understanding. Yes, please, and thank you."

"Then we're good. I love you forever. We were always meant to be," he said.

"Love you more," she said.

The call ended.

Nora sank back into the water, turned on the jets, and let the splashes wash away her tears.

Asher pocketed his phone. While the laundry was in the wash, he went to help Dylan clean, and Gunner was sitting in the little lobby at the garage, waiting for the serviceman to change the oil and winterize Jacob's truck. Gunner had

a mental list of his dad's food choices running in his head, and he was thinking about the flight home to Dallas. He was ready to get back to work.

Chapter 17

THE KINGSTONS WERE UP BEFORE DAWN, DRESSED AND loading up their bags in the SUV. Gunner had a 7:30 a.m. flight to catch, Dylan's flight left at 8:00 a.m., and Asher had blankets and a pillow in the car to make Jacob's ride home easier, and a change of clothes and some slippers for him to come home in. They'd cut off everything he was wearing when he arrived in the ER, and bagged it up for evidence at the time.

They paused once as they were walking out the door, looking back at the shiny floors and gleaming kitchen appliances.

"Looks good," Asher said. "And thank God we still have Dad to come home to at Christmas."

They loaded their bags as Asher locked the door, and then they were gone. By the time they reached Tulia and turned toward Amarillo, the eastern horizon was growing brighter, and when Asher pulled up at the airport to let them out, the sky was bathed in faint shades of yellow and pink.

"Gunner, safe flight. See you at Christmas," he said. "Dylan, safe flight to you, buddy. Give Angie my love. I'll see you around."

"Same to you," they echoed, then took their bags and walked into the terminal, but instead of driving straight to the hospital, Asher parked long enough to call the hangar where he'd left his chopper, asked for a refuel and checkup, and said that he be flying out this afternoon.

Satisfied with their response, he headed for the hospital.

Jacob had showered and shaved but didn't have anything to change into and was hoping Asher would remember to bring him some clothes. He was feeling good enough that he was getting picky about the hospital food and hadn't done justice to the tray of food they'd brought in.

"Jacob! You didn't eat much," the nurse said as she came in to check his vitals.

"Not so hungry today. I just want to go home. Is my doctor making rounds yet?"

She smiled. "He's on the floor. Hold your horses for a bit. He'll get here. Now swing your legs up on that bed and get under the covers."

He sighed. "Yes, ma'am," and did as he was told.

He didn't know what he thought about having a nurse in his home, after all these days with them in the hospital, but he was willing to do what he needed to get back to his old self again.

He turned on the television and leaned back in his bed, and once again, caught the early morning news with a repeat of the FBI bulletin from yesterday. And once again, was in awe of the men that he called sons.

Asher came up the hall carrying the duffel bag with shoes and clothes for his dad, along with his winter coat. He paused at the nurses' desk.

"I'm Asher Kingston. My dad, Jacob Kingston, is supposed to be released this morning. Has his doctor made rounds yet?"

"Doctor Reading is on the floor making rounds, but we don't have orders yet."

"Then I'll wait with Dad until he comes," Asher said, and went down the hall to Jacob's room and walked in.

Jacob's face lit up, and when he saw the bag Asher was carrying, he knew he wasn't going to have to go home with his backside shining.

"Morning, Dad," Asher said. He set the bag down and gave Jacob a quick hug, then took off his coat and pulled up a chair.

"Morning, son. You are a welcome sight."

"I just dropped Gunner and Dylan off at the airport. They're both flying home this morning."

"What about you?" Jacob said. "You need to get back to work, too."

"Oh, I'm flying out this afternoon sometime. I came in the chopper, so I don't have a timeline to meet. It will be ready when I get there. Your nurse's name is Benny Armstrong. He lives in Tulia. You may know him."

Jacob beamed. "You got a male nurse! Thank you. I really appreciate the wonderful care I've been given here, but I'm a bit weary of those bossy little nurses telling me what I can and can't do."

"Now you'll have a bossy man saying the same things, and we expect you to appreciate his wisdom," Asher said.

"Yes, I will. I swear. I have never been this sick or helpless in my life, and I do not want a repeat of it," Jacob said, and then clasped Asher's hand. "I saw the Feds' announcement. I have never been so proud of having you boys for sons. I know you're the one who demanded the clearing of my name, because you were the only one old enough to remember what we all went through, and a simple thank-you isn't enough."

"It's enough for me," Asher said. "Sometime in the near future, we hope to be needing a grandpa. Dylan and Angie are getting married, and so are Nora and me. I don't know

what Dylan and Angie's plans are, but I'm telling you now that Nora and I will just go the justice of the peace route. Losing both parents within the last four years has taken the heart out of her for having a big, elaborate wedding."

"Don't blame her one bit. Brenda demanded the big wedding. The only thing about being married that she really loved was her boys. I look forward to seeing you happily married and raising families. I want someone to call me Poppa. I want babies on my knee before I'm too old to remember what to do with them," Jacob said. "Nearly dying reminded me of how fragile life is, and that nothing is promised."

Before Ash could answer, Doctor Reading walked in.

"Good morning, Jacob. It appears you have a ride waiting for you."

Asher stood. "I brought his going-away clothes. We're just waiting for the okay," he said.

Reading's nurse was right behind him, and pulled up Jacob's most recent numbers while Reading gave him the once-over.

"Well sir, I think we're done with you here. A nurse will bring your release papers and you'll be free to go. Jacob, you are an amazing man. Few would survive what happened to you. I wish you a long and happy life," Reading said as he shook Jacob's hand, and then Asher's. "We know your father's life was in danger for the time that he was here, and we all know what you and your brothers did to secure his safety and clear his name. Remarkable family. All of you," he said, and then he left.

"Well now," Jacob said, struggling with his emotions. "How about you close my door, then help me into some real clothes for a change?"

Asher grinned. "I'd be happy to do that," he said, and shut the door before putting the bag on the bed and removing the clothes.

Jacob was dressed and sitting in the chair, and Asher was sitting on the bed, when a nurse came back with his release papers, and an orderly following, pushing a wheelchair.

"Okay, Dad, I'm going down to bring the car up. Meet you downstairs," and he took off out of the room.

"That is one handsome son you have," the nurse said.

Jacob nodded. "I have three of them—they are my abundance of riches."

The orderly helped him into the wheelchair, while the nurse put the release papers and the odds and ends that came from patient care in his bag, and set it in his lap.

The orderly paused. "Are you comfortable, Mr. Kingston?"

Jacob nodded, and off they rolled.

Asher was waiting at the entrance when they brought Jacob out. He had already notified Benny Armstrong that his dad had been released and they would be home within the hour.

Ash jumped out to open the door, and a quick transfer was made. After reclining the seat and propping a pillow beneath Jacob's arm to ease his shoulder, he buckled the seat belt for his dad.

"Tell me if you hurt or feel nauseated, and we'll adjust accordingly," Asher said.

Jacob shook his head. "I'm good to go, son. Let's go home."

They drove out of the parking lot and into the city traffic, with Jacob talking nonstop and Ash listening and nodding in all the right places. But Jacob's energy swiftly waned, and he was asleep before they passed through Tulia, and still asleep when Ash reached the Tumbleweed Bar.

There was a blue Volvo parked in the lot and a man sitting behind the wheel. He drove up to where Ash had stopped and rolled down the window.

"I'm Benny Armstrong," he said.

"Follow me," Asher said, and led the way around the bar to the house behind it.

Jacob woke up at the sound of Asher's voice, and when he saw that they were home, all he felt was relief.

"Sit tight, Dad," Asher said. "I need to unlock the door first, and then we'll get you inside, okay?"

Jacob nodded. He was already longing to stretch out and couldn't wait to get in his own bed, and then the door opened beside him, and a big burly man with a bald head and a smile wider than Dallas leaned in and unbuckled his seat belt.

"Good morning, Mr. Kingston. I'm your nurse, Benny Armstrong. I'm going to help you out and you lean on me. Let me do all the work and you follow my lead, okay?"

"Okay, and it's Jacob, not mister."

Ash came running back, and together they walked Jacob in, closed the door to keep out the cold, and started walking him past the utility area into the kitchen.

"What a homecoming! My house hasn't been this neat and clean in years," Jacob said.

"Do you want to go to the living room or to your bedroom?" Asher asked.

"Bed, please," Jacob said, and down the hall they went.

They removed his coat and shoes, then stopped. "Dad, do you want to change into pajamas or sweats to rest in?"

"Pajamas, I think. You get them out for Benny. He can help me change. May as well start this partnership off right and strip me down to my altogether."

Benny laughed. "I've seen twenty years' worth of altogethers in my nursing career. One more isn't going to faze me."

Asher was laughing as he left to bring in a quilt and pillow and the duffel bag. He found the doctor's instructions, laid them out on the table, and then stowed the quilt and extra pillow back in one of the spare rooms.

When he got back to Jacob's room, Benny had him in pajamas and tucked neatly into bed, and he'd brought his own bag of tricks, too. Two-way radios, one for each of them for easy communication from anywhere in the house.

"Okay, Jacob. I'll be in the kitchen for a while, learning where everything is. You know how to call for me."

"Yes, I do. Asher, as soon as you get Benny settled, you get yourself back to Amarillo. I don't want to think about you night-flying in that chopper, okay?"

Benny walked out of the room to give them privacy.

Asher sat down on the side of the bed. "Yes, I will, I promise. I'm already packed, and the chopper is serviced and waiting. I wish I didn't have to leave you like this, but you're in good hands. I checked him out twenty ways to Sunday before I even called to see if he was free."

"I would have expected nothing less," Jacob said.

"I am calling Pearl to let her know that you are home, and who's taking care of you, so be prepared for her to show up unannounced to inspect him on her own," Ash said. "And if you ever get a chance, you need to come clean with her, if for no other reason than to clear your conscience there, too. As you once told me, what happened between Nora and me was a shame. A damn shame. The same goes for you and Pearl. Love you, Dad. Be good. Get well, and expect many calls to get updates on your recovery." Then he leaned over and kissed the top of Jacob's head and ruffled his hair.

Jacob grinned. "Safe flight, Asher. I'm going to be fine."

Asher straightened the covers on Jacob's bed, and walked out.

Benny was sitting at the kitchen table reading the doctor's instruction sheets. "I see there were two prescriptions called in."

"I'll pick them up and drop them off before I leave," Ash said. "Now let me run through the rest of the stuff with you

and anything you don't know, ask Dad. He raised all three of us in this house. He knows it inside out."

A few minutes later, Asher was out the door and headed to Belker's to get the meds, and when he went in to pick them up, found them ready and waiting.

"Does this mean Jacob is home?" the pharmacist asked.

"Yes, and for the time being, with a home health nurse on-site. My brothers have already gone home and I'm flying home this afternoon. I have to get home before bad weather sets in, or my chopper will wind up spending the winter at the Amarillo airport."

The man behind Asher overheard, and curiosity got the better of him. "You have a helicopter?" he asked.

"Yep," Asher said, and headed out the door with the meds.

But instead of calling Pearl, he made a knee-jerk decision and stopped at the Rose to tell her goodbye.

Cheryl was at a nearby table when he walked in.

"Hey, Cheryl, is Pearl in the kitchen?"

"Where else?" Cheryl said.

"Would I get in trouble if I popped my head in to say goodbye?"

Cheryl winked. "You'd be in more trouble if you didn't."

Asher gave her a thumbs-up and walked through the dining room and into the kitchen.

The surprise on Pearl's face was obvious. "Everything okay?"

"It's all good, honey," Asher said. "I just brought Dad home. There's a home health nurse on-site with him for a while. His name is Benny Armstrong. I'm dropping off some meds for Dad and then I'm going home."

Pearl wiped her hands and hugged him tight. "Don't you worry about Jacob. There's a whole town full of people who

will have his back. All he has to do is ask and it will be done. Take care of you. We'll take care of your dad."

Asher kissed her on the cheek, got a swat on his backside for his trouble and laughed all the way out the door. He drove back to the house long enough to hand the meds to Benny, and then he was gone.

Three hours later, he was at the hangar in Austin, transferring his bags into his car, and finally heading to his house in rush-hour traffic. The perfect way to be welcomed home.

Walking into his residence was a relief and a letdown. He began by turning up the thermostat, hanging up his coat and Stetson, and leaving his bags in his bedroom to deal with later. After kicking off his boots, he walked sock-footed into the kitchen, got a cold beer out of his fridge, then sent texts to his dad and brothers, letting them know he was back in Austin, and a separate one to Nora.

I'm home, darlin'. Wish you were here.
Love, Ash

When Nora got the text, she sent a two-word reply.

Me, too.

He went to sleep that night with his alarm set for work the next day. He didn't know what his next assignment would be, but he was going to miss working it with his brothers.

Asher's drive to work was hectic as usual, but as he was

walking into the building, he felt the pull of the badge and what it stood for—for the power it gave him to sort through the lies people told, and find a truth that either sets someone free or puts them behind bars where they belong.

He rode the elevator up, walked into the Office of Special Investigation, only to find all the people he worked with gathered, and applauding him as he entered.

He paused. "I take it you missed me?"

They laughed as his boss, Steven Watts, stepped forward. "Come on, Kingston… Big kudos from the FBI? Solved a twenty-one-year-old cold case for them? Caught the perps who tried to kill your father? Way to go!"

"I didn't do it by myself, and you know it. With one brother working homicide for the Dallas PD, and the other owning a construction company threatening to bury the perps in cement for free, they drop at our feet."

The room erupted in laughter.

"Joking aside," Watts said, "we hope your father is okay."

"Brought him home yesterday morning with a home health nurse to attend for a bit. He's on the mend. Enough about me. What's cooking?"

"The case is on your desk, tied up with a pretty bow and a deadline," Watts said.

"Thank you, sir. Just how I like it," Asher said, and headed for his desk.

Gunner's arrival at work was an echo of what Asher experienced.

He walked into the homicide division to applause and big thumps on the back, and two wolf whistles from a couple of female detectives.

He was all smiles until their lieutenant, Moe Daily, walked in.

"Kingston, good to have you back in one piece. Clearly, you have wreaked your usual havoc to the point of embarrassing the Feds, which puts you back on my Christmas list. I hope your father is recovering nicely?"

"Yes, sir. He is," Gunner said.

Moe Daily shifted into a more serious mode. "Although your work was done outside the division, a commendation will still be added to your file. You and your brothers are a force of nature, are they not?"

"Overcompensation for living down the woman who birthed us," he said. "Are there any caramel Long Johns left?"

One of the female detectives who'd whistled at him was waving a little white flag from the back of the room. "I saved one for you. It's on your desk. What do I get in return?"

"Never mind then. You eat it," Gunner said.

She laughed, and the rest laughed with her. They already knew Gunner Kingston took no prisoners when it came to office teasing. He was off-limits on the job, and tight-lipped about what went on when he went home.

Moe Daily saw past the jokes to the shadows in Gunner's eyes, and he had nothing but respect for men who sought justice for their father, and still honorable enough to get the goods on their own mother, and let it be known.

"At any rate, welcome back," Daily said.

Gunner nodded. "Good to be back," he said.

———————

For Dylan, waking up at sunrise with Angie in his arms was a blessing and a relief. She was his heart, and all that home meant to him.

She mumbled something in her sleep, and he leaned over, whispering in her ear. "Shush, baby, sleep. You've held the fort so faithfully. You stay in bed."

"Tired," she mumbled.

He pulled the covers up over her shoulders and slipped into the bathroom to shower and shave. She was still asleep as he dressed for work, then moved into the kitchen. After a cup of coffee and a couple of pieces of toast, he made a to-go thermos of coffee, left her a note on the counter, and headed out the door.

A couple of hours later, Angie woke up to an empty bed and the faint scent of coffee, and smiled. Dylan's homecoming had shortened their sleep time, but she was thoroughly caught up on all the loving she'd been missing.

She vaguely remembered him telling her to stay in bed, which she had. Now she wanted coffee. She got the coffee, and she got a note that made her laugh.

Morning, pretty girl,

You sure know how to put a smile on a man's face. Take the day off. See you this evening.

Love, love, love you.
D

Nora was in high gear.

She'd just had a video call with her boss, explaining her plans. She hadn't expected any issues with her job, or having it be impacted by moving to another location. It was one of the perks of working online.

She was congratulated on the news of her upcoming

wedding, received sympathy for the stitches in her hand, and compliments on the quick sale of the family home, and then a quick end to the call.

It was an eye-opening conversation. It wasn't real sympathy. It was just what one stranger said to another when faced with the need to comment. There was no way to compare it to the love and kindness she'd received when she went home to Crossroads.

She got up and walked to the windows of her office overlooking the city. It was a long way down to the street below. Past time to come down from this ivory tower. Way past time to start life over again with Ash.

That's when she remembered she needed to call Patty about the Jacksons moving into the house early, quickly pulled up the number, and waited for the call to be answered.

"Thomas Realty, Lee speaking."

"Good morning, Lee, this is Nora Borden. Is Patty in?"

"Yes, just a moment while I transfer the call."

Nora heard a few clicks, and then Patty picked up.

"Good morning, Nora!"

"Hi, Patty. Has Sonny signed the contract yet?"

"Yes, he was in before closing yesterday and left escrow money until the deed search has been completed and we can do the final signing. Darndest thing. He didn't just leave the usual percent... He left the entire amount of the house purchase. I told him it wasn't necessary, but he insisted."

"I guessed he might," Nora said, "which is why I'm calling. I'm going to call Sonny this morning and tell him that the Jacksons have my permission to move in right away. We both know it'll take a month to six weeks for all the deed stuff, and there's nothing worse than trying to move in the winter, especially in West Texas with snow on the ground and wind cold enough to freeze spit."

"That's really kind of you, Nora, and of course, these are

your calls to make. Listen, I'm driving into Crossroads this afternoon to pick up the For Sale sign. How about I bring the keys and drop them off at the Yellow Rose. Pearl's connection to Sonny and Maggie should make that okay."

"That would be perfect. Just tell Pearl to give Maggie a call, and she can come get them. You're the best," Nora said. "Take care."

The moment their call ended, she made a call to the ranch. It rang several times, and she was waiting to leave a message when Maggie picked up.

"Hello?"

"Maggie, this is Nora. Hope I didn't catch you at a bad time."

Maggie laughed. "I was working on a portrait, and trying to get enough paint off my hands to pick up the phone."

Nora chuckled. "Sorry to interrupt genius happening, but I have a bit of news I think Chris and Ellen Jackson will like. I've already spoken to Patty Thomas about this. I'm giving Chris and Ellen permission to move in immediately while we're all waiting for the deed search to be finished."

"Oh my God! Nora! How wonderful."

"Well, I kept thinking of how awful it would be trying to move house in the middle of winter. It's setting empty; there's no reason for them not to be there."

"I can't wait to tell Sonny," Maggie said. "You are such a thoughtful, loving person. Chris and Ellen are going to be so excited. What a wonderful Christmas you are giving them!"

"The other thing... Patty is coming to Crossroads this afternoon to pick up her For Sale sign. She is going to leave the house keys with Pearl, at the Rose, so you might want to give Pearl a heads up about that. This way you won't have to drive all the way to Amarillo to get them."

"Even better!" Maggie said. "Blessings to you, Nora. Thank you so much."

"You're welcome," Nora said, and disconnected, then checked that off of her list of things to do.

Sonny came in the back door just as Maggie was hanging up. When she saw him, she went running. "You will never guess!"

He put his hands on her shoulders and closed his eyes. Saw Chris and Ellen moving into the new house and then opened his eyes.

"When do they move?" he asked.

She swatted him on the arm. "I can't believe I even said that to you. You don't have to guess. Agggh."

He grinned. "Just tell me, baby."

"Nora just called and said she's giving permission to Chris and Ellen to move in now. No waiting. Patty Thomas is bringing the house keys to Pearl this afternoon. We can pick them up and give them the keys to their new home immediately."

"That is most kind of her. She has a good heart," he said.

"I have to call Pearl and tell her about the keys, and she can let me know when she has them. Wouldn't it be awesome if they could spend their first night there tonight?"

"It would," Sonny said. "And I will give him the day off tomorrow so they can move their clothes and food and get settled. That's all they have that doesn't belong to the house they're living in now."

"I can't wait to see their faces," Maggie said, and went off to call Pearl.

Four hours later, Maggie got the call from Pearl and made a round trip to Crossroads and back, then went to look for Sonny and found him in the stable with Chris, feeding horses.

"Sonny! I've got them!" she said, and dropped the keys into his outstretched hand, then stood there, looking at Chris and watching his face.

"What?" Chris said.

Sonny passed the keys to Chris. "Nora Borden called this morning. You are officially free to move in. She didn't want you to wind up having to move house in the middle of winter."

He had a smile a mile wide. "Oh, man! This is wonderful. Ellen is going to be so excited."

"Then go home and pack an overnight bag," Sonny said. "Spend the night in your new home, and you have the day off tomorrow to make the official move. Go! I'll finish up."

Chris took off running, and Maggie was jumping with delight.

"Times like this just make my day," she said.

Sonny grinned. "You make my day, every day. Go get out of the cold. I'll be in soon."

They heard Chris's truck start up, and then the roar as he flew up the driveway, looked at each other and laughed.

"We just made his day, too," Sonny said. "Now get! Your nose is getting red from the cold."

The keys to their new house were burning a hole in Chris's pocket as he sped down the blacktop road. It was the fastest two miles he'd ever driven, and he was just as excited as he'd been when he went to tell her that Sonny was buying a house for them to rent.

When he finally reached the little house on the corner of the last block south, he took the turn without bothering to brake and slid sideways in the yard before coming to a halt. Wild rides were nothing. On a horse. In a car. Once a cowboy, always a cowboy.

He killed the engine and got out running. He could smell supper cooking and heard lids banging as he burst into the house.

"Ellen! Honey!"

She came running out of the kitchen. "What now?"

He pulled the keys out of his pocket and dropped them in her hand. "The keys to our new home. Nora Borden told Sonny we should move in now, before winter sets in, and that they'll deal with all the legal work as it goes."

She clutched the keys to her breasts. "Now? As in whenever we want to?"

"Yes, honey. Whenever we want to."

"Supper's almost ready," she said.

"Pack it up. Grab a toothbrush and your nightie. We're eating and sleeping in our new house tonight. Sonny gave me the day off tomorrow so we can move all the rest. This is it, honey! This is the beginning of us!"

Ellen squealed, and then he began dancing her across the floor and into the kitchen.

"This is the last meal you will ever cook in someone else's kitchen, in someone else's pans, and eat on someone else's plates. Come on, I'll help," he said, and together, they packed up what she'd cooked, and then they packed up what amounted to an overnight bag, put all the cookware to soak in the sink, and they were gone.

Driving the few blocks down to Bluebell Street and taking that turn was like finding the end of a rainbow. They pulled up into the drive and went up the steps together, Ellen with their overnight bag, and Chris with the box of food.

He opened the door, set their things down inside, then swooped her up and carried her across the threshold, laughing from the joy of it.

"Just like our honeymoon night," Ellen said.

Chris put her down and kissed her, and then locked the door behind them before carrying the food into the kitchen, turning on the lights as he went.

"You set the table and get the food out. I'll take our bag to our bedroom," Chris said.

Ellen was so giddy she was trembling, but she remembered exactly where the pretty plates were and went straight to the cabinet. The joy of setting plates that matched onto place mats, and getting the flatware out of a drawer, and the salt and pepper shakers out of the spice cabinet was beyond anything she'd ever dreamed for herself.

When Chris came back, the food was on their plates. When he saw she put him at the head of the table, he saw the years ahead, being the man of the house, then turned around and seated her first before he sat down and reached for her hand.

She bowed her head.

And like every meal they'd had together, Chris Jackson blessed the food and the hands who'd prepared it, just like his daddy had taught him to do.

Chapter 18

It had been a slow afternoon at the Yellow Rose, so the cleaning they would normally do after they closed was already done. The cold weather was keeping more people indoors, which turned out good for Pearl. She had other plans. It was time for her to visit Jacob. He was her friend, and not going to see him in person might be construed as a slight.

The second the last customer left the Yellow Rose, she locked the doors and flipped the sign to Closed. Davey, the grill cook, was nearly finished cleaning the kitchen, and she was making a basket of food to take to Jacob. Darla and Cheryl had swept up the floors. When Davey finished, Pearl sent everybody home with a last word to keep warm, then ran upstairs to change.

As always, she showered, fussed a bit with what to wear, and then chided herself for the moment of vanity and put on clean blue jeans and a blue cable-knit sweater, warm socks and a pair of black loafers, and called it done.

Then one look at herself in the mirror, and she wanted to call it off. She never thought about being older, but the mirror didn't lie. Fifty-five was there, and looking back. No more curly blond hair. It was silver now. Visible wrinkles at the corners of her eyes. Life lines, she called them. She applied a bit of rose-colored lipstick, her one bow to fashion, and then went to get her things.

The sun set early in the winter, and it was already dark

outside when she went out the back door of the kitchen, but it was of no consequence. She didn't have far to go. Once the security alarm was set, she was off.

Her heart was pounding as she drove onto the street, then turned right on the highway and headed to the Tumbleweed. The gas station was lit up like the searchlight on a lighthouse—the one bright light for as far as you could see—and still doing business as she passed.

But as she took the turn into the Tumbleweed, the darkened building felt all wrong. Normally, the parking lot would be packed. The bar would be lit from within with all colors of neon lights, and country music from the sound system would be drifting out into the night. The bar was closed, but Jacob was alive somewhere inside, and that's all that would ever matter in her world.

She drove around to the back, saw Jacob's truck and a car, and guessed the car would belong to the nurse. She parked beside it, got out with her basket and purse, and headed up the steps.

To the house that had been built for her.

She knocked three times, and waited.

It was the evening of Jacob's second day home. He was sitting in the living room watching the evening news. Benny had just gone into the kitchen to heat up some food for Jacob before he went home for the night, when he heard a car pulling up at the back door, and then a few moments later, three sharp knocks.

"I'll get it," Benny said, and opened the door to a fairy-size woman with a turned-up nose and a headful of silver curls, carrying an exceedingly large basket.

"I'm Pearl. I came to visit Jacob. I brought food," she

said, handed Benny the basket, and sashayed past him with her chin up, and her blue eyes flashing. It was all bravado. She was scared to the depths of her soul.

Benny stepped aside to let her pass, then carried the basket to the dining table. He'd been forewarned of Pearl, but thought she was too cute and too little to be much of a threat, and followed her into the living room before she had time to sit.

"Jacob, Miss Pearl brought you supper, so I'll just take myself on home now, and see you bright and early in the morning, okay?"

"He'll be fine!" Pearl said. "I'll make sure he's settled before I leave."

Jacob stifled a grin. Benny had just been dismissed.

"Yes, ma'am. Thank you," Benny said, and left the way Pearl had come in.

Pearl sat down in a chair opposite the sofa where Jacob was sitting, keeping a polite distance between them. It took her a few seconds to realize, except for the night he was shot, she hadn't been alone with him like this in well over thirty years.

"You sure look better than the last time I saw you," Pearl said.

Jacob shook his head. "I can only imagine, and I'm really glad you came. It's hard to find the proper words to thank someone for saving your life, but I will owe you forever that you did."

"Oh, Jacob... How could I not?" she said.

He nodded. "Understood, but thank you anyway, for being cautious enough not to ignore a gunshot, and for taking the time to come check on my welfare. It is entirely due to you that I'm still here."

"It was a shock...to see you so hurt and helpless." Her voice shook a little, but she kept talking. "I kept packing

your bar towels on the wound and threatening you with mayhem if you went and died on me. I kept shouting at you, saying that I'd lost you once, and I wasn't going to let that happen again. Not like that."

Jacob heard the hurt in her voice and heard Asher's words echoing in his head—to tell her the truth about what Brenda had done to the both of them.

"There's something I need to confess," he said.

"No. No, you don't. That was a long time ago and you're my friend," she said.

"I need to say it. Secrets are poison. Lies are poison. I am living proof of both, and it needs to be said." He took a deep breath. "All those years ago, I never knew what happened. One day we were fine, and then we weren't. You wouldn't talk to me, and it was over so fast it made my head spin. You wouldn't answer my calls. You wouldn't look at me on the street. I kept wondering what the hell I'd done...what I'd said. All I knew is that I would never have intentionally hurt you." He paused. She hadn't moved, but her gaze was fixed upon his face, so he kept talking. "I don't think I would have ever known if Brenda hadn't gotten herself staggering drunk one New Year's Eve. It was the year Asher turned two. She started talking about what a stunt she'd pulled to 'get me,' as she put it. Laughing at how she'd convinced you I was paying prostitutes for sex. Making sure you saw what she wanted you to see, but putting another spin on it."

Pearl paled, but her gaze never left his face.

"If you remember, I'd only recently opened the bar and moved into the house, and I was overwhelmed by the job. I didn't have a good routine and was wearing myself out by the grunt work. There was a Mexican family who'd moved into one of the trailer houses back then. The man had a wife and four daughters, but no sons. They were all look-ing for work. I needed someone to clean up after closing,

and someone to help me move the heavy kegs and boxes of liquor I was trying to get stocked. When you saw different women leaving the premises after I'd closed, and handing them money as they left, it was me paying daily, to either the wife, or any one of her girls who'd come to clean, and their father, the man I'd hired to help with the heavy lifting, was waiting at the back of the bar to walk them home."

Pearl moaned beneath her breath and clasped her hands over her heart.

"You saw what Brenda said you would see, but with her own ugly spin on it. She laughed and laughed while I stood there, so staggered by what she'd done that I couldn't speak. In one brief moment, the urge to strangle her was huge. She said she would have done worse to get what she wanted, which was me. I yanked the liquor out of her hand and threw it across the bar. I was so mad I was afraid to even put my hands on her. My first instinct was to go tell you. But there was Asher...and I thought, if I left her, I would lose him, too. That was my slap-in-the-face moment. It was too late. Water under the bridge. I blamed myself for not dragging your little ass out of that café and making you tell me what was wrong. It was my bad for not confronting you when it happened. But the bottom line is that Brenda laid waste to everything she did, except the boys. She did love them. But she had a mean streak, and she was, in a way, a coward. She killed herself so she wouldn't have to face her truth."

Tears were rolling down Pearl's cheeks. She just kept shaking her head no and wiping her face with the sleeves of her shirt.

Jacob hurt for her, and with her.

"I'm just so sorry, honey. So sorry I didn't see what she was doing."

Pearl took a deep breath. "And I'm sorry I let the witch she was, poison me as well. I should have talked to you then, but... Ah, well. As you said, water under the bridge."

Jacob patted the cushion beside him. "Come sit by me. I'm harmless, but I need a hug."

It took everything she had to cross the distance between them and sit down beside him. But instead of a hug, he reached for her hand.

"Forgive me?" he asked.

Pearl held his hand against her cheek. "If you'll forgive me."

He was so near to her, and she was still the woman he'd loved, hiding now behind silver curls and teary eyes. He slid his hand behind her head and leaned toward her.

Her eyelids fluttered shut, and then his mouth was on her lips, kissing her, gently, almost reverently, and she could almost convince herself the last thirty years hadn't happened.

"You're so very forgiven," Jacob said, and handed her a couple of tissues from the box at his elbow. "Now, wipe your eyes and tell me what wonderful things you brought for me to eat. I've had all of the hospital food I could stomach. Benny is a good nurse, but a sad cook."

"Come sit at the table. I'll make your plate," Pearl said.

"Only if you'll eat with me," he said.

She nodded. "I'll eat with you, and lay to rest the last of the demons from our past."

She chattered about the day, and how everyone who came into the Rose kept asking about him, and how determined his sons had been to find the men who tried to kill him, and then working so hard to clear the Kingston name.

"You made the right decision when you stayed. You are their touchstone to what a man of honor is supposed to be." And then she smiled. "Lord knows you cannot deny them.

There are visible pieces of you in all of them, right down to the black-haired, blue-eyed giants they are."

"I am proud of them, that's for sure," he said.

"They are men to be proud of," Pearl said, and then glanced at the clock. "It's late. I'll just put these things in the dishwasher for you. Do you need to take medicine before you go to bed?"

"No. Benny made sure of all that before he left. I get around good enough to get myself in bed. I'm getting stronger by the day. And I feel about a thousand pounds lighter now that I am no longer the devil from your past."

Pearl's eyes welled. "You were never that, and it's my fault as much as yours that Brenda was able to trick the both of us."

Jacob reached out and laid his hand over hers. "Water under the bridge, honey. Water under the bridge. She's gone, and we're still here."

"Except there is no 'we', just me and you, and the gas station between us."

Jacob shook his head. "Only if you choose to keep it that way. The decision will always be yours."

Pearl blinked. "Right now, you need to get well. Put your world back together. Open the Tumbleweed so I can get your mopey domino players out of my café, and we'll see what we shall see."

He grinned. "Maybe I'll build a dam under that bridge and put a stop to all that wasted water."

She smiled back. "We shall see what we shall see," she repeated, then cleared the table and retrieved her things. She was putting on her coat as Jacob stood, then followed her to the back door. The empty basket was over her arm as she looked back to make sure he was steady on his feet. "Lock up behind me," she said.

Instead, Jacob reached for her with his good arm, tilted her chin, and kissed her soundly.

"Take care of you," he said, and then opened the door for her.

Pearl's mouth was still tingling. It hadn't been used for kissing a man in a really long time, and she didn't remember what to do. What to say. He was still standing in the doorway watching as she got into her car, and didn't close the door until she was leaving.

She didn't remember the drive home, or climbing the stairs to her apartment, and when she finally got to bed, she couldn't sleep. Her thoughts were jumbled. Her priorities were in peril. Jacob Kingston had just turned her world upside down, and she wasn't all that upset about it.

And down the road, in the back of the Tumbleweed Bar, Jacob had taken himself to bed with hopes and dreams he'd thought had already passed him by.

Asher's first day back on the job was over. He was driving toward his local Whole Foods to pick up a grocery order, thinking his house was going to feel empty until Nora was there to come home to, when a red Audi in the lane to his left suddenly shot across Asher's lane, sideswiping the car in front of him, and then gunning it into the far-right lane in an attempt to exit the off ramp.

Asher slammed on the brakes, and at the same time, tried not to get rear-ended by the car behind him. He hit the red and blue lights on his car, and managed to get into the exit lane. Even as he was calling in the wreck, he saw the red Audi miss the ramp and go airborne, sailing out into the space between the off ramp and the elevated highway he'd just exited, before landing in the middle of traffic on the street below, causing another multicar pileup.

Ash shot down the ramp the Audi driver missed, with

lights still flashing, and pulled off the highway into the parking lot of a service station, popped the trunk to grab a fire extinguisher, and started running toward the nearest smoking car.

Traffic had finally come to a standstill. The hood of the smoking car had popped up during the wreck, and the windshield was shattered. He could see a man and two kids inside, and victims all around crawling out of their wrecked cars, dazed and stumbling, blood dripping from their wounds. People from neighboring businesses were running out of their shops, some of whom were also carrying fire extinguishers.

Asher emptied the fire extinguisher on the smoking car, and then ran to the driver. The man was unconscious, and the little boys in the back seat were crying and in shock.

"Hey, guys, we need to get you out of the car, okay? My name is Officer Kingston. I'm a special investigator for the state of Texas," he said, and showed them his badge, hoping it would lend a measure of trust. He leaned in to unfasten their seat belts, then began checking them for injuries before attempting to move them. "I know you must be scared, but can you tell me your names?"

The little blond with curly hair wiped the snot off his upper lip with the back of his coat sleeve. "I'm Mike Abram. This is my brother, Ray."

"Who's oldest?" Asher asked as he began checking their pulses, and checking their heads for wounds.

"I am. I'm nine," Mike said. "Ray is seven."

Asher's heart skipped. The same ages Dylan and Gunner were when Brenda committed suicide.

"Do you hurt anywhere?" he asked.

"Kind of all over," Mike said.

"All over," Ray echoed.

At that point, the driver began groaning and Asher's

first thought was, *at least he's still alive.* "Is the driver your father?" Asher asked.

They nodded and started crying. "Is he dead?" Mike asked.

"No son, he's not dead. What's his name?"

"Roy Lee Abrams," Mike said.

Asher checked the driver for a pulse. It was steady enough, but the danger of any of these cars blowing up or bursting into flames in the next five seconds was real. "Let's go, boys," he said, and held out his hands. They crawled out into his arms, still crying, and as he turned, saw firemen running through the crowd, and police and EMTs following.

"Over here!" he shouted, and waved down a pair of EMTs. "My name's Kingston. I'm a cop with the attorney general's office. The driver is unconscious. His name is Roy Lee Abrams. These are his sons, Mike and Ray. Where do I take them?"

They pointed to ambulances arriving and lining up along the side of the highway. It was as close as they could get. "First bus is ours. Number ten. That's where we'll take the father. Keep them together. It's a nightmare for family when they wind up at different hospitals."

"On it," Asher said, and started weaving his way through the wrecks with both boys clinging to him, their arms clutched around his neck. "You're both safe, okay? You're going to ride in an ambulance with your daddy."

Ray was sobbing. "I want Mommy."

"The police will call her. They'll let her know where you are, okay?"

Mike shook his head. "Mommy went to heaven today. Daddy was taking us to Grandma's house."

The words were a shot in the heart. Asher pulled them closer, held them tighter. "I'm sorry. I'm so sorry," he kept saying.

When he reached the ambulance, he handed the boys over, flashed his badge, and delivered the information, but when he turned around to leave and saw the boys wrapped together in a blanket, huddled together as if they'd just been abandoned to the world, something inside of him broke.

He walked back to his car with his chest aching. His throat tight with tears as he got into his car, he then drove around to the back of the service station and took a back alley out, and away from the scene.

It was after eight before he got to Whole Foods and picked up his order, then headed home. He didn't think. He just drove.

Forty-five minutes later, he was pulling into his garage. As soon as the door went down, he popped the trunk, gathered up the bags of groceries, and went inside.

The house was just the way he'd left it. But he would never be the same. In his line of work, some days were like that.

He put everything up, then turned on the lights in the hall as he went to his room to lock up his weapon.

He emptied his pockets on top of the dresser, then stripped where he stood and headed for the shower. His heart was pounding as he turned on the water, and only then noticed his hands were shaking. He was coming undone.

It wasn't the weeks of stress from what happened to Jacob. It wasn't even about that damn fool driver who'd set off a chain reaction of death and destruction. It was the little boys. They were the trigger.

All of the shock, and the sadness, and the fear he'd hidden when it had happened to them. Then stepping into shoes too big for a child to wear just to be strong for his dad, for his little brothers. Every side-glance they'd lived with. Every snide remark. Every whisper of gossip. All the shame. Pretending he didn't hear. Didn't know. Didn't care.

The tragedy of those little boys' lives today had hit hard. Hard enough to bring down a wall. Hard enough to make a grown man cry.

Ash stepped beneath the steaming water and ducked his head into the spray. The tears washed away as fast as they fell, until there were no more tears to cry. Then he grabbed the bar of soap and began scrubbing and scrubbing until the shame was all gone.

He said a prayer for Roy Lee Abrams and for his sons, and for the grandma who would step into the gap, and then he turned off the water and got out, dripping all over the bathmat until he remembered that he needed a towel.

He towel-dried his hair, then himself, and walked back into his bedroom and pulled back the covers. He hadn't eaten since morning. He didn't want to close his eyes and relive anything. What he needed was Nora, but was glad she couldn't see him like this.

He put on a pair of sweatpants and a T-shirt, and was on his way to the kitchen when the cell phone he'd left on the kitchen counter began to ring. He ran to answer without looking to see who was calling.

"Hello."

"Hey, you, I hope you weren't asleep, but I had this feeling that I needed to call you. Is everything okay?"

He sighed. "God, Nora, how did you just do that?"

Nora frowned. "Do what, love? What's wrong? Talk to me. A burden shared is always lighter."

"I just… There was a wreck… These kids… I didn't know them… Just saw it all happen and…"

Nora heard the break in his voice, and knew that he had been crying, and it broke her heart. He was rambling. Everything was in bits and pieces. Some of it was from his childhood, some of it was what had just happened to the little boys in the wreck. Talking about stuff she'd never

heard him voice. He'd scared himself and she knew it, so she just listened until he stopped on his own.

"Shit, Nora. I'm not crazy. I just didn't know I'd kept all that inside me. You caught me at a bad moment, or I would have never had the guts to tell you. To even talk about it. I'm sorry, really sorry."

Nora groaned. "You do not ever apologize to me again for being honest. I have bawled off and on all over you, for the entire time you were in Crossroads, and you were there for me every time. I know you were the stoic for everyone in your family, but that's not how we work. We're partners. Not emotional cripples. Me for you. You for me. Understand?"

"Yes."

"I love you. The whole you. Not just the face you turn to the world, no matter how pretty it is. Eat some food. Go to bed. This will all feel different in the morning, because you are no longer the secret keeper. You are not needed in that capacity again," she said. "The long-range forecast for this week is the possibility of bad weather by this weekend. I refuse to be flooded in, trapped for God knows how long here, when I want to be with you. I will be at your house in two days. I will need the code to get into your gated community. A key to get into your house, and the code to deactivate the security alarm."

He started laughing. "Just call me when you leave. Call me when you hit the outskirts of Austin, and I'll make damn sure that I'm there. Okay?"

"Okay, and I love you," Nora said.

"Nora Borden, you are the best thing that has ever happened to me."

"Oh... I haven't happened at all like I'm capable of happening. In the meantime, take care of you," she said.

He was still smiling when the call ended, and then proceeded to do everything she'd just told him to do. He ate

some food, and he went to bed. And when he woke up the next morning, the first thought in his head was the boys and the dad. He knew the hospital they'd been going to, and called a contact in admissions.

"Wendy Farris."

"Wendy, this is Asher Kingston from the AG's office. I need an update on Roy Lee Abrams. I pulled him and his sons out of that second pileup on the freeway last night. What is Abrams' status?"

"Lord. Give me a sec," she said.

He could hear keys clicking, and then she was back online.

"He's in ICU, listed in serious condition. His next of kin was his wife, but she's been listed as deceased."

"Yeah, she died two hours before the wreck. Abrams was taking his kids to a grandmother's house when the wreck happened."

"Oh my God. Wait… Here's added info. Ray Abrams and Mike Abrams, ages seven and nine, respectively, were cleared to go home, and were released to Janice Abrams, paternal grandmother."

Asher sighed with relief. "Thank you. Appreciate the update. I may actually sleep tonight," he said, and disconnected, then went to the kitchen to start coffee before getting dressed for work.

An hour later, he walked into the office, unaware he'd been caught on camera at the crash site, carrying Mike and Ray Abrams to the ambulance.

"Way to go, Kingston," someone said.

"Camera-worthy every time," someone else shouted.

He stopped. "I don't know what the hell you're talking about."

"That wreck. The flying Audi. What a mess, right?"

Asher snapped back. "If that son of a bitch isn't dead, he

will wish he was. There wasn't one damn thing funny about it. He shot straight between me and the car ahead of me. Missed me by inches, and sideswiped the car ahead of me instead, causing that multicar pileup. Then he shot across two more lanes trying to make the exit to the off ramp. I watched the bastard go airborne as I hit my lights to go after him. He landed in the middle of traffic below the overpass, causing the second pileup as well. Those little boys, nine and seven years old. Their mother had just died hours before in a hospital. Their dad was taking them to their grandma's house. The first thing the oldest boy asked me was if his daddy was dead, and then the rest of their tragedy spilled out. I couldn't find the words to answer, and I don't want to talk about it."

He hung his jacket and Stetson on the coat rack behind his desk and sat down.

The room was silent.

A few moments later, someone put a cup of coffee on his desk as they passed by, and another brought him a sweet roll. He didn't acknowledge the gestures or the gifts. His stomach was in knots.

"Meeting in the murder room in five," someone announced, which was where updates and dead ends and any new leads were revealed.

Asher began gathering up what he'd worked on yesterday, and carried the coffee with him as he went, following the other investigators who were working on the same case.

The phone call from Asher last night had been the push that Nora needed. The first thing she did the next morning was contact the leasing agent to notify him that she wanted out of her lease.

He hemmed and hawed for a minute or two, and then asked her when she expected to leave.

"Within the next couple of days. It is something of a family emergency. The furniture will be out within the week of my leaving, and you can check with the building manager to verify I'm gone before you send cleaners to prep for rental."

"Yes, well, of course. That's quite sudden, but we understand how these things happen, and your five-year lease was up for renewal in a couple of months," he said.

"Thank you," Nora said. "I will leave the keys with security before I go. You can pick them up there."

Satisfied that was behind her, she got online and began searching for staging companies, and to her surprise, the Dallas/Fort Worth area was full of them. She called seven, five of which were immediately interested, and explained the requirements that must be met.

She told them she had a penthouse full of fine furniture to sell today, and it had to be picked up within a week, although she would be gone by tomorrow. But it wasn't until after she gave them the address of the building in which she lived, that their interest soared.

Within the hour, she had five different designers, all arriving at the same time, and had given each of them the same speech.

"There are five of you. You will all meet at the security desk and check in. The guard will have your name. It will require your ID to proceed from there. You will all be escorted up at the same time. I will give you twenty minutes to look at everything. You will write down your name and your bid on a piece of paper, fold it, and hand it to me without comment. I will open them all at the same time, and the person with the highest offer gets the lot."

Every person she spoke to asked her the same question. "Who are you?"

"A careful woman with someplace else to be," was the only answer she gave.

After speaking to the last designer, she called down to the front desk, told them what was going to happen at 11:00 a.m. this morning, and gave them the designers' names, and requested an escort to take them up to her penthouse.

Once she had everything set up, she logged out of her computers, locked everything into the desk in her office, and thought about what persona she needed to present to get the highest price for her things.

That's when she remembered the ornate pair of black silk lounging pajamas decorated with a gold-and-white dragon design that she'd brought back from a trip to Japan. She hadn't given them her name, and a bit of international elegance never hurt. She dug out the little gold silk slippers that went with it and got dressed. After she put her hair up, she added mascara and a lipstick called Go-to-Hell Red, then took a picture of herself in a full-length mirror and saved it to send to Asher.

She was in full-on power mode when eleven o'clock rolled around, and within ten minutes, she got a call from the front desk.

"Ma'am, your guests are on the way up."

"Thank you," Nora said, and then stayed sitting until the knock at the door.

She crossed the marbled flooring in the foyer, looked through the peep hole, and then turned the locks and opened the door.

"Thank you, Gage. I'll let you know when they are leaving," and then she smiled. "Please come in."

By their professions alone, the interior designers were not unaccustomed to wealthy clients, but their interest in this place and this woman of secrets was already piqued.

"You may leave your coats in here if you wish. I will be

leading you from room to room, but I will not interfere, or comment in any way. These are your judgments and decisions to make, and yours alone."

The lone man in the group held up his hand. "A question before we start. It is my understanding that you will not be here when we come to move the furniture out. Is that correct?"

"Yes."

"Is there a freight elevator in this building for moving furniture in and out?"

Nora nodded. "Yes, it's how mine was brought in. It will be simple enough for professional movers to take out."

"Thank you," he said.

She explained briefly before they began. "There is a primary bedroom and a secondary bedroom. An office. And then living/dining you see here, and a kitchen and laundry area beyond. You are bidding on the contents of this penthouse. That includes everything but my personal belongings, which will already be with me, and my computers. This way please."

She began moving then from room to room, watching them making notes, and taking pictures, sending texts back and forth, she assumed to people in their office. And every now and then, catching them glaring at each other, knowing the likelihood of winning this weird silent auction hinged on what the four other people would bid.

Finally, they were back where they began. At that point, they were frantically texting back and forth to their offices, then at the end, writing down their name and bid, folding it and bringing it to Nora.

She thanked each of them politely, stepped aside to open each bid, laid them side by side, and then picked up the second one from the bottom.

"Eloise of Lone Star Staging."

The woman smiled and nodded as disappoint fell upon the others.

Nora kept talking. "Eloise, your bid will be valid for the next three hours. I will need your card for further information, and will invoice your office with a bank and account number. Once I receive notice the money has been deposited, I will fax a signed bill of sale to your office. If you fail to meet the timeline and requirements, then Charles of Elegance Incorporated will be notified, and the lot will go to them. Thank you. I'll call down to let them know you're coming," she said, and walked them to the door.

As soon as she turned the locks, she went straight to her bedroom and began undressing. The whole secret act of not revealing her name, and the outfit she'd chosen to wear, had totally sold their desire to have what she owned. She knew what the contents of the penthouse were worth because she'd bought them. But to her, they were just the finery and décor of the prison she'd put herself in. Her future was Ash. And, unless Eloise backed out, Nora was about to be thirty-four thousand dollars to the good, and on her way to Austin by tomorrow.

Chapter 19

BY THE TIME NORA RECEIVED CONFIRMATION OF THE money transfer into her account that same afternoon, she'd already removed the stitches from her hand with a pair of her mother's tiny embroidery scissors and a pair of tweezers, doused it good with alcohol that brought tears to her eyes, and treated herself to a Hershey's kiss to make the ouchie all better.

She emptied her safe, packed the contents in with her winter clothes she was going to take with her, and boxed up her summer clothes, including the silver flatware that had once belonged to her mother, then called the concierge for a luggage cart. She took the boxes down to shipping to be sent via UPS to Asher's address, then went back up to finish packing, boxing up all her office equipment to take with her in the car.

The next morning, she called for the luggage cart again, asked for help getting it down to the parking garage, dropped the apartment keys off at security on the way, and after they'd loaded all her belongings in her car, generously tipped them for their help and thanked them for all the years of their kindness. She was still sitting in her car sending Asher a text when they left.

On my way to you.

As she drove out of the parking garage and into the flow

of traffic, she caught a glimpse of the ivory tower, growing smaller and smaller as the distance between her and her past became longer. A princess escaping her ivory tower. Racing toward the awaiting prince in another kingdom.

Asher was at his desk running background checks on two suspects in an indictment case when he got Nora's text.

"Hot damn," he mumbled, and sent a text back.

Made my day. Safe travels. Text me when you get to Austin. It'll take me a bit to get across the city to my house.

Ryan Gamble, his partner on the case, glanced up thinking Asher had found a link. "What did you find?"

"Someone I lost a long time ago. She's on her way to my house."

Ryan frowned. "Wait! What? Don't tell me you found her online?"

Asher shook his head. "No. I just went home to Crossroads and there she was, back to sell her family property after her parents' deaths."

"You grew up with her?" he asked.

"Every breath I took, she was there. And when I get the second text, I will be AWOL to let her into the house."

Ryan smiled. "Congrats. You should have just given her a key."

"Where I live, you need to know a code to get in the gate, a key to the house, and a code to deactivate my security system. That's not exactly 'welcome home.'"

Ryan's eyes widened. "Damn, man, that's some serious security."

Asher shrugged. "I have trust issues," he said. and went back to work.

───────────

It was just past 1:00 p.m. when Nora drove into Austin. She pulled off the highway into a truck stop for gas, and got her first welcome from the geography and the weather.

It was seventy-one degrees and sunny in Austin, a city with an elevation of less than 500 feet above sea level. And eight hours north in Crossroads, it was in the high forties, and 3,671 feet above sea level.

Distance in Texas was everything.

As soon as she refueled, she drove up to the station and went to find the restrooms, then bought a cold drink and a bag of corn chips to take with her. When she got back in the car, she sent Asher the second text.

INCOMING...leaving an Exxon station via GPS to you.

Asher had skipped his lunch break knowing he would leave work early when Nora arrived. He had just made a printout of phone logs for the State's case he was working on when he got Nora's text. He put the printout on Ryan's desk along with a note, then returned a message.

Best day ever. Ready and waiting.

He sent her the code to get in at the front gate, then left the building.

───────────

It was the longest drive home he'd ever made. The minutes

seemed to drag. He hit too many red lights, and too many detours. Finally, he realized it was the universe telling him to slow down. And once he did, the traffic cleared, and he was home.

He had his gun stashed and was in the living room watching for her car to pull up in his driveway. Her office space awaited, and he'd moved his summer clothes into a closet in another room to make room for her things. Picturing their clothes hanging side by side was yet another facet of their life to come, but going to sleep with her in his arms and waking up to her lying beside him was going to be the real gift.

He glanced at the time, hoping she wasn't lost, and when he looked up, she was pulling into his driveway. He bolted for the kitchen to open the garage door, and saw her waving and smiling as she drove in beside his car and got out.

"I made it!" she said, and seconds later, she was in his arms, being smothered with hugs and kisses. "Are we dreaming, or is this really happening?" she said, as he finally put her down.

"Happening, and better late than never! Show me your hand."

She held it out, palm up.

"You got the stitches out. It looks great, but I'm still carrying things in."

"I took the stitches out, and I am more than happy to let you do all the heavy lifting. I'm about lifted out."

He frowned. "You took them out?"

She nodded. "With my mother's little embroidery scissors and tweezers. It just stung a little, so I poured alcohol on it afterward and made it sting a lot."

Ash burst out laughing. "God, I love you. Grab your purse and coat. I'm coming in behind you with the rest. Our bedroom is the first door on the right, down the hall. Dump

your things, then investigate the rooms on the other side of the hall and find which one suits you for your office. I have a long folding table that will serve for a desk until you find one you like, and we'll have it delivered."

"Yes, okay," she said, and went through the utility room and into the kitchen, staring in delight at the space that was to become her home.

The Mexican-influenced architecture made everything feel warm and homey, while the brilliant colors and hand-made tiles became the jewels adorning the space.

She left her things on an imposing four-poster bed and went across the hall to begin an office search, quickly settling for the largest room at the end of the hall. Perfect for any privacy she would need, and basically soundproof from the sound of daily living going on at the other end of the house.

She had already admired the formal dining room, and was in the living room, trying out every chair and sofa, when Asher walked in.

"Hey, honey, you have one big box labeled *Mom's china.* Would you like to put it in the obviously empty china cabinet in the dining room?"

"Yes, please," she said, and followed him. "That and her silverware were the only things from home that I chose to keep."

"Is the silverware in your car? I didn't see it anywhere."

"I shipped my summer clothes here UPS. It will be in one of those boxes when they arrive."

"Then I'll open the box of dishes and set them on the table for you, but I don't have a clue as to where they should go. The rest of that is out of my wheelhouse. Is it okay if I unpack the clothes in your suitcases? I have extra hangers."

"I packed them with the hangers, and lord, yes, it's okay. Do you have to get back to work?" she asked.

"Not today, baby. Not today. I'm all yours, for whatever you need. Mi casa es su casa."

Nora paused, remembering the day they'd said goodbye after graduation, and the feeling she'd had driving away from him again in Crossroads. No more driving away. No more walls between them ever again. She put her hand on the middle of his chest. His heartbeat was strong and steady, like the man.

"Then I will be needing a happening to happen around sundown, and along about midnight, I might be needing someone to rock me back to sleep. Forewarned is forearmed."

Asher looked at the box of dishes, and then at the look on Nora's face.

"About that happening... I don't think it's gonna wait," he said.

She wrapped her arms around his neck. "I'm all yours, Kingston."

He swooped her up in his arms, and down the hall they went.

Suitcases landed on the floor.

Shoes came off, and then their clothes.

Asher pulled back the covers as Nora stretched out across the bed.

He was hard, and she was waiting, and then the waiting was over as he slid between her legs.

"Mine," he whispered, and began to move.

"Always," Nora said, then wrapped her legs around his waist and pulled him deeper.

The suitcases didn't get unpacked until hours later.

Her mother's china was still in the box while they were having pizza via DoorDash.

It was their first night together in the house that would become *their* home, and they hadn't wasted a moment, making love everywhere but on the kitchen counter and the floors.

Tonight was theirs.

Tomorrow belonged to their jobs, and that reminder came late. Sometime after midnight, Asher set his alarm. Sated by sex and food, they fell asleep in each other's arms.

To Asher's surprise, Nora was AWOL when he got out of the shower. He wrapped a towel around his waist and went looking, and found her in the kitchen making coffee.

"Baby, you didn't have to get up so early," he said.

She was a little teary, but she was smiling. "I didn't want to miss my first morning telling you goodbye and be safe."

He hugged her. "I understand. I'm just as invested in knowing that I'm never coming home to an empty house again. Even if you're somewhere else, I will still know that this place is where you land."

"Can I make you breakfast? I'm not much of a cook, but I do scrambled eggs and toast okay."

"I would be honored," he said. "Don't make a big deal about it. I usually just eat cold cereal, so eggs and toast will be a treat. Skillet's in the drawer beside the stove. Everything else is in the refrigerator. When I get home tonight, we'll get you signed up on my Whole Foods account and DoorDash, and whatever else you like to use. Delivery is good here."

He kissed the tip of her nose and took off to finish dressing, while Nora pulled out a skillet and a rubber spatula to stir with, and then headed for the fridge.

About fifteen minutes later, he was back, black hair neatly combed, blue eyes the same color as the shirt he was

wearing under his brown leather jacket. His sharp-creased denim Wranglers were shiny from the light starch from the cleaners, and he was wearing his holstered gun at his hip. He set his Stetson on the sideboard and shook his head.

"Darlin', you're going to spoil me with this."

She beamed. "Sit. Eat. I don't want all this to make you late."

Then they sat down together and began to talk as they ate.

"What's on your agenda, honey?"

"I'm going to use that table you put up for me and hook up my office, but I'm not logging in until I have the dishes in the china cabinet and the rest of my clothes hung up. After that, it's back to business for me, too. I'll always have my phone with me, but if I'm doing any live video or Zoom meeting, it will be on Mute. I'll hear it vibrating and get back to you the moment I am able."

"Same goes for me," he said. "If I'm on stakeout, sometimes my phone is muted so I don't give myself away. Other times it might be when we're in interrogation. We'll figure it out." He downed the last of his coffee, and got up, leaned over to leave a kiss on her cheek. "Gotta go, love. Oh… Shoot… I need to write down the security code for the house in case you need to run errands. It can be set manually, or set with a remote and disarmed the same way. There's an extra remote in the sideboard."

"I'll figure it out," she said. "I'm all about tech."

Moments later he was gone, and she began cleaning up the kitchen, suddenly anxious to put a little bit of herself into this home. She picked up a clean dish towel and headed for the box with her mother's china and began taking the pieces out one by one, wiping and stacking them on the table, and when the box was empty, she opened the cabinet doors and began filling the shelves with every piece from home. Royal

Doulton Fine Ivory China in the Mandalay pattern. She could almost hear her mother's voice again, cautioning her when she was young.

Be careful of my Royal Doulton, Nora.

"I'm being careful, Mama," Nora said, and she was, even as she set the last piece in place and closed the doors. Then she stepped back, eyeing how they looked against the cherry wood and glass doors.

Satisfied with her effort, she took the empty box to the garage, then headed for her office. She was itching for a project. It was time to set up shop.

Hours later, she had checked in with her boss to let him know she had everything up and running at her new location and was ready for the next assignment. It turned out to be a job on recovering wiped data at a lab facility, caused by a disgruntled worker. The man had been identified and arrested, and Nora's job was trying to recover it from the mainframe, but it wasn't until she found transfer portals leading to a rogue IP address at the thief's home address, that turned the tide.

"Gotcha," she crowed, then picked up the phone and called the home office, identified herself and her ID code, and was put through to the boss.

"Miss Borden, you have news?"

"Yes sir. I found a transfer portal attached to a rogue IP address that is at the same physical address as the man who was arrested. At first, I thought it was just him trying to hide an original location and wondered if the man who was arrested wasn't the thief at all, and that we could be looking at foreign interference. But upon further digging, I believe it was the man under arrest, and I don't think the data was destroyed;

it was transferred, and made it appear as if it had been wiped on the lab mainframe. Tell the authorities to go back to his residence. Search his home from top to bottom. Look for a hidden room, either in the wall or in a basement you don't know about, or an attic that appears to have no access point. There is a whole other functioning system somewhere on that property or that IP address would not exist."

"Interesting catch, and if this pans out, good work! I'll let you know if they locate it, and you can see to the transfer of data back to their mainframe. In the meantime, I'll put you on hold and not give you another case to work until we finalize this."

"Understood," Nora said. The call ended. Satisfied with her day's work, she logged out and went to look for something to snack on.

While she was prowling through the refrigerator, freezer, and pantry, she found a packet of frozen ground beef, a package of taco shells, a packet of taco seasoning, and everything else to make tacos. It wasn't fancy, but it was something she did know how to make. She set the frozen meat in the sink to thaw, then got herself a snack and a cold drink and sat down at the bar and sent Asher a text.

Successful day. Off until tomorrow. I found stuff to make tacos. Are you game enough to trust me?

A minute later she got a reply.

Yum and yes. Running down a lead. I'll let you know when I'm on the way home.

Pleased with herself, she took her snack to the living room and turned on the TV, found the channel for MSNBC, and sat down to catch up on what was happening in the world.

Ash sent a text to his dad, telling him Nora was in the house and laughed at the "told you so" response.

Dylan got a text from Asher midmorning. All it said was, "Nora's in the house." He sent a "finally" response, and couldn't wait to tell Angie there was going to be another woman in the family. She'd already endured several years of holidays in Crossroads and been the only female on the premises. This was going to rock her world.

And when Gunner got the same message, he was both happy and relieved. His response was, "about damn time." He hit Send, then he got out of his car and headed inside the motel to get a look at the body that had just been found.

Forensics was already there gathering evidence. The coroner glanced up.

"Ah, Kingston, just in time."

Gunner grimaced a bit at the stench and made sure he wasn't standing in anything vital. "In time for what?" he said.

"In time to see what's left of the dude before he's finished melting."

"Melting? How?"

"The body has been frozen. I haven't a clue as to how long he's been dead, or who he is. The tips off his fingers have been removed, and the tongue cut out of his mouth. Ten bucks he snitched on someone who wasn't nice."

Gunner frowned then and moved to the foot of the corpse for a better look. "Oh hell, well, there goes the DA's case against the Banner gang. Now we know where the missing witness went. I need to call this in," he said, and walked out.

Not everyone was having a good day.

It was dark before Asher made it home, but when he walked into the house and heard music playing and smelled good food cooking, everything about this day settled within him.

Nora had heard the garage door go up, and then heard it come down, and ran to meet him with a guacamole-loaded tortilla chip as he was walking into the kitchen.

"Starters," she said, and popped it in his mouth.

"Ohmygawd." He chewed and swallowed, then kissed her hello. "That's delicious. The house smells good. You smell good. I am one happy man."

"I smell like tacos. I love you, too. Go put away the cop and come sit. Want a beer with the tacos, or a soft drink?"

"Soft drink. Whatever you're having."

He hung his hat on the hat rack and headed for the bedroom to lock up his weapon and change clothes. He'd repeated this routine for years and years on his own, but never had there been a reward waiting when it was done.

Nora was reheating the taco meat as she pulled out the individual bowls filled with toppings, then made their drinks, and added a roll of paper towels on the table. She couldn't find any paper napkins, and there was no neat way to eat tacos.

As soon as Ash was back, she took the taco shells out of the warming oven and put them on the table along with the condiments and a little jar of hot sauce that looked well used. She poured up the taco meat into a crockery bowl and added a big spoon. It was the last thing to go on the table.

Asher seated her, then sat. The first thing he reached for was her hand.

"Thank you for this. Thank you for giving up your home for me. And thank you for loving me enough to do it."

"I gave up nothing that mattered, and came because we belong together. Is there anything you like on your tacos that I have missed?"

"Just my teeth, and I brought them with me," he said, and then winked.

It made her laugh.

And so they ate, talking a bit about what their days had been like without giving away confidential information.

"I texted the brothers today and told them you were here. Happy wishes all around. I told Dad, too. Another 'told you so' response."

Nora was listening, watching the way his face lit up when he talked about them, and realized getting married by a justice of the peace was inadvertently cheating *them* of out his wedding.

"Ash, honey, I've been thinking about when we get married. When I said I didn't want a wedding, I didn't mean I didn't want them there. I just meant the big church thing and invitations and all that goes with that, so how would we make it work? If we went back to Crossroads, that would be for Jacob's convenience only. If we had it here in Austin, then Gunner and Dylan and Angie would have no problems being here, but Jacob couldn't drive that distance on his own."

As Ash began talking, Nora heard excitement in his voice and relaxed. She'd done the right thing.

"If you want to do that, darlin', then we can get Dad a round-trip ticket, and when he's strong enough to fly, we'll find someone in Crossroads who'll take him to the airport in Amarillo, and then we'll pick him up and take him home. I won't fly the chopper in the winter. Too much danger of stuff freezing up," he said.

Nora nodded. "Yes, that's what I meant. I just didn't explain it properly."

He gave her hand a quick squeeze. "Then that's what we'll do, so we wait for Dad's recovery, then make it happen."

"There we go, happening all over again," she said.

His laughter delighted her, and he delighted her even more when he began making a fourth taco. Tonight was good, and it wasn't even over.

Pearl's first trip to Jacob's house had turned into a regular thing. If Benny didn't bring him to the Yellow Rose for lunch, then she took supper to him at night.

At first no one paid attention. Pearl was always feeding someone in need, and nearly all of her daily customers were locals. They just assumed Jacob's regular appearances at the Rose were all part of his healing—getting out and about again.

But that story went out the window when Jacob walked into the Rose with a bouquet of flowers and gave them to Pearl. She blushed six shades of pink, told Davey the grill cook to shut up when he teased her, then put them on the counter beside the register, and forgot to remove the card.

Love, Jacob was a hard sign to miss.

Neither Pearl nor Jacob commented, but the looks they gave each other were telling, and one day after Pearl had closed the Rose, and everyone was at their clean-up task, Davey asked Pearl a question she hadn't seen coming.

"Hey, Pearl, I know it's none of my business, but if you and Jacob really get together, are you two going to keep living alone?"

Pearl hadn't dared get that far in her head, and the question took her aback. And Pearl, being Pearl, fired off a snappy answer to hush him up.

"If my apartment upstairs winds up empty, you could consider transferring your living quarters from the Crossroads Inn to the Yellow Rose." Then she laughed. "Even then, you'd likely still be late to work."

Everybody laughed, even Davey. "Well, I wouldn't say no if the offer ever came," he said. "The guy in the room next to mine snores the roof off every night."

They laughed again, and the moment passed. Except now the question was in Pearl's mind. Would she want to, if he asked? And the little bee in her bonnet quickly reminded her. *He built the house for me.*

Chapter 20

It was Nora who found out about Jacob and Pearl, when Jacob called to welcome her to the family.

When she answered and heard that big, booming voice, she knew he was well on the way to being healed.

"How's my girl, this morning? Are you all settled into the Austin scene?"

"I'm getting there," she said. "Are you ready for another girl in your family?"

"Aw, honey, I always thought you'd be the first. Right now, I'm about as happy as a man can get. I have my sons. You and Angie are like daughters to me. And I cleared the slate between me and Pearl."

Nora gasped. "Wait. What are you saying? Are you and Pearl back together?"

"Getting there," Jacob said.

"This is the best news, ever! You do know I can't keep this a secret," she said.

He laughed. "It's not a secret in Crossroads, that's for sure. No reason it needs to be. Anyway, I suspect I'm interfering with your work. Next time I see you, I expect a big hug. Tell Asher that I'm proud of you both."

"I will, I will," Nora said. "So glad you called, and even happier that you are still in the world with us."

"Lord have mercy, sugar, so am I," he said.

The call ended, but the smile on Nora's face was still there. "Oh my gosh. OH. MY. GOSH. Jacob and Pearl!"

She did a little two-step across the floor on her way to the office, then sat down and sent a text to Asher.

Your dad called. All is well. More than well. He and Pearl are an item. I think we're going to need two round-trip tickets for our wedding. Jacob and Pearl. The weirdest thing. Brenda broke them up. And the secrets she left behind were the trigger that also brought them back together. Karma is real.

Asher was working a new case, sitting in a parking lot across the street from a dry-cleaning shop, taking pictures of every person who went in empty-handed, without garments to drop off, and exiting the same way. Carrying nothing visible to the eye. Something was changing hands in there, but it wasn't clothes.

As he was waiting, he got Nora's text. His first emotion was pure delight. And then he reread what she wrote about Karma, and got a lump in his throat. She saw the world in a purer way than he ever would, and he was forever grateful that as they were growing up together, she'd seen value in him, when he had not seen it for himself.

This also meant his dad was obviously much better, which meant he and Nora needed to apply for a marriage license. There was a seventy-two-hour waiting period, then they could pick a day, and notify the family.

It also reminded him to swing by Koen and Sons Jewelry. Nora wasn't the only one capable of surprises.

Angie had been giving Nora tips on easy cooking, and when Nora found a digital version of a slow cooker on a shelf in Asher's kitchen, she decided to experiment.

Meat and veggies go in. A set-and-forget timer, and dinner is served. Nothing undercooked. Nothing overcooked. Turns itself to warming when it's done. Martha Stewart she was not, but they weren't going to have to live on scrambled eggs and DoorDash, and that was a plus on any day.

The pot roast and veggies she'd started this morning after talking to Jacob were done and on Warming. The table was set and waiting for Ash to come home. His random arrival times didn't bother her. She'd been her own boss with her own timetable for years and years, while his day was more random. Law enforcement didn't clock out in the middle of emergencies.

She was pouring herself a glass of iced tea when she heard the garage door going up. The brighter light of her life was home!

She set the glass and pitcher back into the fridge and turned just as he walked into the kitchen carrying a bouquet of roses and a very obvious bakery box.

"Asher! How beautiful!"

"For the most beautiful girl," he said, and brushed a kiss across her lips as he handed them to her and set the bakery box on the counter. "Gotta lock up the cop. Be right back!"

"Lock up the cop" had become his byword for storing his weapon. She was fine with locking up the gun, but she loved the cop part of him. She set the flowers at the end of their table so she could see them while they ate and sat down to wait.

When he came back, instead of sitting down, he knelt down on one knee and opened the little black velvet box he was holding.

"I love you, Nora, and since we're already planning a wedding, I felt this huge need to put a ring on it. I lost you once. That will never happen again."

Nora gasped. "Oh, Asher! It's stunning," she said as he slipped it on her finger. "And it fits!"

"I know my woman," he said, then leaned over and sealed it with a kiss.

Nora put her arms around his neck and deepened the kiss.

Their dinner was a hit, as was the Italian crème cake he'd brought home. They were cleaning up the dishes together when he brought up getting married again.

"Can you get off anytime tomorrow so we can do the marriage license thing? It won't take long. I have friends in high places and also in the courthouse," he said.

Nora shook her head. "I'll bet you do, and yes, I will make time. Just text me the address when you're free and I'll meet you there."

"Deal," he said.

That night, when Nora turned back the covers, she found more rose petals in the middle of the bed, and Asher was reaching for her to pull his old football jersey over her head.

"Life won't always be a bed of roses, but as long as we have each other, we'll just keep planting them anyway," he said, then picked her up and laid her down among them.

Nora's heart was pounding as he moved toward her. Yet another facet of this man she never saw coming, and then his mouth was on her breast, and his hand was between her legs. She tried to stay focused, to watch his face as they made love, but what he was doing made her crazy. Her eyes fluttered shut, and she was lost. She was still reeling from

a climax when he slid between her legs, and after that, she was gone.

He left the next morning while she was still asleep, and she woke up to a picture he'd sent.

She was flat on her stomach. Obviously naked, but with the covers pulled up to her waist. One arm was hanging off the side of the bed, and there were dozens of rose petals stuck to her skin.

It came with a heart emoji and a message.

They will wash off. Mine did. It was damn sure worth it.

She burst out laughing and headed for the shower.

The ensuing two weeks were hectic.

During that time, the final papers for the sale of her family house were sent. As promised, the remote signing went off with a hitch. The money from the sale of the house was deposited into her bank account. It was official. She kept imagining the joy for Chris and Ellen, and felt good about the way it had all ended.

After consultations with all involved, Asher and Nora opted to get married the day before Thanksgiving. Gunner had put in a prior request not to be on holiday shift because of his brother's wedding. Construction would come to a halt on all work sites for Dylan and Angie. And for the first time in what Pearl called "forever," the Yellow Rose was going to be closed for three days for the Thanksgiving holidays.

Asher and Nora sent them round-trip tickets from

Amarillo to Austin and back. Dylan and Angie were picking them up at the airport and taking them home with them. Gunner was driving up to Dylan and Angie's the day before the wedding, which was going to be held at Asher and Nora's house.

Wedding cake and champagne afterward, and Thanksgiving dinner with everyone the next evening, back at Asher and Nora's.

———————

Jacob and Pearl were on an adventure. She had never taken a vacation from work, and rarely had she ever closed the Rose. She had never flown. And had it not been for Maggie, would not have had the proper clothes to wear for any of it.

Gunner was midway between Dallas and Austin when Dylan went to pick them up, and Angie stayed home to be there for Gunner's arrival.

There was more turmoil there than at Asher and Nora's. There was no fussing. No florists. No hair stylists to see. Asher was kicked back watching football and Nora was finishing up a quick virus removal for a law office, and wondering what fresh hell the law clerk was getting for using a company computer to cruise dating sites. One click too many on the wrong site, and the virus unloaded into the entire system.

When she finally finished, their system had been cleared and was up and running.

Happy Turkey Day, she thought, and signed off, then went to look for Asher, and followed the noise.

"Who's winning?" she said as she dropped onto the seat beside him.

"We are," he said, and pulled her into his arms.

She laughed. "Have you followed up with your friend in high places? The one who's coming to marry us tomorrow?"

"Yep. He'll be here. Two p.m. sharp."

"Good," she said. "Go back to your game," then did a U-turn on the sofa, put her feet in his lap, pulled a blanket over herself, and snuggled down into the sofa.

At that moment, Asher lost focus on everything about the game and was thinking how freaking awesome women were, to be able to make a nest anywhere, as long as they felt safe. He tucked the blanket around her feet and legs, then turned the sound down on the game and reclined the seat.

Life was perfect.

The weather blessed the day of their wedding, and the family that gathered blessed it more.

Nora's wedding dress was floor length and new. A concoction of simple elegance in white, with long, flowy sleeves. Her bridal bouquet was made of yellow roses, tied together with ribbon the color of bluebonnets. The fragile necklace around her neck had been her mother's. Gunner loaned her a penny for her shoe.

Something old. Something new. Something borrowed. Something blue. And a penny for her shoe.

She had it covered.

And Asher had surprised her yet again.

He owned a tux. Who knew?

And wore it like he'd been born to it. There was still much to learn about the man he had become.

What she didn't know was that Asher was on the same learning curve as Nora. When she showed him the photo she'd taken of herself before the interior designers showed up, and was telling him how she'd set the stage as a woman of mystery, he was shocked at the image and couldn't quit staring—looking for the girl he'd grown up with.

Then she laughed, telling him how she upped the worth of her property by saying nothing about who she was, or why she had three locks on her door and did not receive guests without a security guard bringing them to her door. After that revelation, he guessed there was way more of that woman now, than the girl she had been. And he liked it.

Now they were standing before Asher's justice of the peace, Patrick Fairchild, repeating vows, making promises, and at Asher's instructions days earlier, the word "obey" was not to be used. He was marrying a woman, not a dog, and wasn't having any of it.

At the exchange of rings, the room grew silent. The only sound was Patrick's voice, and the rustle of clothing as Dylan handed Nora's ring to Asher, and Gunner gave Asher's ring to Nora.

Ignoring the ritual Patrick was trying to follow, Asher took her hand and slid the ring up her finger. Then Nora did the same for him.

Single bands. Unadorned. Symbols of unending love.

Patrick sighed, then smiled. "Okay, you two. I now pronounce you man and wife. You may kiss your bride."

"I've been kissing her since we were thirteen. Happy to do it again," Asher said.

Nora laughed, so he kissed her again…because he could.

It was the happiest day of their lives.

She became the target of much hugging and kissing.

Patrick Fairchild stayed long enough to get the marriage certificate signed and witnessed, and he was gone.

During all of the travel arrangements, they'd forgotten all about a wedding cake until it was too late to do much about it, and bought what was there. Cutting a half a sheet cake with the words IT'S A BOY became the next moment of the day.

"Take a picture before we cut it!" Nora cried, and Angie grabbed her phone as they held it up so the words could be read.

"It's either an announcement or a warning," Jacob said, as laughter filled that wonderful kitchen with the jewel colors and handmade tiles. A promise for the years to come.

That night, Nora slept beside her husband, and Asher slept beside his wife, and woke up to the reality of furnishing Thanksgiving for the crowd.

Only this time, Nora was prepared. They weren't eating until evening, and she was ready for the sides and salads that were their contributions.

Pearl and Angie were already cooking turkey and dressing at Dylan's and, to everyone's delight, Gunner was bringing more than himself to the party. He'd transported pecan pies and pumpkin rolls all the way from a Dallas pastry shop.

It was midafternoon when they began to gather, and it was not lost upon any of them what had been lost that year, and what had been found. When they finally sat down at the table in the dining room, they remarked upon the lovely china at their places.

"They were Mom's," Nora said, and then looked at Asher and smiled. Today was just the passing of a torch. One generation to the next.

Pearl sat with her hands in her lap, watching the faces, hearing the laughter, seeing Jacob as the father. Still feeling like she was on the outside, looking in, until Jacob took her hand, and leaned over and whispered in her ear.

"I will build two more rooms on to my house to make room for the daughters-in-law and the grandbabies…yours and mine…if you'll marry me. Don't fuss. Just think about it." And then he lifted her hand and kissed it.

Pearl's eyes widened. Her cheeks flushed, and when she smiled, Jacob smiled back.

Nora saw it, and said nothing, but was hoping it came to something.

The dinner and desserts were a success. The day was ending on a high note, but also on goodbyes. Jacob and Pearl were flying home tomorrow. Gunner was the first to leave, because he was driving home tonight with boxes of leftovers and three pieces of leftover wedding cake, because they'd eaten all the pies.

When he was leaving, Nora slipped the borrowed penny into his coat pocket. "Safe travels, Gunner Kingston, and always watch your back."

"Spoken like a true cop's wife. Asher's got a good one." He winked, then he was gone.

Goodbyes until Christmas were made to Jacob and Pearl, and then everyone was gone, and the house was silent.

Asher saw her standing at the window, watching the taillights of Dylan and Angie's car as they drove away.

He walked up behind her and wrapped his arms around her shoulders as she leaned back against him.

"It's not over, darlin'. It's just the beginning."

Epilogue

Austin—One year later
St. David's Hospital

NORA WAS WELL PAST TEN HOURS IN LABOR, AND ASHER had never left her side.

When they first found out it was a boy, they remembered their wedding cake and laughed, but she was long past laughter. Riding wave after wave of pain of every contraction, her hair soaked from the sweat, her face wet from the tears.

She'd barely caught her breath before the next contraction hit, and then the delivery nurse was giving orders, and her doctor suddenly appeared.

"Looks like that little boy is finally ready to meet the world," he said.

"About damn time," Asher muttered. "My God... Why must there be pain?"

Nora was gripping his hand so tight her nails were digging into his palm, but he wouldn't have let her go if they'd been bleeding.

"I'm here, darlin'. I'm here. Scream if it helps. I'm standing here trying not to cry."

"Oh God... I don't have the breath. Cry for me," she mumbled, and then arched back against the next push.

She heard a nurse say, "The baby's crowning," and thought, *Thank God, thank God. Let it soon be over.*

The doctor was talking fast now, giving orders almost impossible to obey.

"Push harder, Nora. A little more. A little more. Yes, that's it! That's it!"

And between one heartbeat and the next, she felt the weight of him suddenly gone. The room was spinning, and Asher was patting her shoulder and praising her, and all she felt was suddenly empty. The baby she'd been sheltering had just been introduced to a whole new world.

"Is he okay?" she asked, and got an ear-shattering cry for an answer.

"He's okay, and I do believe he's also mad," the doctor said.

Then Nora heard the nurse.

"Doctor, the official time of birth was midnight, but he didn't take a breath until two seconds after."

"It will be recorded as 12:01 a.m., on August 28th," the doctor said.

They were still dealing with Nora, and she was trying to get a glimpse of her son, but there were too many people in the way. Then the crowd parted, and Asher was standing at the foot of the bed, holding their baby, swaddled with blankets.

He had tears on his face, but he was smiling, and then he walked to where she was lying, and laid him in her arms.

"He's beautiful, Mama. You did good. All his fingers and toes."

Nora looked into the face of the child that they had made and smiled, then looked up at Asher, and saw her child's face in the man he would become, then kissed her baby's tiny cheek.

"Welcome to the world, Jacob Thomas. You carry your grandaddies' names, but I pray you become as strong and wonderful as the man who gave you to me."

Keep reading for more small-town romance from *New York Times* bestselling author Sharon Sala in *Sunset*.

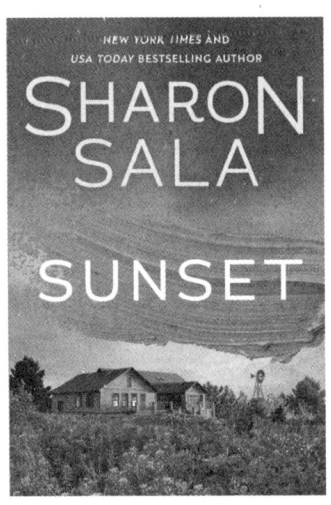

Chapter 1

Bluejacket Hollow, Oklahoma

SATURDAY MORNING BEGAN LIKE EVERY OTHER MORN-
ing on Charlie Bluejacket's farm until his nine-year-
old daughter, Julia, came running in from outside in
hysterics.

"Daddy, Daddy! Butters isn't in his pen, and I can't find
him anywhere!" The little black-and-white pygmy goat was
Julia's shadow, and a family pet.

Her mother, Frances, turned off all the burners at the
stove and took off her apron, as Charlie put down the cup
of coffee he'd been drinking.

Sonny Bluejacket, Charlie's younger brother, had been
living with the family ever since a bull ride at a rodeo
ended his career and nearly his life. He jumped up from
the table, followed the others as they went outside to the
goat pen, expecting to see coyote or cougar tracks, and
blood.

But there was nothing to tell them what had happened.
Just little goat tracks in the pen, and then leading out
through a gate left ajar.

Julia was sobbing. "I shut the gate good last night,
Daddy! I always do."

Sonny was circling the pen looking for signs but saw
nothing but Julia's sneaker tracks. "I'll get the ATV and
head north toward the creek," he said.

Frannie took her daughter by the hand. "We'll go south," she said.

"I'll check the driveway to see if I see tracks there, and if not, I'll go west," Charlie said, and they scattered like quail.

Sonny took off on the ATV, slowly winding his way through the heavily wooded areas around the farm, looking for signs. About a half hour later he rode into a clearing, saw little goat tracks on a patch of bare ground, and got off the ATV.

"Butters Bluejacket, you can't hide from me. I smell you, and I'm not going to chase you down. Get your little self out here now. Julia thinks something ate you, and hurry up. I don't have all day."

Moments later, the little black-and-white goat trotted out of the brush right in front of Sonny, and head-butted one of the front tires.

Sonny laughed. "Look at you being all tough," and as he slipped a lightweight cotton rope around Butters's neck, the little goat began to jump about in protest. "Oh no you don't! You had a chance to ride like a big boy, but you thought you needed to be all tough."

Sonny grabbed him by the horns, rolled him over onto his side, and hogtied the little goat's legs, like a calf at a roping competition.

Butters began protesting loudly, bleating pitifully as Sonny called his brother. "Hey bro, I found Butters. The little squirt came out of the brush and head-butted the ATV. Yeah, that's him making all this noise. I've got him hogtied, and he's riding in my lap all the way back, so you can tell Julia that Uncle Sonny found her baby."

"Good job," Charlie said.

"See you soon," Sonny said, then hopped on the ATV with the little goat in his lap and started the ATV with Butters bleating objections. "Yeah, yeah, I know," Sonny

said. "Sorry about all this, but you shouldn't have run away. Julia thought something ate you, but I think you're too ornery to be tasty."

They rode all the way home with Butters steadily bleating his disapproval. Fifteen minutes later, Sonny arrived and pulled up into the backyard where the family was waiting.

"Come get this noisy critter," Sonny said, and handed him off to Charlie.

"Thank you, Uncle Sonny," Julia cried, and then hurried to catch up to her father, who was carrying the goat back to its pen. There would be some remodeling to the goat pen before nightfall.

Sonny rode the ATV back into the shed, parked and hung the keys up on a nail beside the door, then headed back to the house. From the aroma drifting out the kitchen window, he guessed Frannie had gone back to making breakfast, but now he smelled like goat.

He went inside, bypassed the kitchen to wash up and change clothes before going back to the table. He was headed up the hall toward the kitchen when Frannie called out.

"Sonny! Mailman needs you to sign for something!"

"Coming," he said, and hastened his stride to the front door and went outside to meet him. "Hey Wilson."

Wilson nodded. "Hey, Sonny. I need you to sign for this registered packet."

As soon as Sonny signed, Wilson handed over a large, fat, manila envelope. "Have a good day."

"You, too," Sonny said, glanced at the return address, then went back inside.

"Breakfast is ready," Frannie said.

"Coming," Sonny said, and headed to the kitchen while there was still food left to eat. He laid the packet aside and sat down at the table.

Charlie looked up. "What was it?"

"I don't know. From some law firm in Texas," he said.

"Are you in trouble?" Frances asked, as she put his plate of food down in front of him.

Sonny laughed. "Not that I know of. I left plenty of blood in the dirt back in Texas, but it was mine."

"Open it," Charlie said.

Sonny shrugged. "I will, just as soon as I eat this good food while its hot."

Charlie frowned.

Frances smiled at her husband's impatience and curiosity, and pretended not to see Julia sneaking food into her pocket to take out to Butters's pen later.

The meal progressed until Sonny had taken his last sip of coffee, and then he got up and brought the envelope back to the table. They were all teasing him about everything from being sued for child support for a kid he didn't know he had, to a pillow he'd taken from a motel when he was still on the rodeo circuit. But none of them could have ever guessed the contents of what was inside.

Sonny read the cover letter, then looked up in shock.

"Emmit Cooper died."

George frowned. "Isn't that the bullfighter who nearly got you killed?"

Sonny frowned. "Don't say that. It wasn't Emmit's fault. He stumbled and fell before he could distract the bull. But the bull was mad at me, not Emmit."

"Okay, so he's dead. Why is some lawyer telling you this?" George muttered.

"Because Emmit left everything to me in his will, which includes a thousand-acre spread in West Texas, and a horse operation, including a dozen registered Quarter Horses. I guess you all are finally getting me out of your hair. This is something I never saw coming, but it's my chance to start over."

Frances frowned. "Please tell me you're not going back to the rodeo."

"No way. I'll still be riding and training horses like I've been working horses for the ranchers around here, but these will be mine. This is unexpected, but I wouldn't deny this gift. Emmit had his reasons, and I will honor them," Sonny said.

At that point, his family reluctantly celebrated his good fortune, while Sonny read the rest of the paperwork in detail, then got his laptop and began looking up bus schedules.

About the Author

New York Times and *USA Today* bestselling author Sharon Sala has 148+ books in print, published in eight different genres—romance, young adult, Western, general fiction, mystery, women's fiction, children's books, and nonfiction. First published in 1991, her industry awards include the Janet Dailey Award, five-time Career Achievement winner, five-time winner of the National Readers' Choice Award, five-time winner of the Colorado Romance Writers' Award of Excellence, the Heart of Excellence award, the Booksellers Best Award, the Nora Roberts Lifetime Achievement Award, the Will Rogers Gold Medallion, and the Centennial Award in recognition of her 100th published novel. She lives in Oklahoma, the state where she was born.

Website: sharonsalaauthor.com
Facebook: sharonsala
Instagram: @sharonkaysala_

WELCOME TO JUBILEE, KENTUCKY

Riveting and pulse-pounding small-town romantic suspense
from *New York Times* bestselling author Sharon Sala

Don't Back Down

Army veteran Cameron Pope arrives back in Jubilee, Kentucky, for the first time in years when he becomes embroiled in a deadly hunt for the human traffickers who are destroying the peace of his mountain town. When he's reunited with Rusty Caldwell—a woman from his past he's never stopped thinking about—he wants to believe they can finally be together. Cameron and Rusty will have to find a way to end the feuding between the locals and take down the human trafficking ring if they're to have any chance at happiness.

Last Rites

Eldest brother Aaron Pope returns to his life as a police officer and is settling in just fine. Then Aaron's investigation into an attempted murder leads him right to Dani Owens. She may hold the key to a long-lost part of the Pope family's past, and more importantly, she may hold the key to Aaron's heart.

Heartbeat

Amalie Lincoln moved to Jubilee, Kentucky, to start fresh, build her business, and heal the scars of her past. Little did she know she'd run into Sean Pope, a beloved childhood friend she hasn't seen in decades. On the

day she moves to town, a helicopter explodes under suspicious circumstances, wreaking havoc on the families of Pope Mountain. But as the investigators uncover the truth and the crooks behind the attack set Amalie in their sights, Sean must face the danger or risk losing Amalie forever.

Left Behind

Jubilee PD Officer Wiley Pope thinks he's ruined things with Linette Elgin. But when Wiley walks in on a bank robbery with Linette as one of the hostages, his training and protective instincts kick into full gear. As he and Linette begin anew, Wiley finds himself in over his head with a murder investigation linked to Pope Mountain and an attempted money scheme that results in a seven-year-old girl abandoned at the police station. But the minute the woman signs over her parental rights, Wiley and Linette welcome the wary little girl into their family and show her what real love looks like.

Bad Seed

It's love at first sight when head pastry chef Brendan Pope meets private investigator Harley Banks at the Serenity Inn in Jubilee, Kentucky. Harley is staying there for her latest investigation. But unknown to them both, Harley has a hit man after her, courtesy of the wrong-doer she put behind bars on her last case. The FBI gets involved to clean up the loose ends so Harley can continue the investigation at the inn. But after nearly losing her, Brendan will stop at nothing to make sure Harley is safe and the criminals get their comeuppance.

For more info about Sourcebooks's books and authors, visit:

sourcebooks.com

Also by Sharon Sala

Don't Back Down
Last Rites
Heartbeat
Left Behind
Bad Seed
The Next Best Day

BLESSINGS, GEORGIA
Count Your Blessings (novella)
You and Only You
I'll Stand by You
Saving Jake
A Piece of My Heart
The Color of Love
Come Back to Me
Forever My Hero
A Rainbow Above Us
The Way Back to You
Once in a Blue Moon
Somebody to Love
The Christmas Wish
The Best of Me

CROSSROADS
Sunset